1-9.97

D0782155

Neural Networks

Algorithms, Applications, and Programming Techniques

Neural Networks

Algorithms, Applications, and Programming Techniques

James A. Freeman
David M. Skapura

Loral Space Information Systems
and
Adjunct Faculty, School of Natural and Applied Sciences
University of Houston at Clear Lake

Addison-Wesley Publishing Company

Reading, Massachusetts · Menlo Park, California · New York
Don Mills, Ontario · Wokingham, England · Amsterdam · Bonn
Sydney · Singapore · Tokyo · Madrid · San Juan · Milan · Paris

Library of Congress Cataloging-in-Publication Data
Freeman, James A.
 Neural networks : algorithms, applications, and programming techniques
 / James A. Freeman and David M. Skapura.
  p. cm.
 Includes bibliographical references and index.
 ISBN 0-201-51376-5
 1. Neural networks (Computer science) 2. Algorithms.
 I. Skapura, David M. II. Title.
 QA76.87.F74 1991
 006.3–dc20   90-23758
                                                  CIP

Many of the designations used by manufacturers and sellers to distinguish their products are claimed as trademarks. Where those designations appear in this book, and Addison-Wesley was aware of a trademark claim, the designations have been printed in initial caps or all caps.

The programs and applications presented in this book have been included for their instructional value. They have been tested with care, but are not guaranteed for any particular purpose. The publisher does not offer any warranties or representations, nor does it accept any liabilities with respect to the programs or applications.

Reprinted with corrections July, 1992

8 9 10–MA–9594

P R E F A C E

P

The appearance of digital computers and the development of modern theories of learning and neural processing both occurred at about the same time, during the late 1940s. Since that time, the digital computer has been used as a tool to model individual neurons as well as clusters of neurons, which are called neural networks. A large body of neurophysiological research has accumulated since then. For a good review of this research, see *Neural and Brain Modeling* by Ronald J. MacGregor [21]. The study of artificial neural systems (ANS) on computers remains an active field of biomedical research.

Our interest in this text is not primarily neurological research. Rather, we wish to borrow concepts and ideas from the neuroscience field and to apply them to the solution of problems in other areas of science and engineering. The ANS models that are developed here may or may not have neurological relevance. Therefore, we have broadened the scope of the definition of ANS to include models that have been *inspired* by our current understanding of the brain, but that do not necessarily conform strictly to that understanding.

The first examples of these new systems appeared in the late 1950s. The most common historical reference is to the work done by Frank Rosenblatt on a device called the *perceptron*. There are other examples, however, such as the development of the Adaline by Professor Bernard Widrow.

Unfortunately, ANS technology has not always enjoyed the status in the fields of engineering or computer science that it has gained in the neuroscience community. Early pessimism concerning the limited capability of the perceptron effectively curtailed most research that might have paralleled the neurological research into ANS. From 1969 until the early 1980s, the field languished. The appearance, in 1969, of the book, *Perceptrons*, by Marvin Minsky and Seymour Papert [26], is often credited with causing the demise of this technology. Whether this causal connection actually holds continues to be a subject for debate. Still, during those years, isolated pockets of research continued. Many of the network architectures discussed in this book were developed by researchers who remained active through the lean years. We owe the modern renaissance of neural-network technology to the successful efforts of those persistent workers.

Today, we are witnessing substantial growth in funding for neural-network research and development. Conferences dedicated to neural networks and a new professional society have appeared, and many new educational programs at colleges and universities are beginning to train students in neural-network technology.

In 1986, another book appeared that has had a significant positive effect on the field. *Parallel Distributed Processing (PDP)*, Vols. I and II, by David Rumelhart and James McClelland [23], and the accompanying handbook [22] are the place most often recommended to begin a study of neural networks. Although biased toward physiological and cognitive-psychology issues, it is highly readable and contains a large amount of basic background material.

PDP is certainly not the only book in the field, although many others tend to be compilations of individual papers from professional journals and conferences. That statement is not a criticism of these texts. Researchers in the field publish in a wide variety of journals, making accessibility a problem. Collecting a series of related papers in a single volume can overcome that problem. Nevertheless, there is a continuing need for books that survey the field and are more suitable to be used as textbooks. In this book, we attempt to address that need.

The material from which this book was written was originally developed for a series of short courses and seminars for practicing engineers. For many of our students, the courses provided a first exposure to the technology. Some were computer-science majors with specialties in artificial intelligence, but many came from a variety of engineering backgrounds. Some were recent graduates; others held Ph.Ds. Since it was impossible to prepare separate courses tailored to individual backgrounds, we were faced with the challenge of designing material that would meet the needs of the entire spectrum of our student population. We retain that ambition for the material presented in this book.

This text contains a survey of neural-network architectures that we believe represents a core of knowledge that all practitioners should have. We have attempted, in this text, to supply readers with solid background information, rather than to present the latest research results; the latter task is left to the proceedings and compendia, as described later. Our choice of topics was based on this philosophy.

It is significant that we refer to the readers of this book as *practitioners*. We expect that most of the people who use this book will be using neural networks to solve real problems. For that reason, we have included material on the application of neural networks to engineering problems. Moreover, we have included sections that describe suitable methodologies for simulating neural-network architectures on traditional digital computing systems. We have done so because we believe that the bulk of ANS research and applications will be developed on traditional computers, even though analog VLSI and optical implementations will play key roles in the future.

The book is suitable both for self-study and as a classroom text. The level is appropriate for an advanced undergraduate or beginning graduate course in neural networks. The material should be accessible to students and professionals in a variety of technical disciplines. The mathematical prerequisites are the standard set of courses in calculus, differential equations, and advanced engineering mathematics normally taken during the first 3 years in an engineering curriculum. These prerequisites may make computer-science students uneasy, but the material can easily be tailored by an instructor to suit students' backgrounds. There are mathematical derivations and exercises in the text; however, our approach is to give an understanding of how the networks operate, rather that to concentrate on pure theory.

There is a sufficient amount of material in the text to support a two-semester course. Because each chapter is virtually self-contained, there is considerable flexibility in the choice of topics that could be presented in a single semester. Chapter 1 provides necessary background material for all the remaining chapters; it should be the first chapter studied in any course. The first part of Chapter 6 (Section 6.1) contains background material that is necessary for a complete understanding of Chapters 7 (Self-Organizing Maps) and 8 (Adaptive Resonance Theory). Other than these two dependencies, you are free to move around at will without being concerned about missing required background material.

Chapter 3 (Backpropagation) naturally follows Chapter 2 (Adaline and Madaline) because of the relationship between the delta rule, derived in Chapter 2, and the generalized delta rule, derived in Chapter 3. Nevertheless, these two chapters are sufficiently self-contained that there is no need to treat them in order.

To achieve full benefit from the material, you must do programming of neural-network simulation software and must carry out experiments training the networks to solve problems. For this reason, you should have the ability to program in a high-level language, such as Ada or C. Prior familiarity with the concepts of pointers, arrays, linked lists, and dynamic memory management will be of value. Furthermore, because our simulators emphasize efficiency in order to reduce the amount of time needed to simulate large neural networks, you will find it helpful to have a basic understanding of computer architecture, data structures, and assembly language concepts.

In view of the availability of comercial hardware and software that comes with a development environment for building and experimenting with ANS models, our emphasis on the need to program from scratch requires explanation. Our experience has been that large-scale ANS applications require highly optimized software due to the extreme computational load that neural networks place on computing systems. Specialized environments often place a significant overhead on the system, resulting in decreased performance. Moreover, certain issues—such as design flexibility, portability, and the ability to embed neural-network software into an application—become much less of a concern when programming is done directly in a language such as C.

Chapter 1, Introduction to ANS Technology, provides background material that is common to many of the discussions in following chapters. The two major topics in this chapter are a description of a general neural-network processing model and an overview of simulation techniques. In the description of the processing model, we have adhered, as much as possible, to the notation in the *PDP* series. The simulation overview presents a general framework for the simulations discussed in subsequent chapters.

Following this introductory chapter is a series of chapters, each devoted to a specific network or class of networks. There are nine such chapters:

Chapter 2, Adaline and Madaline

Chapter 3, Backpropagation

Chapter 4, The BAM and the Hopfield Memory

Chapter 5, Simulated Annealing: Networks discussed include the Boltzmann completion and input–output networks

Chapter 6, The Counterpropagation Network

Chapter 7, Self-Organizing Maps: includes the Kohonen topology-preserving map and the feature-map classifier

Chapter 8, Adaptive Resonance Theory: Networks discussed include both ART1 and ART2

Chapter 9, Spatiotemporal Pattern Classification: discusses Hecht–Nielsen's spatiotemporal network

Chapter 10, The Neocognitron

Each of these nine chapters contains a general description of the network architecture and a detailed discussion of the theory of operation of the network. Most chapters contain examples of applications that use the particular network. Chapters 2 through 9 include detailed instructions on how to build software simulations of the networks within the general framework given in Chapter 1. Exercises based on the material are interspersed throughout the text. A list of suggested programming exercises and projects appears at the end of each chapter.

We have chosen not to include the usual pseudocode for the neocognitron network described in Chapter 10. We believe that the complexity of this network makes the neocognitron inappropriate as a programming exercise for students.

To compile this survey, we had to borrow ideas from many different sources. We have attempted to give credit to the original developers of these networks, but it was impossible to define a source for every idea in the text. To help alleviate this deficiency, we have included a list of suggested readings after each chapter. We have not, however, attempted to provide anything approaching an exhaustive bibliography for each of the topics that we discuss.

Each chapter bibliography contains a few references to key sources and supplementary material in support of the chapter. Often, the sources we quote are older references, rather than the newest research on a particular topic. Many of the later research results are easy to find: Since 1987, the majority of technical papers on ANS-related topics has congregated in a few journals and conference proceedings. In particular, the journals *Neural Networks*, published by the International Neural Network Society (INNS), and *Neural Computation*, published by MIT Press, are two important periodicals. A newcomer at the time of this writing is the IEEE special-interest group on neural networks, which has its own periodical.

The primary conference in the United States is the International Joint Conference on Neural Networks, sponsored by the IEEE and INNS. This conference series was inaugurated in June of 1987, sponsored by the IEEE. The conferences have produced a number of large proceedings, which should be the primary source for anyone interested in the field. The proceedings of the annual conference on Neural Information Processing Systems (NIPS), published by Morgan-Kaufmann, is another good source. There are other conferences as well, both in the United States and in Europe. As a comprehensive bibliography of the field, Casey Klimausauskas has compiled *The 1989 Neuro-Computing Bibliography*, published by MIT Press [17].

Finally, we believe this book will be successful if our readers gain

- A firm understanding of the operation of the specific networks presented
- The ability to program simulations of those networks successfully
- The ability to apply neural networks to real engineering and scientific problems
- A sufficient background to permit access to the professional literature
- The enthusiasm that we feel for this relatively new technology and the respect we have for its ability to solve problems that have eluded other approaches

ACKNOWLEDGMENTS

As this page is being written, several associates are outside our offices, discussing the New York Giants' win over the Buffalo Bills in Super Bowl XXV last night. Their comments describing the affair range from the typical superlatives, "The Giants' offensive line overwhelmed the Bills' defense," to denials of any skill, training, or teamwork attributable to the participants, "They were just plain lucky."

By way of analogy, we have now arrived at our Super Bowl. The text is written, the artwork done, the manuscript reviewed, the editing completed, and the book is now ready for typesetting. Undoubtedly, after the book is published many will comment on the quality of the effort, although we hope no one will attribute the quality to "just plain luck." We have survived the arduous process of publishing a textbook, and like the teams that went to the Super Bowl, we have succeeded because of the combined efforts of many, many people. Space does not allow us to mention each person by name, but we are deeply grateful to everyone that has been associated with this project.

There are, however, several individuals that have gone well beyond the normal call of duty, and we would now like to thank these people by name. First of all, Dr. John Engvall and Mr. John Frere of Loral Space Information Systems were kind enough to encourage us in the exploration of neural-network technology and in the development of this book. Mr. Gary McIntire, Ms. Sheryl Knotts, and Mr. Matt Hanson all of the Loral Space Information Systems Artificial Intelligence Laboratory proofread early versions of the manuscript and helped us to debug our algorithms. We would also like to thank our reviewers: Dr. Marijke Augusteijn, Department of Computer Science, University of Colorado; Dr. Daniel Kammen, Division of Biology, California Institute of Technology; Dr. E. L. Perry, Loral Command and Control Systems; Dr. Gerald Tesauro, IBM Thomas J. Watson Research Center; and Dr. John Vittal, GTE Laboratories, Inc. We found their many comments and suggestions quite useful, and we believe that the end product is much better because of their efforts.

We received funding for several of the applications described in the text from sources outside our own company. In that regard, we would like to thank Dr. Hossein Nivi of the Ford Motor Company, and Dr. Jon Erickson, Mr. Ken Baker, and Mr. Robert Savely of the NASA Johnson Space Center.

We are also deeply grateful to our publishers, particularly Mr. Peter Gordon, Ms. Helen Goldstein, and Mr. Mark McFarland, all of whom offered helpful insights and suggestions and also took the risk of publishing two unknown authors. We also owe a great debt to our production staff, specifically, Ms. Loren Hilgenhurst Stevens, Ms. Mona Zeftel, and Ms. Mary Dyer, who guided us through the maze of details associated with publishing a book and to our patient copy editor, Ms. Lyn Dupré, who taught us much about the craft of writing.

Finally, to Peggy, Carolyn, Geoffrey, Deborah, and Danielle, our wives and children, who patiently accepted the fact that we could not be all things to them and published authors, we offer our deepest and most heartfelt thanks.

Houston, Texas   J. A. F.

D. M. S.

CONTENTS

Chapter 10
The Neocognitron   *373*

Introduction to ANS Technology

When the only tool you have is a hammer, every problem you encounter tends to resemble a nail.

—Source unknown

Why can't we build a computer that thinks? Why can't we expect machines that can perform 100 million floating-point calculations per second to be able to comprehend the meaning of shapes in visual images, or even to distinguish between different kinds of similar objects? Why can't that same machine *learn* from experience, rather than repeating forever an explicit set of instructions generated by a human programmer?

These are only a few of the many questions facing computer designers, engineers, and programmers, all of whom are striving to create more "intelligent" computer systems. The inability of the current generation of computer systems to interpret the world at large does not, however, indicate that these machines are completely inadequate. There are many tasks that are ideally suited to solution by conventional computers: scientific and mathematical problem solving; database creation, manipulation, and maintenance; electronic communication; word processing, graphics, and desktop publication; even the simple control functions that add intelligence to and simplify our household tools and appliances are handled quite effectively by today's computers.

In contrast, there are many applications that we would like to automate, but have not automated due to the complexities associated with programming a computer to perform the tasks. To a large extent, the problems are not unsolvable; rather, they are difficult to solve using sequential computer systems. This distinction is important. If the only tool we have is a sequential computer, then we will naturally try to cast every problem in terms of sequential algorithms. Many problems are not suited to this approach, however, causing us to expend

1

a great deal of effort on the development of sophisticated algorithms, perhaps even failing to find an acceptable solution.

In the remainder of this text, we will examine many parallel-processing architectures that provide us with new tools that can be used in a variety of applications. Perhaps, with these tools, we will be able to solve more easily currently difficult-to-solve, or unsolved, problems. Of course, our proverbial hammer will still be extremely useful, but with a full toolbox we should be able to accomplish much more.

As an example of the difficulties we encounter when we try to make a sequential computer system perform an inherently parallel task, consider the problem of visual pattern recognition. Complex patterns consisting of numerous elements that, individually, reveal little of the total pattern, yet collectively represent easily recognizable (by humans) objects, are typical of the kinds of patterns that have proven most difficult for computers to recognize. For example, examine the illustration presented in Figure 1.1. If we focus strictly on the black splotches, the picture is devoid of meaning. Yet, if we allow our perspective to encompass all the components, we can see the image of a commonly recognizable object in the picture. Furthermore, once we see the image, it is difficult for us *not* to see it whenever we again see this picture.

Now, let's consider the techniques we would apply were we to program a conventional computer to recognize the object in that picture. The first thing our program would attempt to do is to locate the primary area or areas of interest in the picture. That is, we would try to segment or cluster the splotches into groups, such that each group could be uniquely associated with one object. We might then attempt to find edges in the image by completing line segments. We could continue by examining the resulting set of edges for consistency, trying to determine whether or not the edges found made sense in the context of the other line segments. Lines that did not abide by some predefined rules describing the way lines and edges appear in the real world would then be attributed to noise in the image and thus would be eliminated. Finally, we would attempt to isolate regions that indicated common textures, thus filling in the holes and completing the image.

The illustration of Figure 1.1 is one of a dalmatian seen in profile, facing left, with head lowered to sniff at the ground. The image indicates the complexity of the type of problem we have been discussing. Since the dog is illustrated as a series of black spots on a white background, how can we write a computer program to determine accurately which spots form the outline of the dog, which spots can be attributed to the spots on his coat, and which spots are simply distractions?

An even better question is this: How is it that we can see the dog in the image quickly, yet a computer cannot perform this discrimination? This question is especially poignant when we consider that the switching time of the components in modern electronic computers are more than seven orders of magnitude faster than the cells that comprise our neurobiological systems. This

Figure 1.1 The picture is an example of a complex pattern. Notice how the image of the object in the foreground blends with the background clutter. Yet, there is enough information in this picture to enable us to perceive the image of a commonly recognizable object. *Source: Photo courtesy of Ron James.*

question is partially answered by the fact that the architecture of the human brain is significantly different from the architecture of a conventional computer. Whereas the response time of the individual neural cells is typically on the order of a few tens of milliseconds, the massive parallelism and interconnectivity observed in the biological systems evidently account for the ability of the brain to perform complex pattern recognition in a few hundred milliseconds.

In many real-world applications, we want our computers to perform complex pattern recognition problems, such as the one just described. Since our conventional computers are obviously not suited to this type of problem, we therefore borrow features from the physiology of the brain as the basis for our new processing models. Hence, the technology has come to be known as **artificial neural systems** (ANS) technology, or simply **neural networks**. Perhaps the models we discuss here will enable us eventually to produce machines that can interpret complex patterns such as the one in Figure 1.1.

In the next section, we will discuss aspects of neurophysiology that contribute to the ANS models we will examine. Before we do that, let's first consider how an ANS might be used to formulate a computer solution to a pattern-matching problem similar to, but much simpler than, the problem of recognizing the dalmation in Figure 1.1. Specifically, the problem we will address is recognition of hand-drawn alphanumeric characters. This example is particularly interesting for two reasons:

- Even though a character set can be defined rigorously, people tend to personalize the manner in which they write the characters. This subtle variation in style is difficult to deal with when an algorithmic pattern-matching approach is used, because it combinatorially increases the size of the legal input space to be examined.

- As we will see in later chapters, the neural-network approach to solving the problem not only can provide a feasible solution, but also can be used to gain insight into the nature of the problem.

We begin by defining a neural-network structure as a collection of *parallel processors* connected together in the form of a directed graph, organized such that the network structure lends itself to the problem being considered. Referring to Figure 1.2 as a typical network diagram, we can schematically represent each **processing element** (or **unit**) in the network as a **node**, with connections between units indicated by the **arcs**. We shall indicate the direction of information flow in the network through the use of the arrowheads on the connections.

To simplify our example, we will restrict the number of characters the neural network must recognize to the 10 decimal digits, $0, 1, \ldots, 9$, rather than using the full ASCII character set. We adopt this constraint only to clarify the example; there is no reason why an ANS could not be used to recognize all characters, regardless of case or style.

Since our objective is to have the neural network determine which of the 10 digits a particular hand-drawn character is, we can create a network structure that has 10 discrete output units (or processors), one for each character to be identified. This strategy simplifies the character-discrimination function of the network, as it allows us to use a network that contains binary units on the **output layer** (e.g., for any given input pattern, our network should activate one and only one of the 10 output units, representing which of the 10 digits that we are attempting to recognize the input most resembles). Furthermore, if we insist that the output units behave according to a simple on–off strategy, the process of converting an input signal to an output signal becomes a simple majority function.

Based on these considerations, we now know that our network should contain 10 binary units as its output structure. Similarly, we must determine how we will model the character input for the network. Keeping in mind that we have already indicated a preference for binary output units, we can again simplify our task if we model the input data as a vector containing binary elements, which will allow us to use a network with only one type of processing unit. To create this type of input, we borrow an idea from the video world and *pixelize* the character. We will arbitrarily size the pixel image as a 10×8 matrix, using a 1 to represent a pixel that is "on," and a 0 to represent a pixel that is "off."

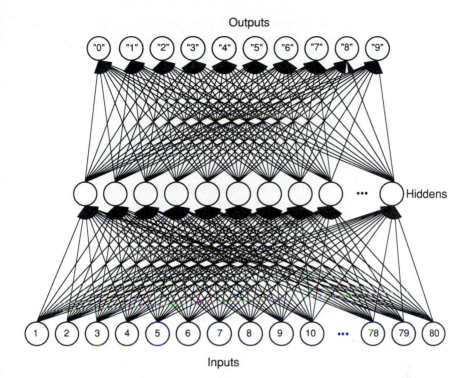

Figure 1.2   This schematic represents the character-recognition problem described in the text. In this example, application of an input pattern on the bottom layer of processors can cause many of the second-layer, or *hidden-layer*, units to activate. The activity on the hidden layer should then cause exactly one of the output-layer units to activate—the one associated with the pattern being identified. You should also note the large number of connections needed for this relatively small network.

Furthermore, we can dissect this matrix into a set of row vectors, which can then be concatenated into a single row vector of dimension 80. Thus, we have now defined the dimension and characteristics of the input pattern for our network.

At this point, all that remains is to size the number of processing units (called **hidden** units) that must be used internally, to connect them to the input and output units already defined using **weighted connections**, and to train the network with example data pairs.[1] This concept of learning by example is extremely important. As we shall see, a significant advantage of an ANS approach to solving a problem is that we need not have a well-defined process for algorithmically converting an input to an output. Rather, all that we need for most

---

[1]Details of how this training is accomplished will occupy much of the remainder of the text.

networks is a collection of representative examples of the desired translation. The ANS then adapts itself to reproduce the desired outputs when presented with the example inputs.

In addition, as our example network illustrates, an ANS is robust in the sense that it will respond with an output even when presented with inputs that it has never seen before, such as patterns containing noise. If the input noise has not obliterated the image of the character, the network will produce a good guess using those portions of the image that were not obscured and the information that it has stored about how the characters are supposed to look. The inherent ability to deal with noisy or obscured patterns is a significant advantage of an ANS approach over a traditional algorithmic solution. It also illustrates a neural-network maxim: The power of an ANS approach lies not necessarily in the elegance of the particular solution, but rather in the generality of the network to *find its own solution* to particular problems, given only examples of the desired behavior.

Once our network is trained adequately, we can show it images of numerals written by people whose writing was not used to train the network. If the training has been adequate, the information propagating through the network will result in a single element at the output having a binary 1 value, and that unit will be the one that corresponds to the numeral that was written. Figure 1.3 illustrates characters that the trained network can recognize, as well as several it cannot.

In the previous discussion, we alluded to two different types of network operation: *training* mode and *production* mode. The distinct nature of these two modes of operation is another useful feature of ANS technology. If we note that the process of training the network is simply a means of encoding information about the problem to be solved, and that the network spends most of its productive time being exercised after the training has completed, we will have uncovered a means of allowing automated systems to evolve *without explicit reprogramming.*

As an example of how we might benefit from this separation, consider a system that utilizes a software simulation of a neural network as part of its programming. In this case, the network would be modeled in the host computer system as a set of data structures that represents the current state of the network. The process of training the network is simply a matter of altering the connection weights systematically to encode the desired input–output relationships. If we code the network simulator such that the data structures used by the network are allocated dynamically, and are initialized by reading of connection-weight data from a disk file, we can also create a network simulator with a similar structure in another, off-line computer system. When the on-line system must change to satisfy new operational requirements, we can develop the new connection weights off-line by training the network simulator in the remote system. Later, we can update the operational system by simply changing the connection-weight initialization file from the previous version to the new version produced by the off-line system.

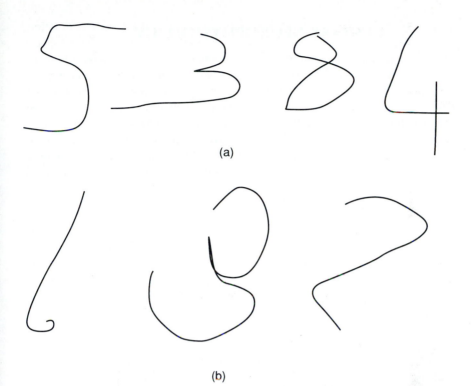

(a)

(b)

Figure 1.3 Handwritten characters vary greatly. (a) These characters were recognized by the network in Figure 1.2; (b) these characters were not recognized.

These examples hint at the ability of neural networks to deal with complex pattern-recognition problems, but they are by no means indicative of the limits of the technology. In later chapters, we will describe networks that can be used to diagnose problems from symptoms, networks that can adapt themselves to model a topological mapping accurately, and even networks that can learn to recognize and reproduce a temporal sequence of patterns. All these networks are based on the simple building blocks discussed previously, and derived from the topics we shall discuss in the next two sections.

Finally, the distinction made between the artificial and natural systems is intentional. We cannot overemphasize the fact that the ANS models we will examine bear only a perfunctory resemblance to their biological counterparts. What is important about these models is that they all exhibit the useful behaviors of learning, recognizing, and applying relationships between objects and patterns of objects in the real world. In this regard, they provide us with a whole new set of tools that we can use to solve "difficult" problems.

1.1   ELEMENTARY NEUROPHYSIOLOGY

From time to time throughout this text, we shall cite specific results from neu-robiology that pertain to a particular ANS architecture. There are also basic concepts that have a more universal significance. In this regard, we look first at individual neurons, then at the synaptic junctions between neurons. We describe the McCulloch–Pitts model of neural computation, and examine its specific re-lationship to our neural-network models. We finish the section with a look at Hebb's theory of learning. Bear in mind that the following discussion is a simplified overview; the subject of neurophysiology is vastly more complicated than is the picture we paint here.

1.1.1   Single-Neuron Physiology

Figure 1.4 depicts the major components of a typical nerve cell in the central nervous system. The membrane of a neuron separates the intracellular plasma from the interstitial fluid external to the cell. The membrane is permeable to certain ionic species, and acts to maintain a potential difference between the

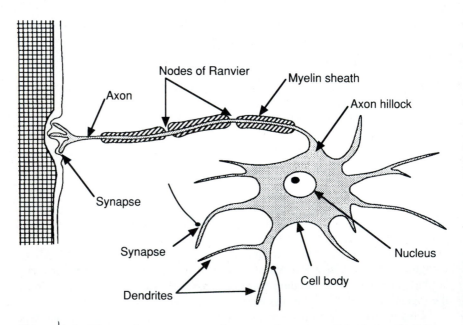

Figure 1.4   The major structures of a typical nerve cell include dendrites, the cell body, and a single axon. The axon of many neurons is surrounded by a membrane called the myelin sheath. Nodes of Ranvier interrupt the myelin sheath periodically along the length of the axon. Synapses connect the axons of one neuron to various parts of other neurons.

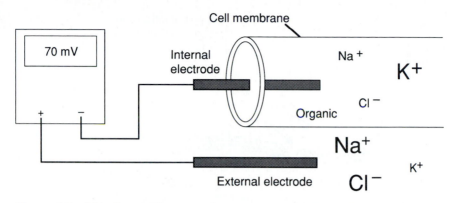

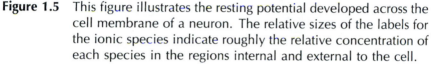

Figure 1.5 This figure illustrates the resting potential developed across the cell membrane of a neuron. The relative sizes of the labels for the ionic species indicate roughly the relative concentration of each species in the regions internal and external to the cell.

intracellular fluid and the extracellular fluid. It accomplishes this task primarily by the action of a sodium–potassium pump. This mechanism transports sodium ions out of the cell and potassium ions into the cell. Other ionic species present are chloride ions and negative organic ions.

All the ionic species can diffuse across the cell membrane, with the exception of the organic ions, which are too large. Since the organic ions cannot diffuse out of the cell, their net negative charge makes chloride diffusion into the cell unfavorable; thus, there will be a higher concentration of chloride ions outside of the cell. The sodium–potassium pump forces a higher concentration of potassium inside the cell and a higher concentration of sodium outside the cell.

The cell membrane is selectively more permeable to potassium ions than to sodium ions. The chemical gradient of potassium tends to cause potassium ions to diffuse out of the cell, but the strong attraction of the negative organic ions tends to keep the potassium inside. The result of these opposing forces is that an equilibrium is reached where there are significantly more sodium and chloride ions outside the cell, and more potassium and organic ions inside the cell. Moreover, the resulting equilibrium leaves a potential difference across the cell membrane of about 70 to 100 millivolts (mV), with the intracellular fluid being more negative. This potential, called the **resting potential** of the cell, is depicted schematically in Figure 1.5.

Figure 1.6 illustrates a neuron with several incoming connections, and the potentials that occur at various locations. The figure shows the axon with a covering called a **myelin sheath.** This insulating layer is interrupted at various points by the **nodes of Ranvier.**

Excitatory inputs to the cell reduce the potential difference across the cell membrane. The resulting depolarization at the **axon hillock** alters the permeability of the cell membrane to sodium ions. As a result, there is a large influx

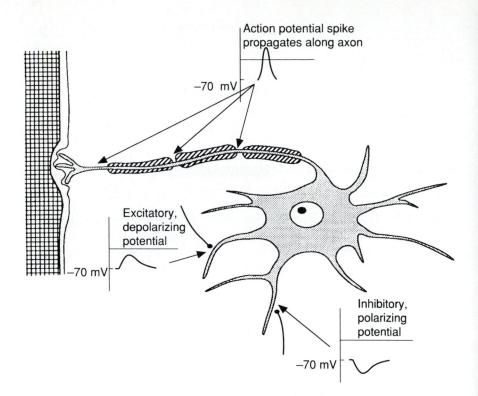

Figure 1.6   Connections to the neuron from other neurons occur at various
                  locations on the cell that are known as synapses.   Nerve
                  impulses through these connecting neurons can result in local
                  changes in the potential in the cell body of the receiving
                  neuron. These potentials, called graded potentials or input
                  potentials, can spread through the main body of the cell. They
                  can be either excitatory (decreasing the polarization of the cell)
                  or inhibitory (increasing the polarization of the cell). The input
                  potentials are summed at the axon hillock. If the amount
                  of depolarization at the axon hillock is sufficient, an action
                  potential is generated; it travels down the axon away from the
                  main cell body.

of positive sodium ions into the cell, contributing further to the depolarization.
This self-generating effect results in the **action potential**.

   Nerve fibers themselves are poor conductors. The transmission of the action
potential down the axon is a result of a sequence of depolarizations that occur
at the nodes of Ranvier. As one node depolarizes, it triggers the depolarization
of the next node. The action potential travels down the fiber in a discontinuous
fashion, from node to node. Once an action potential has passed a given point,

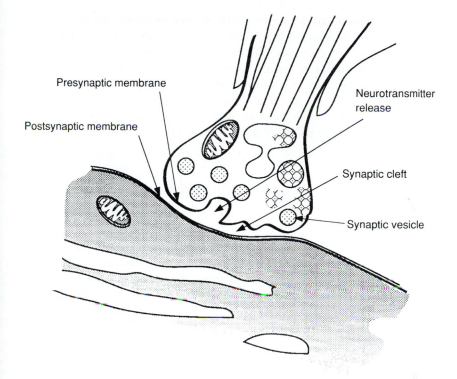

Presynaptic membrane

Postsynaptic membrane

Neurotransmitter release

Synaptic cleft

Synaptic vesicle

Figure 1.7   Neurotransmitters are held in vesicles near the presynaptic membrane. These chemicals are released into the synaptic cleft and diffuse to the postsynaptic membrane, where they are subsequently absorbed.

that point is incapable of being reexcited for about 1 millisecond, while it is restored to its resting potential. This **refractory period** limits the frequency of nerve-pulse transmission to about 1000 per second.

1.1.2   The Synaptic Junction

Let's take a brief look at the activity that occurs at the connection between two neurons called the synaptic junction or **synapse**. Communication between neurons occurs as a result of the release by the presynaptic cell of substances called **neurotransmitters**, and of the subsequent absorption of these substances by the postsynaptic cell. Figure 1.7 shows this activity. When the action potential arrives as the presynaptic membrane, changes in the permeability of the membrane cause an influx of calcium ions. These ions cause the vesicles containing the neurotransmitters to fuse with the presynaptic membrane and to release their neurotransmitters into the synaptic cleft.

The neurotransmitters diffuse across the junction and join to the postsynaptic membrane at certain receptor sites. The chemical action at the receptor sites results in changes in the permeability of the postsynaptic membrane to certain ionic species. An influx of positive species into the cell will tend to depolarize the resting potential; this effect is excitatory. If negative ions enter, a hyperpolarization effect occurs; this effect is inhibitory. Both effects are local effects that spread a short distance into the cell body and are summed at the axon hillock. If the sum is greater than a certain threshold, an action potential is generated.

1.1.3 Neural Circuits and Computation

Figure 1.8 illustrates several basic neural circuits that are found in the central nervous system. Figures 1.8(a) and (b) illustrate the principles of divergence and convergence in neural circuitry. Each neuron sends impulses to many other neurons (divergence), and receives impulses from many neurons (convergence). This simple idea appears to be the foundation for all activity in the central nervous system, and forms the basis for most neural-network models that we shall discuss in later chapters.

Notice the feedback paths in the circuits of Figure 1.8(b), (c), and (d). Since synaptic connections can be either excitatory or inhibitory, these circuits facilitate control systems having either positive or negative feedback. Of course, these simple circuits do not adequately portray the vast complexity of neuroanatomy.

Now that we have an idea of how individual neurons operate and of how they are put together, we can pose a fundamental question: How do these relatively simple concepts combine to give the brain its enormous abilities? The first significant attempt to answer this question was made in 1943, through the seminal work by McCulloch and Pitts [24]. This work is important for many reasons, not the least of which is that the investigators were the first people to treat the brain as a *computational* organism.

The McCulloch–Pitts theory is founded on five assumptions:

1. The activity of a neuron is an all-or-none process.

2. A certain fixed number of synapses (> 1) must be excited within a period of latent addition for a neuron to be excited.

3. The only significant delay within the nervous system is synaptic delay.

4. The activity of any inhibitory synapse absolutely prevents excitation of the neuron at that time.

5. The structure of the interconnection network does not change with time.

Assumption 1 identifies the neurons as being binary: They are either on or off. We can therefore define a predicate, $N_i(t)$, which denotes the assertion that the ith neuron fires at time t. The notation, $\neg N_i(t)$, denotes the assertion that the ith neuron did not fire at time t. Using this notation, we can describe

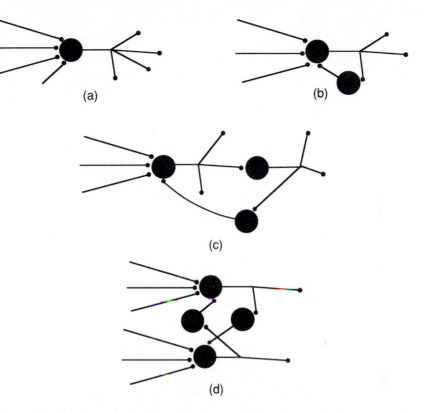

Figure 1.8 These schematics show examples of neural circuits in the central nervous system.   The cell bodies (including the dendrites) are represented by the large circles. Small circles appear at the ends of the axons. Illustrated in (a) and (b) are the concepts of divergence and convergence. Shown in (b), (c), and (d) are examples of circuits with feedback paths.

the action of certain networks using propositional logic. Figure 1.9 shows five simple networks. We can write simple propositional expressions to describe the behavior of the first four (the fifth one appears in Exercise 1.1). Figure 1.9(a) describes precession: neuron 2 fires after neuron 1. The expression is $N_2(t) = N_1(t-1)$. Similarly, the expressions for parts (b) through (d) of this figure are

- $N_3(t) = N_1(t-1) \lor N_2(t-1)$ (disjunction),

- $N_3(t) = N_1(t-1) \& N_2(t-1)$ (conjunction), and

- $N_3(t) = N_1(t-1) \& \neg N_2(t-1)$ (conjoined negation).

One of the powerful proofs in this theory was that *any* network that does not have feedback connections can be described in terms of combinations of these four

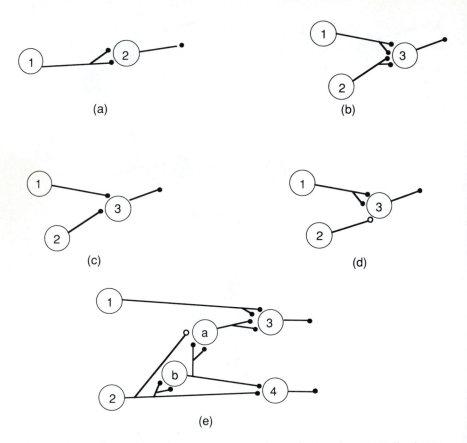

Figure 1.9 These drawings are examples of simple McCulloch–Pitts networks that can be defined in terms of the notation of propositional logic. Large circles with labels represent cell bodies. The small, filled circles represent excitatory connections; the small, open circles represent inhibitory connections. The networks illustrate (a) precession, (b) disjunction, (c) conjunction, and (d) conjoined negation. Shown in (e) is a combination of networks (a)–(d).

simple expressions, and vice versa. Figure 1.9(e) is an example of a network made from a combination of the networks in parts (a) through (d).

Although the McCulloch–Pitts theory has turned out not to be an accurate model of brain activity, the importance of the work cannot be overstated. The theory helped to shape the thinking of many people who were influential in the development of modern computer science. As Anderson and Rosenfeld point out, one critical idea was left unstated in the McCulloch–Pitts paper: Although neurons are simple devices, great computational power can be realized when these neurons are suitably connected and are embedded within the nervous system [2].

Exercise 1.1: Write the propositional expression for $N_3(t)$ and $N_4(t)$, of Figure 1.9(e).

Exercise 1.2: Construct McCulloch–Pitts networks for the following expressions:

1. $N_3(t) = N_2(t-2)\&\neg N_1(t-3)$
2. $N_4(t) = [N_2(t-2)\&\neg N_1(t-2)] \vee [N_3(t-2)\&\neg N_1(t-2)]$
   $\vee [N_2(t-2)\&N_3(t-2)]$

1.1.4 Hebbian Learning

Biological neural systems are not born preprogrammed with all the knowledge and abilities that they will eventually have. A learning process that takes place over a period of time somehow modifies the network to incorporate new information.

In the previous section, we began to see how a relatively simple neuron might result in a sophisticated computational device. In this section, we shall explore a relatively simple learning theory that suggests an elegant answer to this question: How do we learn?

The basic theory comes from a 1949 book by Hebb, *Organization of Behavior*. The main idea was stated in the form of an assumption, which we reproduce here for historical interest:

> When an axon of cell *A* is near enough to excite a cell *B* and repeatedly or persistently takes part in firing it, some growth process or metabolic change takes place in one or both cells such that *A*'s efficiency, as one of the cells firing *B*, is increased. [10, p. 50]

As with the McCulloch–Pitts model, this learning *law* does not tell the whole story. Nevertheless, it appears in one form or another in many of the neural-network models that exist today.

To illustrate the basic idea, we consider the example of classical conditioning, using the familiar experiment of Pavlov. Figure 1.10 shows three idealized neurons that participate in the process.

Suppose that the excitation of C, caused by the sight of food, is sufficient to excite B, causing salivation. Furthermore, suppose that, in the absence of additional stimulation, the excitation of A, resulting from hearing a bell, is not sufficient to cause the firing of B.

Let's allow C to cause B to fire by showing food to the subject, and *while B is still firing,* stimulate A by ringing a bell. Because B is still firing, A is now participating in the excitation of B, even though by itself A would be insufficient to cause B to fire. In this situation, Hebb's assumption dictates that some change occur between A and B, so that A's influence on B is increased.

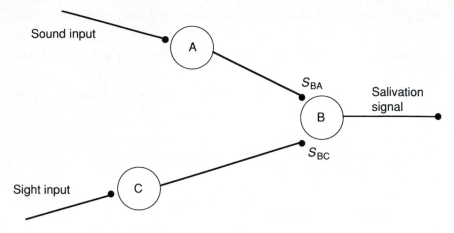

Figure 1.10   Two neurons, A and C, are stimulated by the sensory inputs
of sound and sight, respectively.   The third neuron, B,
causes salivation.   The two synaptic junctions are labeled
S_{BA} and S_{BC}.

If the experiment is repeated often enough, A will eventually be able to cause
B to fire *even in the absence of the visual stimulation from C*. Then, if the bell
is rung, but no food is shown, salivation will still occur, because the excitation
due to A alone is now sufficient to cause B to fire.

Because the connection between neurons is through the synapse, it is reasonable to guess that whatever changes occur during learning take place there.
Hebb theorized that the area of the synaptic junction increased.   More recent
theories assert that an increase in the rate of neurotransmitter release by the
presynaptic cell is responsible.   In any event, changes certainly occur at the
synapse. If either the pre- or postsynaptic cell were altered as a whole, other
responses could be reinforced that are unrelated to the conditioning experiment.

Thus we conclude our brief look at neurophysiology. Before moving on,
however, we reiterate a caution and issue a challenge to you. On the one hand,
although there are many analogies between the basic concepts of neurophysiology and the neural-network models described in this book, we caution you not to
portray these systems as actually modeling the brain. We prefer to say that these
networks have been *inspired* by our current understanding of neurophysiology.
On the other hand, it is often too easy for engineers, in their pursuit of solutions
to specific problems, to ignore completely the neurophysiological foundations
of the technology. We believe that this tendency is unfortunate. Therefore, we
challenge ANS practitioners to keep abreast of the developments in neurobiology so as to be able to incorporate significant results into their systems. After
all, what better model is there than the one example of a neural network with
existing capabilities that far surpass any of our artificial systems?

Exercise 1.3: The analysis of high-dimensional data sets is often a complex task. One way to simplify the task is to use the Karhunen–Loeve (KL) matrix, which is defined as

$$F_{ij} = \frac{1}{N} \sum_{\mu=1}^{N} f_i^{\mu} f_j^{\mu}$$

where N is the number of vectors, and f_i^{μ} is the ith component of the μth vector. The KL matrix extracts the *principal components*, or directions of maximum information (correlation) from a data set. Determine the relationship between the KL formulation and the popular version of the Hebb rule known as the **Oja rule**:

$$\frac{d\phi_i(t)}{dt} = O(t)[I_i(t) - O(t)\phi_i(t)]$$

where $O(t)$ is the output of a simple, linear processing element; $I_i(t)$ are the inputs; and $\phi_i(t)$ are the synaptic strengths. (This exercise was suggested by Dr. Daniel Kammen, California Institute of Technology.)

1.2   FROM NEURONS TO ANS

In this section, we make a transition from some of the ideas gleaned from neurobiology to the idealized structures that form the basis of most ANS models. We first describe a general artificial neuron that incorporates most features we shall need for future discussions of specific models. Later in the section, we take a brief look at a particular example of an ANS called the perceptron. The perceptron was the result of an early attempt to simulate neural computation in order to perform complex tasks. We shall examine in particular what several limitations of this approach are and how they might be overcome.

1.2.1   The General Processing Element

The individual computational elements that make up most artificial neural-system models are rarely called *artificial neurons;* they are more often referred to as nodes, units, or processing elements (PEs). All these terms are used interchangeably throughout this book.

Another point to bear in mind is that it is not always appropriate to think of the processing elements in a neural network as being in a one-to-one relationship with actual biological neurons. It is sometimes better to imagine a single processing element as representative of the collective activity of a group of neurons. Not only will this interpretation help us to avoid the trap of speaking as though our systems were actual brain models, but also it will make the problem more tractable when we *are* attempting to model the behavior of some biological structure.

Figure 1.11 shows our general PE model. Each PE is numbered, the one in the figure being the ith. Having cautioned you not to make too many biological

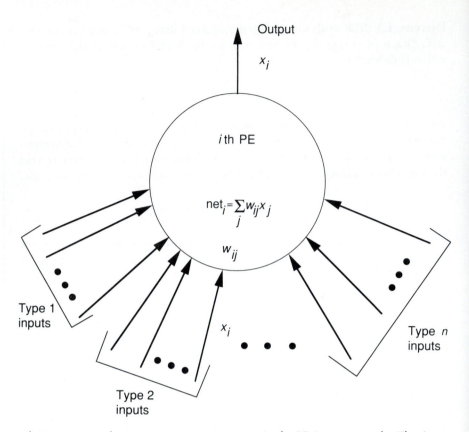

Output

x_i

i th PE

$$\text{net}_i = \sum_j w_{ij} x_j$$

w_{ij}

Type 1
inputs

x_j

Type n
inputs

Type 2
inputs

Figure 1.11   This structure represents a single PE in a network. The input
connections are modeled as arrows from other processing
elements. Each input connection has associated with it a
quantity, w_{ij}, called a weight. There is a single output value,
which can fan out to other units.

analogies, we shall now ignore our own advice and make a few ourselves. For
example, like a real neuron, the PE has many inputs, but has only a single
output, which can fan out to many other PEs in the network. The input the ith
receives from the jth PE is indicated as x_j (note that this value is also the output
of the jth node, just as the output generated by the ith node is labeled x_i). Each
connection to the ith PE has associated with it a quantity called a **weight** or
connection strength. The weight on the connection *from* the jth node *to* the ith
node is denoted w_{ij}. All these quantities have analogues in the standard neuron
model: The output of the PE corresponds to the firing frequency of the neuron,
and the weight corresponds to the strength of the synaptic connection between
neurons. In our models, these quantities will be represented as real numbers.

Notice that the inputs to the PE are segregated into various *types*. This segregation acknowledges that a particular input connection may have one of several effects. An input connection may be excitatory or inhibitory, for example. In our models, excitatory connections have positive weights, and inhibitory connections have negative weights. Other types are possible. The terms **gain, quenching,** and **nonspecific arousal** describe other, special-purpose connections; the characteristics of these other connections will be described later in the book. Excitatory and inhibitory connections are usually considered together, and constitute the most common forms of input to a PE.

Each PE determines a net-input value based on all its input connections. In the absence of special connections, we typically calculate the net input by summing the input values, gated (multiplied) by their corresponding weights. In other words, the net input to the ith unit can be written as

$$\text{net}_i = \sum_j x_j w_{ij} \tag{1.1}$$

where the index, j, runs over all connections to the PE. Note that excitation and inhibition are accounted for automatically by the sign of the weights. This sum-of-products calculation plays an important role in the network simulations that we will be describing later. Because there is often a very large number of interconnects in a network, the speed at which this calculation can be performed usually determines the performance of any given network simulation.

Once the net input is calculated, it is converted to an **activation value,** or simply **activation,** for the PE. We can write this activation value as

$$a_i(t) = F_i(a_i(t-1), \text{net}_i(t)) \tag{1.2}$$

to denote that the activation is an explicit function of the net input. Notice that the current activation may depend on the previous value of the activation, $a(t-1)$.[2] We include this dependence in the definition for generality. In the majority of cases, the activation and net input are identical, and the terms often are used interchangeably. Sometimes, activation and net input are not the same, and we must pay attention to the difference. For the most part, however, we will be able to use activation to mean net input, and vice versa.

Once the activation of the PE is calculated, we can determine the output value by applying an **output function**:

$$x_i = f_i(a_i) \tag{1.3}$$

Since, usually, $a_i = \text{net}_i$, this function is normally written as

$$x_i = f_i(\text{net}_i) \tag{1.4}$$

One reason for belaboring the issue of activation versus net input is that the term **activation function** is sometimes used to refer to the function, f_i, that

---

[2]Because of the emphasis on digital simulations in this text, we generally consider time to be measured in discrete steps. The notation $t-1$ indicates one timestep prior to time t.

converts the net input value, net$_i$, to the node's output value, x_i. In this text, we shall consistently use the term *output function* for $f_i()$ of Eqs. (1.3) and (1.4). Be aware, however, that the literature is not always consistent in this respect.

When we are describing the mathematical basis for network models, it will often be useful to think of the network as a **dynamical system**—that is, as a system that evolves over time. To describe such a network, we shall write differential equations that describe the time rate of change of the outputs of the various PEs. For example, $\dot{x}_i = g_i(x_i, net_i)$ represents a general differential equation for the output of the ith PE, where the dot above the x refers to differentiation with respect to time. Since net$_i$ depends on the outputs of many other units, we actually have a system of coupled differential equations.

As an example, let's look at the equation

$$\dot{x}_i = -x_i + f_i(\text{net}_i)$$

for the output of the ith processing element. We apply some input values to the PE so that net$_i > 0$. If the inputs remain for a sufficiently long time, the output value will reach an equilibrium value, when $\dot{x}_i = 0$, given by

$$x_i = f_i(\text{net}_i)$$

which is identical to Eq. (1.4). We can often assume that input values remain until equilibrium has been achieved.

Once the unit has a nonzero output value, removal of the inputs will cause the output to return to zero. If net$_i = 0$, then

$$\dot{x}_i = -x$$

which means that $x \rightarrow 0$.

It is also useful to view the collection of weight values as a dynamical system. Recall the discussion in the previous section, where we asserted that learning is a result of the modification of the strength of synaptic junctions between neurons. In an ANS, learning usually is accomplished by modification of the weight values. We can write a system of differential equations for the weight values, $\dot{w}_{ij} = G_i(w_{ij}, x_i, x_j, \ldots)$, where G_i represents the **learning law.** The learning process consists of finding weights that encode the knowledge that we want the system to learn. For most realistic systems, it is not easy to determine a closed-form solution for this system of equations. Techniques exist, however, that result in an acceptable approximation to a solution. Proving the existence of stable solutions to such systems of equations is an active area of research in neural networks today, and probably will continue to be so for some time.

1.2.2   Vector Formulation

In many of the network models that we shall discuss, it is useful to describe certain quantities in terms of vectors. Think of a neural network composed of several **layers** of identical processing elements. If a particular layer contains n

units, the outputs of that layer can be thought of as an n-dimensional vector, $\mathbf{x} = (x_1, x_2, \ldots, x_n)^t$, where the t superscript means *transpose*. In our notation, vectors written in boldface type, such as $\mathbf{x}$, will be assumed to be column vectors. When they are written row form, the transpose symbol will be added to indicate that the vector is actually to be thought of as a column vector. Conversely, the notation $\mathbf{x}^t$ indicates a row vector.

Suppose the n-dimensional output vector of the previous paragraph provides the input values to each unit in an m-dimensional layer (a layer with m units). Each unit on the m-dimensional layer will have n weights associated with the connections from the previous layer. Thus, there are m n-dimensional weight vectors associated with this layer; there is one n-dimensional weight vector for each of the m units. The weight vector of the ith unit can be written as $\mathbf{w}_i = (w_{i1}, w_{i2}, \ldots, w_{in})^t$. A superscript can be added to the weight notation to distinguish between weights on different layers.

The net input to the ith unit can be written in terms of the inner product, or dot product, of the input vector and the weight vector. For vectors *of equal dimensions*, the inner product is defined as the sum of the products of the corresponding components of the two vectors. In the notation of the previous section,

$$\text{net}_i = \sum_{j=1}^{n} x_j w_{ij}$$

where n is the number of connections to the ith unit. This equation can be written succinctly in vector notation as

$$\text{net}_i = \mathbf{x} \cdot \mathbf{w}_i$$

or

$$\text{net}_i = \mathbf{x}^t \mathbf{w}_i$$

Also note that, because of the rules of multiplication of vectors,

$$\mathbf{x}^t \mathbf{w}_i = \mathbf{w}_i^t \mathbf{x}$$

We shall often speak of input *vectors* and output *vectors* and weight *vectors*, but we tend to reserve the vector notation for cases where it is particularly appropriate. Additional vector concepts will be introduced later as needed. In the next section, we shall use the notation presented here to describe a neural-network model that has an important place in history: the perceptron.

1.2.3 The Perceptron: Part 1

The device known as the perceptron was invented by psychologist Frank Rosenblatt in the late 1950s. It represented his attempt to "illustrate some of the fundamental properties of intelligent systems in general, without becoming too

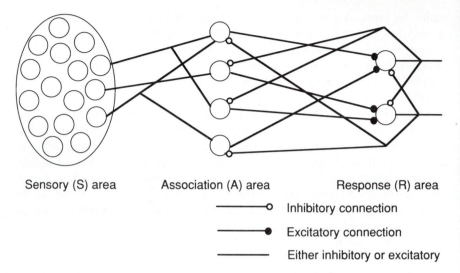

Sensory (S) area   Association (A) area   Response (R) area

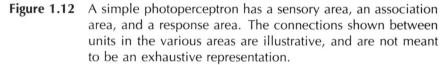

Figure 1.12   A simple photoperceptron has a sensory area, an association
area, and a response area. The connections shown between
units in the various areas are illustrative, and are not meant
to be an exhaustive representation.

deeply enmeshed in the special, and frequently unknown, conditions which hold
for particular biological organisms" [29, p. 387]. Rosenblatt believed that the
connectivity that develops in biological networks contains a large random element. Thus, he took exception to previous analyses, such as the McCulloch–Pitts
model, where symbolic logic was employed to analyze rather idealized structures. Rather, Rosenblatt believed that the most appropriate analysis tool was
probability theory. He developed a theory of **statistical separability** that he used
to characterize the gross properties of these somewhat randomly interconnected
networks.

The **photoperceptron** is a device that responds to optical patterns. We show
an example in Figure 1.12. In this device, light impinges on the **sensory (S)
points** of the retina structure. Each S point responds in an all-or-nothing manner
to the incoming light. Impulses generated by the S points are transmitted to the
associator (A) units in the association layer. Each A unit is connected to a
random set of S points, called the A unit's **source set**, and the connections may
be either excitatory or inhibitory. The connections have the possible values, $+1$,
-1, and 0. When a stimulus pattern appears on the retina, an A unit becomes
active if the sum of its inputs exceeds some threshold value. If active, the A
unit produces an output, which is sent to the next layer of units.

In a similar manner, A units are connected to **response (R) units** in the
response layer. The pattern of connectivity is again random between the layers,
but there is the addition of inhibitory feedback connections from the response

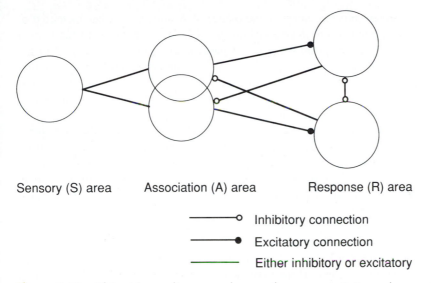

Sensory (S) area   Association (A) area   Response (R) area

```
───────────○   Inhibitory connection
───────────●   Excitatory connection
───────────    Either inhibitory or excitatory
```

Figure 1.13   This Venn diagram shows the connectivity scheme for a simple perceptron.   Each R unit receives excitatory connections from a group of units in the association area that is called the source set of the R unit. Notice that some A units are in the source set for both R units.

layer to the association layer, and of inhibitory connections between R units. The entire connectivity scheme is depicted in the form of a Venn diagram in Figure 1.13 for a simple perceptron with two R units.

This drawing shows that each R unit inhibits the A units in the complement to its own source set. Furthermore, each R unit inhibits the other. These factors aid in the establishment of a single, winning R unit for each stimulus pattern appearing on the retina. The R units respond in much the same way as do the A units. If the sum of their inputs exceeds a threshold, they give an output value of +1; otherwise, the output is −1. An alternative feedback mechanism would connect excitatory feedback connections from each R unit to that R unit's respective source set in the association layer.

A system such as the one just described can be used to classify patterns appearing on the retina into categories, according to the number of response units in the system. Patterns that are sufficiently similar should excite the same R unit. Thus, the problem is one of separability: Is it possible to construct a perceptron such that it can successfully distinguish between different pattern classes? The answer is "yes," but with certain conditions that we shall explore later.

The perceptron was a learning device. In its initial configuration, the perceptron was incapable of distinguishing the patterns of interest; through a *training* process, however, it could learn this capability. In essence, training involved a reinforcement process whereby the output of A units was either increased or decreased depending on whether or not the A units contributed to the correct response of the perceptron for a given pattern. A pattern was applied to the retina, and the stimulus was propagated through the layers until a response unit was activated. If the correct response unit was active, the output of the contributing A units was increased. If the incorrect R unit was active, the output of the contributing A units was decreased.

Using such a scheme, Rosenblatt was able to show that the perceptron could classify patterns successfully in what he termed a *differentiated environment*, where each class consisted of patterns that were in some sense similar to one another. The perceptron was also able to respond consistently to random patterns, but its accuracy diminished as the number of patterns that it attempted to learn increased.

Rosenblatt's work resulted in the proof of an important result known as the **perceptron convergence theorem**. The theorem is proved for a perceptron with one R unit that is learning to differentiate patterns of two distinct classes. It states, in essence, that, if the classification *can* be learned by the perceptron, then the procedure we have described guarantees that it *will* be learned in a finite number of training cycles.

Unfortunately, perceptrons caused a fair amount of controversy at the time they were described. Unrealistic expectations and exaggerated claims no doubt played a part in this controversy. The end result was that the field of artificial neural networks was almost entirely abandoned, except by a few die-hard researchers. We hinted at one of the major problems with perceptrons when we suggested that there were conditions attached to the successful operation of the perceptron. In the next section, we explore and evaluate these considerations.

Exercise 1.4: Consider a perceptron with one R unit and N_a association units, a_μ, which is attempting to learn to differentiate i patterns, S_i, each of which falls into one of two categories. For one category, the R unit gives an output of $+1$; for the other, it gives an output of -1. Let v_μ be the output of the μth A unit. Further, let ρ_i be ± 1, depending on the class of S_i, and let $e_{\mu i}$ be 1 if a_μ is in the source set for S_i, and 0 otherwise. Show that the successful classification of patterns S_i requires that the following condition be satisfied:

$$\sum_{\mu=1}^{N_a} v_\mu e_{\mu i} \rho_i > \theta$$

where θ is the threshold value of the R unit.

1.2.4   The Perceptron: Part 2

In 1969, a book appeared that some people consider to have sounded the death knell for neural networks. The book was aptly entitled *Perceptrons: An Introduction to Computational Geometry* and was written by Marvin Minsky and

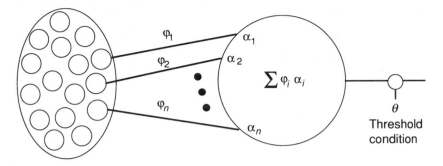

Retina

Figure 1.14 The simple perceptron structure is similar in structure to the general processing element shown in Figure 1.11. Note the addition of a threshold condition on the output. If the net input is greater than the threshold value, the output of the device is +1; otherwise, the output is 0.

Seymour Papert, both of MIT [26]. They presented an astute and detailed analysis of the perceptron in terms of its capabilities and limitations. Whether their intention was to defuse popular support for neural-network research remains a matter for debate. Nevertheless, the analysis is as timely today as it was in 1969, and many of the conclusions and concerns raised continue to be valid.

In particular, one of the points made in the previous section—a point treated in detail in Minsky and Papert's book—is the idea that there are certain restrictions on the class of problems for which the perceptron is suitable. Perceptrons can differentiate patterns only if the patterns are **linearly separable.** The meaning of the term *linearly separable* should become clear shortly. Because many classification problems do not possess linearly separable classes, this condition places a severe restriction on the applicability of the perceptron.

Minsky and Papert departed from the probabilistic approach championed by Rosenblatt, and returned to the ideas of predicate calculus in their analysis of the perceptron. Their idealized perceptron appears in Figure 1.14.

The set $\Phi = \{\varphi_1, \varphi_2, \ldots, \varphi_n\}$ is a set of predicates. In the predicates' simplest form, $\varphi_i = 1$ if the ith point of the retina is on, and $\varphi_i = 0$ otherwise. Each of the input predicates is weighted by a number from the set $\{\alpha_{\varphi_1}, \alpha_{\varphi_2}, \ldots, \alpha_{\varphi_n}\}$. The output, Ψ, is 1 if and only if $\sum_n \alpha_{\varphi_n} \varphi_n > \Theta$, where Θ is the threshold value.

One of the simplest examples of a problem that cannot be solved by a perceptron is the XOR problem. This problem is illustrated in Figure 1.15.

In the network of Figure 1.15, the output function of the output unit is a threshold function

$$f(\text{net}) = \begin{cases} 1 & \text{net} \geq \theta \\ 0 & \text{net} < \theta \end{cases}$$

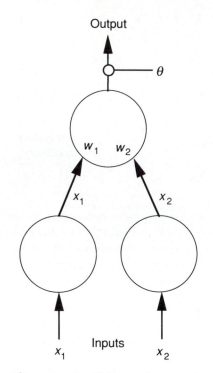

Output

θ

w_1 w_2

x_1 x_2

Inputs

x_1 x_2

x_1	x_2	Output
0	0	0
0	1	1
1	0	1
1	1	0

Figure 1.15   This two-layer network has two nodes on the input layer with input values x_1 and x_2 that can take on values of 0 or 1. We would like the network to be able to respond to the inputs such that the output o is the XOR function of the inputs, as indicated in the table.

where θ is the threshold value. This type of node is called a **linear threshold unit**.

The output-node activation is

$$\text{net} = w_1 x_1 + w_2 x_2$$

and the output value o is

$$o = f(\text{net}) = \begin{cases} 1 & w_1 x_1 + w_2 x_2 \geq \theta \\ 0 & w_1 x_1 + w_2 x_2 < \theta \end{cases}$$

The problem is to select values of the weights such that each pair of input values results in the proper output value. This task cannot be done.

Let's look at the equation

$$\theta = w_1 x_1 + w_2 x_2 \tag{1.5}$$

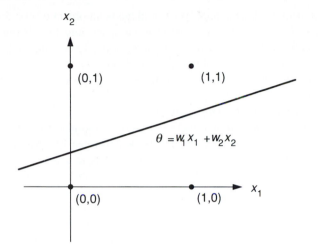

Figure 1.16 This figure shows the x_1, x_2 plane with the four points, $(0,0), (1,0), (0,1),$ and $(1,1)$, which make up the four input vectors for the XOR problem. The line $\theta = w_1 x_1 + w_2 x_2$ divides the plane into two regions but cannot successfully isolate the set of points $(0,0)$ and $(1,1)$ from the points $(0,1)$ and $(1,0)$.

This equation is the equation of a line in the x_1, x_2 plane. That plane is illustrated in Figure 1.16, along with the four points that are the possible inputs to the network. We can think of the problem as one of subdividing this space into regions and then attaching labels to the regions that correspond to the right answer for points in that region. We plot Eq. (1.5) for some values of $\theta, w_1,$ and w_2, as in Figure 1.16. The line can separate the plane into at most two distinct regions. We can then classify points in one region as belonging to the class having an output of 1, and those in the other region as belonging to the class having an output of 0; however, there is no way to arrange the position of the line so that the *correct* two points for each class both lie in the same region. (Try it.) The simple linear threshold unit cannot correctly perform the XOR function.

Exercise 1.5: A linear node is one whose output is equal to its activation. Show that a network such as the one in Figure 1.15, but with a linear output node, also is incapable of solving the XOR problem.

Before showing a way to overcome this difficulty, we digress for a moment to introduce the concept of **hyperplanes**. This idea shows up occasionally in the literature and can be useful in the evaluation of the performance of certain neural networks. We have already used the concept to analyze the XOR problem.

In familiar three-dimensional space, a plane is an object of two dimensions. A single plane can separate three-dimensional space into two distinct regions; two planes can result in three or four distinct regions, depending on their relative orientation, and so on. By extension, in an n-dimensional space, hyperplanes are objects of $n - 1$ dimensions. (An n-dimensional space is usually referred to as a **hyperspace**.) Suitable arrangement of hyperplanes allows an n-dimensional space to be partitioned into various distinct regions.

Many real problems involve the separation of regions of points in a hyperspace into individual categories, or classes, which must be distinguished from other classes. One way to make these distinctions is to select hyperplanes that separate the hyperspace into the proper regions. This task might appear difficult to perform in a high-dimensional space (higher than two, that is)—and it is. Fortunately, as we shall see later, certain neural networks can *learn* the proper partitioning, so we don't have to figure it out in advance.

In a general n-dimensional space, the equation of a hyperplane can be written as

$$\sum_{i=1}^{n} a_i x_i = C$$

where the a_is and C are constants, with at least one $a_i \neq 0$, and the x_is are the coordinates of the space.

Exercise 1.6: What are the general equations for the hyperplanes in two- and three-dimensional spaces? What geometric figures do these equations describe?

Let's return to the XOR problem to see how we might approach a solution. The graph in Figure 1.16 suggests that we could partition the space correctly if we had three regions. One region would belong to one output class, and the other two would belong to the second output class. There is no reason why disjoint regions cannot belong to the same class. Figure 1.17 shows a network of linear threshold units that performs the proper partitioning, along with the corresponding hyperspace diagram. You should verify that the network does indeed give the correct results.

The addition of the two hidden-layer, or middle-layer, units gave the network the needed flexibility to solve the problem. In fact, the existence of this hidden layer gives us the ability to construct networks that can solve complex problems.

This simple example is not intended to imply that all criticisms of the perceptron could be answered by the addition of hidden layers in the structure. It is intended to suggest that the technology continues to evolve toward systems with increasingly powerful computational abilities. Nevertheless, many concerns raised by Minsky and Papert should not be dismissed lightly. You can refer to the epilog of the 1988 reprinting of their book for a synopsis [27]. We briefly describe a second concern here.

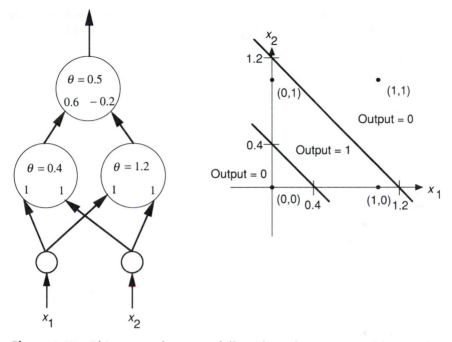

Figure 1.17   This network successfully solves the XOR problem. The hidden layer provides for two lines that can be used to separate the plane into three regions. The two regions containing the points $(0,0)$ and $(1,1)$ are associated with a network output of 0. The central region is associated with a network output of 1.

The subject of that concern is *scaling*. Many demonstrations of neural networks rely on the solution of what Minsky and Papert call *toy* problems— that is, problems that are only shadows of real-world items. Moving from these toy problems to real-world problems is often thought to be only a matter of time; we need only to wait until bigger, faster networks can be constructed. Several of the examples used in this text fall into the category of toy problems. Minsky and Papert claim that many networks suffer undesirable effects when scaled up to a large size. We raise this particular issue here, not because we necessarily believe that scale-up problems will defeat us, but because we wish to call attention to scaling as an issue that still must be resolved. We suspect that scaling problems do exist, but that there is a solution—perhaps one suggested by the architecture of the brain itself.

It seems plausible to us (and to Minsky and Papert) that the brain is composed of many different parallel, distributed systems, performing well-defined functions, but under the control of a serial-processing system at one or more levels. To address the issue of scaling, we may need to learn how to combine small networks and to place them under the control of other networks.

Of course, a "small" network in the brain challenges our current simulation capabilities, so we do not know exactly what the limitations are. The technology, although over 30 years old at this writing, is still emerging and deserves close scrutiny. We should always be aware of both the strengths and the limitations of our tools.

1.3   ANS SIMULATION

We will now consider several techniques for simulating ANS processing models using conventional programming methodologies. After presenting the design guidelines and goals that you should consider when implementing your own neural-network simulators, we will discuss the data structures that will be used throughout the remainder of this text as the basis for the network-simulation algorithms presented as a part of each chapter.

1.3.1   The Need for ANS Simulation

Most of the ANS models that we will examine in subsequent chapters share the basic concepts of distributed and highly interconnected PEs. Each network model will build on these simple concepts, implementing a unique learning law, an interconnection scheme (e.g., fully interconnected, sparsely interconnected, unidirectional, and bidirectional), and a structure, to provide systems that are tailored to specific kinds of problems.

If we are to explore the possibilities of ANS technology, and to determine what its *practical* benefits and limitations are, we must develop a means of testing as many as possible of these different network models. Only then will we be able to determine accurately whether or not an ANS can be used to solve a particular problem. Unfortunately, we do not have access to a computer system designed specifically to perform massively parallel processing, such as is found in all the ANS models we will study. However, we do have access to a tool that can be programmed rapidly to perform any type of algorithmic process, including simulation of a parallel-processing system. This tool is the familiar sequential computer.

Because we will study several different neural-network architectures, it is important for us to consider the aspects of code *portability* and *reusability* early in the implementation of our simulator. Let us therefore focus our attention on the characteristics common to most of the ANS models, and implement those characteristics as data structures that will allow our simulator to migrate to the widest variety of network models possible. The processing that is unique to the different neural-network models can then be implemented to use the data structures we will develop here. In this manner, we reduce to a minimum the amount of reprogramming needed to implement other network models.

1.3.2   Design Guidelines for Simulators

As we begin simulating neural networks, one of the first observations we will usually make is that it is necessary to design the simulation software such that the network can be sized dynamically. Even when we use only one of the network models described in this text, the ability to specify the number of PEs needed "on the fly," and in what organization, is paramount. The justification for this observation is based on the idea that it is not desirable to have to reprogram and recompile an ANS application simply because you want to change the network size. Since dynamic memory-allocation tools exist in most of the current generation of programming languages, we will use them to implement the network data structures.

The next observation you will probably make when designing your own simulator is that, at run time, the computer's central processing unit (CPU) will spend most of its time in the computation of the net_i, the input-activation term described earlier. To understand why this is so, consider how a uniprocessor computer will simulate a neural network. A program will have to be written to allow the CPU to *time multiplex* between units in the network; that is, each unit in the ANS model will share the CPU for some period. As the computer visits each node, it will perform the input computation and output translation function before moving on to the next unit. As we have already seen, the computation that produces the net_i value at each unit is normally a sum-of-products calculation—a very time-consuming operation if there is a large number of inputs at each node.

Compounding the problem, the sum-of-products calculation is done using floating-point numbers, since the network simulation is essentially a digital representation of analog signals. Thus, the CPU will have to perform two floating-point operations (a multiply and an add) for every input to each unit in the network. Given the large number of nodes in some networks, each with potentially hundreds or thousands of inputs, it is easy to see that the computer must be capable of performing several million floating-point operations per second (MFLOPS) to simulate an ANS of moderate size in a reasonable amount of time. Even assuming the computer has the floating-point hardware needed to improve the performance of the simulator, we, as programmers, must optimize the computer's ability to perform this computation by designing our data structures appropriately.

We now offer a final guideline for those readers who will attempt to implement many different network models using the data structures and processing concepts presented here. To a large extent, our simulator design philosophy is based on networks that have a uniform interconnection strategy; that is, units in one layer have all been fully connected to units in another layer. However, many of the networks we present in this text will rely on different interconnection schemes. Units may be only sparsely interconnected, or may have connections to units outside of the next sequential layer. We must take these notions into account as we define our data structures, or we may well end up with a unique set of data structures for each network we implement.

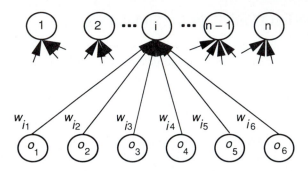

Figure 1.18 A two-layer network illustrating signal propagation is illustrated here. Each unit on the input layer generates a single output signal that is propagated through the connecting weights to each unit on the subsequent layer. Note that for each second-layer unit, the connection weights to the input layer can be modeled as a sequential array (or list) of values.

1.3.3   Array-Based ANS Data Structures

The observation made earlier that data will be processed as a sum of products (or as the *inner product* between two vectors) implies that the network data ought to be arranged in groups of linearly sequential arrays, each containing homogeneous data. The rationale behind this arrangement is that it is much faster to step through an array of data sequentially than it is to have to look up the address of every new value, as would be done if a linked-list approach were used. This grouping also is much more memory efficient than is a linked-list data structure, since there is no need to store pointers in the arrays. However, this efficiency is bought at the expense of algorithm generality, as we shall show later.

As an illustration of why arrays are more efficient than are linked records, consider the neural-network model shown in Figure 1.18. The input value present at the ith node in the upper layer is the sum of the modulated outputs received from every unit in the lower layer. To simulate this structure using data organized in arrays, we can model the connections and node outputs as values in two arrays, which we will call `weights` and `outputs` respectively.[3] The data in these arrays will be sequentially arranged so as to correspond one to one with the item being modeled, as shown in Figure 1.19. Specifically, the output from the first input unit will be stored in the first location in the `outputs` array, the second in the second, and so on. Similarly, the weight associated with the connection between the first input unit and the unit of interest, w_{i1}, will be

---

[3]Symbols that refer to variables, arrays, or code are identified in the text by the use of the typewriter typeface.

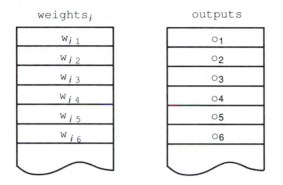

weights$_i$ outputs

weights$_i$
$w_{i\,1}$
$w_{i\,2}$
$w_{i\,3}$
$w_{i\,4}$
$w_{i\,5}$
$w_{i\,6}$

outputs
o_1
o_2
o_3
o_4
o_5
o_6

Figure 1.19 An array data structure is illustrated for the computation of the net$_i$ term. Here, we have organized the connection-weight values as a sequential array of values that map one to one to the array containing unit output values.

located as the first value in the ith `weights` array, `weights[i]`. Notice the index we now associate with the weights array. This index indicates that there will be many such arrays in the network, each containing a set of connection weights. The index here indicates that this array is one of these connection arrays—specifically, the one associated with the inputs to the ith network unit. We will expand on this notion later, as we extend the data structures to model a complete network.

The process needed to compute the aggregate input at the ith unit in the upper layer, net$_i$, is as follows. We begin by setting two pointers to the first location of the `outputs` and `weights[i]` arrays, and setting a local accumulator to zero. We then perform the computation by multiplying the values located in memory at each of the two array pointers, adding the resulting product to the local accumulator, incrementing both of the pointers, and repeating this sequence for all values in the arrays.

In most modern computer systems, this sequence of operations will compile into a two-instruction loop at the machine-code level (four instructions, if we count the compare and branch instructions needed to implement the loop), because the process of incrementing the array pointers can be done automatically as a part of the instruction-addressing mode. Notice that, if either of the arrays contains a structure of data as its elements, rather than a single value, the computation needed to access the next element in the array is no longer an *increment pointer* operation. Thus, the computer must execute additional instructions to compute the location of the next array value, as opposed to simply incrementing a register pointer as part of the instruction addressing mode. For small network applications, the overhead associated with these extra instructions is trivial. For applications that use very large neural networks, however, the overhead time needed for each connection, repeated hundreds of thousands (or perhaps millions) of times, can quickly overwhelm even a dedicated supercomputer. We therefore choose to emphasize efficiency in our simulator design; that is why we indicated earlier that the arrays ought to be constructed with homogeneous data.

This structure will do nicely for the general case of a fully interconnected network, but how can we adapt it to account for networks where the units are not fully interconnected? There are two strategies that can be employed to solve this dilemma:

- Implementation of a parallel index array to specify connectivity
- Use of a universal "zero" value to act as a placeholder connection

In the first case, an array with the same length as the `weights[i]` array is constructed and coexists with the `weights[i]` array. This array contains an integer index specifying the offset into the `outputs` array where the output from the transmitting unit is located. Such a structure, along with the network it describes, is illustrated in Figure 1.20. You should examine the diagram

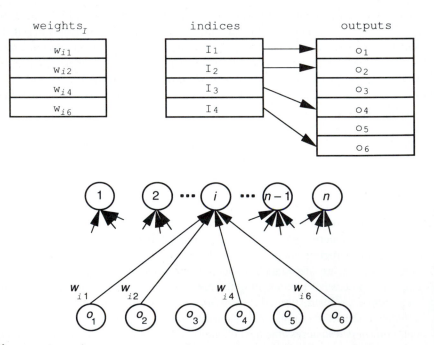

Figure 1.20 This sparse network is implemented using an index array. In this example, we calculate the input value at unit i by multiplying each value in the `weights` array with the value found in the `output` array at the offset indicated by the value in the `indices` array.

carefully to convince yourself that the data structure does implement the network structure shown.

In the second case, if we could specify to the network that a connection had a zero weight, the contribution to the total input of the node that it feeds would be zero. Therefore, the only reason for the existence of this connection would be that it acts as a placeholder, allowing the `weights[i]` array to maintain its one-to-one correspondence of location to connection. The cost of this implementation is the amount of time consumed performing a useless multiply-accumulate operation, and, in very sparsely connected networks, the large amount of wasted memory space. In addition, as we write the code needed to implement the learning law associated with the different network models, our algorithms must take a universal zero value into account and must not allow it to participate in the adaptation process; otherwise, the placeholder connection will be changed as the network adapts and eventually become an active participant in the signal-propagation process.

When is one approach preferable to the other? There is no absolute rule that will cover the wide variety of computers that will be the target machines for many ANS applications. In our experience, though, the break-even point is when the network is missing one-half of its interconnections. The desired approach therefore depends largely on how completely interconnected is the network that is being simulated. Whereas the "placeholder" approach consumes less memory and CPU time when only a relatively few connections are missing, the index array approach is much more efficient in very sparsely connected networks.

1.3.4 Linked-List ANS Data Structures

Many computer languages, such as Ada, LISP, and Modula-2, are designed to implement dynamic memory structures primarily as lists of records containing many different types of data. One type of data common to all records is the pointer type. Each record in the **linked list** will contain a pointer to the next record in the chain, thereby creating a threaded list of records. Each list is then completely described as a set of records that each contain pointers to other similar records, or contain null pointers. Linked lists offer a processing advantage in the algorithm generality they allow for neural-network simulation over the dynamic array structures described previously. Unfortunately, they also suffer from two disadvantages serious enough to limit their applicability to our simulator: excessive memory consumption and a significantly reduced processing rate for signal propagation.

To illustrate the disadvantages in the linked-list approach, we consider the two-layer network model and associated data structure depicted in Figure 1.21. In this example, each network unit is represented by an N_i record, and each connection is modeled as a C_{ij} record. Since each connection is simultaneously part of two unique lists (the input list to a unit on the upper layer and the output list from a unit on the lower layer), each connection record must contain at least two separate pointers to maintain the lists. Obviously, just the memory needed

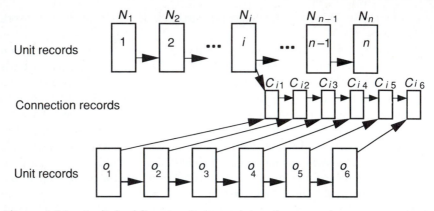

Figure 1.21 A linked-list implementation of a two-layer network is shown here. In this model, each network unit accesses its connections by following pointers from one connection record to the next. Here, the set of connection records modeling the input connections to unit N_i are shown, with links from all input-layer units.

to store those pointers will consume twice as much memory space as is needed to store the connection weight values. This need for extra memory results in roughly a three-fold reduction in the size of the network simulation that can be implemented when compared to the array-based model.[4] Similarly, the need to store pointers is not restricted to this particular structure; it is common to any linked-list data structure.

The linked-list approach is also less efficient than is the array model at run time. The CPU must perform many more data fetches in the linked-list approach (to fetch pointers), whereas in the array structure, the auto-postincrement addressing mode can be used to access the next connection implicitly. For very sparsely connected networks (or a very small network), this overhead is not significant. For a large network, however, the number of extra memory cycles required due to the large number of connections in the network will quickly overwhelm the host computer system for most ANS simulations.

On the bright side, the linked-list data structure is much more tolerant of "nonstandard" network connectivity schemes; that is, once the code has been written to enable the CPU to step through a standard list of input connections, no code modification is required to step through a nonstandard list. In this case, all the overhead is imposed on the software that constructs the original data structure for the network to be simulated. Once it is constructed, the CPU does

---

[4]This description is an obvious oversimplification, since it does not consider potential differences in the amount of memory used by pointers and floating-point numbers, virtual-memory systems, or other techniques for extending physical memory.

not know (or care) whether the connection list implements a fully interconnected network or a sparsely connected network. It simply follows the list to the end, then moves on to the next unit and repeats the process.

1.3.5   Extension of ANS Data Structures

Now that we have defined two possible structures for performing the input computations at each node in the network, we can extend these basic structures to implement an entire network. Since the array structure tends to be more efficient for computing input values at run time on most computers, we will implement the connection weights and node outputs as dynamically allocated arrays. Similarly, any additional parameters required by the different networks and associated with individual connections will also be modeled as arrays that coexist with the connection-weights arrays.

Now we must provide a higher-level structure to enable us to access the various instances of these arrays in a logical and efficient manner. We can easily create an adequate model for our integrated network structure if we adopt a few assumptions about how information is processed in a "standard" neural network:

- Units in the network can always be coerced into layers of units having similar characteristics, even if there is only one unit in some layers.

- All units in any layer must be processed completely before the CPU can begin simulating units in any other layer.

- The number of layers that our network simulator will support is indefinite, limited only by the amount of memory available.

- The processing done at each layer will usually involve the input connections to a node, and will only rarely involve output connections from a node (see Chapter 3 for an exception to this assumption).

Based on these assumptions, let us presume that the *layer* will be the network structure that binds the units together. Then, a layer will consist of a record that contains pointers to the various arrays that store the information about the nodes on that layer. Such a layer model is presented in Figure 1.22. Notice that, whereas the layer record will locate the node output array directly, the connection arrays are accessed indirectly through an intermediate array of pointers. The reason for this intermediate structure is again related to our desire to optimize the data structures for efficient computation of the net$_i$ value for each node. Since each node on the layer will produce exactly one output, the outputs for all the nodes on any layer can be stored in a single array. However, each node will also have many input connections, each with weights unique to that node. We must therefore construct our data structures to allow input-weight arrays to be identified uniquely with specific nodes on the layer. The intermediate `weight_pointer` array satisfies the need to associate input weights with the appropriate node (via the position of the pointer in the intermediate array),

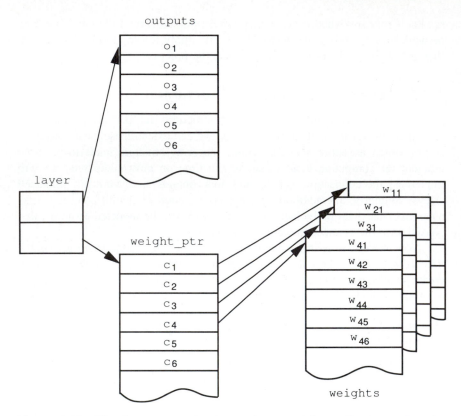

Figure 1.22   The layer structure is used to model a collection of nodes with similar function. In this example, the weight values of all input connections to the first processing unit (o_1) are stored sequentially in the w_{1j} array, connections to the second unit (o_2) in the w_{2j} array, and so on, enabling rapid sequential access to these values during the input computation operation.

while allowing the input weights for each node to be modeled as sequential arrays, thus maintaining the desired efficiency in the network data structures.

Finally, let us consider how we might model an entire network. Since we have decided that any network can be constructed from a set of layers, we will model the network as a record that contains both global data, and pointers to locate the first and last elements in a dynamically allocated array of layer records. This approach allows us to create a network of arbitrary depth while providing us with a means of immediate access to the two most commonly accessed layers in the network—the input and output layers.

Such a data structure, along with the network structure it represents, is depicted in Figure 1.23. By modeling the data in this way, we will allow for

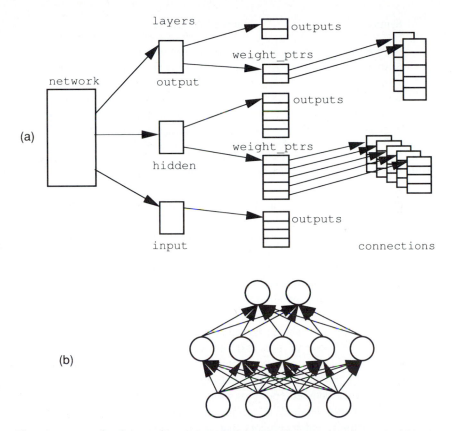

Figure 1.23   The figure shows a neural network (a) as implemented by our data structures, and (b) as represented schematically.

networks of arbitrary size and complexity, while optimizing the data structures for efficient run-time operation in the *inner loop*, the computation of the net$_i$ term for each node in the network.

1.3.6   A Final Note on ANS Simulation

Before we move on to examine specific ANS models, we must mention that the earlier discussion of the ANS simulator data structures is meant to provide you with only an insight into how to go about simulating neural networks on conventional computers. We have specifically avoided any detailed discussion of the data structures needed to implement a simulator (such as might be found in a conventional computer-science textbook). Likewise, we have avoided any analysis of how much more efficient one technique may be over another. We have taken this approach because we believe that it is more important to convey

Syntax	Intended Meaning
^type	a pointer to an object type
^type[]	a pointer to the first object in an array
record.slot	access a field "slot" in a record
pointer^.name	access a field "name" through a pointer
length(^type[])	get number of items in the array
{ text }	curly braces enclose comments

Table 1.1 Pseudocode language definitions.

the ideas of *what* must be done to simulate an ANS model, than to advocate *how* to implement that model.

This philosophy carries through the remainder of the text as well, specifically in the sections in each chapter that describe how to implement the learning algorithms for the network being discussed. Rather than presenting algorithms that might indicate a preference for a specific computer language, we have opted to develop our own pseudocode descriptions for the algorithms.[5] We hope that you will have little difficulty translating our simulator algorithms to your own preferrred data structures and programming languages.

Part of the purpose of this text, however, is to illustrate the design of the algorithms needed to construct simulators for the various neural-network models we shall present. For that reason, the algorithms developed in this text will be rather detailed, perhaps more so than some people prefer. We have elected to use detailed algorithms so that we can illustrate, wherever possible, algorithmic enhancements that should be made to improve the performance of the simulator. However, with this detail comes a responsibility. Since we have elected to present *pseudocode* algorithms, we are obligated to develop a syntax that precisely describes the actions we intend the computer to perform. For that reason, you should become comfortable with the notations described in Table 1.1, as we will adhere to this syntax in the description of the various algorithms and data structures throughout the remainder of this text.

One final note for programmers who prefer the C language. You should be aware of the fundamental differences between the mathematical summations that will be described in the ANS-specific chapters that follow, and the C **for(;;)** construct. Although it is mathematically correct to describe a summation with an index, i, starting at 1 and running through n, in C it is preferable to use arrays that start at index 0 and run through $n - 1$. Those readers that will be writing simulators in C must account for this difference in their code, and should be alert to this difference as they read the theoretical sections of this text.

---

[5]We have thus ensured that we have offended everyone equally.

Suggested Readings

There are many books appearing that cover various aspects of ANS technology from widely differing perspectives. We shall not attempt to give an exhaustive bibliography here; rather, we shall indicate sources that we have found to be useful, for one reason or another.

Neurocomputing: Foundations of Research is an excellent source of papers having an historical interest, as well as of more modern works [2]. Perhaps the most widely read books are the PDP series, edited by Rumelhart and Mc-Clelland [23, 22]. Volume III of that series contains a disk with software that can be used for experiments with the technology. An earlier work, *Parallel Models of Associative Memory*, contains papers of the same type as those found in the PDP series [13]. We have also included in the bibliography other books, some that are collections and some that are monographs, on the general topic of ANS [1, 7, 6, 8, 12, 16, 25, 27, 28, 31]. On a less technical level is the recent work by Caudill and Butler, which provides an excellent review of the subject [5]. An excellent introduction to neurophysiology is given by Lavine [19]. This book presents the basic terminology and technical details of neurophysiology without the excruciating detail of a medical text. A more comprehensive review of neural modeling is given in the book by McGregor [21]. For a cognitive-psychology viewpoint, the works by Anderson and Baron are both well written and thought provoking [3, 4].

An excellent review article is that by Richard Lippmann [20]. This article gives an overview of several of the algorithms presented in later chapters of this text. You might also want to read the *Scientific American* article by David Tank and John Hopfield [30]. Two other well-written and informative review articles appear in the first edition of the journal *Neural Networks* [9, 18]. For a comparison between traditional classification techniques and neural-network classifiers, see the papers by Huang and Lippmann [15, 14]. You can get an idea of the types of applications to which neural-network technology may apply from the paper by Hecht-Nielsen [11].

Bibliography

[1] Igor Aleksander, editor. *Neural Computing Architectures*. MIT Press, Cambridge, MA, 1989.

[2] James A. Anderson and Edward Rosenfeld, editors. *Neurocomputing: Foundations of Research*. MIT Press, Cambridge, MA, 1988.

[3] John R. Anderson. *The Architecture of Cognition*. Cognitive Science Series. Harvard University Press, Cambridge, MA, 1983.

[4] Robert J. Baron. *The Cerebral Computer*. Lawrence Erlbaum Associates, Hillsdale, NJ, 1987.

[5] Maureen Caudill and Charles Butler. *Naturally Intelligent Systems*. MIT Press, Cambridge, MA, 1990.

[6] John S. Denker, editor. *Neural Networks for Computing: AIP Conference Proceedings 151*. American Institute of Physics, New York, 1986.

[7] Rolf Eckmiller and Christoph v. d. Malsburg, editors. *Neural Computers*. NATO ASI Series F: Computer and Systems Sciences. Springer-Verlag, Berlin, 1988.

[8] Stephen Grossberg, editor. *Neural Networks and Natural Intelligence*. MIT Press, Cambridge, MA, 1988.

[9] Stephen Grossberg. Nonlinear neural networks: Principles, mechanisms, and architectures. *Neural Networks*, 1(1):17–62, 1988.

[10] Donald O. Hebb. *The Organization of Behavior*. Wiley, New York, 1949.

[11] Robert Hecht-Nielsen. Neurocomputer applications. In Rolf Eckmiller and Christoph v.d. Malsburg, editors, *Neural Computers*, pages 445–454. Springer-Verlag, 1988. NATO ASI Series F: Computers and System Sciences Vol. 41.

[12] Robert Hecht-Nielsen. *Neurocomputing*. Addison-Wesley, Reading, MA, 1990.

[13] Geoffrey E. Hinton and James A. Anderson, editors. *Parallel Models of Associative Memory*. Lawrence Erlbaum Associates, Hillsdale, NJ, 1981.

[14] Willian Y. Huang and Richard P. Lippmann. Comparison between neural net and conventional classifiers. In *Proceedings of the IEEE First International Conference on Neural Networks*, San Diego, CA, pp. iv.485–iv.494 June 1987.

[15] Willian Y. Huang and Richard P. Lippmann. Neural net and traditional classifiers. In *Proceedings of the Conference on Neural Information Processing Systems*, Denver, CO, November 1987.

[16] Tarun Khanna. *Foundations of Neural Networks*. Addison-Wesley, Reading, MA, 1990.

[17] C. Klimasauskas. *The 1989 Neuro-Computing Bibliography*, MIT Press, Cambridge, MA, 1989.

[18] Teuvo Kohonen. An introduction to neural computing. *Neural Networks*, 1(1):3–16, 1988.

[19] Robert A. Lavine. *Neurophysiology: The Fundamentals*. The Collamore Press, Lexington, MA, 1983.

[20] Richard P. Lippmann. An introduction to computing with neural nets. *IEEE ASSP Magazine*, pp. 4–22, April 1987.

[21] Ronald J. MacGregor. *Neural and Brain Modeling*. Academic Press, San Diego, CA, 1987.

[22] James McClelland and David Rumelhart. *Explorations in Parallel Distributed Processing*. MIT Press, Cambridge, MA, 1986.

[23] James McClelland and David Rumelhart. *Parallel Distributed Processing*, volumes 1 and 2. MIT Press, Cambridge, MA, 1986.

[24] Warren S. McCulloch and Walter Pitts. A logical calculus of the ideas immanent in nervous activity. *Bulletin of Mathematical Biophysics*, 5:115–133, 1943.

[25] Carver A. Mead and M. A. Mahowald. A silicon model of early visual processing. *Neural Networks*, 1(1):91–98, 1988.

[26] Marvin Minsky and Seymour Papert. *Perceptrons*. MIT Press, Cambridge, MA, 1969.

[27] Marvin Minsky and Seymour Papert. *Perceptrons: Expanded Edition*. MIT Press, Cambridge, MA, 1988.

[28] Yoh-Han Pao. *Adaptive Pattern Recognition and Neural Networks*. Addison-Wesley, Reading, MA, 1989.

[29] Frank Rosenblatt. The perceptron: A probabilistic model for information storage and organization in the brain. *Psychological Review*, 65:386–408, 1958.

[30] David W. Tank and John J. Hopfield. Collective computation in neuronlike circuits. *Scientific American*, 257(6):104–114, 1987.

[31] Philip D. Wasserman. *Neural Computing: Theory and Practice*. Van Nostrand Reinhold, New York, 1989.

C H A P T E R

Adaline and Madaline

Signal processing developed as an engineering discipline with the advent of electronic communication. Initially, analog filters using resistor–inductor–capacitor (RLC) circuits were designed to remove noise from the communication signals. Today, signal processing has evolved into a many-faceted technology, with the emphasis having shifted from tuned circuit implementation to digital signal processors (DSPs) that can perform the same types of filtering applications by executing convolution filters implemented in software. The basis for the industry remains the design and implementation of filters to perform noise removal from information-bearing signals.

In this chapter, we will focus on a specific type of filter, called the **Adaline** (and the multiple-Adaline, or **Madaline**) developed by Bernard Widrow of Stanford University. As we will see, the Adaline model is similar to that of a single PE in an ANS.

2.1 REVIEW OF SIGNAL PROCESSING

We begin our discussion of the Adaline and Madaline networks with a review of basic signal-processing theory. An understanding of this material is essential if we are to appreciate the operation and applications of these networks. However, this material is also typically covered as part of an undergraduate curriculum in information coding and data communication. Therefore, readers already comfortable with signal-processing concepts may skip this first section without fear of missing material relevant to the Adaline and Madaline topics. For those readers who are not familiar with the techniques commonly used to implement electronic communications and signal processing, we shall begin by describing briefly the data-encoding and modulation schemes used in an amplitude-modulation (AM) radio transmission. As part of this discussion, we shall illustrate the need for filters in the communications industry. We will then review the concepts of the frequency domain, the four basic filter types, and Fourier analysis. This preliminary section concludes with a brief overview of digital signal processing, because many of the concepts realized in digital filters are directly applicable to the Adaline and Madaline (and many other) neural networks.

2.1.1   Signal Processing and Filters

Signal processing is an engineering discipline that deals primarily with the implementation of filters to remove or reduce unwanted frequency components from an information-bearing signal. Let's consider, for example, an AM radio broadcast. Electronic communication techniques, whether for audio signals or other data, consist of signal *encoding* and *modulation*. Information to be transmitted—in this case, audible sounds, such as voice or music—can be encoded electronically by an analog signal that exactly reproduces the frequencies and amplitudes of the original sounds. Since the sounds being encoded represent a continuum from silence through voice to music, the instantaneous frequency of the encoded signal will vary with time, ranging from 0 to approximately 10,000 hertz (Hz).

Rather than attempt to transmit this encoded signal directly, we transform the signal into a form more suitable for radio transmission. We accomplish this transformation by modulating the amplitude of a high-frequency *carrier* signal with the analog information signal. This process is illustrated in Figure 2.1. Here, the carrier is nothing more than a sine wave with a frequency much greater than the information signal. For AM radio, the carrier frequency will be in the range of 550 to 1600 kilohertz (KHz). Since the frequency of the carrier is significantly greater than is the maximum frequency of the information signal, little information is lost by this modulation. The modulated signal can then be transmitted to a receiving station (or broadcast to anyone with a radio receiver), where the signal is demodulated and is reproduced as sound.

The most obvious reason for a filter in AM radio is that different people have different preferences in music and entertainment. Therefore, the government and the communication industry have allowed many different radio stations to operate in the same geographical area, so that everyone's tastes in entertainment can be accommodated. With so many different radio stations all broadcasting in close proximity, how is it that we can listen to only one station at a time? The answer is to allow each receiver to be tuned by the user to a selectable frequency. In tuning the radio, we are essentially changing the frequency-response characteristics of a *bandpass* filter inside the radio. This filter allows only the signals from the station in which we are interested to pass, while eliminating all the other signals being broadcast within the spectrum of the AM radio.

To illustrate how the bandpass filter operates, we will change our reference from the time domain to the frequency domain. We begin by constructing a two-axis graph, where the *x* axis represents increasing frequencies and the *y* axis represents decreasing attenuation in a unit called the decibel (dB). Such a

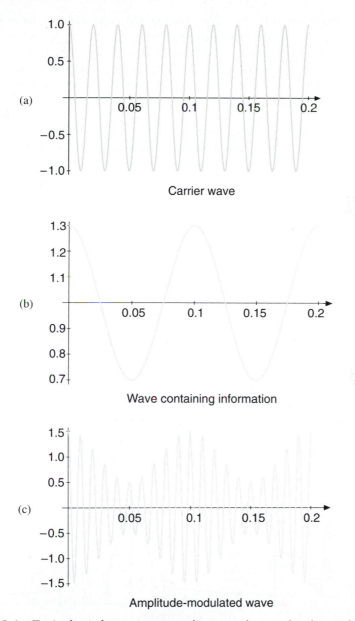

Figure 2.1   Typical   information-encoding   and   amplitude-modulation
techniques for electronic communication are shown. (a) The
carrier wave has a frequency much higher than that of (b) the
information-bearing signal. (c) The carrier wave is modulated
by the information-bearing signal.

graph is illustrated in Figure 2.2(a). For the AM radio example, let us imagine that there are seven AM radio stations, labeled A through G, operating in the area where we are listening. The frequencies at which these stations transmit are graphed as vertical lines located on the frequency axis at the point corresponding to their transmitting, or carrier, frequency. The amplitude of the lines, as illustrated in Figure 2.2(a), is almost 0 dB, indicating that each station is transmitting at full power, and each can be received equally well.

Now we will tune a bandpass filter to select one of the seven stations. The frequency response of a typical bandpass filter is illustrated in Figure 2.2(b). Notice that the frequency-response curve is such that all frequencies that fall outside the inverted notch are attenuated to very small magnitudes, whereas frequencies within the passband are allowed to pass with very little attenuation—hence the name "bandpass filter." To tune our radio receiver to any one of the seven broadcasting stations, we simply adjust the frequency response of the filter such that the carrier frequency of the desired station is within the passband.

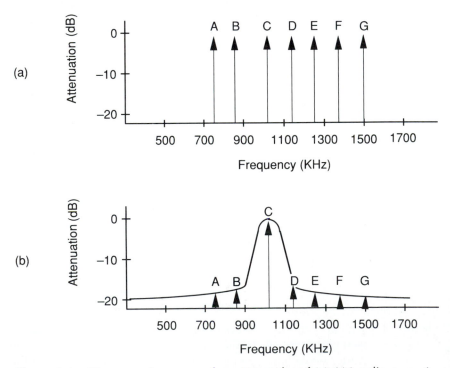

Figure 2.2 These are frequency domain graphs of (a) AM radio reception of seven different stations, (b) the frequency response of the tuning filter and the magnitude of the received signals after filtering.

As another example of the use of filters in the communication industry, consider the problem of echo suppression in long-distance telephone communication. As indicated in Figure 2.3, the problem is caused by the interaction between the amplifiers and series coupling used on both ends of the line, and the delay time required to transmit the voice information between the switching office and the communications satellite in geostationary orbit, 23,000 miles above the earth. Specifically, you hear an echo of your own voice in the telephone when you speak. The signal carrying your voice arrives at the receiving telephone approximately 270 milliseconds after you speak. This delay is the amount of time required by the microwave signal to travel the 46,000 miles between the transmitting station, the satellite, and the receiving station on the ground. Once received and routed to the destination telephone, the signal is again amplified and reproduced as sound on the receiving handset. Unfortunately, it is also often picked up by the transmitter at the receiving end, due to imperfections in the devices used to decouple the incoming signals. It can then be reamplified and fed back to you approximately 1/2 second after you spoke. The result is echo. Obviously, a simple bandpass filter cannot be used to remove the echo, because there is no way to distinguish the echoed signal from valid signals.

To solve problems such as these, the communications industry has developed many different types of filters. These filters not only are used in elec-

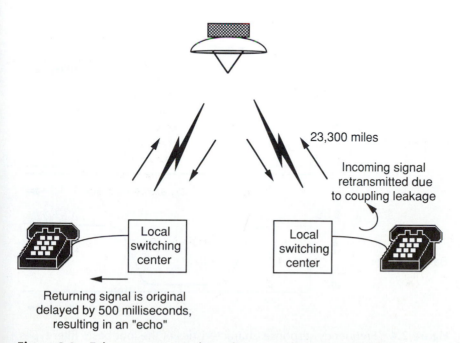

Figure 2.3   Echo can occur in long-distance telecommunications.

tronic communications, but also have an application base that includes radar and sonar imaging, electronic warfare, and medical technology. However, all the application-specific filter implementations can be grouped into four general filter types: lowpass, highpass, bandpass, and bandstop. The characteristic frequency response of these filters is depicted in Figure 2.4. The adaptive filter, which is the subject of the remainder of the chapter, has characteristics unique to the application it serves. It can reproduce the characteristics of any of the four basic filter types, alone or in combination. As we shall show later, the adaptive filter is ideally suited to the telephone-echo problem just discussed.

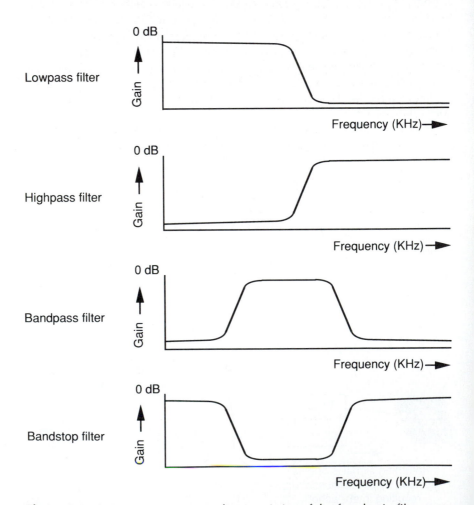

Figure 2.4   Frequency-response characteristics of the four basic filter types are shown.

2.1.2   Fourier Analysis and the Frequency Domain

To analyze a signal-processing problem that requires a filter, we must leave the time domain and find a tool for translating our filter models into the frequency domain, because most of the signals we will analyze cannot be completely understood in the time domain. For example, most signals consist not only of a fundamental frequency, but also harmonics that must be considered, or they consist of many discrete frequency components that must be accounted for by the filters we design. There are many tools that we can use to help understand the frequency-domain nature of signals. One of the most commonly used is the Fourier series. It has been shown that any periodic signal can be modeled as an infinite series of sines and cosines. The Fourier series, which describes the frequency-domain nature of periodic signals, is given by the equation

$$x(t) = \sum_{n=0}^{\infty} a_n \cos(2\pi n f_0 t) + \sum_{n=1}^{\infty} b_n \sin(2\pi n f_0 t)$$

where f_0 is the fundamental frequency of the signal in the time domain, and the coefficients, a_n and b_n, are needed to modulate the amplitude of the individual terms of the series.

This series is useful for describing the discrete frequency components that comprise a nontrivial periodic signal. As an illustration, a square wave can be decomposed into a summation of frequency elements containing nothing more than sine waves of different amplitude and frequency, as is illustrated in Figure 2.5. Since a square wave is useful for representing binary information in data transmission, it is important that we understand the frequency-domain nature of such a signal. From inspection in the time domain, we can observe that the square wave is ideally suited to binary data representation because there are two distinct states (a 1 and a 0), and the transition time between states is negligible.

It is difficult, however, to obtain a perfect square wave in any practical electronic circuit, due in part to the effects of the transmitting media on the signal. To illustrate why this is so, consider the Fourier series expansion

$$x(t) = \sin(2\pi f_0 t) + \frac{1}{3} \sin(6\pi f_0 t) + \frac{1}{5} \sin(10\pi f_0 t) + \dots$$

which describes a typical square wave.

As illustrated in Figure 2.5, if we algebraically add together the first three sinusoidal components of this Fourier series, we produce a signal that already strongly resembles the square wave. However, we should notice that the resultant signal also exhibits *ripples* in both active regions. These ripples will remain to some extent, unless we complete the infinite series. Since that is obviously not practical, we must eventually truncate the series and settle for some amount of ripple in the resulting signal.

It turns out that this truncation exactly corresponds to the behavior we observed when transmitting a square wave across an electromagnetic media. As it is impossible to have a medium of infinite bandwidth, it follows that it is impossible to transmit all the frequency components of a square wave. Thus,

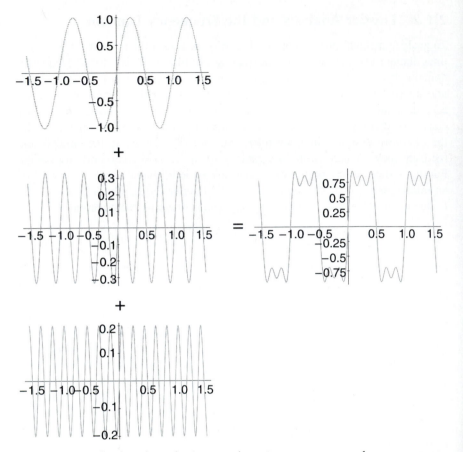

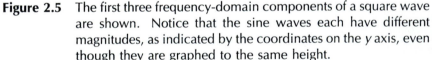

Figure 2.5   The first three frequency-domain components of a square wave are shown. Notice that the sine waves each have different magnitudes, as indicated by the coordinates on the y axis, even though they are graphed to the same height.

when we transmit a periodic square wave, we can observe the frequency-domain effects in the time-domain signal as *overshoot*, *undershoot*, and *ripple*.

This example shows that the Fourier series can be a powerful tool in helping us to understand the frequency-domain nature of any periodic signal, and to predict ahead of time what transmission effects we must consider as we design filters for our signal-processing applications.

We can also apply Fourier analysis to aperiodic signals, by evaluating the Fourier integral, which is given by

$$X(f) = \int_{-\infty}^{\infty} x(t)e^{-j2\pi ft} \, dt.$$

We will not, however, belabor this point. Our purpose here is merely to understand the frequency-domain nature of signals. Readers interested in investigating Fourier analysis further are referred to Kaplan [4].

2.1.3 Filter Implementation and Digital Signal Processing

Early implementations of the four basic filters were predominantly tuned RLC circuits. This approach had a basic limitation, however, in that the filters had only a very small range of adjustability. Aside from our being able to change the resonant frequency of the filter by adjusting a variable capacitor or inductor, the filters were pretty much fixed once implemented, leaving little room for change as applications became more sophisticated.

The next step in the evolution of filter design came about with the advent of digital computer systems, and, just recently, with the availability of microcomputer chips with architectures custom-tailored for signal-processing applications. The basic concept underlying digital filter implementation is the idea that a continuous analog signal can be sampled periodically, quantized, and processed by a fairly standard computer system. This approach, illustrated in Figure 2.6, overcame the limitation of fixed implementation, because changing the filter was simply a matter of rewriting the software for the computer. We will therefore concentrate on what goes on within the software simulation of the analog filter.

We assume that the computer implementation of the filter is a discrete-time, linear, time-invariant system. Systems that satisfy these constraints can perform a transformation on an input signal, based on some predefined criteria,

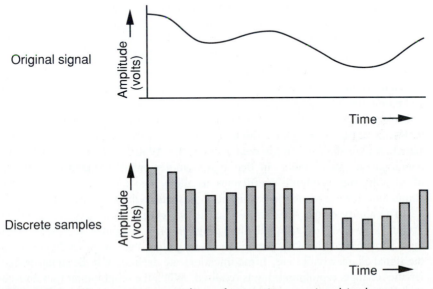

Figure 2.6   Discrete-time sampling of a continuous signal is shown.

to produce an output that corresponds to the input as though it had passed through an analog filter. Thus, a computer, executing a program that applies a given transformation operation, R, to discrete, digitized approximations of a continuous input signal, $x(n)$, can produce an output value $y(n)$ for each input sample, where n is the discrete timestep variable. In its role in performing this transformation, the computer can be thought of as a digital filter. Moreover, any filter can be completely characterized by its response, $h(n)$, to the unit impulse function, represented as $\delta(n)$. More precisely,

$$h(n) = R[\delta(n)]$$

The benefit of this formulation is that, once the system response to the unit impulse is known, the system output for *any* input is given by

$$y(n) = R[x(n)]$$

$$= \sum_{i=-\infty}^{\infty} h(i)x(n-i)$$

where $x(n)$ is the system input.

This equation is meaningful to us in that it describes a convolution sum between the input signal and the unit impulse response of the system. The process can be pictured as a window sliding past a scene of interest. As illustrated in Figure 2.7, for each time step, the system output is produced by transposing and shifting $h(n)$ one position to the right. The summation is then performed over all nonzero values of $x(n)$ for the finite length of the filter. In this manner, we can realize the filter by repetitively performing floating-point multiplications and additions, coupled with sample time delays and shift operations. Repetitive, mathematical operations are what computers do best; therefore, the convolution sum provides us with a mechanism for building the digital equivalent of analog filters. Readers interested in learning more about digital signal processing are referred to Oppenheim and Schafer [5] or Hamming [3].

It is sufficient for our purposes to note that the convolution sum is a sum-of-products operation similar to the type of operation an ANS PE performs when computing its input activation signal. Specifically, the Adaline uses exactly this sum-of-products calculation, without the sample time delays and shift operations, to determine how much input stimulation it receives from an instantaneous input signal. As we shall see in the next section, the Adaline extends the basic filter operation one step further, in that it has implemented within itself a means of adapting the weighting coefficients to allow it to increase or decrease the stimulation it receives the next time it is presented with the same signal.

The ability of the Adaline to adapt its weighting coefficients is extremely useful. When writing a digital filter program on a computer, the programmer must know exactly how to specify the filtering algorithm and what the details of the signal characteristics are. If modifications are desired, or if the signal characteristics change, reprogramming is required. When the programmer uses an Adaline, the problem shifts to one of being able to specify the desired output signal,

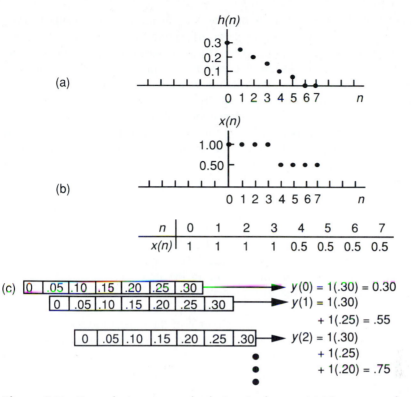

n	0	1	2	3	4	5	6	7
$x(n)$	1	1	1	1	0.5	0.5	0.5	0.5

Figure 2.7   Convolution sum calculation is shown. (a) The process begins by determining the desired response of the filter to the unit impulse function at eight discrete timesteps. (b) The input signal is sampled and quantized eight times. (c) The output of the filter is produced for each timestep by multiplication of each term in (a) with the corresponding value of (b) for all valid timesteps.

given a particular input signal. The Adaline takes the input and the desired output, and adjusts itself so that it can perform the desired transformation. Furthermore, if the signal characteristics change, the Adaline can adapt automatically. We shall now expand these ideas, and begin our investigation of the Adaline.

2.2   ADALINE AND THE ADAPTIVE LINEAR COMBINER

The Adaline is a device consisting of a single processing element; as such, it is not technically a neural *network*. Nevertheless, it is a very important structure that deserves close study. Moreover, we will show how it can form the basis of a network in a later section.

The term *Adaline* is an acronym; however, its meaning has changed somewhat over the years. Initially called the ADAptive LInear NEuron, it became the ADAptive LINear Element, when neural networks fell out of favor in the late 1960s. It is almost identical in structure to the general PE described in Chapter 1. Figure 2.8 shows the Adaline structure. There are two basic modifications required to make the general PE structure into an Adaline. The first modification is the addition of a connection with weight, w_0, which we refer to as the **bias** term. This term is a weight on a connection that has its input value always equal to 1. The inclusion of such a term is largely a matter of experience. We show it here for completeness, but it will not appear in the discussion of the next sections. We shall resurrect the idea of a bias term in Chapter 3, on the backpropagation network.

The second modification is the addition of a bipolar condition on the output. The dashed box in Figure 2.8 encloses a part of the Adaline called the **adaptive linear combiner** (ALC). If the output of the ALC is positive, the Adaline output is $+1$. If the ALC output is negative, the Adaline output is -1. Because much of the interesting processing takes place in the ALC portion of the Adaline, we shall concentrate on the ALC. Later, we shall add back the binary output condition.

The processing done by the ALC is that of the typical processing element described in the previous chapter. The ALC performs a sum-of-products calcu-

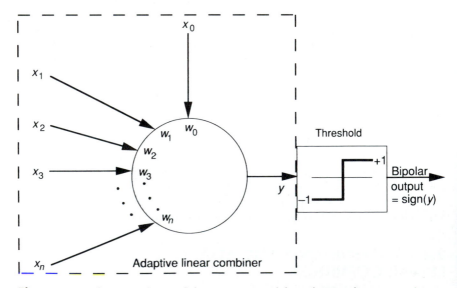

Figure 2.8   The complete Adaline consists of the adaptive linear combiner, in the dashed box, and a bipolar output function. The adaptive linear combiner resembles the general PE described in Chapter 1.

lation using the input and weight vectors, and applies an output function to get a single output value. Using the notation in Figure 2.8,

$$y = w_0 + \sum_{j=1}^{n} w_j x_j$$

where w_0 is the bias weight. If we make the identification, $x_0 = 1$, we can rewrite the preceding equation as

$$y = \sum_{j=0}^{n} w_j x_j$$

or, in vector notation,

$$y = \mathbf{w}^t \mathbf{x} \tag{2.1}$$

The output function in this case is the identity function, as is the activation function. The use of the identity function as both output and activation functions means that the output is the same as the activation, which is the same as the net input to the unit.

The Adaline (or the ALC) is ADAptive in the sense that there exists a well-defined procedure for modifying the weights in order to allow the device to give the *correct* output value for the given input. What output value is *correct* depends on the particular processing function being performed by the device. The Adaline (or the ALC) is LInear because the output is a simple linear function of the input values. It is a NEuron only in the very limited sense of the PEs described in the previous chapter. The Adaline could also be said to be a LINear Element, avoiding the NEuron issue altogether. In the next section, we look at a method to *train* the Adaline to perform a given processing function.

2.2.1   The LMS Learning Rule

Given an input vector, $\mathbf{x}$, it is straightforward to determine a set of weights, $\mathbf{w}$, which will result in a particular output value, y. Suppose we have a set of input vectors, $\{\mathbf{x}_1, \mathbf{x}_2, \ldots, \mathbf{x}_L\}$, each having its own, perhaps unique, *correct* or *desired* output value, $d_k, k = 1, L$. The problem of finding a single weight vector that can successfully associate each input vector with its desired output value is no longer simple. In this section, we develop a method called the least-mean-square (LMS) learning rule, which is one method of finding the desired weight vector. We refer to this process of finding the weight vector as *training* the ALC. The learning rule can be embedded in the device itself, which can then *self-adapt* as inputs and desired outputs are presented to it. Small adjustments are made to the weight values as each input–output combination is processed until the ALC gives correct outputs. In a sense, this procedure is a true training procedure, because we do not need to calculate the value of the weight vector explicitly. Before describing the training process in detail, let's perform the calculation manually.

Calculation of w*.   To begin, let's state the problem a little differently: Given
examples, $(\mathbf{x}_1, d_1), (\mathbf{x}_2, d_2), \ldots, (\mathbf{x}_L, d_L)$, of some processing function that associates input vectors, $\mathbf{x}_k$, with (or *maps* to) the desired output values, d_k, what
is the *best* weight vector, $\mathbf{w}^*$, for an ALC that performs this mapping?

To answer this question, we must first define what it is that constitutes the
best weight vector. Clearly, once the best weight vector is found, we would
like the application of each input vector to result in the precise, corresponding
output value. Thus, we want to eliminate, or at least to minimize, the difference
between the desired output and the actual output for each input vector. The
approach we select here is to minimize the mean squared error for the set of
input vectors.

If the actual output value is y_k for the kth input vector, then the corresponding error term is $\varepsilon_k = d_k - y_k$. The mean squared error, or expectation
value of the error, is defined by

$$\langle \varepsilon_k^2 \rangle = \frac{1}{L} \sum_{k=1}^{L} \varepsilon_k^2 \tag{2.2}$$

where L is the number of input vectors in the **training set.**[1]

Using Eq. (2.1), we can expand the mean squared error as follows:

$$\langle \varepsilon_k^2 \rangle = \langle (d_k - \mathbf{w}^t \mathbf{x}_k)^2 \rangle \tag{2.3}$$
$$= \langle d_k^2 \rangle + \mathbf{w}^t \langle \mathbf{x}_k \mathbf{x}_k^t \rangle \mathbf{w} - 2 \langle d_k \mathbf{x}_k^t \rangle \mathbf{w} \tag{2.4}$$

In going from Eq. (2.3) to Eq. (2.4), we have made the assumption that the
training set is statistically stationary, meaning that any expectation values vary
slowly with respect to time. This assumption allows us to factor out the weight
vectors from the expectation value terms in Eq. (2.4).

Exercise 2.1: Give the details of the derivation that leads from Eq. (2.3), to
Eq. (2.4) along with the justification for each step. Why are the factors d_k and
$\mathbf{x}_k^t$ left together in the last term in Eq. (2.4), rather than shown as the product
of the two separate expectation values?

Define a matrix $\mathbf{R} = \langle \mathbf{x}_k \mathbf{x}_k^t \rangle$, called the **input correlation matrix**, and a
vector $\mathbf{p} = \langle d_k \mathbf{x}_k \rangle$. Further, make the identification $\xi = \langle \varepsilon_k^2 \rangle$. Using these
definitions, we can rewrite Eq. (2.4) as

$$\xi = \langle d_k^2 \rangle + \mathbf{w}^t \mathbf{R} \mathbf{w} - 2 \mathbf{p}^t \mathbf{w} \tag{2.5}$$

This equation shows ξ as an explicit function of the weight vector, $\mathbf{w}$. In other
words, $\xi = \xi(\mathbf{w})$.

---

[1]Widrow and Stearns use the notation, $E[\varepsilon_k^2]$, for the expectation value; also, the term *exemplars*
will sometimes be seen as a synonym for *training set*.

To find the weight vector corresponding to the minimum mean squared error, we differentiate Eq. (2.5), evaluate the result at $\mathbf{w}^*$, and set the result equal to zero:

$$\frac{\partial \xi(\mathbf{w})}{\partial \mathbf{w}} = 2\mathbf{R}\mathbf{w} - 2\mathbf{p} \tag{2.6}$$

$$2\mathbf{R}\mathbf{w}^* - 2\mathbf{p} = 0$$

$$\mathbf{R}\mathbf{w}^* = \mathbf{p} \tag{2.7}$$

$$\mathbf{w}^* = \mathbf{R}^{-1}\mathbf{p} \tag{2.8}$$

Notice that, although ξ is a scalar, $\frac{\partial \xi(\mathbf{w})}{\partial \mathbf{w}}$ is a vector. Equation (2.6) is an expression of the gradient of ξ, $\nabla\xi$, which is the vector

$$\nabla\xi = \left[\frac{\partial \xi}{\partial w_1}, \frac{\partial \xi}{\partial w_2}, \ldots, \frac{\partial \xi}{\partial w_n} \right]^t \tag{2.9}$$

All that we have done by the procedure is to show that we can find a point where the slope of the function, $\xi(\mathbf{w})$, is zero. In general, that point may be a minimum or a maximum point. In the example that follows, we show a simple case where the ALC has only two weights. In that situation, the graph of $\xi(\mathbf{w})$ is a paraboloid. Furthermore, it must be concave upward, since all combinations of weights must result in a nonnegative value for the mean squared error, ξ. This result is general and is obtained regardless of the dimension of the weight vector. In the case of dimensions higher than two, the paraboloid is known as a hyperparaboloid.

Suppose we have an ALC with two inputs and various other quantities defined as follows:

$$\mathbf{R} = \begin{bmatrix} 3 & 1 \\ 1 & 4 \end{bmatrix} \quad \mathbf{p} = \begin{bmatrix} 4 \\ 5 \end{bmatrix} \quad \langle d_k^2 \rangle = 10$$

Rather than inverting $\mathbf{R}$, we use Eq. (2.7) to find the optimum weight vector:

$$\begin{bmatrix} 3 & 1 \\ 1 & 4 \end{bmatrix} \begin{bmatrix} w_1^* \\ w_2^* \end{bmatrix} = \begin{bmatrix} 4 \\ 5 \end{bmatrix}$$

This equation results in two equations for w_1^* and w_2^*:

$$3w_1^* + w_2^* = 4$$

$$w_1^* + 4w_2^* = 5$$

The solution is $\mathbf{w}^* = (1, 1)^t$. The graph of ξ as a function of the two weights is shown in Figure 2.9.

Exercise 2.2: Show that the minimum value of the mean squared error can be written as

$$\xi_{\min} = \langle d_k^2 \rangle - \mathbf{p}^t \mathbf{w}^*$$

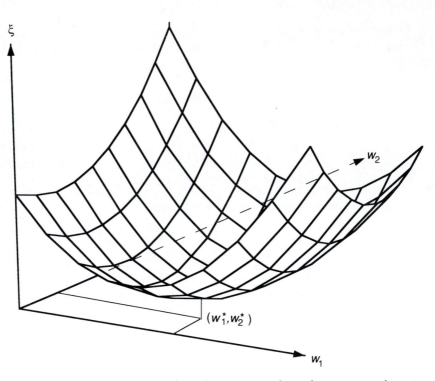

Figure 2.9 For an ALC with only two weights, the error surface is a
paraboloid. The weights that minimize the error occur at the
bottom of the paraboloidal surface.

Exercise 2.3: Determine an explicit equation for ξ as a function of w_1 and w_2
using the example in the text. Use it to find $\nabla\xi$, the optimum weight vector,
$\mathbf{w}^*$, the minimum mean squared error, $\xi_{\min}$, and prove that the paraboloid is
concave upward.

In the next section, we shall examine a method for finding the optimum
weight vector by an iterative procedure. This procedure allows us to avoid the
often-difficult calculations necessary to determine the weights manually.

Finding $\mathbf{w}^*$ by the Method of Steepest Descent.   As you might imagine, the
analytical calculation to determine the optimum weights for a problem is rather
difficult in general. Not only does the matrix manipulation get cumbersome for
large dimensions, but also each component of $\mathbf{R}$ and $\mathbf{p}$ is itself an expectation
value. Thus, explicit calculations of $\mathbf{R}$ and $\mathbf{p}$ require knowledge of the statistics
of the input signals. A better approach would be to let the ALC find the optimum
weights itself by having it *search* over the weight surface to find the minimum.
A purely random search might not be productive or efficient, so we shall add
some intelligence to the procedure.

Begin by assigning arbitrary values to the weights. From that point on the weight surface, determine the direction of the steepest slope in the downward direction. Change the weights slightly so that the new weight vector lies farther down the surface. Repeat the process until the minimum has been reached. This procedure is illustrated in Figure 2.10. Implicit in this method is the assumption that we *know* what the weight surface looks like in advance. We do not know, but we will see shortly how to get around this problem.

Typically, the weight vector does not initially move directly toward the minimum point. The cross-section of the paraboloidal weight surface is usually elliptical, so the negative gradient may not point directly at the minimum point, at least initially. The situation is illustrated more clearly in the contour plot of the weight surface in Figure 2.11.

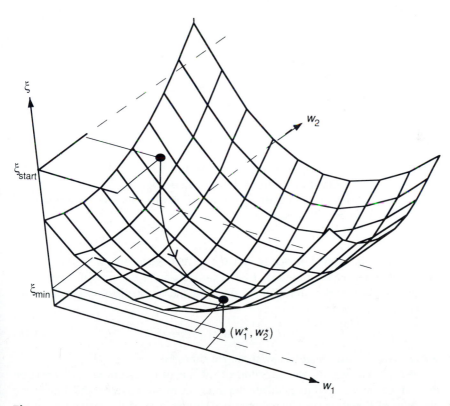

Figure 2.10 We can use this diagram to visualize the steepest-descent method. An initial selection for the weight vector results in an error, ξ_{start}. The steepest-descent method consists of sliding this point down the surface toward the bottom, always moving in the direction of the steepest downward slope.

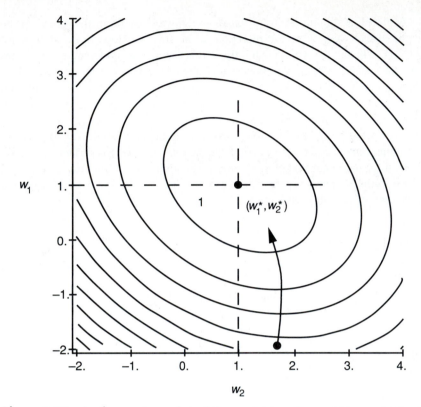

Figure 2.11   In the contour plot of the weight surface of Figure 2.10, the direction of steepest descent is perpendicular to the contour lines at each point, and this direction does not always point to the minimum point.

Because the weight vector is variable in this procedure, we write it as an explicit function of the timestep, t. The initial weight vector is denoted $\mathbf{w}(0)$, and the weight vector at timestep t is $\mathbf{w}(t)$. At each step, the next weight vector is calculated according to

$$\mathbf{w}(t+1) = \mathbf{w}(t) + \Delta\mathbf{w}(t) \tag{2.10}$$

where $\Delta\mathbf{w}(t)$ is the change in $\mathbf{w}$ at the tth timestep.

We are looking for the direction of the steepest descent at each point on the surface, so we need to calculate the gradient of the surface (which gives the direction of the steepest *upward* slope). The negative of the gradient is in the direction of steepest descent. To get the magnitude of the change, multiply the gradient by a suitable constant, μ. The appropriate value for μ will be discussed later. This procedure results in the following expression:

$$\mathbf{w}(t+1) = \mathbf{w}(t) - \mu\nabla\xi(\mathbf{w}(t)) \tag{2.11}$$

All that is necessary to complete the discussion is to determine the value of $\nabla \xi(\mathbf{w}(t))$ at each successive iteration step.

The value of $\nabla \xi(\mathbf{w}(t))$ was determined analytically in the previous section. Equation (2.6) or Eq. (2.9) could be used here to determine $\nabla \xi(\mathbf{w}(t))$, but we would have the same problem that we had with the analytical determination of $\mathbf{w}^*$: We would need to know both $\mathbf{R}$ and $\mathbf{p}$ in advance. This knowledge is equivalent to knowing what the weight surface looks like in advance. To circumvent this difficulty, we use an approximation for the gradient that can be determined from information that is known explicitly at each iteration.

For each step in the iteration process, we perform the following:

1. Apply an input vector, $\mathbf{x}_k$, to the Adaline inputs.

2. Determine the value of the error squared, $\varepsilon_k^2(t)$, using the current value of the weight vector

$$\varepsilon_k^2(t) = (d_k - \mathbf{w}^t(t)\mathbf{x}_k)^2 \tag{2.12}$$

3. Calculate an approximation to $\nabla \xi(t)$, by using $\varepsilon_k^2(t)$ as an approximation for $\langle \varepsilon_k^2 \rangle$:

$$\nabla \varepsilon_k^2(t) \approx \nabla \langle \varepsilon_k^2 \rangle \tag{2.13}$$

$$\nabla \varepsilon_k^2(t) = -2\varepsilon_k(t)\mathbf{x}_k \tag{2.14}$$

where we have used Eq. (2.12) to calculate the gradient explicitly.

4. Update the weight vector according to Eq. (2.11) using Eq. (2.14) as the approximation for the gradient:

$$\mathbf{w}(t+1) = \mathbf{w}(t) + 2\mu \varepsilon_k \mathbf{x}_k \tag{2.15}$$

5. Repeat steps 1 through 4 with the next input vector, until the error has been reduced to an acceptable value.

Equation (2.15) is an expression of the LMS algorithm. The parameter μ determines the stability and speed of convergence of the weight vector toward the minimum-error value.

Because an approximation of the gradient has been used in Eq. (2.15), the path that the weight vector takes as it moves down the weight surface toward the minimum will not be as smooth as that indicated in Figure 2.11. Figure 2.12 shows an example of how a search path might look with the LMS algorithm of Eq. (2.15). Changes in the weight vector must be kept relatively small on each iteration. If changes are too large, the weight vector could wander about the surface, never finding the minimum, or finding it only by accident rather than as a result of a steady convergence toward it. The function of the parameter μ is to prevent this aimless searching. In the next section, we shall discuss the parameter, μ, and other practical considerations.

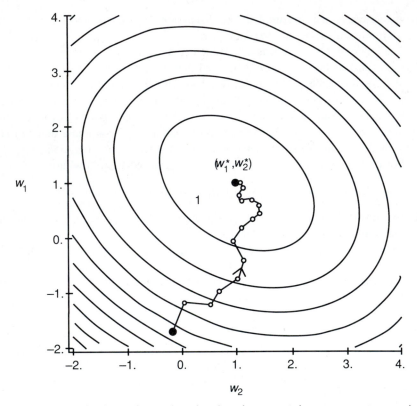

Figure 2.12 The hypothetical path taken by a weight vector as it searches for the minimum error using the LMS algorithm is not a smooth curve because the gradient is being approximated at each point. Note also that step sizes get smaller as the minimum-error solution is approached.

2.2.2   Practical Considerations

There are several questions to consider when we are attempting to use the ALC to solve a particular problem:

- How many training vectors are required to solve a particular problem?

- How is the *expected output* generated for each training vector?

- What is the appropriate dimension of the weight vector?

- What should be the initial values for the weights?

- Is a bias weight required?

- What happens if the signal statistics vary with time?

- What is the appropriate value for μ?

- How do we determine when to stop training?

The answers to these questions depend on the specific problem being addressed, so it is difficult to give well-defined responses that apply in all cases. Moreover, for a specific case, the answers are not necessarily independent.

Consider the dimension of the weight vector. If there are a well-defined number of inputs—say, from multiple sensors—then there would be one weight for each input. The question would be whether to add a bias weight. Figure 2.13 depicts this case, with the bias term added, in a somewhat standard form that shows the variability of the weights, the error term, and the feedback from the output to the weights. As for the bias term itself, including it sometimes helps convergence of the weights to an acceptable solution. It is perhaps best thought of as an extra *degree of freedom*, and its use is largely a matter of experimentation with the specific application.

A situation different from the previous paragraph arises if there is only a single input signal, say from a single electrocardiograph (EKG) sensor. For

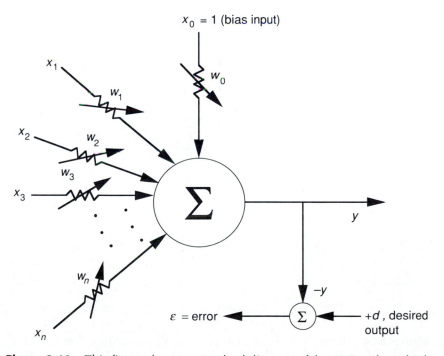

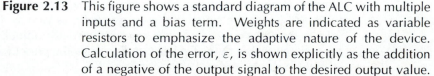

Figure 2.13   This figure shows a standard diagram of the ALC with multiple inputs and a bias term. Weights are indicated as variable resistors to emphasize the adaptive nature of the device. Calculation of the error, ε, is shown explicitly as the addition of a negative of the output signal to the desired output value.

example, an ALC can be used to remove noise from the input signal in order to give a cleaner signal at the output. In a case such as this one, the ALC is arranged in a configuration known as a **transversal filter.** In this configuration, the input signal is sampled at several points in time, rather than from several sensors at a single time. Figure 2.14 shows the ALC arranged as a transverse filter.

For the transversal filter, each additional sample in time represents another degree of freedom that can be used to fit the input signal to the desired output signal. Thus, if you cannot get a good fit with a small number of samples, try a few more. On the other hand, if you get good convergence with your first

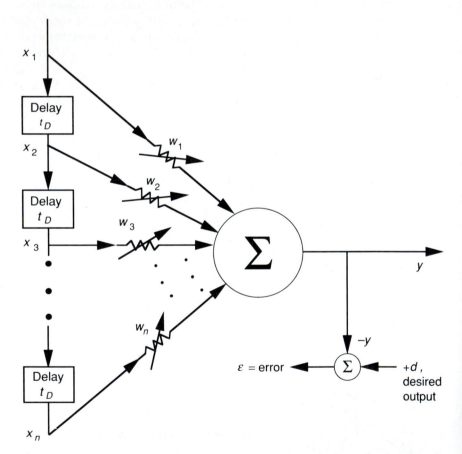

Figure 2.14   In an ALC arranged as a transversal filter, the individual samples are provided by $n-1$, presumably equal, time delays, t_D. The ALC sees the signal at the current time, as well as its value at the previous $n-1$ sample times. When data is initially applied, remember to wait at least nt_D for data to be present at all of the ALC's inputs.

choice, try one with fewer samples to see whether you get a significant speedup in convergence and still have satisfactory results (you may be surprised to find that the results are better in some cases). Moreover, the bias weight is probably superfluous in this case.

Earlier, we alluded to a relationship between training time and the dimension of the weight vector, especially for the software simulations that we consider in this text: More weights generally mean longer training times. This equation must be constantly balanced against other factors, such as the acceptability of the solution. As stated in the previous paragraph, using more weights does not always result in a better solution. Furthermore, there are other factors that affect both the training time and the acceptability of the solution.

The parameter μ is one factor that has a significant effect on training. If μ is too large, convergence will never take place, no matter how long is the training period. If the statistics of the input signal are known, it is possible to show that the value of μ is restricted to the range

$$\frac{1}{\lambda_{\max}} > \mu > 0$$

where $\lambda_{\max}$ is the largest eigenvalue of the matrix $\mathbf{R}$, the input correlation matrix discussed in Section 2.4.1. [9]. Although it is not always reasonable to expect these statistics to be known, there are cases where they can be estimated. The text by Widrow and Stearns contains many examples. In this text, we propose a more heuristic approach: Pick a value for μ such that a weight does not change by more than a small fraction of its current value. This rule is admittedly vague, but experience appears to be the best teacher for selecting an appropriate value for μ.

As training proceeds, the error value ε_k will diminish (hopefully), resulting in smaller and smaller weight changes, and, hence, in a slower convergence toward the minimum of the weight surface. It is sometimes useful to increase the value of μ during these periods to speed convergence. Bear in mind, however, that a larger μ may mean that the weights might *bounce around* the bottom of the weight surface, giving an overall error that is unacceptable. Here again, experience is necessary to enable us to judge effectively.

One method of compensating for differences in problems is to use normalized input vectors. Instead of $\mathbf{x}_k$, use $\mathbf{x}_k/|\mathbf{x}_k|$. Another tactic is to scale the desired output value. These methods help particularly when we are selecting initial weight values or a value for μ. In most cases, weights can be initialized to random values of small real numbers—say, between -1.0 and 1.0. The value of μ is usually best kept significantly less than 1; a value of 0.1 or even 0.05 may be reasonable for some problems, but values considerably less may be required.

The question of when to stop training is largely a matter of the requirements on the output of the system. You determine the amount of error that you can tolerate on the output signal, and train until the observed error is consistently less than the required value. Since the mean squared error is the value used to derive the training algorithm, that is the quantity that usually determines when a system has converged to its minimum error solution. Alternatively, observing individual errors is often necessary, since the system performance may have a requirement that no error exceed a certain amount. Nevertheless, a mean squared error that falls as the iteration number increases is probably your best indication that the system is converging toward a solution.

We usually assume that the input signals are statistically stationary, and, therefore, $\langle \varepsilon_k^2 \rangle$ is essentially a constant *after the optimum weight values have been determined*. During training, $\langle \varepsilon_k^2 \rangle$ will hopefully decrease toward a stable solution. Suppose, however, that the input signal statistics change somewhat over time, or undergo some discontinuity: Additional training would be required to compensate.

One way to deal with this situation is to cease or resume training conditionally, based on the current value of $\langle \varepsilon_k^2 \rangle$. If the signal statistics change, training can be reinitiated until $\langle \varepsilon_k^2 \rangle$ is again reduced to an acceptable value. This method presumes that a method of error measurement is available.

Provided that the input signals are statistically stationary, choosing the number of input vectors to use during training may be relatively simple. You can use real, time-sequenced inputs as training vectors, provided that you know the desired output for each input vector. If it is possible to identify a sample of input vectors that adequately reproduces the statistical distribution of the actual inputs, it may be possible to train on this set in a shorter time. The accuracy of the training depends on how well the selected set of training vectors models the distribution of the entire input signal space.

The other, related question is how to go about determining the desired output for a given input vector. As with many questions discussed in this section, this depends on the specific details of the problem. Fortunately, for some problems, knowing the desired result is easy compared to finding an algorithm for transforming the inputs into the desired result. The ALC will often solve the difficult part. The "easy" part is left to the engineer.

Exercise 2.4: A lowpass filter can be constructed with an Adaline having two weights. Consider a simple case of the removal of a random noise from a constant signal. The constant signal level is $C = 3$, and the random noise signal has a constant power, $\langle r^2 \rangle = n = 0.025$. Assume that the random noise is completely uncorrelated with the constant input signal. Calculate the optimum weight vector and the mean squared error in the output after the optimum weight vector has been found. By finding the eigenvalues of the matrix, $\mathbf{R}$, determine the maximum value of the constant μ for use in the LMS algorithm.

2.3 APPLICATIONS OF ADAPTIVE SIGNAL PROCESSING

Up to now, we have been concerned with the Adaline minus the threshold condition on the output. In Section 2.4, on the Madaline, we will replace the threshold condition and examine networks of Adalines. In this section, we will look at a few examples of adaptive signal processing using only the ALC portion of the Adaline.

2.3.1 Echo Cancellation in Telephone Circuits

You may have experienced the phenomenon of echo in telephone conversations: you hear the words you speak into the mouthpiece a fraction of a second later in the earphone of the telephone. The echo tends to be most noticeable on long-distance calls, especially those over satellite links where transmission delays can be a significant fraction of a second.

Telephone circuits contain devices called **hybrids** that are intended to isolate incoming signals from outgoing signals, thus avoiding the echo effect. Unfortunately, these circuits do not always perform perfectly, due to causes such as impedance mismatches, resulting in some echo back to the speaker. Even when the echo signal has been attenuated by a substantial amount, it still may be audible, and hence an annoyance to the speaker.

Certain echo-suppression devices rely on relays that open and close circuits in the outgoing lines so that incoming voice signals are not sent back to the speaker. When transmission delays are long, as with satellite communications, these echo suppressors can result in a loss of parts of words. This choppy-speech effect is perhaps more familiar than the echo effect. An adaptive filter can be used to remove the echo effect without the choppiness of the relays used in other echo suppression circuits [9, 7].

Figure 2.15 is a block diagram of a telephone circuit with an adaptive filter used as an echo-suppression device. The echo is caused by a leakage of the incoming voice signal to the output line through the hybrid circuit. This leakage adds to the output signal coming from the microphone. The output of the adaptive filter, y, is subtracted from the outgoing signal, $s + n'$, where s is the outgoing pure voice signal and n' is the *noise*, or echo caused by leakage of the incoming voice signal through the hybrid circuit. The success of the echo cancellation depends on how well the adaptive filter can mimic the leakage through the hybrid circuit.

Notice that the input to the filter is a copy of the incoming signal, n, and that the error is a copy of the outgoing signal,

$$\varepsilon = s + n' - y \tag{2.16}$$

We assume that y is correlated with the noise, n', but not with the pure voice signal, s. If the quantity, $n' - y$, is nonzero, some echo still remains in the outgoing signal. Squaring and taking expectation values of both sides of Eq. (2.16) gives

$$\langle \varepsilon^2 \rangle = \langle s^2 \rangle + \langle (n' - y)^2 \rangle + 2\langle s(n' - y) \rangle \tag{2.17}$$
$$= \langle s^2 \rangle + \langle (n' - y)^2 \rangle \tag{2.18}$$

Equation (2.18) follows, since s is not correlated with either y or n', resulting in the last term in Eq. (2.17) being equal to zero.

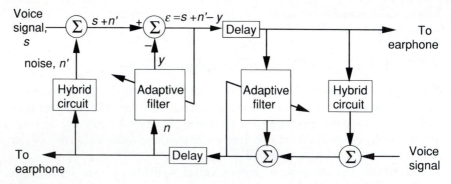

Figure 2.15 This figure is a schematic of a telephone circuit using an adaptive filter to cancel echo. The adaptive filter is depicted as a box; the slanted arrow represents the adjustable weights.

The signal power, $\langle s^2 \rangle$, is determined by the source of the voice signal—say, some amplifier at the telephone switching station local to the sender. Thus, $\langle s^2 \rangle$ is not directly affected by changes in $\langle \varepsilon^2 \rangle$. The adaptive filter attempts to minimize $\langle \varepsilon^2 \rangle$, and, in doing so, minimizes $\langle (n' - y)^2 \rangle$, the power of the uncanceled noise on the outgoing line.

Since there is only one input to the adaptive filter, the device would be configured as a transverse filter. Widrow and Stearns [9] suggest sampling the incoming signal at a rate of 8 KHz and using 128 weight values.

2.3.2 Other Applications

Rather than go into the details of the many applications that can be addressed by these adaptive filters, we refer you once again to the excellent text by Widrow and Stearns. In this section, we shall simply suggest a few broad areas where adaptive filters can be used in addition to the echo-cancellation application we have discussed.

Figure 2.16 shows an adaptive filter that is used to *predict* the future value of a signal based on its present value. A second example is shown in Figure 2.17. In this example, the adaptive filter learns to reproduce the output from some *plant* based on inputs to the system. This configuration has many uses as an adaptive control system. The *plant* could represent many things, including a human operator. In that case, the adaptive filter could learn how to respond to changing conditions by *watching* the human operator. Eventually, such a device might result in an automated control system, leaving the human free for more important tasks.[2]

Another useful application of these devices is in adaptive beam-forming antenna arrays. Although the term *antenna* is usually associated with electro-

---

[2]Such as training another adaptive filter with the Standard & Poors 500.

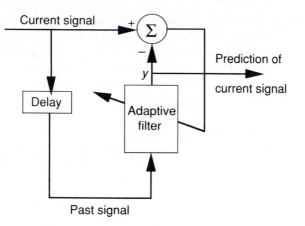

Current signal

Σ

Prediction of
current signal

y

Delay

Adaptive
filter

Past signal

Figure 2.16   This schematic shows an adaptive filter used to predict signal values. The input signal used to train the network is a delayed value of the actual signal; that is, it is the signal at some past time. The expected output is the current value of the signal. The adaptive filter attempts to minimize the error between its output and the current signal, based on an input of the signal value from some time in the past. Once the filter is correctly predicting the current signal based on the past signal, the current signal can be used directly as an input without the delay. The filter will then make a prediction of the future signal value.

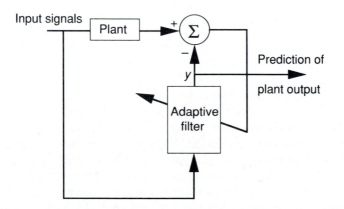

Input signals

Plant

Σ

Prediction of
plant output

y

Adaptive
filter

Figure 2.17   This example shows an adaptive filter used to model the output from a system, called the *plant*. Inputs to the filter are the same as those to the plant. The filter adjusts its weights based on the difference between its output and the output of the plant.

magnetic radiation, we broaden the definition here to include any spatial array of sensors. The basic task here is to learn to steer the array. At any given time, a signal may be arriving from any given direction, but antennae usually are directional in their reception characteristics: They respond to signals in some directions, but not in others. The antenna array with adaptive filters learns to adjust its directional characteristics in order to respond to the incoming signal no matter what the direction is, while reducing its response to unwanted noise signals coming in from other directions.

Of course, we have only touched on the number of applications for these devices. Unlike many other neural-network architectures, this is a relatively mature device with a long history of success. In the next section, we replace the binary output condition on the ALC circuit so that the latter becomes, once again, the complete Adaline.

2.4 THE MADALINE

As you can see from the discussion in Chapter 1, the Adaline resembles the perceptron closely; it also has some of the same limitations as the perceptron. For example, a two-input Adaline cannot compute the XOR function. Combining Adalines in a layered structure can overcome this difficulty, as we did in Chapter 1 with the perceptron. Such a structure is illustrated in Figure 2.18.

Exercise 2.5: What logic function is being computed by the single Adaline in the output layer of Figure 2.18? Construct a three-input Adaline that computes the majority function.

2.4.1 Madaline Architecture

Madaline is the acronym for Many Adalines. Arranged in a multilayered architecture as illustrated in Figure 2.19, the Madaline resembles the general neural-network structure shown in Chapter 1. In this configuration, the Madaline could be presented with a large-dimensional input vector—say, the pixel values from a raster scan. With suitable training, the network could be taught to respond with a binary +1 on one of several output nodes, each of which corresponds to a different category of input image. Examples of such categorization are {cat, dog, armadillo, javelina} and {Flogger, Tom Cat, Eagle, Fulcrum}. In such a network, each of four nodes in the output layer corresponds to a single class. For a given input pattern, a node would have a +1 output if the input pattern corresponded to the class represented by that particular node. The other three nodes would have a −1 output. If the input pattern were not a member of any known class, the results from the network could be ambiguous.

To train such a network, we might be tempted to begin with the LMS algorithm at the output layer. Since the network is presumably trained with previously identified input patterns, the *desired* output vector is known. What

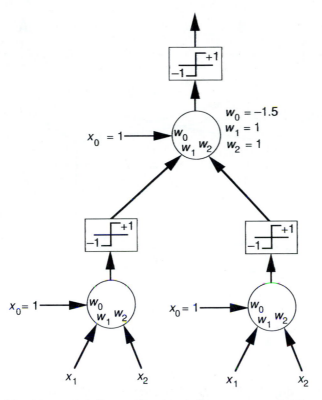

Figure 2.18   Many Adalines (the Madaline) can compute the XOR function of two inputs. Note the addition of the bias terms to each Adaline. A positive analog output from an ALC results in a +1 output from the associated Adaline; a negative analog output results in a −1. Likewise, any inputs to the device that are binary in nature must use ±1 rather than 1 and 0.

we do not know is the *desired* output for a given node on one of the hidden layers. Furthermore, the LMS algorithm would operate on the analog outputs of the ALC, not on the bipolar output values of the Adaline. For these reasons, a different training strategy has been developed for the Madaline.

2.4.2   The MRII Training Algorithm

It is possible to devise a method of training a Madaline-like structure based on the LMS algorithm; however, the method relies on replacing the linear threshold output function with a continuously differentiable function (the threshold function is discontinuous at 0; hence, it is not differentiable there). We will take up the study of this method in the next chapter. For now, we consider a method known as Madaline rule II (MRII). The original Madaline rule was an earlier

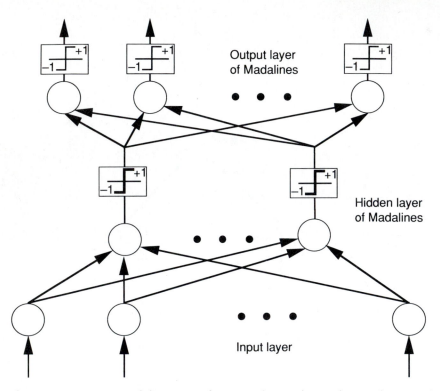

Figure 2.19   Many Adalines can be joined in a layered neural network such as this one.

method that we shall not discuss here. Details can be found in references given at the end of this chapter.

MRII resembles a trial-and-error procedure with added intelligence in the form of a **minimum disturbance principle.** Since the output of the network is a series of bipolar units, training amounts to reducing the number of incorrect output nodes for each training input pattern. The minimum disturbance principle enforces the notion that those nodes that can affect the output error while incurring the least change in their weights should have precedence in the learning procedure. This principle is embodied in the following algorithm:

1. Apply a training vector to the inputs of the Madaline and propagate it through to the output units.

2. Count the number of incorrect values in the output layer; call this number the error.

3. For all units on the output layer,

   a. Select the first previously unselected node whose *analog* output is clos-est to zero. (This node is the node that can reverse its bipolar output with the least change in its weights—hence the term *minimum distur-bance.*)

 b. Change the weights on the selected unit such that the bipolar output of the unit changes.

 c. Propagate the input vector forward from the inputs to the outputs once again.

 d. If the weight change results in a reduction in the number of errors, accept the weight change; otherwise, restore the original weights.

4. Repeat step 3 for all layers except the input layer.

5. For all units on the output layer,

 a. Select the previously unselected pair of units whose analog outputs are closest to zero.

 b. Apply a weight correction to both units, in order to change the bipolar output of each.

 c. Propagate the input vector forward from the inputs to the outputs.

 d. If the weight change results in a reduction in the number of errors, accept the weight change; otherwise, restore the original weights.

6. Repeat step 5 for all layers except the input layer.

If necessary, the sequence in steps 5 and 6 can be repeated with triplets of units, or quadruplets of units, or even larger combinations, until satisfactory results are obtained. Preliminary indications are that pairs are adequate for modest-sized networks with up to 25 units per layer [8].

At the time of this writing, the MRII was still undergoing experimentation to determine its convergence characteristics and other properties. Moreover, a new learning algorithm, MRIII, has been developed. MRIII is similar to MRII, but the individual units have a continuous output function, rather than the bipolar threshold function [2]. In the next section, we shall use a Madaline architecture to examine a specific problem in pattern recognition.

2.4.3   A Madaline for Translation-Invariant Pattern Recognition

Various Madaline structures have been used recently to demonstrate the applicability of this architecture to adaptive pattern recognition having the properties of translation invariance, rotation invariance, and scale invariance. These three properties are essential to any robust system that would be called on to recognize objects in the field of view of optical or infrared sensors, for example. Remember, however, that even humans do not always instantly recognize objects that have been rotated to unfamiliar orientations, or that have been scaled significantly smaller or larger than their everyday size. The point is that there may be alternatives to *training in* instantaneous recognition at all angles and scale factors. Be that as it may, it is possible to build neural-network devices that exhibit these characteristics to some degree.

Figure 2.20 shows a portion of a network that is used to implement translation-invariant recognition of a pattern [7]. The **retina** is a 5-by-5-pixel array on which bit-mapped representation of patterns, such as the letters of the alphabet, can be placed. The portion of the network shown is called a **slab**. Unlike a layer, a slab does not communicate with other slabs in the network, as will be seen shortly. Each Adaline in the slab receives the identical 25 inputs from the retina, and computes a bipolar output in the usual fashion; however, the weights on the 25 Adalines share a unique relationship.

Consider the weights on the top-left Adaline as being arranged in a square matrix duplicating the pixel array on the retina. The Adaline to the immediate

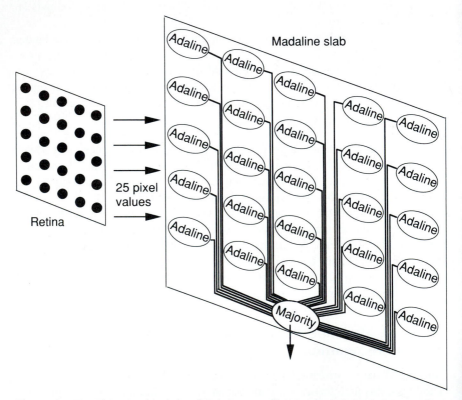

Figure 2.20   This single slab of Adalines will give the same output (either +1 or −1) for a particular pattern on the retina, regardless of the horizontal or vertical alignment of that pattern on the retina. All 25 individual Adalines are connected to a single Adaline that computes the majority function: If most of the inputs are +1, the majority element responds with a +1 output. The network derives its translation-invariance properties from the particular configuration of the weights. See the text for details.

right of the top-left pixel has the identical set of weight values, but translated one pixel to the right: The rightmost column of weights on the first unit wraps around to the left to become the leftmost column on the second unit. Similarly, the unit below the top-left unit also has the identical weights, but translated one pixel down. The bottom row of weights on the first unit becomes the top row of the unit under it. This translation continues across each row and down each column in a similar manner. Figure 2.21 illustrates some of these weight matrices. Because of this relationship among the weight matrices, a single pattern on the retina will elicit identical responses from the slab, independent

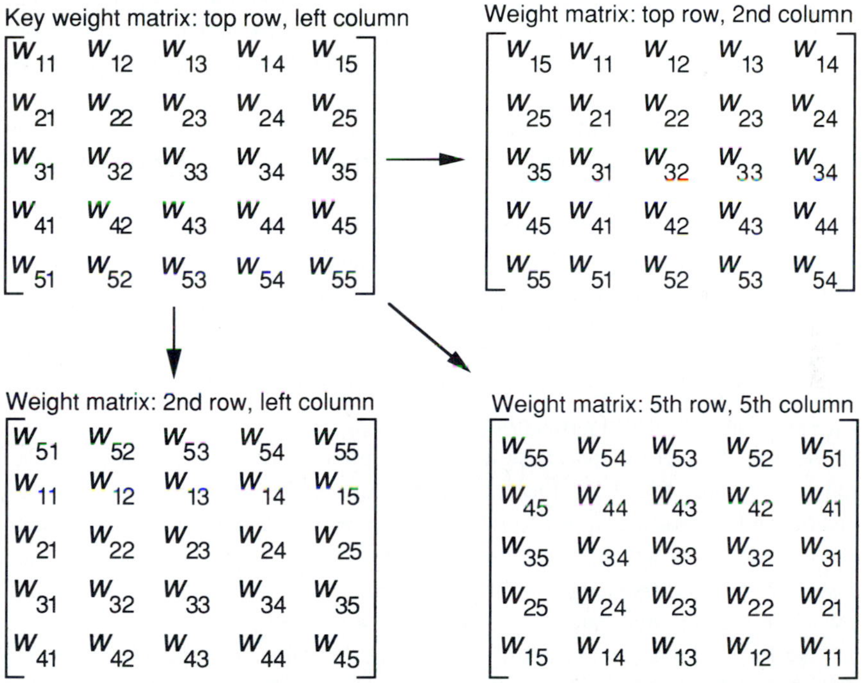

Key weight matrix: top row, left column

$$\begin{bmatrix} W_{11} & W_{12} & W_{13} & W_{14} & W_{15} \\ W_{21} & W_{22} & W_{23} & W_{24} & W_{25} \\ W_{31} & W_{32} & W_{33} & W_{34} & W_{35} \\ W_{41} & W_{42} & W_{43} & W_{44} & W_{45} \\ W_{51} & W_{52} & W_{53} & W_{54} & W_{55} \end{bmatrix}$$

Weight matrix: top row, 2nd column

$$\begin{bmatrix} W_{15} & W_{11} & W_{12} & W_{13} & W_{14} \\ W_{25} & W_{21} & W_{22} & W_{23} & W_{24} \\ W_{35} & W_{31} & W_{32} & W_{33} & W_{34} \\ W_{45} & W_{41} & W_{42} & W_{43} & W_{44} \\ W_{55} & W_{51} & W_{52} & W_{53} & W_{54} \end{bmatrix}$$

Weight matrix: 2nd row, left column

$$\begin{bmatrix} W_{51} & W_{52} & W_{53} & W_{54} & W_{55} \\ W_{11} & W_{12} & W_{13} & W_{14} & W_{15} \\ W_{21} & W_{22} & W_{23} & W_{24} & W_{25} \\ W_{31} & W_{32} & W_{33} & W_{34} & W_{35} \\ W_{41} & W_{42} & W_{43} & W_{44} & W_{45} \end{bmatrix}$$

Weight matrix: 5th row, 5th column

$$\begin{bmatrix} W_{55} & W_{54} & W_{53} & W_{52} & W_{51} \\ W_{45} & W_{44} & W_{43} & W_{42} & W_{41} \\ W_{35} & W_{34} & W_{33} & W_{32} & W_{31} \\ W_{25} & W_{24} & W_{23} & W_{22} & W_{21} \\ W_{15} & W_{14} & W_{13} & W_{12} & W_{11} \end{bmatrix}$$

Figure 2.21 The weight matrix in the upper left is the key weight matrix. All other weight matrices on the slab are derived from this matrix. The matrix to the right of the key weight matrix represents the matrix on the Adaline directly to the right of the one with the key weight matrix. Notice that the fifth column of the key weight matrix has wrapped around to become the first column, with the other columns shifting one space to the right. The matrix below the key weight matrix is the one on the Adaline directly below the Adaline with the key weight matrix. The matrix diagonal to the key weight matrix represents the matrix on the Adaline at the lower right of the slab.

of the pattern's translational position on the retina. We encourage you to reflect on this result for a moment (perhaps several moments), to convince yourself of its validity.

The *majority* node is a single Adaline that computes a binary output based on the outputs of the majority of the Adalines connecting to it. Because of the translational relationship among the weight vectors, the placement of a particular pattern at any location on the retina will result in the identical output from the majority element (we impose the restriction that patterns that extend beyond the retina boundaries will wrap around to the opposite side, just as the various weight matrices are derived from the key weight matrix.). Of course, a pattern different from the first may elicit a different response from the majority element. Because only two responses are possible, the slab can differentiate two classes on input patterns. In terms of hyperspace, a slab is capable of dividing hyperspace into two regions.

To overcome the limitation of only two possible classes, the retina can be connected to multiple slabs, each having different **key weight matrices** (Widrow and Winter's term for the weight matrix on the top-left element of each slab). Given the binary nature of the output of each slab, a system of n slabs could differentiate 2^n different pattern classes. Figure 2.22 shows four such slabs producing a four-dimensional output capable of distinguishing 16 different input-pattern classes with translational invariance.

Let's review the basic operation of the translation invariance network in terms of a specific example. Consider the 16 letters A $\rightarrow$ P, as the input patterns we would like to identify regardless of their up–down or left–right translation on the 5-by-5-pixel retina. These translated retina patterns are the inputs to the slabs of the network. Each retina pattern results in an output pattern from the invariance network that maps to one of the 16 input classes (in this case, each class represents a letter). By using a lookup table, or other method, we can associate the 16 possible outputs from the invariance network with one of the 16 possible letters that can be identified by the network.

So far, nothing has been said concerning the values of the weights on the Adalines of the various slabs in the system. That is because it is not actually necessary to train those nodes in the usual sense. In fact, each key weight matrix can be chosen at random, provided that each input-pattern class result in a unique output vector from the invariance network. Using the example of the previous paragraph, any translation of one of the letters should result in the same output from the invariance network. Furthermore, any pattern from a different class (i.e., a different letter) must result in a different output vector from the network. This requirement means that, if you pick a random key weight matrix for a particular slab and find that two letters give the same output pattern, you can simply pick a different weight matrix.

As an alternative to random selection of key weight matrices, it may be possible to optimize selection by employing a training procedure based on the MRII. Investigations in this area are ongoing at the time of this writing [7].

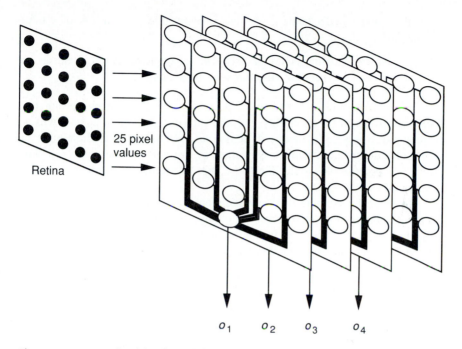

25 pixel values

Retina

o_1 o_2 o_3 o_4

Figure 2.22 Each of the four slabs in the system depicted here will produce a +1 or a −1 output value for every pattern that appears on the retina. The output vector is a four-digit binary number, so the system can potentially differentiate up to 16 different classes of input patterns.

2.5 SIMULATING THE ADALINE

As we shall for the implementation of all other network simulators we will present, we shall begin this section by describing how the general data structures are used to model the Adaline unit and Madaline network. Once the basic architecture has been presented, we will describe the algorithmic process needed to propagate signals through the Adaline. The section concludes with a discussion of the algorithms needed to cause the Adaline to self-adapt according to the learning laws described previously.

2.5.1 Adaline Data Structures

It is appropriate that the Adaline is the first test of the simulator data structures we presented in Chapter 1 for two reasons:

1. Since the forward propagation of signals through the single Adaline is virtually identical to the forward propagation process in most of the other networks we will study, it is beneficial for us to observe the Adaline to

gain a better understanding of what is happening in each unit of a larger network.

2. Because the Adaline is not a network, its implementation exercises the versatility of the network structures we have defined.

As we have already seen, the Adaline is only a single processing unit. Therefore, some of the generality we built into our network structures will not be required. Specifically, there will be no real need to handle multiple units and layers of units for the Adaline. Nevertheless, we will include the use of those structures, because we would like to be able to extend the Adaline easily into the Madaline.

We begin by defining our network record as a structure that will contain all the parameters that will be used globally, as well as pointers to locate the dynamic arrays that will contain the network data. In the case of the Adaline, a good candidate structure for this record will take the form

```
record Adaline =
   mu : float;              {Storage for stability term}
   input: ^layer;           {Pointer to input layer}
   output : ^layer;         {Pointer to output layer}
end record
```

Note that, even though there is only one unit in the Adaline, we will use two layers to model the network. Thus, the `input` and `output` pointers will point to different layer records. We do this because we will use the `input` layer as storage for holding the input signal vector to the Adaline. There will be no connections associated with this layer, as the input will be provided by some other process in the system (e.g., a time-multiplexed analog-to-digital converter, or an array of sensors).

Conversely, the `output` layer will contain one weight array to model the connections between the `input` and the `output` (recall that our data structures presume that PEs process input connections primarily). Keeping in mind that we would like to extend this structure easily to handle the Madaline network, we will retain the indirection to the connection weight array provided by the `weight_ptr` array described in Chapter 1. Notice that, in the case of the Adaline, however, the `weight_ptr` array will contain only one value, the pointer to the input connection array.

There is one other thing to consider that may vary between Adaline units. As we have seen previously, there are two parts to the Adaline structure: the linear ALC and the bipolar Adaline units. To distinguish between them, we define an enumerated type to classify each Adaline neuron:

```
type NODE_TYPE : {linear, binary};
```

We now have everything we need to define the `layer` record structure for the Adaline. A prototype structure for this record is as follows.

```
record layer =
  activation : NODE_TYPE {kind of Adaline node}
  outs: ^float[];           {pointer to unit output array}
  weights : ^^float[]; {indirect access to weight arrays}
end record
```

Finally, three dynamically allocated arrays are needed to contain the output of the Adaline unit, the `weight_ptrs` and the connection `weights` values. We will not specify the structure of these arrays, other than to indicate that the `outs` and `weights` arrays will both contain floating-point values, whereas the `weight_ptr` array will store memory addresses and must therefore contain memory pointer types. The entire data structure for the Adaline simulator is depicted in Figure 2.23.

2.5.2 Signal Propagation Through the Adaline

If signals are to be propagated through the Adaline successfully, two activities must occur: We must obtain the input signal vector to stimulate the Adaline, and the Adaline must perform its input-summation and output-transformation functions. Since the origin of the input signal vector is somewhat application specific, we will presume that the user will provide the code necessary to keep the data located in the `outs` array in the `Adaline.inputs` layer current.

We shall now concentrate on the matter of computing the input stimulation value and transforming it to the appropriate output. We can accomplish this task through the application of two algorithmic functions, which we will name `sum_inputs` and `compute_output`. The algorithms for these functions are as follows:

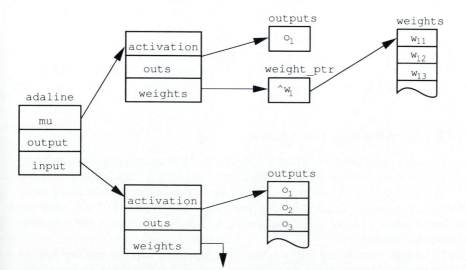

Figure 2.23 The Adaline simulator data structure is shown.

```
function sum_inputs (INPUTS : ^float[];
                     WEIGHTS : ^^float[])
return float
   var sum : float;        {local accumulator}
       temp : float;       {scratch memory}
       ins : ^float[];     {local pointer}
       wts : ^float[];     {local pointer}
         i : integer;      {iteration counter}

   begin
     sum = 0;              {initialize accumulator}
     ins = INPUTS;         {locate input array}
     wts = WEIGHTS^;       {locate connection array}

     for i = 1 to length(wts) do
                              {for all weights in array}
         temp = ins[i] * wts[i]; {modulate input}
         sum = sum + temp;       {sum modulated inputs}
       end do

      return(sum);         {return the modulated sum}
   end function;


function compute_output (INPUT : float;
                         ACT : NODE_TYPE) return float

   begin
     if (ACT = linear)    {if the Adaline is a linear unit}
     then return (INPUT)    {then just return the input}
     else                   {otherwise}
        if (INPUT >= 0.0)   {if the input is positive}
        then return (1.0)   {then return a binary true}
        else return (-1.0); {else return a binary false}
     end function;
```

2.5.3   Adapting the Adaline

Now that our simulator can forward propagate signal information, we turn our attention to the implementation of the learning algorithms. Here again we assume that the input signal pattern is placed in the appropriate array by an application-specific process. During training, however, we will need to know what the target output d_k is for every input vector, so that we can compute the error term for the Adaline.

Recall that, during training, the LMS algorithm requires that the Adaline update its weights after every forward propagation for a new input pattern. We must also consider that the Adaline application may need to adapt the

Adaline *while it is running*. Based on these observations, there is no need to store or accumulate errors across all patterns within the training algorithm. Thus, we can design the training algorithm merely to adapt the weights for a single pattern. However, this design decision places on the application program the responsibility for determining when the Adaline has trained sufficiently.

This approach is usually acceptable because of the advantages it offers over the implementation of a self-contained training loop. Specifically, it means that we can use the same training function to adapt the Adaline initially or while it is on-line. The generality of the algorithm is a particularly useful feature, in that the application program merely needs to detect a condition requiring adaptation. It can then sample the input that caused the error and generate the correct response "on the fly," provided we have some way of knowing that the error is increasing and can generate the correct desired values to accommodate retraining. These values, in turn, can then be input to the Adaline training algorithm, thus allowing adaptation at run time. Finally, it also reduces the housekeeping chores that must be performed by the simulator, since we will not need to maintain a list of expected outputs for all training patterns.

We must now define algorithms to compute the squared error term ($\varepsilon^2(t)$), the approximation of the gradient of the error surface, and to update the connection weights to the Adaline. We can again simplify matters by combining the computation of the error and the update of the connection weights into one function, as there is no need to compute the former without performing the latter. We now present the algorithms to accomplish these functions:

```
function compute_error (A : Adaline;  TARGET : float)
return float
   var temp1 : float;        {scratch memory}
       temp2 : float;        {scratch memory}
       err : float;          {error term for unit}

   begin
     temp1 = sum_inputs (A.input.outs, A.output.weights);
     temp2 = compute_output (temp1, A.output^.activation);
     err = absolute (TARGET - temp2); {fast error}
     return (err);                    {return error}
   end function;

function update_weights (A : Adaline;  ERR : float)
return void
   var grad : float;         {the gradient of the error}
       ins : ^float[];       {pointer to inputs array}
       wts : ^float[];       {pointer to weights array}
        i : integer;         {iteration counter}
```

```
begin
  ins = A.input.outs;      {locate start of input vector}
  wts = A.output.weights^;
                            {locate start of connections}

  for i = 1 to length(wts) do {for all connections, do}
    grad = -2 * err * ins[i];  {approximate gradient}
    wts[i] = wts[i] - grad * A.mu;
                                    {update connection}
  end do;
end function;
```

2.5.4   Completing the Adaline Simulator

The algorithms we have just defined are sufficient to implement an Adaline simulator in both learning and operational modes. To offer a clean interface to any external program that must call our simulator to perform an Adaline function, we can combine the modules we have described into two higher-level functions. These functions will perform the two types of activities the Adaline must perform: forward_propagate and adapt_Adaline.

```
function forward_propagate (A : Adaline) return void
   var temp1 : float;              {scratch memory}

  begin
    temp1 = sum_inputs (A.inputs.outs,
    A.outputs.weights);
    A.outputs.outs[1] = compute_output (temp1,
    A.node_type);
  end function;

function adapt_Adaline (A : Adaline;  TARGET : float)
return float
   var err : float;                         {train until small}

  begin
     forward_propagate (A);              {Apply input signal}
     err = compute_error (A, TARGET); {Compute error}
     update_weights (A, err);         {Adapt Adaline}
     return(err);
  end function;
```

2.5.5   Madaline Simulator Implementation

As we have discussed earlier, the Madaline network is simply a collection of binary Adaline units, connected together in a layered structure. However, even though they share the same type of processing unit, the learning strategies implemented for the Madaline are significantly different, as described in Section 2.5.2. Providing that as a guide, along with the discussion of the data structures needed, we leave the algorithm development for the Madaline network to you as an exercise.

In this regard, you should note that the layered structure of the Madaline lends itself directly to our simulator data structures. As illustrated in Figure 2.24, we can implement a layer of Adaline units as easily as we created a single Adaline. The major differences here will be the length of the `outs` arrays in the `layer` records (since there will be more than one Adaline output per layer), and the length and number of connection arrays (there will be one `weights` array for each Adaline in the `layer`, and the `weight_ptr` array will be extended by one slot for each new `weights` array).

Similarly, there will be more `layer` records as the depth of the Madaline increases, and, for each layer, there will be a corresponding increase in the number of `outs`, `weights`, and `weight_ptr` arrays. Based on these observations, one fact that becomes immediately perceptible is the combinatorial growth of both memory consumed and computer time required to support a linear growth in network size. This relationship between computer resources and model sizing is true not only for the Madaline, but for all ANS models we will study. It is for these reasons that we have stressed optimization in data structures.

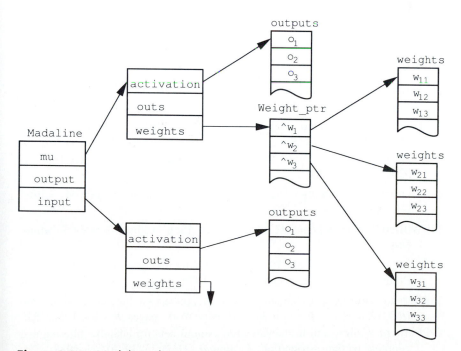

Figure 2.24   Madaline data structures are shown.

Programming Exercises

2.1. Extend the Adaline simulator to include the bias unit, θ, as described in the text.

2.2. Extend the simulator to implement a three-layer Madaline using the algorithms discussed in Section 2.3.2. Be sure to use the binary Adaline type. Test the operation of your simulator by training it to solve the XOR problem described in the text.

2.3. We have indicated that the network stability term, μ, can greatly affect the ability of the Adaline to converge on a solution. Using four different values for μ of your own choosing, train an Adaline to eliminate noise from an input sinusoid ranging from 0 to 2π (one way to do this is to use a scaled random-number generator to provide the noise). Graph the curve of training iterations versus μ.

Suggested Readings

The authoritative text by Widrow and Stearns is the standard reference to the material contained in this chapter [9]. The original delta-rule derivation is contained in a 1960 paper by Widrow and Hoff [6], which is also reprinted in the collection edited by Anderson and Rosenfeld [1].

Bibliography

[1] James A. Anderson and Edward Rosenfeld, editors. *Neurocomputing: Foundations of Research*. MIT Press, Cambridge, MA, 1988.

[2] David Andes, Bernard Widrow, Michael Lehr, and Eric Wan. MRIII: A robust algorithm for training analog neural networks. In *Proceedings of the International Joint Conference on Neural Networks*, pages I-533–I-536, January 1990.

[3] Richard W. Hamming. *Digital Filters*. Prentice-Hall, Englewood Cliffs, NJ, 1983.

[4] Wilfred Kaplan. *Advanced Calculus*, 3rd edition. Addison-Wesley, Reading, MA, 1984.

[5] Alan V. Oppenheim and Ronald W. Schafer. *Digital Signal Processing*. Prentice-Hall, Englewood Cliffs, NJ, 1975.

[6] Bernard Widrow and Marcian E. Hoff. Adaptive switching circuits. In *1960 IRE WESCON Convention Record*, New York, pages 96–104, 1960. IRE.

[7] Bernard Widrow and Rodney Winter. Neural nets for adaptive filtering and adaptive pattern recognition. *Computer*, 21(3):25–39, March 1988.

[8] Rodney Winter and Bernard Widrow. MADALINE RULE II: A training algorithm for neural networks. In *Proceedings of the IEEE Second International Conference on Neural Networks*, San Diego, CA, I:401–408, July 1988.

[9] Bernard Widrow and Samuel D. Stearns. *Adaptive Signal Processing*. Signal Processing Series. Prentice-Hall, Englewood Cliffs, NJ, 1985.

Backpropagation

There are many potential computer applications that are difficult to implement because there are many problems unsuited to solution by a sequential process. Applications that must perform some complex data translation, yet have no predefined mapping function to describe the translation process, or those that must provide a "best guess" as output when presented with noisy input data are but two examples of problems of this type.

An ANS that we have found to be useful in addressing problems requiring recognition of complex patterns and performing nontrivial mapping functions is the backpropagation network (BPN), formalized first by Werbos [11], and later by Parker [8] and by Rummelhart and McClelland [7]. This network, illustrated generically in Figure 3.1, is designed to operate as a multilayer, feedforward network, using the supervised mode of learning.

The chapter begins with a discussion of an example of a problem mapping character image to ASCII, which appears simple, but can quickly overwhelm traditional approaches. Then, we look at how the backpropagation network operates to solve such a problem. Following that discussion is a detailed derivation of the equations that govern the learning process in the backpropagation network. From there, we describe some practical applications of the BPN as described in the literature. The chapter concludes with details of the BPN software simulator within the context of the general design given in Chapter 1.

3.1 THE BACKPROPAGATION NETWORK

To illustrate some problems that often arise when we are attempting to automate complex pattern-recognition applications, let us consider the design of a computer program that must translate a 5×7 matrix of binary numbers representing the bit-mapped pixel image of an alphanumeric character to its equivalent eight-bit ASCII code. This basic problem, pictured in Figure 3.2, appears to be relatively trivial at first glance. Since there is no obvious mathematical function

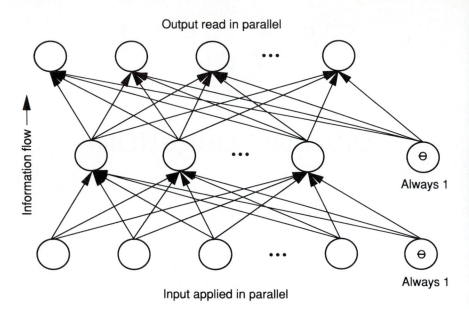

Figure 3.1   The general backpropagation network architecture is shown.

that will perform the desired translation, and because it would undoubtedly take too much time (both human and computer time) to perform a pixel-by-pixel correlation, the best algorithmic solution would be to use a lookup table.

The lookup table needed to solve this problem would be a one-dimensional linear array of ordered pairs, each taking the form:

```
record AELEMENT =
    pattern : long integer;
    ascii : byte;
end record;
```

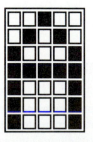

$= 00100010101010001111111000110001100001_2$

$= 1151FC631_{16}$

$= 65_{10}$ ASCII

Figure 3.2   Each character image is mapped to its corresponding ASCII code.

The first is the numeric equivalent of the bit-pattern code, which we generate by moving the seven rows of the matrix to a single row and considering the result to be a 35-bit binary number. The second is the ASCII code associated with the character. The array would contain exactly the same number of ordered-pairs as there were characters to convert. The algorithm needed to perform the conversion process would take the following form:

```
function TRANSLATE(INPUT : long integer;
              LUT : ^AELEMENT[]) return ascii;
{performs pixel-matrix to ASCII character conversion}

var TABLE : ^AELEMENT[];
    found : boolean;
    i : integer;

  begin
    TABLE = LUT;       {locate translation table}
    found = false;     {translation not found yet}

    for i = 1 to length(TABLE) do {for all items in table}
        if TABLE[i].pattern = INPUT
        then Found = True; Exit;
                               {translation found, quit loop}
      end;

    If Found
    Then return TABLE[i].ascii    {return ascii}
    Else return 0
  end;
```

Although the lookup-table approach is reasonably fast and easy to maintain, there are many situations that occur in real systems that cannot be handled by this method. For example, consider the same pixel-image–to–ASCII conversion process in a more realistic environment. Let's suppose that our character image scanner alters a random pixel in the input image matrix due to noise when the image was read. This single pixel error would cause the lookup algorithm to return either a null or the wrong ASCII code, since the match between the input pattern and the target pattern must be exact.

Now consider the amount of additional software (and, hence, CPU time) that must be added to the lookup-table algorithm to improve the ability of the computer to "guess" at which character the noisy image should have been. Single-bit errors are fairly easy to find and correct. Multibit errors become increasingly difficult as the number of bit errors grows. To complicate matters even further, how could our software compensate for noise on the image if that noise happened to make an "O" look like a "Q", or an "E" look like an "F"? If our character-conversion system had to produce an accurate output all the time,

an inordinate amount of CPU time would be spent eliminating noise from the
input pattern prior to attempting to translate it to ASCII.

One solution to this dilemma is to take advantage of the parallel nature of
neural networks to reduce the time required by a sequential processor to perform
the mapping. In addition, system-development time can be reduced because the
network can *learn* the proper algorithm without having someone deduce that
algorithm in advance.

3.1.1   The Backpropagation Approach

Problems such as the noisy image-to-ASCII example are difficult to solve by
computer due to the basic incompatibility between the machine and the problem.
Most of today's computer systems have been designed to perform mathematical and logic functions at speeds that are incomprehensible to humans. Even
the relatively unsophisticated desktop microcomputers commonplace today can
perform hundreds of thousands of numeric comparisons or combinations every
second.

However, as our previous example illustrated, mathematical prowess is not
what is needed to recognize complex patterns in noisy environments. In fact,
an algorithmic search of even a relatively small input space can prove to be
time-consuming. The problem is the sequential nature of the computer itself;
the "fetch–execute" cycle of the von Neumann architecture allows the machine
to perform only one operation at a time. In most cases, the time required
by the computer to perform each instruction is so short (typically about one-
millionth of a second) that the aggregate time required for even a large program
is insignificant to the human users. However, for applications that must search
through a large input space, or attempt to correlate all possible permutations of
a complex pattern, the time required by even a very fast machine can quickly
become intolerable.

What we need is a new processing system that can examine all the pixels in
the image in parallel. Ideally, such a system would not have to be programmed
explicitly; rather, it would adapt itself to "learn" the relationship between a set of
example patterns, and would be able to apply the same relationship to new input
patterns. This system would be able to focus on the features of an arbitrary input
that resemble other patterns seen previously, such as those pixels in the noisy
image that "look" like a known character, and to ignore the noise. Fortunately,
such a system exists; we call this system the **backpropagation network** (BPN).

3.1.2   BPN Operation

In Section 3.2, we will cover the details of the mechanics of backpropagation.
A summary description of the network operation is appropriate here, to illustrate
how the BPN can be used to solve complex pattern-matching problems. To begin
with, the network *learns* a predefined set of input–output example pairs by using
a two-phase *propagate–adapt* cycle. After an input pattern has been applied as
a stimulus to the first layer of network units, it is propagated through each upper

layer until an output is generated. This output pattern is then compared to the desired output, and an error signal is computed for each output unit.

The error signals are then transmitted backward from the output layer to each node in the intermediate layer that contributes directly to the output. However, each unit in the intermediate layer receives only a portion of the total error signal, based roughly on the relative contribution the unit made to the original output. This process repeats, layer by layer, until each node in the network has received an error signal that describes its relative contribution to the total error. Based on the error signal received, connection weights are then updated by each unit to cause the network to converge toward a state that allows all the training patterns to be encoded.

The significance of this process is that, as the network trains, the nodes in the intermediate layers organize themselves such that different nodes learn to recognize different features of the total input space. After training, when presented with an arbitrary input pattern that is noisy or incomplete, the units in the hidden layers of the network will respond with an active output if the new input contains a pattern that resembles the feature the individual units learned to recognize during training. Conversely, hidden-layer units have a tendency to inhibit their outputs if the input pattern does not contain the feature that they were trained to recognize.

As the signals propagate through the different layers in the network, the activity pattern present at each upper layer can be thought of as a pattern with features that can be recognized by units in the subsequent layer. The output pattern generated can be thought of as a feature map that provides an indication of the presence or absence of many different feature combinations at the input. The total effect of this behavior is that the BPN provides an effective means of allowing a computer system to examine data patterns that may be incomplete or noisy, and to recognize subtle patterns from the partial input.

Several researchers have shown that during training, BPNs tend to develop internal relationships between nodes so as to organize the training data into classes of patterns [5]. This tendency can be extrapolated to the hypothesis that all hidden-layer units in the BPN are somehow associated with specific features of the input pattern as a result of training. Exactly what the association is may or may not be evident to the human observer. What is important is that the network has found an internal representation that enables it to generate the desired outputs when given the training inputs. This same internal representation can be applied to inputs that were not used during training. The BPN will classify these previously unseen inputs according to the features they share with the training examples.

3.2 THE GENERALIZED DELTA RULE

In this section, we present the formal mathematical description of BPN operation. We shall present a detailed derivation of the **generalized delta rule** (GDR), which is the learning algorithm for the network.

Figure 3.3 serves as the reference for most of the discussion. The BPN is a layered, feedforward network that is fully interconnected by layers. Thus, there are no feedback connections and no connections that bypass one layer to go directly to a later layer. Although only three layers are used in the discussion, more than one hidden layer is permissible.

A neural network is called a **mapping network** if it is able to compute some functional relationship between its input and its output. For example, if the input to a network is the value of an angle, and the output is the cosine of that angle, the network performs the mapping $\theta \rightarrow \cos(\theta)$. For such a simple function, we do not need a neural network; however, we might want to perform a complicated mapping where we do not know how to describe the functional relationship in advance, but we do know of examples of the correct mapping.

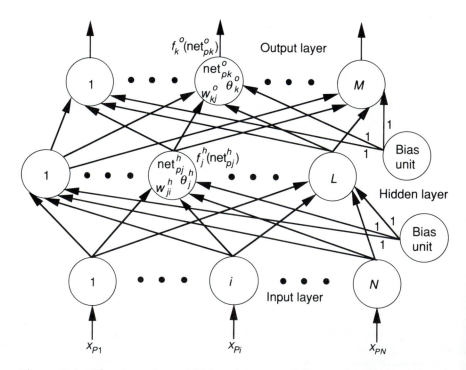

Figure 3.3   The three-layer BPN architecture follows closely the general network description given in Chapter 1. The bias weights, θ_j^h, and θ_k^o, and the bias units are optional. The bias units provide a fictitious input value of 1 on a connection to the bias weight. We can then treat the bias weight (or simply, bias) like any other weight: It contributes to the net-input value to the unit, and it participates in the learning process like any other weight.

In this situation, the power of a neural network to discover its own algorithms is extremely useful.

Suppose we have a set of P vector-pairs, $(\mathbf{x}_1, \mathbf{y}_1)$, $(\mathbf{x}_2, \mathbf{y}_2)$,..., $(\mathbf{x}_P, \mathbf{y}_P)$, which are examples of a functional mapping $\mathbf{y} = \phi(\mathbf{x}) : \mathbf{x} \in \mathbf{R}^N, \mathbf{y} \in \mathbf{R}^M$. We want to train the network so that it will learn an approximation $\mathbf{o} = \mathbf{y}' = \phi'(\mathbf{x})$. We shall derive a method of doing this training that usually works, provided the training-vector pairs have been chosen properly and there is a sufficient number of them. (Definitions of *properly* and *sufficient* will be given in Section 3.3.) Remember that learning in a neural network means finding an appropriate set of weights. The learning technique that we describe here resembles the problem of finding the equation of a line that best fits a number of known points. Moreover, it is a generalization of the LMS rule that we discussed in Chapter 2. For a line-fitting problem, we would probably use a least-squares approximation. Because the relationship we are trying to map is likely to be nonlinear, as well as multidimensional, we employ an iterative version of the simple least-squares method, called a *steepest-descent technique*.

To begin, let's review the equations for information processing in the three-layer network in Figure 3.3. An input vector, $\mathbf{x}_p = (x_{p1}, x_{p2}, \ldots, x_{pN})^t$, is applied to the input layer of the network. The input units distribute the values to the hidden-layer units. The net input to the jth hidden unit is

$$\text{net}_{pj}^h = \sum_{i=1}^{N} w_{ji}^h x_{pi} + \theta_j^h \tag{3.1}$$

where w_{ji}^h is the weight on the connection from the ith input unit, and θ_j^h is the bias term discussed in Chapter 2. The "h" superscript refers to quantities on the hidden layer. Assume that the activation of this node is equal to the net input; then, the output of this node is

$$i_{pj} = f_j^h(\text{net}_{pj}^h) \tag{3.2}$$

The equations for the output nodes are

$$\text{net}_{pk}^o = \sum_{j=1}^{L} w_{kj}^o i_{pj} + \theta_k^o \tag{3.3}$$

$$o_{pk} = f_k^o(\text{net}_{pk}^o) \tag{3.4}$$

where the "o" superscript refers to quantities on the output layer.

The initial set of weight values represents a first guess as to the proper weights for the problem. Unlike some methods, the technique we employ here does not depend on making a *good* first guess. There are guidelines for selecting the initial weights, however, and we shall discuss them in Section 3.3. The basic procedure for training the network is embodied in the following description:

1. Apply an input vector to the network and calculate the corresponding output values.

2. Compare the actual outputs with the correct outputs and determine a measure of the error.

3. Determine in which direction (+ or −) to change each weight in order to reduce the error.

4. Determine the amount by which to change each weight.

5. Apply the corrections to the weights.

6. Repeat items 1 through 5 with all the training vectors until the error for all vectors in the training set is reduced to an acceptable value.

In Chapter 2, we described an iterative weight-change law for network with no hidden units and linear output units, called the LMS rule or delta rule:

$$w(t+1)_i = w(t)_i + 2\mu\varepsilon_k x_{ki} \tag{3.5}$$

where μ is a positive constant, x_{ki} is the ith component of the kth training vector, and ε_k is the difference between the actual output and the correct value, $\varepsilon_k = (d_k - y_k)$. Equation 3.5 is just the component form of Eq. (2.15).

A similar equation results when the network has more than two layers, or when the output functions are nonlinear. We shall derive the results explicitly in the next sections.

3.2.1   Update of Output-Layer Weights

In the derivation of the delta rule, the error for the kth input vector is $\varepsilon_k = (d_k - y_k)$, where the desired output is d_k and the actual output is y_k. In this chapter, we adopt a slightly different notation that is somewhat inconsistent with the notation we used in Chapter 2. Because there are multiple units in a layer, a single error value, such as ε_k, will not suffice for the BPN. We shall define the error at a single output unit to be $\delta_{pk} = (y_{pk} - o_{pk})$, where the subscript "$p$" refers to the pth training vector, and "k" refers to the kth output unit. In this case, y_{pk} is the desired output value, and o_{pk} is the actual output from the kth unit. The error that is minimized by the GDR is the sum of the squares of the errors for all output units:

$$E_p = \frac{1}{2}\sum_{k=1}^{M} \delta_{pk}^2 \tag{3.6}$$

The factor of $\frac{1}{2}$ in Eq. (3.6) is there for convenience in calculating derivatives later. Since an arbitrary constant will appear in the final result, the presence of this factor does not invalidate the derivation.

To determine the direction in which to change the weights, we calculate the negative of the gradient of E_p, ∇E_p, with respect to the weights, w_{kj}. Then, we can adjust the values of the weights such that the total error is reduced. It is often useful to think of E_p as a surface in weight space. Figure 3.4 shows a simple example where the network has only two weights.

To keep things simple, we consider each component of ∇E_p separately. From Eq. (3.6) and the definition of δ_{pk},

$$E_p = \frac{1}{2} \sum_k (y_{pk} - o_{pk})^2 \tag{3.7}$$

and

$$\frac{\partial E_p}{\partial w_{kj}^o} = -(y_{pk} - o_{pk}) \frac{\partial f_k^o}{\partial(\text{net}_{pk}^o)} \frac{\partial(\text{net}_{pk}^o)}{\partial w_{kj}^o} \tag{3.8}$$

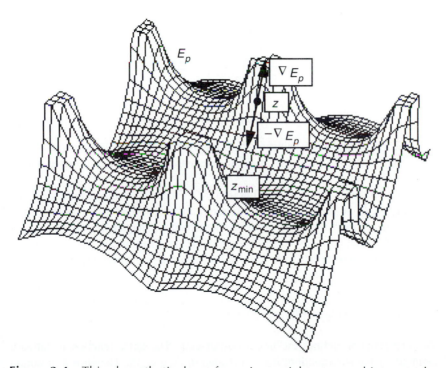

Figure 3.4 This hypothetical surface in weight space hints at the complexity of these surfaces in comparison with the relatively simple hyperparaboloid of the Adaline (see Chapter 2). The gradient, ∇E_p, at point **z** appears along with the negative of the gradient. Weight changes should occur in the direction of the negative gradient, which is the direction of the *steepest descent* of the surface at the point **z**. Furthermore, weight changes should be made iteratively until E_p reaches the minimum point $\mathbf{z}_{\min}$.

where we have used Eq. (3.4) for the output value, o_{pk}, and the chain rule for partial derivatives. For the moment, we shall not try to evaluate the derivative of f_k^o, but instead will write it simply as $f_k^{o'}(\text{net}_{pk}^o)$. The last factor in Eq. (3.8) is

$$\frac{\partial(\text{net}_{pk}^o)}{\partial w_{kj}^o} = \left(\frac{\partial}{\partial w_{kj}^o}\sum_{j=1}^{L} w_{kj}^o i_{pj} + \theta_k^o\right) = i_{pj} \tag{3.9}$$

Combining Eqs. (3.8) and (3.9), we have for the negative gradient

$$-\frac{\partial E_p}{\partial w_{kj}^o} = (y_{pk} - o_{pk})f_k^{o'}(\text{net}_{pk}^o)i_{pj} \tag{3.10}$$

As far as the magnitude of the weight change is concerned, we take it to be proportional to the negative gradient. Thus, the weights on the output layer are updated according to

$$w_{kj}^o(t+1) = w_{kj}^o(t) + \Delta_p w_{kj}^o(t) \tag{3.11}$$

where

$$\Delta_p w_{kj}^o = \eta(y_{pk} - o_{pk})f_k^{o'}(\text{net}_{pk}^o)i_{pj} \tag{3.12}$$

The factor η is called the **learning-rate parameter**. We shall discuss the value of η in Section 3.3. For now, it is sufficient to note that it is positive and is usually less than 1.

Let's go back to look at the function $f_k^{o'}$. First, notice the requirement that the function f_k^o be differentiable. This requirement eliminates the possibility of using a linear threshold unit such as we described in Chapter 2, since the output function for such a unit is not differentiable at the threshold value.

There are two forms of the output function that are of interest here:

- $f_k^o(\text{net}_{jk}^o) = \text{net}_{jk}^o$

- $f_k^o(\text{net}_{jk}^o) = (1 + e^{-\text{net}_{jk}^o})^{-1}$

The first function defines the linear output unit. The latter function is called a sigmoid, or logistic function; it is illustrated in Figure 3.5. The choice of output function depends on how you choose to represent the output data. For example, if you want the output units to be binary, you use a sigmoid output function, since the sigmoid is output-limiting and quasi-bistable but is also differentiable. In other cases, either a linear or a sigmoid output function is appropriate.

In the first case, $f_k^{o'} = 1$; in the second case, $f_k^{o'} = f_k^o(1 - f_k^o) = o_{pk}(1 - o_{pk})$. For these two cases, we have

$$w_{kj}^o(t+1) = w_{kj}^o(t) + \eta(y_{pk} - o_{pk})i_{pj} \tag{3.13}$$

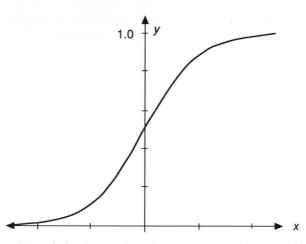

Figure 3.5   This graph shows the characteristic S-shape of the sigmoid function.

for the linear output, and

$$w_{kj}^o(t+1) = w_{kj}^o(t) + \eta(y_{pk} - o_{pk})o_{pk}(1 - o_{pk})i_{pj} \qquad (3.14)$$

for the sigmoidal output.

We want to summarize the weight-update equations by defining a quantity

$$\delta_{pk}^o = (y_{pk} - o_{pk})f_k^{o\prime}(\text{net}_{pk}^o)$$
$$= \delta_{pk}f_k^{o\prime}(\text{net}_{pk}^o) \qquad (3.15)$$

We can then write the weight-update equation as

$$w_{kj}^o(t+1) = w_{kj}^o(t) + \eta\delta_{pk}^o i_{pj} \qquad (3.16)$$

regardless of the functional form of the output function, f_k^o.

We wish to make a comment regarding the relationship between the gradient-descent method described here and the least-squares technique. If we were trying to make the generalized delta rule entirely analogous to a least-squares method, we would not actually change any of the weight values until all of the training patterns had been presented to the network once. We would simply accumulate the changes as each pattern was processed, sum them, and make one update to the weights. We would then repeat the process until the error was acceptably low. The error that this process minimizes is

$$E = \sum_{p=1}^{P} E_p \qquad (3.17)$$

where P is the number of patterns in the training set. In practice, we have found little advantage to this strict adherence to analogy with the least-squares method. Moreover, you must store a large amount of information to use this method. We recommend that you perform weight updates as each training pattern is processed.

Exercise 3.1: A certain network has output nodes called **quadratic neurons**. The net input to such a neuron is

$$\text{net}_k = \sum_j w_{kj}(i_j - v_{kj})^2$$

The output function is sigmoidal. Both w_{kj} and v_{kj} are weights, and i_j is the jth input value. Assume that the w weights and v weights are independent.

a. Determine the weight-update equations for both types of weights.

b. What is the significance of this type of node? Hint: Consider a single unit of the type described here, having two inputs and a linear-threshold function output. With what geometric figure does this unit partition the input space?

(This exercise was suggested by Gary McIntire, Loral Space Information Systems, who derived and implemented this network.)

3.2.2   Updates of Hidden-Layer Weights

We would like to repeat for the hidden layer the same type of calculation as we did for the output layer. A problem arises when we try to determine a measure of the error of the outputs of the hidden-layer units. We know what the actual output is, but we have no way of knowing in advance what the correct output should be for these units. Intuitively, the total error, E_p, must somehow be related to the output values on the hidden layer. We can verify our intuition by going back to Eq. (3.7):

$$E_p = \frac{1}{2} \sum_k (y_{pk} - o_{pk})^2$$

$$= \frac{1}{2} \sum_k (y_{pk} - f_k^o(\text{net}_{pk}^o))^2$$

$$= \frac{1}{2} \sum_k (y_{pk} - f_k^o(\sum_j w_{kj}^o i_{pj} + \theta_k^o))^2$$

We know that i_{pj} depends on the weights on the hidden layer through Eqs. (3.1) and (3.2). We can exploit this fact to calculate the gradient of E_p with respect to the hidden-layer weights.

$$\frac{\partial E_p}{\partial w_{ji}^h} = \frac{1}{2} \sum_k \frac{\partial}{\partial w_{ji}^h} (y_{pk} - o_{pk})^2$$

$$= -\sum_k (y_{pk} - o_{pk}) \frac{\partial o_{pk}}{\partial(\text{net}_{pk}^o)} \frac{\partial(\text{net}_{pk}^o)}{\partial i_{pj}} \frac{\partial i_{pj}}{\partial(\text{net}_{pj}^h)} \frac{\partial(\text{net}_{pj}^h)}{\partial w_{ji}^h} \qquad (3.18)$$

Each of the factors in Eq. (3.18) can be calculated explicitly from previous equations. The result is

$$\frac{\partial E_p}{\partial w_{ji}^h} = -\sum_k (y_{pk} - o_{pk}) f_k^{o\prime}(\text{net}_{pk}^o) w_{kj}^o f_j^{h\prime}(\text{net}_{pj}^h) x_{pi} \tag{3.19}$$

Exercise 3.2: Verify the steps between Eqs. (3.18) and (3.19). |

We update the hidden-layer weights in proportion to the negative of Eq. (3.19):

$$\Delta_p w_{ji}^h = \eta f_j^{h\prime}(\text{net}_{pj}^h) x_{pi} \sum_k (y_{pk} - o_{pk}) f_k^{o\prime}(\text{net}_{pk}^o) w_{kj}^o \tag{3.20}$$

where η is once again the learning rate.

We can use the definition of δ_{pk}^o given in the previous section to write

$$\Delta_p w_{ji}^h = \eta f_j^{h\prime}(\text{net}_{pj}^h) x_{pi} \sum_k \delta_{pk}^o w_{kj}^o \tag{3.21}$$

Notice that every weight update on the hidden layer depends on *all* the error terms, δ_{pk}^o, on the output layer. This result is where the notion of *back-propagation* arises. The known errors on the output layer are *propagated back* to the hidden layer to determine the appropriate weight changes on that layer. By defining a hidden-layer error term

$$\delta_{pj}^h = f_j^{h\prime}(\text{net}_{pj}^h) \sum_k \delta_{pk}^o w_{kj}^o \tag{3.22}$$

we cause the weight update equations to become analogous to those for the output layer:

$$w_{ji}^h(t + 1) = w_{ji}^h(t) + \eta \delta_{pj}^h x_i \tag{3.23}$$

Finally, so that we close the circle on the GDR, notice that both Eq. (3.16) in the previous section and Eq. (3.23) in this section have the same form as Eq. (3.5), the delta rule.

Exercise 3.3: Refer to the description of the quadratic neuron given in Exercise 3.1. Determine the weight-update equations for hidden-layer units for both w and v weights.

Exercise 3.4: Consider a network with two hidden layers instead of one. Determine the weight-update equations for units on the first hidden layer (the one between the input units and the second hidden layer).

3.2.3   BPN Summary

To reduce the need to flip pages to find the appropriate equations, we collect all of the relevant equations for the BPN here. They are presented in the order in which they would be used during training for a single training-vector pair.

1. Apply the input vector, $\mathbf{x}_p = (x_{p1}, x_{p2}, \ldots, x_{pN})^t$ to the input units.

2. Calculate the net-input values to the hidden layer units:

$$\text{net}_{pj}^h = \sum_{i=1}^{N} w_{ji}^h x_{pi} + \theta_j^h$$

3. Calculate the outputs from the hidden layer:

$$i_{pj} = f_j^h(\text{net}_{pj}^h)$$

4. Move to the output layer. Calculate the net-input values to each unit:

$$\text{net}_{pk}^o = \sum_{j=1}^{L} w_{kj}^o i_{pj} + \theta_k^o$$

5. Calculate the outputs:

$$o_{pk} = f_k^o(\text{net}_{pk}^o)$$

6. Calculate the error terms for the output units:

$$\delta_{pk}^o = (y_{pk} - o_{pk})f_k^{o'}(\text{net}_{pk}^o)$$

7. Calculate the error terms for the hidden units:

$$\delta_{pj}^h = f_j^{h'}(\text{net}_{pj}^h)\sum_k \delta_{pk}^o w_{kj}^o$$

Notice that the error terms on the hidden units are calculated *before* the connection weights to the output-layer units have been updated.

8. Update weights on the output layer:

$$w_{kj}^o(t + 1) = w_{kj}^o(t) + \eta \delta_{pk}^o i_{pj}$$

9. Update weights on the hidden layer:

$$w_{ji}^h(t + 1) = w_{ji}^h(t) + \eta \delta_{pj}^h x_i$$

The order of the weight updates on an individual layer is not important.

Be sure to calculate the error term

$$E_p = \frac{1}{2}\sum_{k=1}^{M} \delta_{pk}^2$$

since this quantity is the measure of how well the network is learning. When the error is acceptably small for each of the training-vector pairs, training can be discontinued.

3.3   PRACTICAL CONSIDERATIONS

There are some topics that we omitted from previous sections so as not to divert your attention from the main ideas. Before moving on to the discussion of applications and the simulator, let's pick up these loose ends.

3.3.1   Training Data

We promised a definition of the terms *sufficient* and *properly* regarding the selection of training-vector pairs for the BPN. Unfortunately, there is no single definition that applies to all cases. As with many aspects of neural-network systems, experience is often the best teacher. As you gain facility with using networks, you will also gain an appreciation for how to select and prepare training sets. Thus, we shall give only a few guidelines here.

In general, you can use as many data as you have available to train the network, although you may not need to use them all. From the available training data, a small subset is often all that you need to train a network successfully. The remaining data can be used to test the network to verify that the network can perform the desired mapping on input vectors it has never encountered during training.

If you are training a network to perform in a noisy environment, such as the pixel-image–to–ASCII example, then include some noisy input vectors in the data set. Sometimes the addition of noise to the input vectors during training helps the network to converge even if no noise is expected on the inputs.

The BPN is good at generalization. What we mean by *generalization* here is that, given several different input vectors, all belonging to the same class, a BPN will learn to key off of significant similarities in the input vectors. Irrelevant data will be ignored. As an example, suppose we want to train a network to determine whether a bipolar number of length 5 is even or odd. With only a small set of examples used for training, the BPN will adjust its weights so that a classification will be made solely on the basis of the value of the least significant bit in the number: The network learns to ignore the irrelevant data in the other bits.

In contrast to generalization, the BPN will not extrapolate well. If a BPN is inadequately or insufficiently trained on a particular class of input vectors, subsequent identification of members of that class may be unreliable. Make sure that the training data cover the entire expected input space. During the training process, select training-vector pairs randomly from the set, if the problem lends itself to this strategy. In any event, do not train the network completely with input vectors of one class, and then switch to another class: The network will *forget* the original training.

If the output function is sigmoidal, then you will have to scale the output values. Because of the form of the sigmoid function, the network outputs can never reach 0 or 1. Therefore, use values such as 0.1 and 0.9 to represent the smallest and largest output values. You can also shift the sigmoid so that, for example, the limiting values become ± 0.4. Moreover, you can change the slope of the linear portion of the sigmoid curve by including a multiplicative constant in the exponential. There are many such possibilities that depend largely on the problem being solved.

3.3.2 Network Sizing

Just how many nodes are needed to solve a particular problem? Are three layers always sufficient? As with the questions concerning proper training data, there are no strict answers to questions such as these. Generally, three layers are sufficient. Sometimes, however, a problem seems to be easier to solve with more than one hidden layer. In this case, *easier* means that the network learns faster.

The size of the input layer is usually dictated by the nature of the application. You can often determine the number of output nodes by deciding whether you want analog values or binary values on the output units. Section 3.4 contains two examples that illustrate both of these situations.

Determining the number of units to use in the hidden layer is not usually as straightforward as it is for the input and output layers. The main idea is to use as few hidden-layer units as possible, because each unit adds to the load on the CPU during simulations. Of course, in a system that is fully implemented in hardware (one processor per processing element), additional CPU loading is not as much of a consideration (interprocessor communication may be a problem, however). We hesitate to offer specific guidelines except to say that, in our experience, for networks of reasonable size (hundreds or thousands of inputs), the size of the hidden layer needs to be only a relatively small fraction of that of the input layer. If the network fails to converge to a solution it may be that more hidden nodes are required. If it does converge, you might try fewer hidden nodes and settle on a size on the basis of overall system performance.

It is also possible to remove hidden units that are superfluous. If you examine the weight values on the hidden nodes periodically as the network trains, you will see that weights on certain nodes change very little from their starting values. These nodes may not be participating in the learning process, and fewer hidden units may suffice. There is also an automatic method, developed by Rumelhart, for pruning unneeded nodes from the network.[1]

3.3.3 Weights and Learning Parameters

Weights should be initialized to small, random values—say between ± 0.5—as should the bias terms, θ_i, that appear in the equations for the net input to a unit. It is common practice to treat this bias value as another weight, which is

---

[1]Unscheduled talk given at the Second International Conference on Neural Networks, San Diego, June 1988.

connected to a fictitious unit that always has an output of 1. To see how this scheme works, recall Eq. (3.3):

$$\text{net}^o_{pk} = \sum_{j=1}^{L} w^o_{kj} i_{pj} + \theta^o_k$$

By making the definitions, $\theta^o_k \equiv w^o_{k(L+1)}$ and $i_{p(L+1)} \equiv 1$, we can write

$$\text{net}^o_{pk} = \sum_{j=1}^{L+1} w^o_{kj} i_{pj}$$

So θ^o_k is treated just like a weight, and it participates in the learning process as a weight. Another possibility is simply to remove the bias terms altogether; their use is optional.

Selection of a value for the learning rate parameter, η, has a significant effect on the network performance. Usually, η must be a small number—on the order of 0.05 to 0.25—to ensure that the network will settle to a solution. A small value of η means that the network will have to make a large number of iterations, but that is the price to be paid. It is often possible to increase the size of η as learning proceeds. Increasing η as the network error decreases will often help to speed convergence by increasing the step size as the error reaches a minimum, but the network may bounce around too far from the actual minimum value if η gets too large.

Another way to increase the speed of convergence is to use a technique called **momentum**. When calculating the weight-change value, $\Delta_p w$, we add a fraction of the *previous* change. This additional term tends to keep the weight changes going in the same direction—hence the term *momentum*. The weight-change equations on the output layer then become

$$w^o_{kj}(t+1) = w^o_{kj}(t) + \eta \delta^o_{pk} i_{pj} + \alpha \Delta_p w^o_{kj}(t-1) \qquad \textbf{(3.24)}$$

with a similar equation on the hidden layer. In Eq. (3.24), α is the momentum parameter, and it is usually set to a positive value less than 1. The use of the momentum term is also optional.

A final topic concerns the possibility of converging to a **local minimum** in weight space. Figure 3.6 illustrates the idea. Once a network settles on a minimum, whether local or global, learning ceases. If a local minimum is reached, the error at the network outputs may still be unacceptably high. Fortunately, this problem does not appear to cause much difficulty in practice. If a network stops learning before reaching an acceptable solution, a change in the number of hidden nodes or in the learning parameters will often fix the problem; or we can simply start over with a different set of initial weights. When a network reaches an acceptable solution, there is no guarantee that it *has* reached the global minimum rather than a local one. If the solution is acceptable from an error standpoint, it does not matter whether the minimum is global or local, or even whether the training was halted at some point before a true minimum was reached.

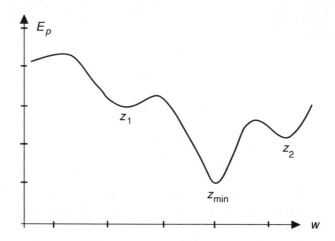

Figure 3.6   This graph shows a cross-section of a hypothetical error surface
in weight space. The point, z_{min}, is called the **global minimum**.
Notice, however, that there are other minimum points, z_1 and
z_2. A gradient-descent search for the global minimum might
accidentally find one of these local minima instead of the
global minimum.

Exercise 3.5: Consider a three-layer BPN with all weights initialized to the
same value on every unit. Prove that this network will never be able to learn
anything. Interpret this result in terms of the error surface in weight space.

3.4   BPN APPLICATIONS

The BPN is a versatile tool that is readily applied to a number of diverse
problems. To a large extent, its versatility is due to the general nature of the
network learning process. As we discussed in the previous section, there are
only two equations needed to backpropagate error signals within the network;
which of the two is used depends on whether the processing unit receiving the
error signal contributes directly to the output. Those units that do not connect
directly to the output use the same error-propagation mechanism regardless of
where they are in the network structure.

   The generality offered by this common process allows arrangement and
connectivity of individual units within the network that can vary dramatically.
Similarly, due to the variety of network structures that can be created and
trained successfully using the backpropagation algorithms, this network-learning
technique can be applied to many different kinds of problems. In the remainder
of this section, we will describe two such applications, selected to illustrate the
diversity of the BPN network architecture.

3.4.1 Data Compression

As our first example, let's consider the common problem of data compression. Specifically, we would like to try to find a way to reduce the data needed to encode and reproduce accurately a moderately high-resolution video image, so that we might transmit these images over low- to medium-bandwidth communication equipment. Although there are many algorithmic approaches to performing data compression, most of these are designed to deal with static data, such as ASCII text, or with display images that are fairly consistent, such as computer graphics. Because video data rarely contain regular, well-defined forms (and even less frequently contain empty space), video data compression is a difficult problem from an algorithmic viewpoint.

Conversely, as originally described in [1], a neural-network approach is ideal for a video data-reduction application, because a BPN can be trained easily to map a set of patterns from an n-dimensional space to an m-dimensional space. Since any video image can be thought of as a matrix of picture elements (pixels), it naturally follows that the image can also be conceptualized as a vector in n-space. If we limit the video to be encoded to monochromatic, images can be represented as vectors of elements, each representing the gray-scale value of a single pixel (0 through 255).

Network Architecture for Data Compression. The first step in solving this problem is to try to find a way to structure our network so that it will perform the desired data compression. We would like to select a network architecture that provides a reasonable data-reduction factor (say, four-to-one), while still enabling us to recover a close approximation of the original image from the encoded form. The network illustrated in Figure 3.7 will satisfy both of these requirements.

At first glance, it may seem unusual that the proposed network will have a one-to-one correspondence between input and output units. After all, did we not indicate that data compression was the desired objective? On further investigation, the strategy implied by the network architecture becomes apparent; since there are fewer hidden units than input units, the hidden layer must represent the compressed form of the data. This is exactly the plan of attack.

By providing an image vector as the input stimulation pattern, the network will propagate the input through the hidden units to the output. Since the hidden layer contains only one-quarter of the number of processing units as the input layer, the output values produced by the hidden-layer units can be thought of as the encoded form of the input. Furthermore, by propagating the output of the hidden-layer units forward to the output layer, we have implemented a mechanism for reconstructing the original image from the encoded form, as well as for training the network.

During training, the network will be shown examples of random pixel vectors taken from representative video images. Each vector will be used as both

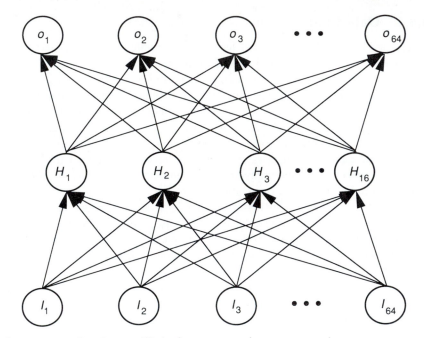

Figure 3.7   This BPN will do four-to-one data compression.

the input to the network and the target output.   Using the backpropagation
process, the network will develop the internal weight coding so that the image is compressed into one-quarter of its original size at the outputs of the
hidden units.   If we then read out the values produced by the hidden-layer
units in our network and transmit those values to our receiving station, we
can reconstruct the original image by propagating the compressed image to
the output units in an identical network.   Such a system is depicted in Figure 3.8.

Network Sizing.   There are two problems remaining to be solved for this application: the first is the network-sizing problem, and the second is the generation of the sample data sets needed to train the network. We will address the
network-sizing aspect first.

It is unrealistic to expect to create a network that will contain an input
unit for every pixel in a single video image. Even if we restricted ourselves to
the relatively low resolution of the 525-line scan rate specified by the National
Television Standard Code (NTSC) for commercial television, our network would
have to have 336,000 input units (525 lines $\times$ 640 pixels). Moreover, the entire
network would contain roughly 750,000 processing units ($336000 + 336000/4 +$
336000) and 50 billion connections. As we have mentioned in earlier chapters,
simulating a network containing a large number of units and a vast number

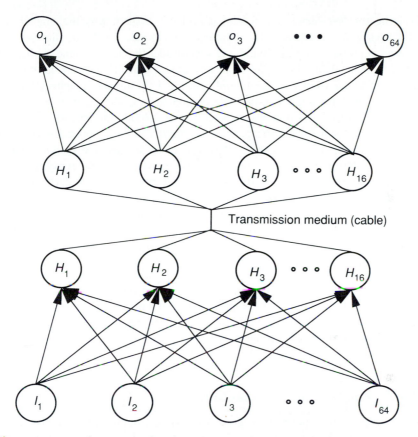

Figure 3.8 In this example, the output activity pattern from the second layer of units is transferred to a receiving station, where it is applied as the output of another layer of units that forms the top half of the three-layer network. The receiving network then reconstructs the transmitted image from the compressed form, using the inverse mapping function contained in the connection weights to the top half of the network.

of connections on anything less than a dedicated supercomputer is much too time-consuming to be considered practical.

Our sizing strategy is therefore somewhat less ambitious; we will restrict the size of our input and output spaces to 64 pixels. Thus, the hidden layer will contain 16 units. Although this might appear to be a significant compromise over the full image network, the smaller network offers two practical benefits over its larger counterpart:

- It is easy to simulate on small computers.

- It makes obtaining training data for the smaller network easier.

Training the Network.   By now, it is probably evident why the smaller network is easier to simulate. Why obtaining training data for the smaller network
is easier is probably not as obvious. If we consider the nature of the application
the network is attempting to address, we can see that the network is trying to
learn a mapping from n-space to $n/4$-space and the inverse mapping back to
n-space. Since the number of possible permutations of the input pattern is significantly smaller in 64 dimensions than it is in 336,000 dimensions, it follows
that far fewer random training patterns are needed for the network to learn to
reproduce the input in 64-space.[2] It is also easier to generate random images
for training the network by using 64 inputs, because a single complete video
image can be subdivided into about 5000 8×8 pixel matrices, each of which
can be used to train the network.

Based on these observations, our approach of downsizing the network has
solved both of the remaining issues. We now have a network that is easy to
manage and that offers a means of acquiring the training data sets from readily
obtainable sources.

Exercise 3.6: Assume that the system described in this section has been built
using a BPN simulator on a single-processor computer. What are the processing
requirements to allow entire video images to be sent at standard frame rates
(30 Hz interlaced, 60 Hz noninterlaced)?

3.4.2   Paint-Quality Inspection

Visual inspection of painted surfaces, such as automobile body panels, is currently a very time-consuming and labor-intensive process. To reduce the amount
of time required to perform this inspection, one of the major U.S. automobile
manufacturers reflects a laser beam off the painted panel and on to a projection
screen. Since the light source is a coherent beam, the amount of scatter observed in the reflected image of the laser provides an indication of the quality of
the paint finish on the car. A poor paint job is one that contains ripples, looks
like "orange peel," or lacks shine. A laser beam reflected off a panel with a
poor finish will therefore be relatively diffuse. Conversely, a good-quality paint
finish will be relatively smooth and will exhibit a bright luster. A laser light
reflected off a high-quality paint finish will appear to an observer as very close
to uniform throughout its image. Figure 3.9 illustrates the kind of differences
typically observed as a result of performing this test.

We have now seen how it might be possible to automate the quality inspection of a painted surface. However, our system design has presumed that

---

[2]Encoding all of the patterns in 64-space is obviously not feasible. Practically, the best encoding
we can hope for using an ANS is an output mapping that resembles the desired output within some
margin of error.

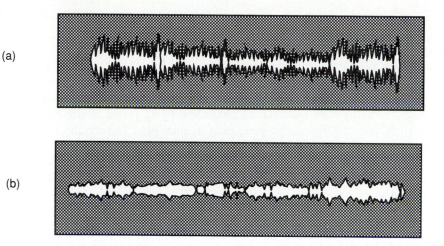

(a)

(b)

Figure 3.9 The scatter typically observed when a laser beam is reflected off painted sheet-metal surfaces. (a) A poor-quality paint finish. (b) A better-quality paint finish.

there is an "observer" present to assess the paint quality by performing a visual inspection of the reflected laser image. In the past, this part of the inspection process would have been performed primarily by humans, because conventional computer-programming techniques that could be used to automate the "observation" and scoring process suffered from a lack of flexibility and were not particularly robust.[3] To illustrate why an algorithmic analysis of the reflected laser image might be considered inflexible, consider that such a program would have to examine every pixel in the input image, correlate features of each pixel (such as brightness) with those observed in a multitude of neighboring pixels, and assess the coherency of the image *as a whole*. Small, localized perturbations in the image might represent relatively minor problems, such as a fingerprint on the paint panel. The complexity of such a program makes it difficult to modify.

By using a BPN to perform the quality-scoring application, we have constructed a system that captures the expertise of the human inspectors, and is relatively easy to maintain and update. To improve the performance of the system, we have coupled algorithmic techniques to simplify the problem, illustrating once again that difficult problems are much easier to solve when we can work with a complete set of tools. We shall now describe the system we developed to address this application.

---

[3]An algorithmic solution to this problem *does* exist, and has been successfully applied to the problem described. However, the amount of time (and hence money) needed to maintain and update that system, should the need arise, probably would be prohibitive.

Automatic Paint QA System Concept.   To automate the paint inspection process, a video system was easily substituted for the human visual system. However, we were then faced with the problem of trying to create a BPN to examine
and score the paint quality given the video input. To accomplish the examination, we constructed the system illustrated in Figure 3.10. The input video image
was run through a video frame-grabber to record a *snapshot* of the reflected laser
image. This snapshot contained an image 400-by-75 pixels in size, each pixel
stored as one of 256 values representing its intensity. To keep the size of the
network needed to solve the problem manageable, we elected to take 10 sample
images from the snapshot, each sample consisting of a 30-by-30-pixel square
centered on a region of the image with the brightest intensity. This approach
allowed us to reduce the input size of the BPN to 900 units (down from the
30,000 units that would have been required to process the entire image). The
desired output was to be a numerical score in the range of 1 through 20 (a
1 represented the best possible paint finish; a 20 represented the worst). To
produce that type of score, we constructed the BPN with one output unit—that
unit producing a linear output that was interpreted as the scaled paint score.
Internally, 50 sigmoidal units were used on a single hidden layer. In addition,
the input and hidden layers each contained threshold ($[\theta]$) units used to bias the
units on the hidden and output layers, respectively.

Once the network was constructed (and trained), 10 sample images were
taken from the snapshot using two different sampling techniques. In the first
test, the samples were selected randomly from the image (in the sense that their
position on the *beam image* was random); in the second test, 10 sequential
samples were taken, so as to ensure that the entire beam was examined.[4] In
both cases, the input sample was propagated through the trained BPN, and the
score produced as output by the network was averaged across the 10 trials. The
average score, as well as the range of scores produced, were then provided to
the user for comparison and interpretation.

Training the Paint QA Network.   At the time of the development of this application, this network was significantly larger than any other network we had yet
trained. Consider the size of the network used: 901 inputs, 51 hiddens, 1 output,
producing a network with 45,101 connections, each modeled as a floating-point
number. Similarly, the unit output values were modeled as floating-point numbers, since each element in the input vector represented a pixel intensity value
(scaled between 0 and 1), and the network output unit was linear.

The number of training patterns with which we had to work was a function
of the number of control paint panels to which we had access (18), as well as of
the number of sample images we needed from each panel to acquire a relatively
complete training set (approximately 6600 images per panel). During training,

---

[4]Results of the tests were consistent with scores assessed for the same paint panels by the human
experts, within a relatively minor error range, regardless of the sample-selection technique used.

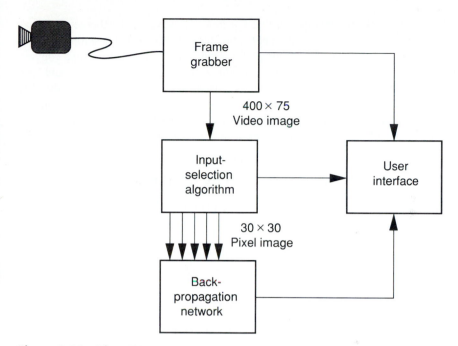

Figure 3.10   The BPN system is constructed to perform paint-quality assessment. In this example, the BPN was merely a software simulation of the network described in the text. Inputs were provided to the network through an array structure located in system memory by a pointer argument supplied as input to the simulation routine.

the samples were presented to the network randomly to ensure that no single paint panel dominated the training.

From these numbers, we can see that there was a great deal of computer time consumed during the training process. For example, one training *epoch* (a single training pass through all training patterns) required the host computer to perform approximately 13.5 million connection updates, which translates into roughly 360,000 floating-point operations (FLOPS) per pattern (2 FLOPS per connection during forward propagation, 6 FLOPS during error propagation), or 108 million FLOPS per epoch. You can now understand why we have emphasized efficiency in our simulator design.

Exercise 3.7: Estimate the number of floating-point operations required to simulate a BPN that used the entire 400-by-75-pixel image as input. Assume 50 hidden-layer units and one output unit, with threshold units on the input and hidden layers as described previously.

We performed the network training for this application on a dedicated LISP computer workstation. It required almost *2 weeks* of uninterrupted computation for the network to converge on that machine. However, once the network was trained, we ported the paint QA application to an 80386-based desktop computer by simply transferring the network connection weights to a disk file and copying the file onto the disk on the desktop machine. Then, for demonstration and later paint QA applications, the network was utilized in a production mode only. The dual-phased nature of the BPN allowed the latter to be employed in a relatively low-cost delivery system, without loss of any of the benefits associated with a neural-network solution as compared to traditional software techniques.

3.5   THE BACKPROPAGATION SIMULATOR

In this section, we shall describe the adaptations to the general-purpose neural simulator presented in Chapter 1, and shall present the detailed algorithms needed to implement a BPN simulator. We shall begin with a brief review of the general signal- and error-propagation process through the BPN, then shall relate that process to the design of the simulator program.

3.5.1   Review of Signal Propagation

In a BPN, signals flow bidirectionally, but in only one direction at a time. During training, there are two types of signals present in the network: during the first half-cycle, modulated output signals flow from input to output; during the second half-cycle, error signals flow from output layer to input layer. In the production mode, only the feedforward, modulated output signal is utilized.

Several assumptions have been incorporated into the design of this simulator. First, the output function on all hidden- and output-layer units is assumed to be the sigmoid function. This assumption is also implicit in the pseudocode for calculating error terms for each unit. In addition, we have included the momentum term in the weight-update calculations. These assumptions imply the need to store weight updates at one iteration, for use on the next iteration. Finally, bias values have not been included in the calculations. The addition of these is left as an exercise at the end of the chapter.

In this network model, the input units are fan-out processors only. That is, the units in the input layer perform no data conversion on the network input pattern. They simply act to hold the components of the input vector within the network structure. Thus, the training process begins when an externally provided input pattern is applied to the input layer of units. Forward signal propagation then occurs according to the following sequence of activities:

1. Locate the first processing unit in the layer immediately above the current layer.

2. Set the current input total to zero.

3. Compute the product of the first input connection weight and the output from the transmitting unit.

4. Add that product to the cumulative total.

5. Repeat steps 3 and 4 for each input connection.

6. Compute the output value for this unit by applying the output function $f(x) = 1/(1 + e^{-x})$, where $x = $ input total.

7. Repeat steps 2 through 6 for each unit in this layer.

8. Repeat steps 1 through 7 for each layer in the network.

Once an output value has been calculated for every unit in the network, the values computed for the units in the output layer are compared to the desired output pattern, element by element. At each output unit, an error value is calculated. These error terms are then fed back to all other units in the network structure through the following sequence of steps:

1. Locate the first processing unit in the layer immediately below the output layer.

2. Set the current error total to zero.

3. Compute the product of the first output connection weight and the error provided by the unit in the upper layer.

4. Add that product to the cumulative error.

5. Repeat steps 3 and 4 for each output connection.

6. Multiply the cumulative error by $o(1 - o)$, where o is the output value of the hidden layer unit produced during the feedforward operation.

7. Repeat steps 2 through 6 for each unit on this layer.

8. Repeat steps 1 through 7 for each layer.

9. Locate the first processing unit in the layer above the input layer.

10. Compute the weight change value for the first input connection to this unit by adding a fraction of the cumulative error at this unit to the input value to this unit.

11. Modify the weight change term by adding a momentum term equal to a fraction of the weight change value from the previous iteration.

12. Save the new weight change value as the old weight change value for this connection.

13. Change the connection weight by adding the new connection weight change value to the old connection weight.

14. Repeat steps 10 through 13 for each input connection to this unit.

15. Repeat steps 10 through 14 for each unit in this layer.

16. Repeat steps 10 through 15 for each layer in the network.

3.5.2   BPN Special Considerations

In Chapter 1, we emphasized that our simulator was designed to optimize the signal-propagation process through the network by organizing the input connections to each unit as linear sequential arrays. Thus, it becomes possible to perform the input sum-of-products calculation in a relatively straightforward manner. We simply step through the appropriate connection and unit output arrays, summing products as we go. Unfortunately, this structure does not lend itself easily to the backpropagation of errors that must be performed by this network.

To understand why there is a problem, consider that the *output* connections from each unit are being used to sum the error products during the learning process. Thus, we must jump between arrays to access output connection values that are contained in input connection arrays to the units above, rather than stepping through arrays as we did during the forward-propagation phase. Because the computer must now explicitly compute where to find the next connection value, error propagation is much less efficient, and, hence, training is significantly slower than is production-mode operation.

3.5.3   BPN Data Structures

We begin our discussion of the BPN simulator with a presentation of the backpropagation network data structures that we will require. Although the BPN is similar in structure to the Madaline network described in Chapter 2, it is also different in that it requires the use of several additional parameters that must be stored on a connection or network unit basis. Based on our knowledge of how the BPN operates, we shall now propose a record of data that will define the top-level structure of the BPN simulator:

```
record BPN =
  INUNITS : ^layer;          {locate input layer}
  OUTUNITS : ^layer;         {locate output units}
  LAYERS : ^layer[];         {dynamically sized network}
  alpha,                     {the momentum term}
  eta : float;               {the learning rate}
end record;
```

Figure 3.11 illustrates the relationship between the network record and all subordinate structures, which we shall now discuss. As we complete our discussion of the data structures, you should refer to Figure 3.11 to clarify some of the more subtle points.

Inspection of the BPN record structure reveals that this structure is designed to allow us to create networks containing more than just three layers of units. In practice, BPNs that *require* more than three layers to solve a problem are not prevalent. However, there are several examples cited in the literature referenced at the end of this chapter where multilayer BPNs were utilized, so we

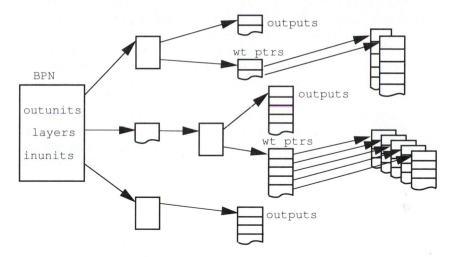

Figure 3.11 The BPN data structure is shown without the arrays for the `error` and `last_delta` terms for clarity. As before, the network is defined by a record containing pointers to the subordinate structures, as well as network-specific parameters. In this diagram, only three layers are illustrated, although many more hidden layers could be added by simple extension of the `layer_ptr` array.

have included the capability to construct networks of this type in our simulator design.

It is obvious that the BPN record contains the information that is of global interest to the units in the network—specifically, the alpha (α) and eta (η) terms. However, we must now define the layer structure that we will use to construct the remainder of the network, since it is the basis for locating all information used to define the units on each layer. To define the layer structure, we must remember that the BPN has two different types of operation, and that different information is needed in each phase. Thus, the layer structure contains pointers to two different sets of arrays: one set used during forward propagation, and one set used during error propagation. Armed with this understanding, we can now define the layer structure for the BPN:

```
record layer =
  outputs : ^float[];        {locate output array}
  weights : ^^float[];       {locate connection array(s)}
  errors : ^float[];         {locate error terms for layer}
  last_delta : ^^float[];    {locate previous delta terms}
end record;
```

During the forward-propagation phase, the network will use the information contained in the `outputs` and `weights` arrays, just as we saw in the design of the Adaline simulator. However, during the backpropagation phase, the BPN requires access to an array of error terms (one for each of the units on the layer) and to the list of change parameters used during the previous learning pass (stored on a connection basis). By combining the access mechanisms to all these terms in the layer structure, we can continue to keep processing efficient, at least during the forward-propagation phase, as our data structures will be exactly as described in Chapter 1. Unfortunately, activity during the backpropagation phase will be inefficient, because we will be accessing different arrays rather than accessing sequential locations within the arrays. However, we will have to live with the inefficiency incurred here since we have elected to model the network as a set of arrays.

3.5.4   Forward Signal-Propagation Algorithms

The following four algorithms will implement the feedforward signal-propagation process in our network simulator model. They are presented in a bottom-up fashion, meaning that each is defined before it is used.

The first procedure will serve as the interface routine between the host computer and the BPN simulation. It assumes that the user has defined an array of floating-point numbers that indicate the pattern to be applied to the network as inputs.

```
procedure set_inputs (INPUTS, NET_IN : ^float[])
{copy the input values into the net input layer}

var
  temp1:^float[];    {a local pointer}
  temp2:^float[];    {a local pointer}
  i : integer;       {iteration counter}

begin
  temp1 = NET_IN;           {locate net input layer}
  temp2 = INPUTS;           {locate input values}

  for i = 1 to length(NET_IN) do
                            {for all input values, do}
      temp1[i] = temp2[i];  {copy input to net input}
    end do;
end;
```

The next routine performs the forward signal propagation between any two layers, located by the pointer values passed into the routine. This routine embodies the calculations done in Eqs. (3.1) and (3.2) for the hidden layer, and in Eqs. (3.3) and (3.4) for the output layer.

```
procedure propagate_layer (LOWER, UPPER: ^layer)
{propagate signals from the lower to the upper layer}

var
   inputs   : ^float[];    {size input layer}
   current  : ^float[];    {size current layer}
   connects : ^float[];    {step through inputs}
   sum : real;             {accumulate products}
   i, j : integer;         {iteration counters}

begin
   inputs = LOWER^.outputs;    {locate lower layer}
   current = UPPER^.outputs;   {locate upper layer}

   for i = 1 to length(current) do
                              {for all units in layer}
      sum = 0;                 {reset accumulator}
      connects = UPPER^.weights^[i];
                              {find start of wt. array}

      for j = 1 to length(inputs) do
                              {for all inputs to unit}
         sum = sum + inputs[j] * connects[j];
                                  {accumulate products}
      end do;

      current[i] = 1.0 / (1.0 + exp(-sum));
                                      {generate output}
   end do;
end;
```

The next procedure performs the forward signal propagation for the entire network. It assumes the input layer contains a valid input pattern, placed there by a higher-level call to set_inputs.

```
procedure propagate_forward (NET: BPN)
{perform the forward signal propagation for net}

var
   upper : ^layer;    {pointer to upper layer}
   lower : ^layer;    {pointer to lower layer}
   i : integer;       {layer counter}

begin
   for i = 1 to length(NET.layers) do      {for all layers}
      lower = NET.layers[i];   {get pointer to input layer}
      upper = NET.layers[i+1]; {get pointer to next layer}
      propagate_layer (lower, upper);   {propagate forward}
   end do;
end;
```

The final routine needed for forward propagation will extract the output values generated by the network and copy them into an external array specified by the calling program. This routine is the complement of the `set_input` routine described earlier.

```
procedure get_outputs (NET_OUTS, OUTPUTS : ^float[])
{copy the net out values into the outputs specified.}

var
 temp1:^float[];        {a local pointer}
 temp2:^float[];        {a local pointer}

begin
  temp1 = NET_OUTS;     {locate net output layer}
  temp2 = OUTPUTS;      {locate output values array}

  for i = 1 to length(NET_OUTS) do   {for all outputs, do}
        temp2[i] = temp1[i];         {copy net output}
  end do;                            {to output array}
end;
```

3.5.5   Error-Propagation Routines

The backward propagation of error terms is similar to the forward propagation of signals. The major difference here is that error signals, once computed, are being backpropagated through output connections from a unit, rather than through input connections.

If we allow an extra array to contain error terms associated with each unit within a layer, similar to our data structure for unit outputs, the error-propagation procedure can be accomplished in three routines. The first will compute the error term for each unit on the output layer. The second will backpropagate errors from a layer with known errors to the layer immediately below. The third will use the error term at any unit to update the output connection values from that unit.

The pseudocode designs for these routines are as follows. The first calculates the values of δ_{pk}^o on the output layer, according to Eq. (3.15).

```
procedure compute_output_error (NET : BPN;
                                TARGET: ^float[])
{compare output to target, update errors accordingly}

var
  errors : ^float;      {used to store error values}
  outputs : ^float;     {access to network outputs}

begin
  errors = NET.OUTUNITS^.errors;      {find error array}
```

```
        outputs = NET.OUTUNITS^.outputs;
                                {get pointer to unit outputs}

        for i = 1 to length(outputs) do   {for all output units}
            errors[i] = outputs[i]*(1-outputs[i])
                            *(TARGET[i]-outputs[i]);
        end do;
    end;
```

In the backpropagation network, the terms η and α will be used globally to govern the update of all connections. For that reason, we have extended the network record to include these parameters. We will refer to these values as "eta" and "alpha" respectively. We now provide an algorithm for backpropagating the error term to any unit below the output layer in the network structure. This routine calculates δ^h_{pj} for hidden-layer units according to Eq. (3.22).

```
    procedure backpropagate_error (UPPER,LOWER: ^layer)
    {backpropagate errors from an upper to a lower layer}

    var
        senders : ^float[];        {source errors}
        receivers : ^float[];      {receiving errors}
        connects : ^float[];       {pointer to connection arrays}
        unit : float;              {unit output value}
        i, j : integer;            {indices}

    begin
        senders = UPPER^.errors;       {known errors}
        receivers = LOWER^.errors;     {errors to be computed}

        for i = 1 to length(receivers) do
                                    {for all receiving units}
            receivers[i] = 0;          {init error accumulator}

            for j = 1 to length(senders) do
                                    {for all sending units}
                connects = UPPER^.weights^[j];
                                    {locate connection array}
                receivers[i] = receivers[i] + senders[j]
                            * connects[i];
            end do;
            unit = LOWER^.outputs[i];       {get unit output}
            receivers[i] = receivers[i] * unit * (1-unit);
        end do;
    end;
```

Finally, we must now step through the network structure once more to adjust connection weights. We move from the input layer to the output layer.

Here again, to improve performance, we process only input connections, so our simulator can once more step through sequential arrays, rather than jumping from array to array as we had to do in the backpropagate_error procedure. This routine incorporates the momentum term discussed in Section 3.4.3. Specifically, alpha is the momentum parameter, and delta refers to the weight change values; see Eq. (3.24).

```
procedure adjust_weights (NET:BPN)
{update all connection weights based on new error values}

var
    current : ^layer;       {access layer data record}
    inputs : ^float[];      {array of input values}
    units : ^float[];       {access units in layer}
    weights : ^float[];     {connections to unit}
    delta : ^float[];       {pointer to delta arrays}
    error : ^float[];       {pointer to error arrays}
    i, j, k : integer;      {iteration indices}


begin
    for i = 2 to length(NET.layers) do
                        {starting at first computed layer}
        current = NET.layers[i];
                        {get pointer to layer}
        units = NET.layers[i]^.outputs;
                        {step through units}

        inputs = NET.layers[i-1]^.outputs;
                                    {access input array}


        for j = 1 to length(units) do
                                {for all units in layer}
            weights = current.weights[j];
                                {find input connections }
            delta = current.lastdeltas[j]; {locate last delta}
            error = NET.layers[i]^.errors;
                                    {access unit errors}
            for k = 1 to length(weights) do
                                    {for all connections}
                weights[k] = weights[k] + (inputs[k]*NET.eta
                                        *error[j]) +
                                    (NET.alpha * delta[k]);
                delta[k] = inputs[k]*NET.eta*error[j]
            end do;
        end do;
    end do;
end;
```

3.5.6 The Complete BPN Simulator

We have now implemented the algorithms needed to perform the backpropagation function. All that remains is to implement a top-level routine that calls our signal-propagation procedures in the correct sequence to allow the simulator to be used. For production-mode operation after training, this routine would take the following general form:

```
begin
  call set_inputs to stimulate the network with an input.
  call propagate_forward to generate an output.
  call get_outputs to examine the output generated.
end
```

During training, the routine would be extended to this form:

```
begin
  while network error is larger than some predefined limit
    do
      call set_inputs to apply a training input.
      call propagate_forward to generate an output.
      call compute_output_error to determine errors.
      call backpropagate_error to update error values.
      call adjust_weights to modify the network.
    end do
end.
```

Programming Exercises

3.1. Implement the backpropagation network simulator using the pseudocode examples provided. Test the network by training it to solve the character-recognition problem described in Section 3.1. Use a 5-by-7-character matrix as input, and train the network to recognize all 36 alphanumeric characters (uppercase letters and 10 digits). Describe the network's tolerance to noisy inputs after training is complete.

3.2. Modify the BPN simulator developed in Programming Exercise 3.1 to implement linear units in the output layer only. Rerun the character-recognition example, and compare the network response with the results obtained in Programming Exercise 3.1. Be sure to compare both the training and the production behaviors of the networks.

3.3. Using the XOR problem described in Chapter 1, determine how many hidden units are needed by a sigmoidal, three-layer BPN to learn the four conditions completely.

3.4. The BPN simulator adjusts its internal connection status after every training pattern. Modify the simulator design to implement true steepest descent by adjusting weights only after all training patterns have been examined. Test your modifications on the XOR problem set from Chapter 1, and on the character-identification problem described in this chapter.

3.5. Modify your BPN simulator to incorporate the bias terms. Follow the suggestion in Section 3.4.3 and consider the bias terms to be weights connected to a fictitious unit that always has an output of 1. Train the network using the character-recognition example. Note any differences in the training or performance of the network when compared to those of earlier implementations.

Suggested Readings

Both Chapter 8 of PDP [7] and Chapter 5 of the PDP Handbook [6] contain discussions of backpropagation and of the generalized delta rule. They are good supplements to the material in this chapter. The books by Wasserman [10] and Hecht-Nielsen [4] also contain treatments of the backpropagation algorithm. Early accounts of the algorithm can be found in the report by Parker [8] and the thesis by Werbos [11].

Cottrell and colleagues [1] describe the image-compression technique discussed in Section 4 of this chapter. Gorman and Sejnowski [3] have used backpropagation to classify SONAR signals. This article is particularly interesting for its analysis of the weights on the hidden units in their network. A famous demonstration system that uses a backpropagation network is Terry Sejnowski's NETtalk [9]. In this system, a neural network replaces a conventional system that translates ASCII text into phonemes for eventual speech production. Audio tapes of the system while it is learning are mindful of the behavior patterns seen in human children while they are learning to talk. An example of a commercial visual-inspection system is given in the paper by Glover [2].

Because the backpropagation algorithm is so expensive computationally, people have made numerous attempts to speed convergence. Many of these attempts are documented in the various proceedings of IEEE/INNS conferences. We hesitate to recommend any particular method, since we have not yet found one that results in a network as capable as the original.

Bibliography

[1] G. W. Cottrell, P. Munro, and D. Zipser. Image compression by back propagation: An example of extensional programming. Technical Report ICS 8702, Institute for Cognitive Science, University of California, San Diego, CA, February 1987.

[2] David E. Glover. Optical Fourier/electronic neurocomputer machine vision inspection system. In *Proceedings of the Vision '88 Conference*, Dearborn, MI, June 1988. Society of Manufacturing Engineers.

[3] R. Paul Gorman and Terrence J. Sejnowski. Analysis of hidden units in a layered network trained to classify sonar targets. *Neural Networks*, 1(1):76–90, 1988.

[4] Robert Hecht-Nielsen. *Neurocomputing*. Addison-Wesley, Reading, MA, 1990.

[5] Geoffrey E. Hinton and Terrence J. Sejnowski. Neural network architectures for AI. Tutorial No. MP2, AAAI87, Seattle, WA, July 1987.

[6] James McClelland and David Rumelhart. *Explorations in Parallel Distributed Processing*. MIT Press, Cambridge, MA, 1986.

[7] James McClelland and David Rumelhart. *Parallel Distributed Processing*, volumes 1 and 2. MIT Press, Cambridge, MA, 1986.

[8] D. B. Parker. Learning logic. Technical Report TR-47, Center for Computational Research in Economics and Management Science, MIT, Cambridge, MA, April 1985.

[9] Terrence J. Sejnowski and Charles R. Rosenberg. Parallel networks that learn to pronounce English text. *Complex Systems*, 1:145–168, 1987.

[10] Philip D. Wasserman. *Neural Computing: Theory and Practice*. Van Nostrand Reinhold, New York, 1989.

[11] P. Werbos. *Beyond Regression: New Tools for Prediction and Analysis in the Behavioral Sciences*. PhD thesis, Harvard, Cambridge, MA, August 1974.

The BAM and the Hopfield Memory

The subject of this chapter is a type of ANS called an **associative memory**. When you read a bit further, you may wonder why the backpropagation network discussed in the previous chapter was not included in this category. In fact, the definition of an associative memory, which we shall present shortly, does apply to the backpropagation network in certain circumstances. Nevertheless, we have chosen to delay the formal discussion of associative memories until now. Our definitions and discussion will be slanted toward the two varieties of memories treated in this chapter: the **bidirectional associative memory** (BAM), and the **Hopfield memory**. You should be able to generalize the discussion to cover other network models.

The concept of an associative memory is a fairly intuitive one: Associative memory appears to be one of the primary functions of the brain. We easily *associate* the face of a friend with that friend's name, or a name with a telephone number.

Many devices exhibit associative-memory characteristics. For example, the memory bank in a computer is a type of associative memory: it associates addresses with data. An object-oriented program (OOP) with inheritance can exhibit another type of associative memory. Given a datum, the OOP associates other data with it, through the OOP's inheritance network. This type of memory is called a content-addressable memory (CAM). The CAM associates data with addresses of other data; it does the opposite of the computer memory bank.

The Hopfield memory, in particular, played an important role in the current resurgence of interest in the field of ANS. Probably as much as any other single factor, the efforts of John Hopfield, of the California Institute of Technology, have had a profound, stimulating effect on the scientific community in the area of ANS. Before describing the BAM and the Hopfield memory, we shall present a few definitions in the next section.

4.1 ASSOCIATIVE-MEMORY DEFINITIONS

In this section, we review some basic definitions and concepts related to associative memories. We shall begin with a discussion of **Hamming distance**, not because the concept is likely to be new to you, but because we want to relate it to the more familiar Euclidean distance, in order to make the notion of Hamming *distance* more plausible. Then we shall discuss a simple associative memory called the **linear associator**.

4.1.1 Hamming Distance

Figure 4.1 shows a set of points which form the three-dimensional **Hamming cube.** In general, *Hamming space* can be defined by the expression

$$\mathbf{H}^n = \{\mathbf{x} = (x_1, x_2, \ldots, x_n)^t \in \mathbf{R}^n : x_i \in (\pm 1)\} \tag{4.1}$$

In words, n-dimensional Hamming space is the set of n-dimensional vectors, with each component an element of the real numbers, **R**, subject to the condition that each component is restricted to the values ± 1. This space has 2^n points, all equidistant from the origin of Euclidean space.

Many neural-network models use the concept of the distance between two vectors. There are, however, many different measures of distance. In this section, we shall define the distance measure known as *Hamming distance* and shall show its relationship to the familiar Euclidean distance between points. In later chapters, we shall explore other distance measures.

Let $\mathbf{x} = (x_1, x_2, \ldots, x_n)^t$ and $\mathbf{y} = (y_1, y_2, \ldots, y_n)^t$ be two vectors in n-dimensional Euclidean space, subject to the restriction that $x_i, y_i \in \{\pm 1\}$, so that $\mathbf{x}$ and $\mathbf{y}$ are also vectors in n-dimensional Hamming space. The Euclidean distance between the two vector endpoints is

$$d = \sqrt{(x_1 - y_1)^2 + (x_2 - y_2)^2 + \cdots + (x_n - y_n)^2}$$

Since $x_i, y_i \in \{\pm 1\}$, then $(x_i - y_i)^2 \in \{0, 4\}$:

$$(x_i - y_i)^2 = \begin{cases} 0 & x_i = y_i \\ 4 & x_i \neq y_i \end{cases}$$

Thus, the Euclidean distance can be written as

$$d = \sqrt{4(\text{\# mismatched components of } \mathbf{x} \text{ and } \mathbf{y})}$$

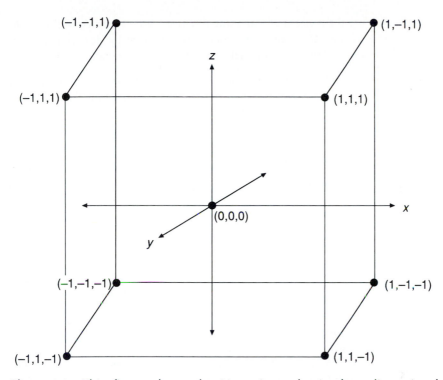

Figure 4.1 This figure shows the Hamming cube in three-dimensional space. The entire three-dimensional Hamming space, $\mathbf{H}^3$, comprises the eight points having coordinate values of either -1 or $+1$. In this three-dimensional space, no other points exist.

We define the Hamming distance as

$$h = \#\text{ mismatched components of } \mathbf{x} \text{ and } \mathbf{y} \tag{4.2}$$

or the number of *bits* that are different between $\mathbf{x}$ and $\mathbf{y}$.[1]

The Hamming distance is related to the Euclidean distance by the equation

$$d = 2\sqrt{h} \tag{4.3}$$

or

$$h = \frac{d^2}{4} \tag{4.4}$$

---

[1]Even though the components of the vectors are ± 1, rather than 0 and 1, we shall use the term *bits* to represent one of the vector components. We shall refer to vectors having components of ± 1 as being **bipolar**, rather than binary. We shall reserve the term *binary* for vectors whose components are 0 and 1.

We shall use the concept of Hamming distance a little later in our discussion of the BAM. In the next section, we shall take a look at the formal definition of the associative memory and the details of the linear-associator model.

Exercise 4.1: Determine the Euclidean distance between $(1, 1, 1, 1, 1)^t$ and $(-1, -1, 1, -1, 1)^t$. Use this result to determine the Hamming distance with Eq. (4.4).

4.1.2 The Linear Associator

Suppose we have L pairs of vectors, $\{(\mathbf{x}_1, \mathbf{y}_1), (\mathbf{x}_2, \mathbf{y}_2), \ldots, (\mathbf{x}_L, \mathbf{y}_L)\}$, with $\mathbf{x}_i \in \mathbf{R}^n$, and $\mathbf{y}_i \in \mathbf{R}^m$. We call these vectors **exemplars**, because we will use them as examples of correct associations. We can distinguish three types of associative memories:

1. **Heteroassociative memory:** Implements a mapping, Φ, of $\mathbf{x}$ to $\mathbf{y}$ such that $\Phi(\mathbf{x}_i) = \mathbf{y}_i$, and, if an arbitrary $\mathbf{x}$ is *closer* to $\mathbf{x}_i$ than to any other $\mathbf{x}_j$, $j = 1, \ldots, L$, then $\Phi(\mathbf{x}) = \mathbf{y}_i$. In this and the following definitions, *closer* means with respect to Hamming distance.

2. **Interpolative associative memory:** Implements a mapping, Φ, of $\mathbf{x}$ to $\mathbf{y}$ such that $\Phi(\mathbf{x}_i) = \mathbf{y}_i$, but, if the input vector differs from one of the exemplars by the vector $\mathbf{d}$, such that $\mathbf{x} = \mathbf{x}_i + \mathbf{d}$, then the output of the memory also differs from one of the exemplars by some vector $\mathbf{e}$: $\Phi(\mathbf{x}) = \Phi(\mathbf{x}_i + \mathbf{d}) = \mathbf{y}_i + \mathbf{e}$.

3. **Autoassociative memory:** Assumes $\mathbf{y}_i = \mathbf{x}_i$ and implements a mapping, Φ, of $\mathbf{x}$ to $\mathbf{x}$ such that $\Phi(\mathbf{x}_i) = \mathbf{x}_i$, and, if some arbitrary $\mathbf{x}$ is *closer* to $\mathbf{x}_i$ than to any other $\mathbf{x}_j$, $j = 1, \ldots, L$, then $\Phi(\mathbf{x}) = \mathbf{x}_i$.

Building such a memory is not such a difficult task mathematically if we make the further restriction that the vectors, $\mathbf{x}_i$, form an orthonormal set.[2] To build an interpolative associative memory, we define the function

$$\Phi(\mathbf{x}) = (\mathbf{y}_1 \mathbf{x}_1^t + \mathbf{y}_2 \mathbf{x}_2^t + \cdots + \mathbf{y}_L \mathbf{x}_L^t)\mathbf{x} \tag{4.5}$$

If $\mathbf{x}_i$ is the input vector, then $\Phi(\mathbf{x}_i) = \mathbf{y}_i$, since the set of $\mathbf{x}$ vectors is orthonormal. This result can be seen from the following example. Let $\mathbf{x}_2$ be the input vector. Then, from Eq. (4.5),

$$\Phi(\mathbf{x}_2) = (\mathbf{y}_1 \mathbf{x}_1^t + \mathbf{y}_2 \mathbf{x}_2^t + \cdots + \mathbf{y}_L \mathbf{x}_L^t)\mathbf{x}_2$$
$$\Phi(\mathbf{x}_2) = \mathbf{y}_1 \mathbf{x}_1^t \mathbf{x}_2 + \mathbf{y}_2 \mathbf{x}_2^t \mathbf{x}_2 + \cdots + \mathbf{y}_L \mathbf{x}_L^t \mathbf{x}_2$$
$$\Phi(\mathbf{x}_2) = \mathbf{y}_1 \delta_{12} + \mathbf{y}_2 \delta_{22} + \cdots + \mathbf{y}_L \delta_{L2}$$

---

[2]Such a set is defined by the relationship, $\mathbf{x}_i^t \mathbf{x}_j = \delta_{ij}$, where $\delta_{ij} = 1$ if $i = j$, and $\delta_{ij} = 0$ if $i \neq j$.

All the δ_{ij} terms in the preceding expression vanish, except for δ_{22}, which is equal to 1. The result is perfect recall of $\mathbf{y}_2$:

$$\Phi(\mathbf{x}_2) = \mathbf{y}_2$$

If the input vector is different from one of the exemplars, such that $\mathbf{x} = \mathbf{x}_i + \mathbf{d}$, then the output is

$$\Phi(\mathbf{x}) = \Phi(\mathbf{x}_i + \mathbf{d}) = \mathbf{y}_i + \mathbf{e}$$

where

$$\mathbf{e} = (\mathbf{y}_1\mathbf{x}_1^t + \mathbf{y}_2\mathbf{x}_2^t + \cdots + \mathbf{y}_L\mathbf{x}_L^t)\mathbf{d}$$

Note that there is nothing in the discussion of the linear associator that requires that the input or output vectors be members of Hamming space: The only requirement is that they be orthonormal. Furthermore, notice that there was no training involved in the definition of the linear associator. The function that mapped $\mathbf{x}$ into $\mathbf{y}$ was defined by the mathematical expression in Eq. (4.5). Most of the models we discuss in this chapter share this characteristic; that is, they are not trained in the sense that an Adaline or backpropagation network is trained.

In the next section, we take up the discussion of BAM. This model utilizes the distributed processing approach, discussed in the previous chapters, to implement an associative memory.

4.2 THE BAM

The BAM consists of two layers of processing elements that are fully interconnected between the layers. The units may, or may not, have feedback connections to themselves. The general case is illustrated in Figure 4.2.

4.2.1 BAM Architecture

As in other neural network architectures, in the BAM architecture there are weights associated with the connections between processing elements. Unlike in many other architectures, these weights can be determined in advance if all of the training vectors can be identified.

We can borrow the procedure from the linear-associator model to construct the weight matrix. Given L vector pairs that constitute the set of exemplars that we would like to store, we can construct the matrix:

$$\mathbf{w} = \mathbf{y}_1\mathbf{x}_1^t + \mathbf{y}_2\mathbf{x}_2^t + \cdots + \mathbf{y}_L\mathbf{x}_L^t \tag{4.6}$$

This equation gives the weights on the connections *from* the $\mathbf{x}$ layer *to* the $\mathbf{y}$ layer. For example, the value w_{23} is the weight on the connection from the

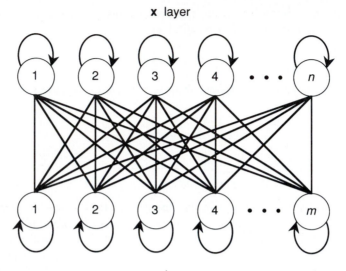

x layer

y layer

Figure 4.2 The BAM shown here has n units on the **x** layer, and m units
on the **y** layer. For convenience, we shall call the **x** vector
the input vector, and call the **y** vector the output vector. In
this network, $\mathbf{x} \in \mathbf{H}^n$, and $\mathbf{y} \in \mathbf{H}^m$. All connections between
units are bidirectional, with weights at each end. Information
passes back and forth from one layer to the other, through these
connections. Feedback connections at each unit may not be
present in all BAM architectures.

third unit on the **x** layer to the second unit on the **y** layer. To construct the
weights for the **x** layer units, we simply take the transpose of the weight matrix, $\mathbf{w}^t$.

We can make the BAM into an *autoassociative memory* by constructing the
weight matrix as

$$\mathbf{w} = \mathbf{x}_1\mathbf{x}_1^t + \mathbf{x}_2\mathbf{x}_2^t + \cdots + \mathbf{x}_L\mathbf{x}_L^t$$

In this case, the weight matrix is square and symmetric.

4.2.2   BAM Processing

Once the weight matrix has been constructed, the BAM can be used to recall
information (e.g., a telephone number), when presented with some key information (a name corresponding to a particular telephone number). If the desired
information is only partially known in advance or is *noisy* (a misspelled name
such as "Simth"), the BAM may be able to complete the information (giving
the proper spelling, "Smith," and the correct telephone number).

To recall information using the BAM, we perform the following steps:

1. Apply an initial vector pair, $(\mathbf{x}_0, \mathbf{y}_0)$, to the processing elements of the BAM.

2. Propagate the information from the $\mathbf{x}$ layer to the $\mathbf{y}$ layer, and update the values on the $\mathbf{y}$-layer units. We shall see how this propagation is done shortly.[3]

3. Propagate the updated $\mathbf{y}$ information back to the $\mathbf{x}$ layer and update the units there.

4. Repeat steps 2 and 3 until there is no further change in the units on each layer.

This algorithm is what gives the BAM its bidirectional nature. The terms *input* and *output* refer to different quantities, depending on the current direction of the propagation. For example, in going from $\mathbf{y}$ to $\mathbf{x}$, the $\mathbf{y}$ vector is considered as the input to the network, and the $\mathbf{x}$ vector is the output. The opposite is true when propagating from $\mathbf{x}$ to $\mathbf{y}$.

If all goes well, the final, stable state will recall one of the exemplars used to construct the weight matrix. Since, in this example, we assume we know something about the desired $\mathbf{x}$ vector, but perhaps know nothing about the associated $\mathbf{y}$ vector, we hope that the final output is the exemplar whose $\mathbf{x}_i$ vector is closest in Hamming distance to the original input vector, $\mathbf{x}_0$. This scenario works well provided we have not overloaded the BAM with exemplars. If we try to put too much information in a given BAM, a phenomenon known as **crosstalk** occurs between exemplar patterns. Crosstalk occurs when exemplar patterns are too *close* to each other. The interaction between these patterns can result in the creation of *spurious* stable states. In that case, the BAM could stabilize on meaningless vectors. If we think in terms of a surface in weight space, as we did in Chapters 2 and 3, the spurious stable states correspond to minima that appear between the minima that correspond to the exemplars.

4.2.3 BAM Mathematics

The basic processing done by each unit of the BAM is similar to that done by the general processing element discussed in the first chapter. The units compute sums of products of the inputs and weights to determine a net-input value, net. On the $\mathbf{y}$ layer,

$$\mathbf{net}^y = \mathbf{wx} \tag{4.7}$$

where $\mathbf{net}^y$ is the vector of net-input values on the $\mathbf{y}$ layer. In terms of the individual units, y_i,

$$\mathrm{net}_i^y = \sum_{j=1}^n w_{ij} x_j \tag{4.8}$$

---

[3] Although we consistently begin with the $\mathbf{x}$-to-$\mathbf{y}$ propagation, you could begin in the other direction.

On the x layer,

$$\mathbf{net}^x = \mathbf{w}^t \mathbf{y} \tag{4.9}$$

$$\mathrm{net}_i^x = \sum_{j=1}^{m} y_j w_{ji} \tag{4.10}$$

The quantities n and m are the dimensions of the **x** and **y** layers, respectively.
    The output value for each processing element depends on the net input value, and on the *current* output value on the layer. The new value of **y** at timestep $t + 1$, $\mathbf{y}(t + 1)$, is related to the value of **y** at timestep t, $\mathbf{y}(t)$, by

$$y_i(t+1) = \begin{cases} +1 & \mathrm{net}_i^y > 0 \\ y_i(t) & \mathrm{net}_i^y = 0 \\ -1 & \mathrm{net}_i^y < 0 \end{cases} \tag{4.11}$$

Similarly, $\mathbf{x}(t + 1)$ is related to $\mathbf{x}(t)$ by

$$x_i(t+1) = \begin{cases} +1 & \mathrm{net}_i^x > 0 \\ x_i(t) & \mathrm{net}_i^x = 0 \\ -1 & \mathrm{net}_i^x < 0 \end{cases} \tag{4.12}$$

Let's illustrate BAM processing with a specific example. Let

$$\mathbf{x}_1 = (1, -1, -1, 1, -1, 1, 1, -1, -1, 1)^t \quad \text{and} \quad \mathbf{y}_1 = (1, -1, -1, -1, -1, 1)^t$$
$$\mathbf{x}_2 = (1, 1, 1, -1, -1, -1, 1, 1, -1, -1)^t \quad \text{and} \quad \mathbf{y}_2 = (1, 1, 1, 1, -1, -1)^t$$

We have purposely made these vectors rather long to minimize the possibility of crosstalk. Hand calculation of the weight matrix is tedious when the vectors are long, but the weight matrix is fairly sparse.
    The weight matrix is calculated from Eq. (4.6). The result is

$$\mathbf{w} = \begin{pmatrix} 2 & 0 & 0 & 0 & -2 & 0 & 2 & 0 & -2 & 0 \\ 0 & 2 & 2 & -2 & 0 & -2 & 0 & 2 & 0 & -2 \\ 0 & 2 & 2 & -2 & 0 & -2 & 0 & 2 & 0 & -2 \\ 0 & 2 & 2 & -2 & 0 & -2 & 0 & 2 & 0 & -2 \\ -2 & 0 & 0 & 0 & 2 & 0 & -2 & 0 & 2 & 0 \\ 0 & -2 & -2 & 2 & 0 & 2 & 0 & -2 & 0 & 2 \end{pmatrix}$$

For our first trial, we choose an $\mathbf{x}$ vector with a Hamming distance of 1 from $\mathbf{x}_1$: $\mathbf{x}_0 = (-1, -1, -1, 1, -1, 1, 1, -1, -1, 1)^t$. This situation could represent noise on the input vector. The starting $\mathbf{y}_0$ vector is one of the training vectors, $\mathbf{y}_2$: $\mathbf{y}_0 = (1, 1, 1, 1, -1, -1)^t$. (Note that in a realistic problem, you may not have prior knowledge of the output vector. Use a random bipolar vector if necessary.)

We will propagate first from $\mathbf{x}$ to $\mathbf{y}$. The net inputs to the $\mathbf{y}$ units are $\mathbf{net}^y = (4, -12, -12, -12, -4, 12)^t$. The new $\mathbf{y}$ vector is $\mathbf{y}_{new} = (1, -1, -1, -1, -1, 1)^t$, which is also one of the training vectors. Propagating back to the $\mathbf{x}$ layer we get $\mathbf{x}_{new} = (1, -1, -1, 1, -1, 1, 1, -1, -1, 1)^t$. Further passes result in no change, so we are finished. The BAM successfully recalled the first training set.

Exercise 4.2: Repeat the calculation just shown, but begin with the y-to-x propagation. Is the result what you expected?

For our second example, we choose the following initial vectors:

$$\mathbf{x}_0 = (-1, 1, 1, -1, 1, 1, 1, -1, 1, -1)^t$$
$$\mathbf{y}_0 = (-1, 1, -1, 1, -1, -1)^t$$

The Hamming distances of the $\mathbf{x}_0$ vector from the training vectors are $h(\mathbf{x}_0, \mathbf{x}_1) = 7$ and $h(\mathbf{x}_0, \mathbf{x}_2) = 5$. For the $\mathbf{y}_0$ vector, the values are $h(\mathbf{y}_0, \mathbf{y}_1) = 4$ and $h(\mathbf{y}_0, \mathbf{y}_2) = 2$. Based on these results, we might expect that the BAM would settle on the second exemplar as a final solution.

We start again by propagating from $\mathbf{x}$ to $\mathbf{y}$, and the new $\mathbf{y}$ vector is $\mathbf{y}_{new} = (-1, 1, 1, 1, 1, -1)^t$. Propagating back from $\mathbf{y}$ to $\mathbf{x}$, we get $\mathbf{x}_{new} = (-1, 1, 1, -1, 1, -1, -1, 1, 1, -1)^t$. Further propagation does not change the results. If you examine these output vectors, you will notice that they do not match any of the exemplars. Furthermore, they are actually the complement of the first training set, $(\mathbf{x}_{new}, \mathbf{y}_{new}) = (\mathbf{x}_1^c, \mathbf{y}_1^c)$, where the "$c$" superscript refers to the complement. This example illustrates a basic property of the BAM: If you encode an exemplar, $(\mathbf{x}, \mathbf{y})$, you also encode its complement, $(\mathbf{x}^c, \mathbf{y}^c)$.

The best way to familiarize yourself with the properties of a BAM is to work through many examples. Thus, we recommend the following exercises.

Exercise 4.3: Using the same weight matrix as in Exercise 4.2, experiment with several different input vectors to investigate the characteristics of the BAM. In particular, evaluate the difference between starting with x-to-y propagation, and y-to-x propagation. Pick starting vectors that have various Hamming distances from the exemplar vectors. In addition, try adding more exemplars to the weight matrix. You can add more exemplars to the weight matrix by a simple additive process. How many exemplars can you add before crosstalk becomes a significant problem?

Exercise 4.4: Construct an autoassociative BAM using the following training vectors:

$$\mathbf{x}_1 = (1, -1, -1, 1, -1, 1)^t \quad \text{and} \quad \mathbf{x}_2 = (1, 1, 1, -1, -1, -1)^t$$

Determine the output using $\mathbf{x}_0 = (1, 1, 1, 1, -1, 1)^t$, which is a Hamming distance of two from each training vector. Try $\mathbf{x}_0 = (-1, 1, 1, -1, 1, -1)^t$, which is a complement of one of the training vectors. Experiment with this network in accordance with the instructions in Exercise 4.3. In addition, try setting the diagonal elements of the weight matrix equal to zero. Does doing so have any effect on the operation of the BAM?

4.2.4 BAM Energy Function

In the previous two chapters, we discussed an iterative process for finding weight values that are appropriate for a particular application. During those discussions, each point in *weight space* had associated with it a certain error value. The learning process was an iterative attempt to find the weights which minimized the error. To gain an understanding of the process, we examined simple cases having two weights so that each weight vector corresponded to a point on an error surface in three dimensions. The height of the surface at each point determined the error associated with that weight vector. To minimize the error, we began at some given starting point and moved along the surface until we reached the deepest valley on the surface. This minimum point corresponded to the weights that resulted in the smallest error value. Once these weights were found, no further changes were permitted and training was complete.

During the training process, the weights form a dynamical system. That is, the weights change as a function of time, and those changes can be represented as a set of coupled differential equations.

For the BAM that we have been discussing in the last few sections, a slightly different situation occurs. The weights are calculated in advance, and are not part of a dynamical system. On the other hand, an unknown pattern presented to the BAM may require several passes before the network stabilizes on a final result. In this situation, the **x** and **y** vectors change as a function of time, and they form a dynamical system.

In both of the dynamical systems described, we are interested in several aspects of system behavior: Does a solution exist? If it does, will the system converge to it in a finite time? What is the solution? Up to now we have been primarily concerned with the last of those three questions. We shall now look at the first two.

For the simple examples discussed so far, the question of the existence of a solution is academic. We found solutions; therefore, they must exist. Nevertheless, we may have been simply lucky in our choice of problems. It is still a valid question to ask whether a BAM, or for that matter, any other network, will *always* converge to a stable solution. The technique discussed here is fairly easy to apply to the BAM. Unfortunately, many network architectures do not have convergence proofs. The lack of such a proof does not mean that the network will not function properly, but there is no guarantee that it will converge for any given problem.

In the theory of dynamical systems, a theorem can be proved concerning the existence of stable states that uses the concept of a function called a **Lyapunov function**, or **energy function**. We shall present a nonrigorous version here, which is useful for our purposes. If a bounded function of the state variables of a dynamical system can be found, such that all state changes result in a decrease in the value of the function, then the system has a stable solution.[4] This function is called a Lyapunov function, or energy function. In the case of the BAM, such a function exists. We shall call it the **BAM energy function**; it has the form

$$E(\mathbf{x}, \mathbf{y}) = -\mathbf{y}^t \mathbf{w} \mathbf{x} \tag{4.13}$$

or, in terms of components,

$$E = -\sum_{i=1}^{m} \sum_{j=1}^{n} y_i w_{ij} x_j \tag{4.14}$$

We shall now state an important theorem about the BAM energy function that will help to answer our questions about the existence of stable solutions of the BAM processing equations. The theorem has three parts:

1. Any change in $\mathbf{x}$ or $\mathbf{y}$ during BAM processing results in a decrease in E.

2. E is bounded below by $E_{\min} = -\sum_{i,j} |w_{ij}|$.

3. When E changes, it must change by a finite amount.

Items 1 and 2 prove that E is a Lyapunov function, and that the dynamical system has a stable state. In particular, item 2 shows that E can decrease only to a certain value; it can't continue down to negative infinity, so that eventually the $\mathbf{x}$ and $\mathbf{y}$ vectors must stop changing. Item 3 prevents the possibility that changes in E might be infinitesimally small, resulting in an infinite amount of time spent before the minimum E is reached.

In essence, the weight matrix determines the contour of a surface, or landscape, with hills and valleys, much like the ones we have discussed in previous chapters. Figure 4.3 illustrates a cross-sectional view of such a surface. The analogy of the E function as an energy function results from an analysis of how the BAM operates. The initial state of the BAM is determined by the choice of the starting vectors, ($\mathbf{x}$ and $\mathbf{y}$). As the BAM processes the data, $\mathbf{x}$ and $\mathbf{y}$ change, resulting in movement of the energy over the landscape, which is guaranteed by the BAM energy theorem to be downward.

---

[4]See Hirsch and Smale [3] or Beltrami [1] for a more rigorous version of the theorem.

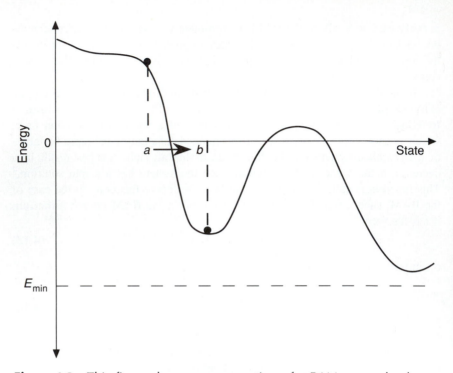

Figure 4.3 This figure shows a cross-section of a BAM energy landscape in two dimensions. The particular topography results from the choice of exemplar vectors that go into making up the weight matrix. During processing, the BAM energy value will move from its starting point down the energy hill to the nearest minimum, while the BAM outputs move from state a to state b. Notice that the minima reached need not be the global, or lowest, minima on the landscape.

Initially, the changes in the calculated values of $E(\mathbf{x}, \mathbf{y})$ are large. As the $\mathbf{x}$ and $\mathbf{y}$ vectors reach their stable state, the value of E changes by smaller amounts, and eventually stops changing when the minimum point is reached. This situation corresponds to a physical system such as a ball rolling down a hill into a valley, but with enough friction that, by the time the ball reaches the bottom, it has no more energy and therefore it stops. Thus, the BAM resembles a dissipative dynamic system in which the E function corresponds to the energy of the physical system. Remember that the weight matrix determines the contour of this energy landscape; that is, it determines how many energy valleys there are, how far apart they are, how deep they are, and whether there are any unexpected valleys (i.e., spurious states).

We need to clarify one point. We have been illustrating these concepts using a two-dimensional cross-section of an energy landscape, and using the familiar term *valley* to refer to the locations of the minima. A more precise term would be *basin*. In fact, the literature on dynamical systems refers to these locations as *basins of attraction*.

To solidify the concept of BAM energy, we return to the examples of the previous section. First, notice that according to part two of the BAM energy theorem, the minimum value of E is -64, found by summing the negatives of all the magnitudes of the components of the matrix. A calculation of E for each of the two training vectors shows that both pairs sit at the bottom of basins having this same value of E. Our first trial vectors were $\mathbf{x}_0 = (-1, -1, -1, 1, -1, 1, 1, -1, -1, 1)^t$ and $\mathbf{y}_0 = (1, 1, 1, 1, -1, -1)^t$. The energy of this system is $E = -\mathbf{y}_0^t \mathbf{w} \mathbf{x}_0 = 40$.

The first propagation results in $\mathbf{y}_{\text{new}} = (1, -1, -1, -1, -1, 1)^t$, and a new energy value $E = -\mathbf{y}_{\text{new}}^t \mathbf{w} \mathbf{x}_0 = -56$. Propagation back to the $\mathbf{x}$ layer resulted in $\mathbf{x}_{\text{new}} = (1, -1, -1, 1, -1, 1, 1, -1, -1, 1)^t$. The energy is now $E = -\mathbf{y}_{\text{new}}^t \mathbf{w} \mathbf{x}_{\text{new}} = -64$. At this point, no further passes through the system are necessary, since -64 is the lowest possible energy. Since any further change in $\mathbf{x}$ or $\mathbf{y}$ would lower the energy, according to the theorem, no such changes are possible.

Exercise 4.5: Perform the BAM energy calculation on the second example from Section 4.2.3.

Proof of the BAM Energy Theorem. In this section, we prove the first part of the BAM energy theorem. We present this proof because it is both clever and easy to understand. The proof is not essential to your understanding of the remaining material, so you may skip it if you wish.

We begin with Eq. (4.14), which is reproduced here:

$$E = -\sum_{i=1}^{m}\sum_{j=1}^{n} y_i w_{ij} x_j$$

According to the theorem, any change in $\mathbf{x}$ or $\mathbf{y}$ must result in a decrease in the value of E. For simplicity, we first consider a change in a single component of $\mathbf{y}$, specifically y_k.

We can rewrite Eq. (4.14) showing the term with y_k explicitly:

$$E = -\sum_{j=1}^{n} y_k w_{kj} x_j - \sum_{\substack{i=1 \\ i \neq k}}^{m}\sum_{j=1}^{n} y_i w_{ij} x_j \tag{4.15}$$

Now, make the change $y_k \rightarrow y_k^{\text{new}}$. The new energy value is

$$E^{\text{new}} = -\sum_{j=1}^{n} y_k^{\text{new}} w_{kj} x_j - \sum_{\substack{i=1 \\ i \neq k}}^{m}\sum_{j=1}^{n} y_i w_{ij} x_j \tag{4.16}$$

Since only y_k has changed, the second terms on the right sides of Eqs. (4.15) and (4.16) are identical. In that case we can write the change in energy as

$$\Delta E = (E^{\text{new}} - E) = (y_k - y_k^{\text{new}}) \sum_{j=1}^{n} w_{kj} x_j \qquad (4.17)$$

For convenience, we recall the state-change equations that determine the new value of y_k:

$$y_k^{\text{new}} = \begin{cases} +1 & \sum_{j=1}^{n} w_{kj} x_j > 0 \\ y_k & \sum_{j=1}^{n} w_{kj} x_j = 0 \\ -1 & \sum_{j=1}^{n} w_{kj} x_j < 0 \end{cases}$$

There are two possible changes of y_k to consider. Suppose $y_k = +1$, and it changes to -1; in this case, $(y_k - y_k^{\text{new}}) > 0$. But, according to the procedure for calculating y_k^{new}, this transition can occur only if $\sum_{j=1}^{n} w_{kj} x_j < 0$. Therefore, the value of ΔE is the product of one factor that is greater than zero and one that is less than zero. The result is that $\Delta E < 0$.

The second possibility is that $y_k = -1$ and $y_k^{\text{new}} = +1$. Then, $(y_k - y_k^{\text{new}}) < 0$, but this transition occurs only if $\sum_{j=1}^{n} w_{kj} x_j > 0$. Again, ΔE is the product of one factor less than zero and one greater than zero. In both cases where y_k changes, ΔE decreases. Note that, for the case where y_k does not change, both factors in the equation for ΔE are zero, so the energy does not change unless one of the vectors changes.

Equation (4.17) can be extended to cover the situation where more than one component of the **y** vector changes. If we write $\Delta y_i = (y_i - y_i^{\text{new}})$, then the equation that replaces Eq. (4.17) for the general case where any or all components of **y** can change is

$$\Delta E = (E^{\text{new}} - E) = \sum_{i=1}^{m} \Delta y_i \sum_{j=1}^{n} w_{ij} x_j \qquad (4.18)$$

This equation is a sum of m terms, one for each possible Δy_i, which are either negative or zero depending on whether or not y_i changed. Thus, in the general case, E must decrease if **y** changes.

Exercise 4.6: Prove part 2 of the BAM energy theorem.

Exercise 4.7: Prove part 3 of the BAM energy theorem.

Exercise 4.8: Suppose we have defined an autoassociative BAM whose weight matrix is calculated according to

$$\mathbf{w} = \mathbf{x}_1 \mathbf{x}_1^t + \mathbf{x}_2 \mathbf{x}_2^t + \cdots + \mathbf{x}_L \mathbf{x}_L^t$$

where the $\mathbf{x}_i$ are not necessarily orthonormal. Show that the weight matrix can be written as

$$\mathbf{w} = \alpha \mathbf{I} + \mathbf{S}$$

where α is a constant, $\mathbf{I}$ is the identity matrix, and $\mathbf{S}$ is identical to the weight matrix, but with zeros on the diagonal. For an arbitrary input vector, $\mathbf{x}$, show that the value of the BAM energy function is

$$E = -\beta - \mathbf{x}^t \mathbf{S} \mathbf{x}$$

where β is a constant. From this result, deduce that the change in energy, ΔE, during a state change, is independent of the diagonal elements on the weight matrix.

4.3   THE HOPFIELD MEMORY

In this section we describe two versions of an ANS, which we call the *Hopfield memory*. We shall show that you can consider the Hopfield memory as a derivative of the BAM, although we doubt that that was the way the Hopfield memory originated. The two versions are the **discrete Hopfield memory**, and the **continuous Hopfield memory**, depending on whether the unit outputs are a discrete or a continuous function of the inputs respectively.

4.3.1   Discrete Hopfield Memory

In the discussion of the previous sections, we defined an autoassociative BAM as one which stored and recalled a set of vectors $\{\mathbf{x}_1, \mathbf{x}_2, \ldots, \mathbf{x}_L\}$. The prescription for determining the weights was to calculate the correlation matrix:

$$\mathbf{w} = \sum_{i=1}^{L} \mathbf{x}_i \mathbf{x}_i^t$$

Figure 4.4 illustrates a BAM that performs this autoassociative function.

We pointed out in the previous section that the weight matrix for an autoassociative memory is square and symmetric, which means, for example, that the weights w_{12} and w_{21} are equal. Since each of the two layers has the same number of units, and the connection weight from the nth unit on layer 1 to the nth unit on layer 2 is the same as the connection weight from the nth unit on layer 2 back to the nth unit on layer 1, it is possible to reduce the autoassociative BAM structure to one having only a single layer. Figure 4.5 illustrates this structure. A somewhat different rendering appears in Figure 4.6. The figure shows a fully connected network, without the feedback from each unit to itself.

The major difference between the architecture of Figure 4.5 and that of Figure 4.6 is the existence of the external input signals, I_i. This addition modifies the calculation of the net input to a given unit by the inclusion of the I_i term. In this case,

$$\text{net}_i = \sum_{j=1}^{n} w_{ij} x_j + I_i \qquad \textbf{(4.19)}$$

x layer

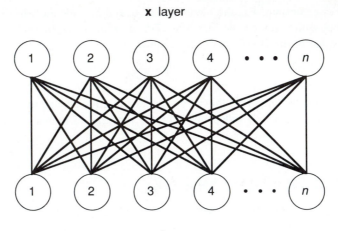

x layer

Figure 4.4   The autoassociative BAM architecture has an equal number of
units on each layer. Note that we have omitted the feedback
terms to each unit.

x layer

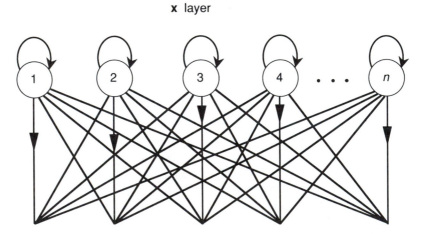

Figure 4.5   The autoassociative BAM can be reduced to a single-layer
structure. Notice that, when the reduction is carried out, the
feedback connections to each unit reappear.

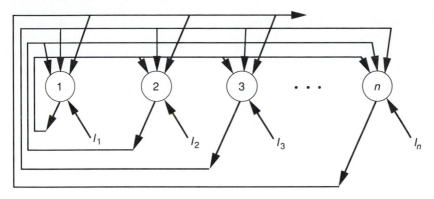

Figure 4.6 This figure shows the Hopfield-memory architecture without the feedback connections to each unit. Eliminating these connections explicitly forces the weight matrix to have zeros on the diagonal. We have also added external input signals, I_i, to each unit.

Moreover, we can allow the threshold condition on the output value to take on a value other than zero. Then, instead of Eq. (4.12), we would have

$$x_i(t+1) = \begin{cases} +1 & \text{net}_i > U_i \\ x_i(t) & \text{net}_i = U_i \\ -1 & \text{net}_i < U_i \end{cases} \qquad (4.20)$$

where U_i is the threshold condition for the ith unit.

A final point concerns the use of binary $(0, +1)$ vectors rather than bipolar $(-1, +1)$ vectors. Hopfield's original papers used binary $(0, 1)$ vectors, whereas we have used the bipolar form up to now. To facilitate the reading of the original papers, we want to be able to shift to binary vectors, $\mathbf{v}_i$. All that is required is that we modify a few equations slightly. To calculate the weight matrix, we use

$$\mathbf{w} = (2\mathbf{v}_1 - \vec{1})(2\mathbf{v}_1 - \vec{1})^t + (2\mathbf{v}_1 - \vec{1})(2\mathbf{v}_2 - \vec{1})^t + \cdots + (2\mathbf{v}_L - \vec{1})(2\mathbf{v}_L - \vec{1})^t \quad (4.21)$$

where $\vec{1}$ is the vector with all 1's as components. The expression $(2\mathbf{v}_i - \vec{1})$ converts the binary vector, $\mathbf{v}_i$ into the equivalent bipolar vector, so the weight matrix is the same as that calculated with the original bipolar vectors. The second change occurs when we apply the threshold: If $\text{net}_i < U_i$ then $v_i = 0$ rather than -1.

The energy equation is modified by the addition of the I_i and U_i terms. Furthermore, we now explicitly define the diagonal elements of the weight matrix to be zero. The energy equation for the network is

$$E = -\frac{1}{2}\sum_i \sum_{\substack{j \\ j \neq i}} v_i w_{ij} v_j - \sum_i I_i v_i + \sum_i U_i v_i \qquad (4.22)$$

The factor of $\frac{1}{2}$ did not appear in the energy equation of the BAM. In the BAM, both forward and backward passes contributed equally to the total energy of the system. In the Hopfield memory, there is only a single layer, hence, half the energy that there is in the BAM.

Exercise 4.9: Beginning with Eq. (4.22), show that the Hopfield network will always converge to a stable state by proving a theorem similar to the BAM energy theorem of the previous section. This exercise assumes that you have read the section on the proof of the BAM energy theorem.

4.3.2   Continuous Hopfield Model

Hopfield's intent was to extend his discrete-memory model by incorporating some results from neurobiology that make his PEs more closely resemble actual neurons. For example, it is known that real neurons have a continuous, graded output response as a function of their inputs, rather than the two-state, on-or-off binary output. By using this modification and others, Hopfield constructed a new, continuous-memory model that had the same useful properties of an associative memory that the discrete model showed. Moreover, there is an analogous electronic circuit using nonlinear amplifiers and resistors, which suggests the possibility of building these associative memory circuits using VLSI technology.

To develop the continuous model, we shall define u_i to be the net input to the ith PE. One possible biological analog of u_i is the summed action potentials at the axon hillock of a neuron. In the case of the neuron, the output of the cell would be a series of potential spikes whose mean frequency versus total action potential resembles the sigmoid curve in Figure 4.7(a). For use in the Hopfield model, the PE output function is

$$v_i = g_i(\lambda u_i) = \frac{1}{2}\left(1 + \tanh(\lambda u_i)\right) \tag{4.23}$$

where λ is a constant called the **gain parameter**. This relationship is illustrated in Figure 4.7(b) for several values of the gain parameter, λ.

In real neurons, there will be a time delay between the appearance of the outputs, v_j, of other cells, and the resulting net input, u_i, to a cell. This delay is caused by the resistance and capacitance of the cell membrane and the finite conductance of the synapse between the jth and ith cells. These ideas are incorporated into the circuit shown in Figure 4.8.

Each amplifier has an input resistance, ρ, and an input capacitance, C, as shown. Also shown are the external signals, I_i. In the case of an actual circuit, the external signals would supply a constant current to each amplifier.

The net-input current to each amplifier is the sum of the individual current contributions from other units, plus the external-input current, minus leakage across the input resistor, ρ. The contribution from each connecting unit is the voltage value across the resistor at the connection, divided by the connection

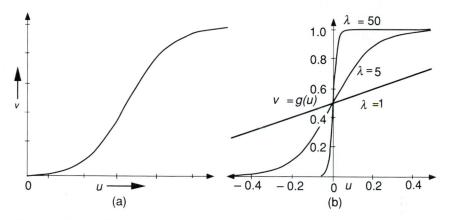

Figure 4.7   (a) This sigmoid curve approximates the output of a neuron in response to the total action potential. (b) This series of graphs has been drawn using Eq. (4.23), for three different values of the gain parameter, λ. Note that, for large values of the gain, the function approaches the step function used in the discrete model.

resistance. For the connection from the jth unit to the ith, this contribution would be $(v_j - u_i)/R_{ij} = (v_j - u_i)T_{ij}$. The leakage current is u_i/ρ. Thus, the total contribution from all connecting units and the external input is

$$I_{T_i} = \sum_j (v_j - u_i)T_{ij} - \frac{u_i}{\rho} + I_i$$

Rearranging slightly gives

$$I_{T_i} = \sum_j T_{ij}v_j - \frac{u_i}{R_i} + I_i$$

where $\frac{1}{R_i} = \frac{1}{\rho} + \sum_j \frac{1}{R_{ij}}$ is the parallel combination of the input resistor and the connection-matrix resistors. We can treat the circuit as a transient RC circuit, and can find the value of u_i from the equation that describes the charging of the capacitor as a result of the net-input current. That equation is

$$C\frac{du_i}{dt} = \sum_j T_{ij}v_j - \frac{u_i}{R_i} + I_i \qquad (4.24)$$

These equations, one for each unit in the memory circuit, completely describe the time evolution of the system. If each PE is given an initial value, $u_i(0)$, these equations can be solved on a digital computer using the numerical techniques for initial value problems. Do not forget to apply the output function, Eq. (4.23), to each u_i to obtain the corresponding amplifier output, v_i.

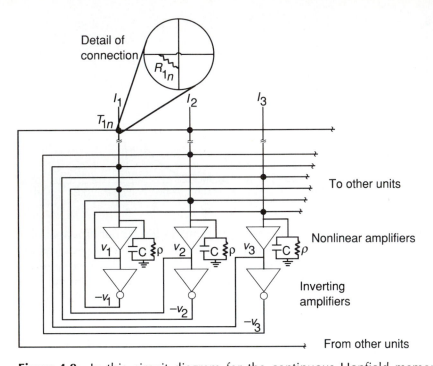

Figure 4.8   In this circuit diagram for the continuous Hopfield memory, amplifiers with a sigmoid output characteristic are used as the PEs. The black circles at the intersection points of the lines represent connections between PEs. At each connection, we place a resistor having a value $R_{ij} = 1/|T_{ij}|$, where we have used Hopfield's notation T_{ij} to represent the weight matrix. Since all real resistor values are positive, inverting amplifiers are used to simulate inhibitory signals. Thus, a PE consists of two amplifiers. If the output of a particular element excites some other element, then the connection is made with the signal from the noninverting amplifier. If the connection is inhibitory, it is made from the inverting amplifier.

Continuous-Model Energy Function.   Like the BAM, the discrete Hopfield memory always converges to a stable point in Hamming space: one of the 2^n vertices of the Hamming hypercube.[5] The energy function that allows us to analyze the continuous model is

$$E = -\frac{1}{2} \sum_i \sum_{\substack{j \\ j \neq i}} T_{ij} v_i v_j + \frac{1}{\lambda} \sum_i \frac{1}{R_i} \int_0^{v_i} g_i^{-1}(v) dv - \sum_i I_i v_i \qquad (4.25)$$

---

[5]As we are now working with binary vectors, rather than bipolar, we must think of the Hamming hypercube as being made up of points whose values are $\{0, +1\}$ rather than ± 1.

In Eq. (4.25), $g^{-1}(v) = u$ is the inverse of the function $v = g(u)$. It is graphed in Figure 4.9, along with the integral of $g^{-1}(v)$, as a function of v.

To show that Eq. (4.25) is an appropriate Lyapunov function for the system, we shall take the time derivative of Eq. (4.25) assuming T_{ij} is symmetric:

$$\frac{dE}{dt} = -\sum_i \frac{dv_i}{dt} \left(\sum_j T_{ij} v_j - \frac{u_i}{R_i} + I_i \right). \tag{4.26}$$

Notice that the quantity in parentheses in Eq. (4.26) is identical to the right-hand side of Eq. (4.24). Then,

$$\frac{dE}{dt} = -\sum_i C \frac{dv_i}{dt} \frac{du_i}{dt}$$

Because $u_i = g_i^{-1}(v_i)$, we can use the chain rule to write

$$\frac{du_i}{dt} = \frac{dg_i^{-1}(v_i)}{dv_i} \frac{dv_i}{dt}$$

and Eq. (4.26) becomes

$$\frac{dE}{dt} = -\sum_i C \frac{dg_i^{-1}(v_i)}{dv_i} \left(\frac{dv_i}{dt} \right)^2 \tag{4.27}$$

Figure 4.9(a) shows that $g_i^{-1}(v_i)$ is a monotonically increasing function of v_i and therefore its derivative is positive everywhere. All the factors in the summation of Eq. (4.27) are positive, so dE/dt must decrease as the system evolves. The

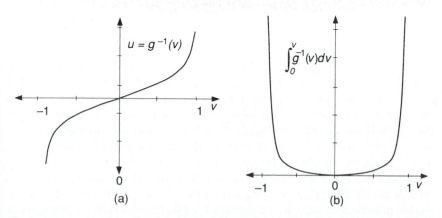

Figure 4.9 (a) The graph shows the inverse of the nonlinear output function. (b) The graph shows the integral of the nonlinear output function.

system eventually reaches a stable configuration, where $dE/dt = dv_i/dt = 0$. We have assumed, for this argument, that E is bounded. It would be necessary to establish this fact to ensure that E will eventually stop changing.

Effects of the Nonlinear Output Function. If we make the assumption that the external inputs I_i are all zero, then the energy equation for the continuous model, Eq. (4.25), is identical to that of the discrete model, Eq. (4.22), except for the contribution

$$\frac{1}{\lambda} \sum_i \frac{1}{R_i} \int_0^{v_i} g_i^{-1}(v) dv. \tag{4.28}$$

This term alters the energy landscape such that the stable points of the system no longer lie exactly at the corners of the Hamming hypercube. The value of the gain parameter determines how close the stable points come to the hypercube corners. In the limit of very high gain, $\lambda \to \infty$, Eq. (4.28) is driven to zero, and the continuous model becomes identical to the discrete model. For finite gain, the stable points move toward the interior of the hypercube. As the gain becomes smaller, these stable points may coalesce. Ultimately, as $\lambda \to 0$, only a single stable point exists for the system. Thus, prudent choice of the gain parameter is necessary for successful operation.

4.3.3   The Traveling-Salesperson Problem

In this section, we shall examine the application of the continuous Hopfield memory to a class of problems known as *optimization problems*. Simply put, these problems are typically posed in terms of finding the best way to do something, subject to certain constraints. The *best* solution is generally defined by a specific criterion. For example, there might be a cost associated with each potential solution, and the *best* solution is the one that minimizes the cost while still fulfilling all the requirements for an acceptable solution. In fact, in many cases optimization problems are described in terms of a **cost function**.

One such optimization problem is the traveling-salesperson problem (TSP). In its simplest form, a salesperson must make a circuit through a certain number of cities, visiting each only once, while minimizing the total distance traveled. The problem is to find the right sequence of cities to visit. The constraints are that all cities are visited, each is visited only once, and the salesperson returns to the starting point at the end of the trip. The cost function to be minimized is the total distance traveled in the course of the trip.

Notice that *minimum distance* is not a constraint in this problem. Constraints *must* be satisfied, whereas minimum distance is only a desirable end. We can include minimum distance as a constraint if we distinguish between two types of constraints: weak and strong. Weak constraints, such as minimum distance for the TSP, are conditions that we desire, but may not achieve. Strong constraints are conditions that must be satisfied, or the solution we obtain will be invalid.

The TSP is computationally intensive if an exhaustive search is to be performed comparing all possible routes to find the best one. For an n-city tour, there are $n!$ possible paths. Due to degeneracies, the number of distinct solutions is less than $n!$. The term *distinct* in this case refers to tours with different total distances. For a given tour, it does not matter which of the n cities is the starting point, in terms of the total distance traveled. This degeneracy reduces the number of distinct tours by a factor of n. Similarly, for a given circuit, it does not matter in which of two directions the salesperson travels. This fact further reduces the number of distinct tours by a factor of two. Thus, for an n-city tour, there are $n!/2n$ distinct circuits to consider.

For a five-city tour, there would be $120/10 = 12$ distinct tours—hardly a problem worthy of solution by a computer! A 10-city tour, however, has $3628800/20 = 181440$ distinct tours; a 30-city tour has over 4×10^{30} possibilities. Adding a single city to a tour results in an increase in the number of distinct tours by a factor of

$$\frac{(n+1)!/2(n+1)}{n!/2n} = n$$

Thus, a 31-city tour requires that we examine 31 times as many tours as we must for a 30-city tour. The amount of computation time required by a digital computer to solve this problem grows exponentially with the number of cities. The problem belongs to a class of problems known as NP-complete [2]. Because of the computational burden, it is often the case with optimization problems that a *good* solution found quickly is more desirable than the *best* solution found too late to be of use.

The Hopfield memory is well suited for this type of problem. The characteristic of interest is the rapid minimization of an energy function, E. Although the network is guaranteed to converge to a minimum of the energy function, there is no guarantee that it will converge to the *lowest* energy minimum: The solution will likely be a good one, but not necessarily the best. Because the PEs in the memory operate in parallel (in the actual circuit), computation time is minimized. In fact, adding another city would not significantly affect the time required to determine a solution, assuming the existence of the actual circuits with parallel PEs (the simulation of this system on a digital computer may still require a considerable amount of time).

To use the Hopfield memory for this application, we must find a way to map the problem onto the network architecture. This task is not a simple one. For example, there is no longer a set of well-defined vectors whose correlation matrix determines the connection weights for the network.

The first item is to develop a representation of the problem solutions that fits an architecture having a single array of PEs. We develop it by allowing a set of n PEs (for an n-city tour) to represent the n possible positions for a given city in the sequence of the tour. For a five-city tour, the outputs of five PEs could convey this information. For example, the five elements: 0 0 0 1 0 would indicate that the city in question was the fourth to be visited on the tour (we assume the high-gain limit for this discussion). There would be five such groups, each having information about the position of one city. Figure 4.10 illustrates this representation.

We shall follow the matrix format of Figure 4.10(b) henceforth, so the outputs will be labeled v_{Xi}, where the "X" subscript refers to the city, and the "i" subscript refers to a position on the tour. To account for the constraint that the tour begin and end at the same city, we must define $v_{X(n+1)} = v_{X1}$ and $v_{X0} = v_{Xn}$. The need for these definitions will become clear shortly.

To define the connection weight matrix, we shall begin with the energy function. Once it is defined, a suitable connection-weight matrix can be deduced.

An energy function must be constructed that satisfies the following criteria:

1. Energy minima must favor states that have each city only once on the tour.

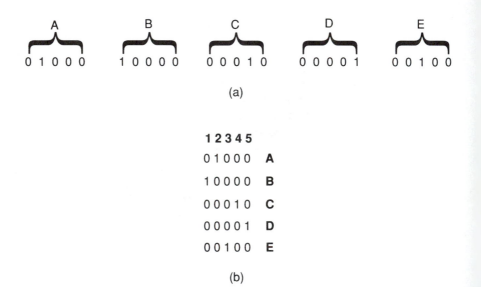

(a)

$$
\begin{array}{l}
\mathbf{1\,2\,3\,4\,5} \\
0\,1\,0\,0\,0 \quad \mathbf{A} \\
1\,0\,0\,0\,0 \quad \mathbf{B} \\
0\,0\,0\,1\,0 \quad \mathbf{C} \\
0\,0\,0\,0\,1 \quad \mathbf{D} \\
0\,0\,1\,0\,0 \quad \mathbf{E}
\end{array}
$$

(b)

Figure 4.10   (a) In this representation scheme for the output vectors in a five-city TSP problem, five units are associated with each of the five cities. The cities are labeled A through E. The position of the 1 within any group of five represents the location of that particular city in the sequence of the tour. For this example, the sequence is B–A–E–C–D, with the return to B assumed. Notice that $N = n^2$ PEs are required to represent the information for an n-city tour. (b) This matrix provides an alternative way of looking at the units. The PEs are arranged in a two-dimensional matrix configuration, with each row representing a city and each column representing a position on the sequence of the tour.

2. Energy minima must favor states that have each position on the tour only once. For example, two different cities cannot be the second city on the tour.

3. Energy minima must favor states that include all n cities.

4. Energy minima must favor states with the shortest total distances.

The energy function that satisfies these conditions is not easy to construct. We shall state the entire function, then analyze each term to show its contribution. The energy equation is

$$
E = \frac{A}{2} \sum_{X=1}^{n} \sum_{i=1}^{n} \sum_{\substack{j=1 \\ j \neq i}}^{n} v_{Xi} v_{Xj} + \frac{B}{2} \sum_{i=1}^{n} \sum_{X=1}^{n} \sum_{\substack{Y=1 \\ Y \neq X}}^{n} v_{Xi} v_{Yi}
$$

$$
+ \frac{C}{2} \left(\sum_{X=1}^{n} \sum_{i=1}^{n} v_{Xi} - n \right)^{2} \tag{4.29}
$$

$$
+ \frac{D}{2} \sum_{X=1}^{n} \sum_{\substack{Y=1 \\ Y \neq X}}^{n} \sum_{i=1}^{n} d_{XY} v_{Xi} (v_{Y,i+1} + v_{Y,i-1}).
$$

In the last term of this equation, if $i = 1$, then the quantity v_{Y0} appears. If $i = n$, then the quantity $v_{Y,n+1}$ appears. These results establish the need for the definitions, $v_{X(n+1)} = v_{X1}$ and $v_{X0} = v_{Xn}$, discussed previously.

Before we dissect this rather formidable energy equation, first note that d_{XY} represents the distance between city X and city Y, and that $d_{XY} = d_{YX}$. Furthermore, if the parameters, A, B, C, and D, are positive, then E is nonnegative.[6]

Let's take the first term in Eq. (4.29) and consider the five-city tour proposed in Figure 4.10. The product terms, $v_{Xi} v_{Xj}$, refer to a single city, X. The inner two sums result in a sum of products, $v_{Xi} v_{Xj}$, for all combinations of i and j as long as $i \neq j$. After the network has stabilized on a solution, and in the high-gain limit where $v \in \{0, 1\}$, all such terms will be zero if and only if there is a single $v_{Xi} = 1$ and all other $v_{Xi} = 0$. That is, the contribution of the first term in Eq. (4.29) will be zero if and only if a single city appears in each row of the PE matrix. This condition corresponds to the constraint that each city appear only once on the tour. Any other situation results in a positive value for this term in the energy equation.

Using a similar analysis, we can show that the second term in Eq. (4.29) can be shown to be zero, if and only if each column of the PE matrix contains a single value of 1. This condition corresponds to the second constraint on the problem; that each position on the tour has a unique city associated with it.

In the third term, $\sum_X \sum_i v_{Xi}$ is a simple summation of all n^2 output values. There should be only n of these terms that have a value of 1; all others

---

[6]The parameters, A, B, C, and D, in Eq. (4.29) have nothing to do with the cities labeled A, B, C, and D.

should be zero. Then the third term will be zero, since $\sum_X \sum_i v_{Xi} = n$. If more or less than n terms are equal to 1, then the sum will be greater or less than n, and the contribution of the third term in Eq. (4.29) will be greater than zero.

The final term in Eq. (4.29) computes a value proportional to the distance traveled on the tour. Thus, a minimum distance tour results in a minimum contribution of this term to the energy function.

Exercise 4.10: For the five-city example in Figure 4.10(b), show that the fourth term in Eq. (4.29) is

$$D(d_{BA} + d_{AE} + d_{EC} + d_{CD} + d_{DB})$$

The result of this analysis is that the energy function of Eq. (4.29) will be minimized only when a solution satisfies all four of the constraints (three strong, one weak) listed previously. Now we wish to construct a weight matrix that corresponds to this energy function so that the network will compute solutions properly.

As is often the case, it is easier to specify what the network should *not* do than to say what it should do. Therefore, the connection weight matrix is defined solely in terms of inhibitions between PEs. Instead of the double index that has been used up to now to describe the weight matrix, we adopt a four-index scheme that corresponds to the double-index scheme on the output vectors. The connection-matrix elements are the n^2 by n^2 quantities, $T_{Xi,Yj}$, where X and Y refer to the cities, and i and j refer to the positions on the tour.

The first term of the energy function is zero if and only if no more than one element in each row of the output-unit matrix is 1. This situation is favored if, when one unit in a row is on (i.e., it has a large output value relative to the others), then it inhibits the other units in the same row. This situation is essentially a *winner-take-all* competition, where the rich get richer at the expense of the poor. Consider the quantity

$$-A\delta_{XY}(1 - \delta_{ij})$$

where $\delta_{uv} = 1$ if $u = v$, and $\delta_{uv} = 0$ if $u \neq v$. The first delta is zero except on a single row where $X = Y$. The quantity in parentheses is 1 unless $i = j$. That factor ensures that a unit inhibits all other units on its row but does not inhibit itself. Therefore, if this quantity represented a connection weight between units, all units on a particular row would have an inhibitory connection of strength $-A$ to all other units on the same row. As the network evolved toward a solution, if one unit on a row began to show a larger output value than the others, it would tend to inhibit the other units on the same row. This situation is called *lateral inhibition*.

The second term in the energy function is zero if and only if a single unit in each column of the output-unit matrix is 1. The quantity

$$-B\delta_{ij}(1 - \delta_{XY})$$

causes a lateral inhibition between units on each column. The first delta ensures that this inhibition is confined to each column, where $i = j$. The second delta ensures that each unit does not inhibit itself.

The contribution of the third term in the energy equation is perhaps not so intuitive as the first two. Because it involves a sum of all of the outputs, it has a rather *global* character, unlike the first two terms, which were localized to rows and columns. Thus, we include a **global inhibition**, $-C$, such that each unit in the network is inhibited by this constant amount.

Finally, recall that the last term in the energy function contains information about the distance traveled on the tour. The desire to minimize this term can be translated into connections between units that inhibit the selection of adjacent cities in proportion to the distance between those cities. Consider the term

$$-Dd_{XY}(\delta_{j,i+1} + \delta_{j,i-1})$$

For a given column, j (i.e., for a given position on the tour), the two delta terms ensure that inhibitory connections are made only to units on adjacent columns. Units on adjacent columns represent cities that might come either before or after the cities on column j. The factor $-Dd_{XY}$ ensures that the units representing cities farther apart will receive the largest inhibitory signal.

We can now define the entire connection matrix by adding the contributions of the previous four paragraphs:

$$T_{Xi,Yj} = -A\delta_{XY}(1-\delta_{ij}) - B\delta_{ij}(1-\delta_{XY}) - C - Dd_{XY}(\delta_{j,i+1}+\delta_{j,i-1}) \quad \textbf{(4.30)}$$

The inhibitory connections between units are illustrated graphically in Figure 4.11.

To find a solution to the TSP, we must return to the equations that describe the time evolution of the network. Equation (4.24) is the one we want:

$$C\frac{du_i}{dt} = \sum_{j=1}^{N} T_{ij}v_j - \frac{u_i}{R_i} + I_i$$

Here, we have used N as the summation limit to avoid confusion with the n previously defined. Because all of the terms in T_{ij} contain arbitrary constants, and I_i can be adjusted to any desired values, we can divide this equation by C and write

$$\frac{du_i}{dt} = \sum_{j=1}^{N} T_{ij}v_j - \frac{u_i}{\tau} + I_i$$

where $\tau = RC$, the system time constant, and we have assumed that $R_i = R$ for all i.

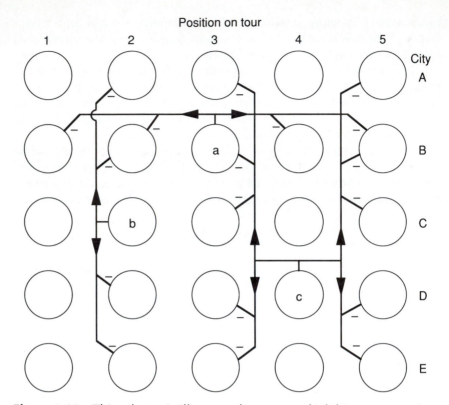

Figure 4.11   This schematic illustrates the pattern of inhibitory connections between PEs for the TSP problem: Unit a illustrates the inhibition between units on a single row, unit b shows the inhibition within a single column, and unit c shows the inhibition of units in adjacent columns. The global inhibition is not shown.

A digital simulation of this system requires that we integrate the above set of equations numerically. For a sufficiently small value of Δt, we can write

$$\frac{\Delta u_i}{\Delta t} = \sum_{j=1}^{N} T_{ij} v_j - \frac{u_i}{\tau} + I_i$$

(4.31)

$$\Delta u_i = \left(\sum_{j=1}^{N} T_{ij} v_j - \frac{u_i}{\tau} + I_i \right) \Delta t$$

Then, we can iteratively update the u_i values according to

$$u_i(t+1) = u_i(t) + \Delta u_i \qquad (4.32)$$

where Δu_i is given by Eq. (4.31). The final output values are then calculated using the output function

$$v_i = g_i(u_i)$$

Notice that, in these equations, we have returned to the subscript notation used in the discussion of the general system: v_i rather than v_{Yj}.

In the double-subscript notation, we have

$$u_{Xi}(t + 1) = u_{Xi}(t) + \Delta u_{Xi} \tag{4.33}$$

and

$$v_{Xi} = g_{Xi}(u_{Xi}) = \frac{1}{2}(1 + \tanh(\lambda u_{Xi})) \tag{4.34}$$

If we substitute $T_{Xi,Yj}$ from Eq. (4.30) into Eq. (4.31), and define the external inputs as $I_{Xi} = Cn'$, with n' a constant, and C equal to the C in Eq. (4.30), the result takes on an interesting form (see Exercise 4.11):

$$\Delta u_{Xi} = \left[-\frac{u_{Xi}}{\tau} - A\sum_{\substack{j=1 \\ j \neq i}}^{n} v_{Xj} - B\sum_{\substack{Y=1 \\ Y \neq X}}^{n} v_{Yi} - C\left(\sum_{X=1}^{n}\sum_{j=1}^{n} v_{Xj} - n'\right) \right.$$

$$\tag{4.35}$$

$$\left. - D\sum_{\substack{Y=1 \\ Y \neq X}}^{n} d_{XY}(v_{Y,i+1} + v_{Y,i-1}) \right]\Delta t$$

Exercise 4.11: Assume that $n' = n$ in Eq. (4.35). Then, the sum of terms, $-A(\ldots) - B(\ldots) - C(\ldots) - D(\ldots)$, has a simple relationship to the TSP energy function in Eq. (4.29). What is that relationship?

Exercise 4.12: Using the double-subscript notation on the outputs of the PEs, v_{C3} refers to the output of the unit that represents city C in position 3 of the tour. This unit is also element v_{33} of the output-unit matrix. What is the general equation that converts the dual subscripts of the matrix notation, v_{jk} into the proper single subscript of the vector notation, v_i?

Exercise 4.13: There are 25 possible connections to unit $v_{C3} = v_{33}$ from other units in the five-city tour problem. Determine the values of the resistors, $R_{ij} = 1/|T_{ij}|$, that form those connections.

To complete the solution of the TSP, suitable values for the constants must be chosen, along with the initial values of the u_{Xi}. Hopfield [6] provides parameters suitable for a 10-city problem: $A = B = 500$, $C = 200$, $D = 500$, $\tau = 1$, $\lambda = 50$, and $n' = 15$. Notice that it is not necessary to choose $n' = n$. Because n' enters the equations through the external inputs, $I_i = Cn'$, it can be used as another adjustable parameter. These parameters must be empirically chosen, and those for a 10-city tour will not necessarily work for tours of different sizes.

We might be tempted to make all of the initial values of the u_{Xi} equal to a constant u_{00} such that, at $t = 0$,

$$\sum_X \sum_i v_{Xi} = 10$$

because that is what we expect that particular sum to be when the network has stabilized on a solution. Assigning initial values in that manner, however, has the effect of placing the system on an unstable equilibrium point, much like a ball placed at the exact top of a hill. Without at least a slight nudge, the ball would remain there forever. Given that nudge, however, the ball would roll down the hill. We can give our TSP system a nudge by adding a random noise term to the u_{00} values, so that $u_{Xi} = u_{00} + \delta u_{Xi}$, where δu_{Xi} is the random noise term, which may be different for each unit.

In the ball-on-the-hill analogy, the *direction* of the nudge determines the direction in which the ball rolls off the hill. Likewise, different random-noise selections for the initial u_{Xi} values may result in different final stable states. Refer back to the discussion of optimization problems earlier in this section, where we said that a good solution now may be better than the best solution later. Hopfield's solution to the TSP may not always find the best solution (the one with the shortest distance possible), but repeated trials have shown that the network generally settles on tours at or near the minimum distance. Figure 4.12 shows a graphical representation of how a network would evolve toward a solution.

We have discussed this example at great length to show both the power and the complexity of the Hopfield network. The example also illustrates a general principle about neural networks: For a given problem, finding an appropriate representation of the data or constraints is often the most difficult part of the solution.

4.4   SIMULATING THE BAM

As you may already suspect, the implementation of the BAM network simulator will be straightforward. The only difficulty is the implementation of bidirectional connections between the layers, and, with a little finesse, this is a relatively easy problem to overcome. We shall begin by describing the general nature of the problems associated with modeling bidirectional connections in a sequential memory array. From there, we will present the data structures needed to overcome these problems while remaining compatible with our basic simulator. We conclude this section with a presentation of the algorithms needed to implement the BAM.

4.4.1   Bidirectional-Connection Considerations

Let us first consider the basic data structures we have defined for our simulator. We have assumed that all network PEs will be organized into layers, with connections primarily between the layers. Further, we have decided that the

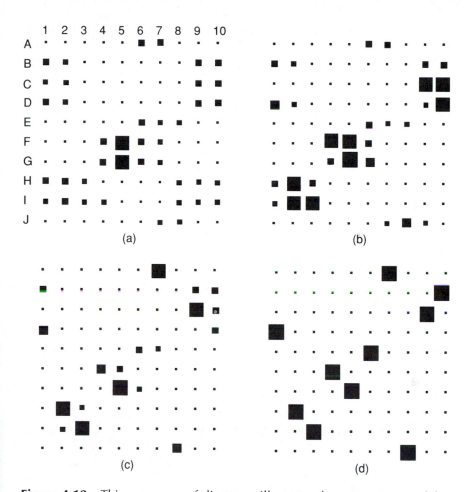

Figure 4.12   This sequence of diagrams illustrates the convergence of the Hopfield network for a 10-city TSP tour. The output values, v_{Xi}, are represented as squares at each location in the output-unit matrix. The size of the square is proportional to the magnitude of the output value. (a, b, c) At the intermediate steps, the system has not yet settled on a valid tour. The magnitude of the output values for these intermediate steps can be thought of as the current estimate of the confidence that a particular city will end up in a particular position on the tour. (d) The network has stabilized on the valid tour, DHIFGEAJCB. *Source: Reprinted with permission of Springer-Verlag, Heidelberg, from J. J. Hopfield and D. W. Tank, "Neural computation of decisions in optimization problems."* Biological Cybernetics, *52:141–152, 1985.*

individual PEs within any layer will be simulated by processing *inputs*, with no provision for processing output connections. With respect to modeling bidirectional connections, we are faced with the dilemma of using a single connection as input to two different PEs. Thus, our parallel array structures for modeling network connections are no longer valid.

As an example, consider the weight matrix illustrated on page 136 as part of the discussion in Section 4.2. For clarity, we will consider this matrix as being an $R \times C$ array, where

$$R = \text{rows} = 6$$

and

$$C = \text{columns} = 10.$$

Next, consider the implementation of this matrix in computer memory, as depicted in Figure 4.13. Since memory is organized as a one-dimensional linear array of cells (or bytes, words, etc.), most modern computer languages will allocate and maintain this matrix as a one-dimensional array of R vectors, each C cells long, arranged sequentially in the computer memory.[7] In this implementation, access to each row vector requires at least one multiplication (row index $\times$ number of columns per row) and an addition (to determine the memory address of the row, offset from the base address of the array). However, once the beginning of the row has been located, access to the individual components within the vector is simply an increment operation.

In the column-vector case, access to the data is not quite as easy. Simply put, each component of the column vector must be accessed by performance of a multiplication (as before, to access the appropriate row), plus an addition to locate the appropriate cell. The penalty imposed by this approach is such that, for the entire column vector to be accessed, R multiplications must be performed. To access each element in the matrix as a component of a column vector, we must do $R \times C$ multiplications, or one for each element—a time-consuming process.

4.4.2   BAM Simulator Data Structures

Since we have chosen to use the array-based model for our basic network data structure, we are faced with the complicated (and CPU-time-consuming) problem of accessing the network weight matrix first as a set of row vectors for the propagation from layer **x** to layer **y**, then accessing weights as a set of column vectors for the propagation in the other direction. Further complicating the situation is the fact that we have chosen to isolate the weight vectors in our network data structure, accessing each array indirectly through the intermediate

---

[7]FORTRAN, which uses a column-major array organization, is the notable exception.

`weight_ptr` array. If we hold strictly to this scheme, we must significantly modify the design of our simulator to allow access to the connections from both layers of PEs, a situation illustrated in Figure 4.14. As shown in this diagram, all the connection weights will be contained in a set of arrays associated with one layer of PEs. The connections back to the other layer must then be individually accessed by indexing into each array to extract the appropriate element.

To solve this dilemma, let's now consider a slight modification to the conceptual model of the BAM. Until now, we have considered the connections between the layers as one set of *bidirectional* paths; that is, signals can pass

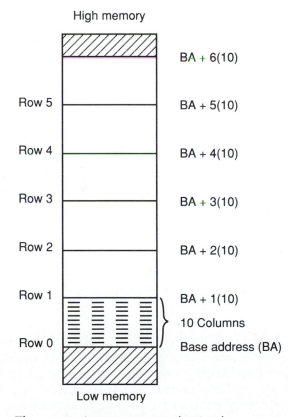

Figure 4.13 The row-major structure used to implement a matrix is shown. In this technique, memory is allocated sequentially so that column values within the same row are adjacent. This structure allows the computer to step through all values in a single row by simply incrementing a memory pointer.

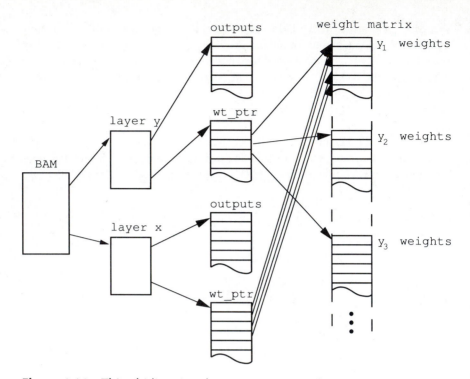

Figure 4.14   This bidirectional connection implementation uses our standard data structures. Here, the connection arrays located by the layer **y** structure are identical to those previously described for the backpropagation simulator. However, the pointers associated with the layer **x** structure locate the connection in the first `weights` array that is associated with the column weight vector. Hence, stepping through connections to layer **x** requires locating the connection in each `weights` array at the same offset from the beginning of array as the first connection.

from layer **x** *to* layer **y** as well as *from* layer **y** *to* layer **x**. If we instead consider the connections as two sets of *unidirectional* paths, we can logically implement the same network if we simply connect the outputs of the **x** layer to the inputs on the **y** layer, and, similarly, connect the outputs of the **y** layer to the inputs on the **x** layer. To complete this model, we must initialize the connections from **x** to **y** with the predetermined weight matrix, while the connections from **y** to **x** must contain the transpose of the weight matrix. This strategy allows us to process only *inputs* at each PE, and, since the connections are always accessed in the desired row-major form, allows efficient signal propagation through the simulator, regardless of direction.

The disadvantage to this approach is that it consumes twice as much memory as does the single-matrix implementation. There is not much that we can do to solve this problem other than reverting to the single-matrix model. Even a linked-list implementation will not solve the problem, as it will require approximately three times the memory of the single-matrix model. Thus, in terms of memory consumption, the single-matrix model is the most efficient implementation. However, as we have already seen, there are performance issues that must be considered when we use the single matrix. We therefore choose to implement the double matrix, because run-time performance, especially in a large network application, must be good enough to prevent long periods of *dead time* while the human operator waits for the computer to arrive at a solution.

The remainder of the network is completely compatible with our generic network data structures. For the BAM, we begin by defining a network with two layers:

```
record BAM =
  X : ^layer;          {pointer to first layer record}
  Y : ^layer;          {pointer to second layer record}
end record;
```

As before, we now consider the implementation of the layers themselves. In the case of the BAM, a layer structure is simply a record used to contain pointers to the `outputs` and `weight_ptr` arrays. Such a record is defined by the structure

```
record LAYER =
  OUTS : ^integer[];       {pointer to node outputs array}
  WEIGHTS : ^^integer[];   {pointer to weight_ptr array}
end record;
```

Notice that we have specified integer values for the `outputs` and `weights` in the network. This is a benefit derived from the binary nature of the network, and from the fact that the individual connection weights are given by the dot product between two integer vectors, resulting in an integer value. We use integers in this model, since most computers can process integer values much faster than they can floating-point values. Hence, the performance improvement of the simulator for large BAM applications justifies the use of integers.

We now define the three arrays needed to store the node `outputs`, the connection `weights`, and the intermediate `weight_ptr`. These arrays will be sized dynamically to conform to the desired BAM network structure. In the case of the `outputs` arrays, one will contain x integer values, whereas the other must be sized to contain y integers. The `weight_ptr` array will contain a memory pointer for each PE on the layer; that is, x pointers will be required to locate the connection arrays for each node on the x layer, and y pointers for the connections to the y layer.

Conversely, each of the `weights` arrays must be sized to accommodate an integer value for each connection *to* the layer *from* the input layer. Thus, each weights array on the x layer will contain y values, whereas the weights arrays on the y layer will each contain x values. The complete BAM data structure is illustrated in Figure 4.15.

4.4.3   BAM Initialization Algorithms

As we have noted earlier, the BAM is different from most of the other ANS networks discussed in this text, in that it is not *trained*; rather, it is *initialized*. Specifically, it is initialized from the set of training vectors that it will be required to recall. To develop this algorithm, we use the formula used previously to generate the weight matrix for the BAM, given by Eq. (4.6), and repeated here

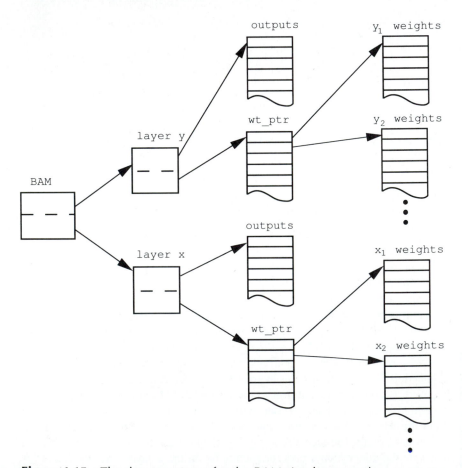

Figure 4.15   The data structures for the BAM simulator are shown. Notice the difference in the implementation of the connection arrays in this model and in the single-matrix model described earlier.

for reference:

$$\mathbf{w} = \mathbf{y}_1\mathbf{x}_1^t + \mathbf{y}_2\mathbf{x}_2^t + \cdots + \mathbf{y}_L\mathbf{x}_L^t$$

We can translate this general formula into one that can be used to determine any specific connection weight, given L training pairs to be encoded in the BAM. This new equation, which will form the basis of the routine that we will use to initialize the connection weights in the BAM simulation, is given by

$$w_{RC} = \sum_{i=1}^{L} \mathbf{y}_i[r]\, \mathbf{x}_i[c] \qquad (4.36)$$

where the variables r and c denote the row and column position of the weight value of interest. We assume that, for purposes of computer simulation, each of the training vectors $\mathbf{x}$ and $\mathbf{y}$ are one-dimensional arrays of length C and R, respectively. We also presume that the calculation will be performed only to determine the weights for the connections *from* layer $\mathbf{x}$ *to* layer $\mathbf{y}$. Once the values for these connections are determined, the connections from $\mathbf{y}$ to $\mathbf{x}$ are simply the transpose of this weight matrix.

Using this equation, we can now write a routine to determine any weight value for the BAM. The following algorithm presumes that all the training pairs to be encoded are contained in two external, two-dimensional matrices named XT and YT. These arrays will contain the patterns to be encoded in the BAM, organized as L instances of either $\mathbf{x}$ or $\mathbf{y}$ vectors. Thus, the dimensions of the XT and YT initialization matrices are $L \times C$ and $L \times R$ respectively.

```
function weight (r,c,L:integer; XT,YT:^integer[][])
                    return integer;
{determine and return weight value for position r,c}

var i : integer;           {loop iteration counter}
    x,y : ^integer[][];    {local array pointers}
    sum : integer;         {local accumulator}

begin
  sum = 0;                 {initialize accumulator}
  x = XT;                  {initialize x pointer}
  y = YT;                  {initialize y pointer}

  for i = 1 to L do        {for all training pairs}
      sum = sum + y[i][r] * x[i][c];
  end do;

  return (sum);            {return the result}
end function;
```

The `weight` function allows us to compute the value to be associated with any particular connection. We will now extend that basic function into a general routine to initialize all the `weights` arrays for all the input connections

to the PEs in layer **y**. This algorithm uses two functions, called `rows_in` and
`cols_in`, that return the number of rows and columns in a given matrix. The
implementation of these two algorithms is left to the reader as an exercise.

```
procedure initialize (Y:^layer; XT,YT:^integer[][]);
{initialize all input connections to a layer, Y}

var connects: ^integer[];   {connection pointer}
    units: ^integer[];      {pointers into weight_ptrs}
    L,R,C : integer;        {size-of variables}
    i, j: integer;          {iteration counters}

begin
  units = Y^.WEIGHTS;       {locate weight_ptr array}
  L = rows_in (XT);         {number of training patterns}
  R = cols_in (YT);         {dimension of Y vector}
  C = cols_in (XT);         {dimension of X vector}

  for i = 1 to length(units) do {for all units on layer}
      connects = unit[i];   {get pointer to weight array}

      for j = 1 to length(connects) do
                              {for all connections to unit}
          connects[j] = weight (R,C,L,XT,YT);
                                    {initialize weight}
      end do;
  end do;
end procedure;
```

We indicated earlier that the connections from layer **y** to layer **x** could be
initialized by use of the transpose of the weight matrix computed for the inputs
to layer **y**. We could develop another routine to copy data from one set of
arrays to another, but inspection of the `initialize` algorithm just described
indicates that another algorithm will not be needed. By substituting the **x** layer
record for the **y**, and swapping the order of the two input training arrays, we can
use `initialize` to initialize the input connections to the **x** layer as well, and
we will have reduced the amount of code needed to implement the simulator.
On the other hand, the transpose operation is a relatively easy algorithm to write,
and, since it involves only copying data from one array to another, it is also
extremely fast. We therefore leave to you the choice of which of these two
approaches to use to complete the BAM initialization.

4.4.4 BAM Signal Propagation

Now that we have created and initialized the BAM, we need only to implement
an algorithm to perform the signal propagation through the network. Here again,
we would like this routine to be general enough to propagate signals to either
layer of the BAM. We will therefore design the routine such that the direction

of signal propagation will be determined by the order of the input arguments to the routine. For simplicity, we also assume that the layer outputs arrays have been initialized to contain the patterns to be propagated.

Before we proceed, however, note that the desired algorithm generality implies that this routine will not be sufficient to implement completely the iterated signal-propagation function needed to allow the BAM to stabilize. This iteration must be performed by a higher-level routine. We will therefore design the unidirectional BAM propagation routine as a function that returns the number of patterns changed in the receiving layer, so that the iterated propagation routine can easily determine when to stop.

With these concerns in mind, we can now design the unidirectional signal-propagation routine. Such a routine will take this general form:

```
function propagate (X,Y:^layer) return integer;
{propagate signals from layer X to layer Y}

var changes, i, j: integer;    {local counters}
    ins, outs : ^integer[];    {local pointers}
    connects : ^integer[];     {locate connections}
    sum : integer;             {sum of products}

begin
  outs = Y^.OUTS;              {locate start of Y array}

  changes = 0;                 {initialize counter}

  for i = 1 to length(outs) do  {for all output units}
     ins = X^.OUTS;                {locate X outputs}
     connects= Y^.WEIGHTS[i];      {find connections}
     sum = 0;                      {initial sum}

     for j = 1 to length(ins) do  {for all inputs}
         sum = sum + ins[j] * connects[j];
     end do;

     if (sum < 0)                 {if negative sum}
     then sum = -1                {use -1 as output}
     else if (sum > 0)            {if positive sum}
          then sum = 1            {use 1 as output}
          else sum = outs[i]; {else use old output}

     if (sum != outs[i])          {if unit changed}
     then changes = changes + 1;

     outs[i] = sum;               {store new output}
  end do;

  return (changes);              {number of changes}
end function;
```

To complete the BAM simulator, we will need a top-level routine to perform the bidirectional signal propagation. We will use the `propagate` routine described previously to perform the signal propagation between layers, and we will iterate until no units change state on two successive passes, as that will indicate that the BAM has stabilized. Here again, we assume that the input vectors have been initialized by an external process prior to calling `recall`.

```
procedure recall (net:BAM);
{propagate signals in the BAM until stabilized}

var delta : integer;        {how many units change}

begin
  delta = 100;              {arbitrary non-zero value}

  while (delta != 0)        {until two successive passes}
    do
      delta = 0;            {reset to zero}
      delta = delta + propagate (net^.X, net^.Y);
      delta = delta + propagate (net^.Y, net^.X);
    end do;
end procedure;
```

Programming Exercises

4.1. Define the pseudocode algorithms for the functions `rows_in` and `cols_in` as described in the text.

4.2. Implement the BAM simulator described in Section 4.4, adding a routine to initialize the input vectors from patterns read from a data file. Test the BAM with the two training vectors described in Exercise 4.4 in Section 4.2.3.

4.3. Modify the BAM simulator so that the initial direction of signal propagation can be specified by the user at run time. Repeat Exercise 4.2, starting signal propagation first *from* **x** *to* **y**, then *from* **y** *to* **x**. Describe the results for each case.

4.4. Develop an encoding scheme to represent the following training pairs for a BAM application. Initialize your simulator with the training data, and then apply a "noisy" input pattern to the input (Hint: One way to do this exercise is to encode each character as a seven-bit ASCII code, letting -1 represent a logic 0 and $+1$ represent a logic 1). Does your BAM return the correct results?

X	Y
CAT	TABBY
DOG	ROVER
FLY	PESKY

Suggested Readings

Introductory articles on the BAM, by Bart Kosko, appear in the IEEE ICNN proceedings and *Byte* magazine [9, 10]. Two of Kosko's papers discuss how to make the BAM weights adaptive [8, 11].

The *Scientific American* article by Tank and Hopfield provides a good introduction to the Hopfield network as we have discussed the latter in this chapter [13]. It is also worthwhile to review some of the earlier papers that discuss the development of the network and the use of the network for optimization problems such as the TSP [4, 5, 6, 7].

The issue of the information storage capacity of associative memories is treated in detail in the paper by Kuh and Dickinson [12].

The paper by Tagliarini and Page, on "solving constraint satisfaction problems with neural networks," is a good complement to the discussion of the TSP in this chapter [14].

Bibliography

[1] Edward J. Beltrami. *Mathematics for Dynamic Modeling*. Academic Press, Orlando, FL, 1987.

[2] M. R. Garey and D. S. Johnson. *Computers and Intractability*. W. H. Freeman, New York, 1979.

[3] Morris W. Hirsch and Stephen Smale. *Differential Equations, Dynamical Systems, and Linear Algebra*. Academic Press, New York, 1974.

[4] John J. Hopfield. Neural networks and physical systems with emergent collective computational abilities. *Proc. Natl. Acad. Sci. USA*, 79:2554–2558, April 1982. Biophysics.

[5] John J. Hopfield. Neurons with graded response have collective computational properties like those of two-state neurons. *Proc. Natl. Acad. Sci. USA*, 81:3088–3092, May 1984. Biophysics.

[6] John J. Hopfield and David W. Tank. "Neural" computation of decisions in optimization problems. *Biological Cybernetics*, 52:141–152, 1985.

[7] John J. Hopfield and David W. Tank. Computing with neural circuits: A model. *Science*, 233:625–633, August 1986.

[8] Bart Kosko. Adaptive bidirectional associative memories. *Applied Optics*, 26(23):4947–4960, December 1987.

[9] Bart Kosko. Competitive bidirectional associative memories. In *Proceedings of the IEEE First International Conference on Neural Networks*, San Diego, CA, II: 759–766, June 1987.

[10] Bart Kosko. Constructing an associative memory. *Byte*, 12(10):137–144, September 1987.

[11] Bart Kosko. Bidirectional associative memories. *IEEE Transactions on Systems, Man, and Cybernetics*, 18(1):49–60, January–February 1988.

[12] Anthony Kuh and Bradley W. Dickinson. Information capacity of associative memories. *IEEE Transactions on Information Theory*, 35(1):59–68, January 1989.

[13] David W. Tank and John J. Hopfield. Collective computation in neuronlike circuits. *Scientific American*, 257(6):104–114, December 1987.

[14] Gene A. Tagliarini and Edward W. Page. Solving constraint satisfaction problems with neural networks. In *Proceedings of the First IEEE Conference on Neural Networks*, San Diego, CA, III: 741–747, June 1987.

C H A P T E R

Simulated Annealing

The neural networks discussed in Chapters 2, 3, and 4 relied on the minimization of some function during either the learning process (Adaline and back-propagation) or the recall process (BAM and Hopfield network). The technique employed to perform this minimization is essentially the opposite of a standard heuristic used to find the maximum of a function. That technique is known as **hill climbing**.

The term *hill climbing* derives from a simple analogy. Imagine that you are standing at some unknown location in an area of hilly terrain, with the goal of walking up to the highest peak. The problem is that it is foggy and you cannot see more than a few feet in any direction. Barring obvious solutions, such as waiting for the fog to lift, a logical way to proceed would be to begin walking in the steepest upward direction possible. If you walk only upward at each step, you will eventually reach a spot where the only possible way to go is down. At this point, you are at the top of a hill. The question that remains is whether this hill is indeed the highest hill possible. Unfortunately, without further extensive exploration, that question cannot be answered.

The methods we have used to minimize energy or error functions in previous chapters often suffer from a similar problem: If only downward steps are allowed, when the minimum is reached it may not be the lowest minimum possible. The lowest minimum is referred to as the **global minimum**, and any other minimum that exists is called a **local minimum**.

It is not always necessary, or even desirable, to reach the global minimum during a search. In one instance, it is impossible to reach any but the global minimum. In the case of the Adaline, the error surface was shown to be a hyperparaboloid with a single minimum. Thus, finding a local minimum is impossible. In the BAM and discrete Hopfield model, we store *items* at the vertices of the Hamming hypercube, each of which occupies a minimum of the energy surface. When recalling an item, we begin with some partial information and seek the local minimum nearest to the starting point. Hopefully, the item stored at that local minimum will represent the complete item of interest. The point we reach may or may not lie at the global minimum of the energy function. Thus, we do not care whether the minimum that we reach is global; we desire only that it correspond to the data in which we are interested.

The generalized delta rule, used as the learning algorithm for the back-propagation network, performs gradient descent down an error surface with a topology that is not well understood. It is possible, as is seen occasionally in practice, that the system will end up in a local minimum. The effect is that the network appears to stop learning; that is, the error does not continue to decrease with additional training. Whether or not this situation is acceptable depends on the value of the error when the minimum is reached. If the error is acceptable, then it does not matter whether or not the minimum is global. If the error is unacceptable, the problem often can be remedied by retraining of the network with different learning parameters, or with a different random weight initialization. In the case of backpropagation, we see that finding the global minimum is desirable, but we can live with a local minimum in many cases.

A further example of local-minima effects is found in the continuous Hop-field memory as the latter is used to perform an optimization calculation. The traveling-salesperson problem is a well-defined problem subject to certain con-straints. The salesperson *must* visit each city once and only once on the tour. This restriction is known as a *strong constraint*. A violation of this constraint is not permitted in any real solution. An additional constraint is that the to-tal distance traveled must be minimized. Failure to find the solution with the absolute minimum distance does not invalidate the solution completely. Any solution that does not have the minimum distance results in a penalty or cost increase. It is up to the individual to decide how much cost is acceptable in return for a relatively quick solution. The minimum-distance requirement is an example of a *weak constraint*; it is desirable, but not absolutely necessary. Finding the absolute shortest route corresponds to finding the global minimum of the energy function. As with backpropagation, we would like to find the global minimum, but will settle for a local minimum, provided the cost is not too high.

In the following sections, we shall present one method for reducing the possibility of falling into a local minimum. That method is called **simulated annealing** because of its strong analogy to the physical annealing process done to metals and other substances. Along the way, we shall briefly explore a few concepts in information theory, and discuss the relationship between information theory and a branch of physics known as *statistical mechanics*. Because we do not expect that you are an information theorist or a physicist, the discussion is somewhat brief. However, we do assume a knowledge of basic probability theory, a discussion of which can be found in many fundamental texts.

5.1 INFORMATION THEORY AND STATISTICAL MECHANICS

In this section we shall present a few topics from the fields of information theory and statistical mechanics. We choose to discuss only those topics that have relevance to the discussion of simulated annealing, so that the treatment is brief.

5.1.1 Information-Theory Concepts

Every computer scientist understands what a **bit** is. It is a **binary digit**, a thing that has a value of either 1 or 0. Memory in a digital computer is implemented as a series of bits joined together logically to form *bytes*, or *words*. In the mathematical discipline of information theory, however, a bit is something else. Suppose some event, e, occurs with some probability, $P(e)$. If we observe that e has occurred, then, according to information theory, we have received

$$I(e) = \log_2 \frac{1}{P(e)} \tag{5.1}$$

bits of information, where $\log_2$ refers to the log to the base 2.

You may need to get used to this notion. For example, suppose that $P(e) = 1/2$, so there is a 50-percent chance that the event occurs. In that case, $I(e) = \log_2 2 = 1$ bit. We can, therefore, define a bit as the amount of information received when one of two equally probable alternatives is specified. If we know for sure that an event will occur, its occurrence provides us with no information: $\log_2 1 = 0$. Some reflection on these ideas will help you to understand the intent of Eq. (5.1). The most information is received when we have absolutely no clue regarding whether the event will occur. Notice also that bits can occur in fractional quantities.

Suppose we have an information source, which has a sequential output of symbols from the set, $S = \{s_1, s_2, \ldots, s_q\}$, with each symbol occurring with a fixed probability, $\{P(s_1), P(s_2), \ldots, P(s_q)\}$. A simple example would be an automatic character generator that types letters according to a certain probability distribution. If the probability of sending each symbol is independent of symbols previously sent, then we have what is called a **zero-memory source**. For such an information source, the amount of information received from each symbol is

$$I(s_i) = \log_2 \frac{1}{P(s_i)} \tag{5.2}$$

The average amount of information received per symbol is

$$\langle I \rangle = \sum_{i=1}^{q} P(s_i) I(s_i) \tag{5.3}$$

$$= -\sum_{i=1}^{q} P(s_i) \log_2 P(s_i)$$

Equation (5.3) is the definition of the **entropy**, $H(S)$, of the source, S:

$$H(S) = -\sum_{i=1}^{q} P(s_i) \log_2 P(s_i) \qquad (5.4)$$

In a physical system, entropy is associated with a measure of disorder in the system. It is the same in information theory. The most disorderly system is the one where all symbols occur with equal probability. Thus, the maximum information (maximum entropy) is received from such a system.

Exercise 5.1: Show that the average amount of information received from a zero-memory source having q symbols occurring with equal probabilities, $1/q$, is

$$H = +\log_2 q \qquad (5.5)$$

Exercise 5.2: Consider two sources, each of which sends a sequence of symbols whose possible values are the 26 letters of the English alphabet and the "space" character. The first source, S_1, sends the letters with equal probability. The second source, S_2, sends letters with the probabilities equal to their relative frequency of occurrence in English text. Which source transmits the most information? How many bits of information per symbol are transmitted by each source on the average?

We can demonstrate explicitly that the maximum entropy occurs for a source whose symbol probabilities are all equal. Suppose we have two sources, S_1 and S_2, each containing q symbols, where the symbol probabilities are $\{P_{1i}\}$ and $\{P_{2i}\}$, $i = 1,\ldots,q$, and the probabilities are normalized so that $\sum_i P_{1i} = \sum_i P_{2i} = 1$. The difference in entropy between these two sources is

$$H_1 - H_2 = -\sum_{i=1}^{q} [P_{1i} \log_2 P_{1i} - P_{2i} \log_2 P_{2i}]$$

By using the trick of adding and subtracting the same quantity from the right side of the equation, we can write

$$H_1 - H_2 = -\sum_{i=1}^{q} [P_{1i} \log_2 P_{1i} + P_{1i} \log_2 P_{2i} - P_{1i} \log_2 P_{2i} - P_{2i} \log_2 P_{2i}]$$

$$= -\sum_{i=1}^{q} [P_{1i} \log_2 \frac{P_{1i}}{P_{2i}} + (P_{1i} - P_{2i}) \log_2 P_{2i}] \qquad (5.6)$$

$$= -\sum_{i=1}^{q} P_{1i} \log_2 \frac{P_{1i}}{P_{2i}} - \sum_{i=1}^{q} (P_{1i} - P_{2i}) \log_2 P_{2i}$$

If we identify S_2 as a source with equiprobable symbols, then $H_2 = H = +\log_2 q$, as in Eq. (5.5). Since $\log_2 P_{2i} = \log_2 \frac{1}{q}$ is independent of i, and

$\sum_i (P_{1i} - P_{2i}) = \sum_i P_{1i} - \sum_i P_{2i} = 1 - 1 = 0$, the second sum in Eq. (5.6) is zero. We are left with

$$H_1 + (-\log_2 q) = -\sum_{i=1}^{q} P_{1i} \log_2 \frac{P_{1i}}{P_{2i}}$$

or

$$H_1 + (-\log_2 q) = \sum_{i=1}^{q} P_{1i} \log_2 \frac{P_{2i}}{P_{1i}} \tag{5.7}$$

We shall now employ the inequality, $\log_2 x \le x - 1$. Using this inequality, we know that the right side of Eq. (5.7) obeys the inequality

$$\sum_{i=1}^{q} P_{1i} \log_2 \frac{P_{2i}}{P_{1i}} \le \sum_{i=1}^{q} P_{1i}(\frac{P_{2i}}{P_{1i}} - 1)$$

$$\le \sum_{i=1}^{q} P_{2i} - \sum_{i-1}^{q} P_{1i}$$

$$\le 0$$

Then

$$H_1 - (+\log_2 q) \le 0 \tag{5.8}$$

The only way the equality can hold in Eq. (5.8) is if S_1 is also an equiprobable source, so that $H_1 = +\log_2 q$. Otherwise, the entropy of S_1 is always going to be less than the source with equiprobable symbols.

The right side of Eq. (5.7) has a meaning independent of whether S_2 is a source with equiprobable symbols. Given any two arbitrary sources, S_1 and S_2, we can define the quantity

$$G = \sum_{i=1}^{q} P_{1i} \log_2 \frac{P_{1i}}{P_{2i}} \tag{5.9}$$

which is the negative of the right side of Eq. (5.7). The quantity G is called the **information gain** or **asymmetric divergence** between two sources. If we expand Eq. (5.9), G *almost* looks like the difference in entropies between two sources:

$$G = \sum_{i=1}^{q} P_{1i} \log_2 P_{1i} - \sum_{i=1}^{q} P_{1i} \log_2 P_{2i} \tag{5.10}$$

The second term on the right side of Eq. (5.10), however, is not the entropy of a source. The $\log_2 P_{2i}$ terms are weighted by the S_1 probabilities, P_{1i}, rather than by the S_2 probabilities, P_{2i}.

G can be thought of as a measure of the distance, in bits, *from* source S_2 *to* source S_1. That distance calculation has the symbol probabilities of S_2 weighted according to their relative importance in matching the symbol probabilities in

S_1. In other words, the calculation of the effective distance from S_2 to S_1 places more emphasis on those symbols that have a higher probability of occurrence in S_1, which is why the term *asymmetric* was used in the definition of G. If the identities of P_{1i} and P_{2i} were reversed in Eqs. (5.9) and (5.10), the calculated value of G would be different. In that case, we would be finding the distance *from S_1 to S_2*, instead of the other way around.

We now conclude our brief introduction to information theory. In the next section, we discuss some elementary concepts in statistical mechanics. You should be alert to similarities between the discussion in the present section and that in the next.

5.1.2   Statistical-Mechanics Concepts

Statistical mechanics is a branch of physics that deals with systems containing a large number of particles, usually so large that the gross properties of the system cannot be determined by evaluation of the contributions of each particle individually. Instead, overall properties are determined by the average behavior of a number of identical systems. A collection of identical systems is called an **ensemble**, and is characterized by the average of its constituent systems, along with the statistical fluctuations about the average. For example, the average energy of an ensemble is the statistical average of the energies of the ensemble's constituent systems, each weighted by the probability that the system has a particular energy. If P_r is the probability that a system has an energy, E_r, then the average energy of the ensemble of such systems is

$$\langle E \rangle = \sum_r P_r E_r \qquad (5.11)$$

An important class of systems are those that are in thermal contact with a much larger system called a **heat reservoir**. A heat reservoir is characterized by the fact that any thermal interaction with the smaller system in question results in only infinitesimal changes in the properties of the reservoir, whereas the smaller system may undergo substantial change, until an equilibrium condition is reached. An example would be a warm bottle of wine submersed in a large, cold lake. As an equilibrium is reached, the temperature of the wine might change considerably, whereas the overall temperature of the lake probably would change by only an immeasurable amount.[1]

If we were to examine a large number of identical wine bottles, immersed in identical cold lakes (or the same lake if it were very big compared to the total volume of wine), we would find some variation in the total energy contained in the wine of different bottles. Furthermore, we would find that the probability,

---

[1] We have been using terms such as *energy, equilibrium*, and *temperature* without supplying precise definitions. We are relying on your intuitive understanding of these concepts, and of others that will appear later, so that we can avoid a lengthy treatment of the subject at hand.

P_r, that a wine bottle was at a certain energy, E_r, was proportional to an exponential factor:

$$P_r = Ce^{-\beta E_r}$$

where β is a parameter that depends on the temperature of the lake. Since the sum of all such probabilities must be 1, $\sum_r P_r = 1$, the proportionality constant must be

$$C = \left(\sum_r e^{-\beta E_r} \right)^{-1}$$

so

$$P_r = \frac{e^{-\beta E_r}}{\sum_r e^{-\beta E_r}} \tag{5.12}$$

The quantity, C^{-1}, has a special name and symbol in statistical mechanics: It is called the **partition function**, and the usual symbol for it is Z:

$$Z = \sum_r e^{-\beta E_r} \tag{5.13}$$

We can write the average energy of our wine bottle as

$$\langle E \rangle = \frac{\sum_r e^{-\beta E_r} E_r}{Z} \tag{5.14}$$

The exponential factor, $e^{-\beta E_r}$, is called the **Boltzmann factor**, and the probability distribution in Eq. (5.12) is called the **Boltzmann distribution**. Ensembles whose properties follow the Boltzmann distribution are called **canonical ensembles**. The factor β is related to the *absolute* temperature (temperature in Kelvins) by

$$\beta = (k_B T)^{-1} \tag{5.15}$$

where k_B is a constant known as the **Boltzmann constant**.

In a physical system, entropy is defined by essentially the same relationship that we saw in the section on information theory:

$$S = -k_B \sum_r P_r \ln P_r \tag{5.16}$$

Although we discussed information theory first, the development of statistical mechanics preceded that of information theory. The development of information theory began essentially with the recognition of the relationship between statistical mechanics and information through the concept of entropy [7]. Equation (5.16) differs from the information-theory definition of entropy in Eq. (5.4) by only a constant multiplier. Note that the conversion between the natural log and the base-2 log is given by

$$\ln x = \log_e x = \frac{\log_2 x}{\log_2 e}$$

In the previous section, we showed that the maximum entropy (information) is obtained from a source with equiprobable symbols. We can make a similar argument for physical systems. Suppose we have two systems with entropies $S_1 = -k_B \sum_r P_{1r} \ln P_{1r}$ and $S_2 = -k_B \sum_r P_{2r} \ln P_{2r}$, such that both systems have the same average energy:

$$\langle E_1 \rangle = \sum_r P_{1r} E_r = \sum_r P_{2r} E_r = \langle E_2 \rangle$$

Furthermore, assume that the P_{2r} probabilities follow the canonical distribution in Eq. (5.12). By performing an analysis identical to that of the previous section, we can show that the difference in entropies of the two systems is given by

$$S_1 - S_2 = k_B \sum_r P_{1r} \ln \frac{P_{2r}}{P_{1r}} \qquad (5.17)$$

Using the inequality, $\ln x \leq x - 1$, we can show that S_1 will always be less than S_2 unless P_{1r} also follows the canonical distribution.

Exercise 5.3: Derive Eq. (5.17) assuming that P_{2r} is the canonical distribution. Using the inequality, $\ln x \leq x - 1$, show that the maximum entropy for the system, S_1, with a given average energy, occurs when the probability distribution of that system is the canonical distribution.

In previous chapters, we have exploited the analogy of an energy function associated with various neural networks, and we have seen in this chapter that the concept of entropy applies to both physical and information systems. We wish to extend the analogy along the following lines: If our neural networks have energy and entropy, is it possible to define a *temperature* parameter that has meaning for neural networks? If so, what is the benefit to be gained by defining such a parameter? Can we place our neural network in contact with a fictitious *heat reservoir*, and again, is there some advantage to this analogy? These questions, and their answers, form the basis of the discussion in the next section.

5.1.3   Annealing: Real and Simulated

Our intuition should tell us that a lump of material at a high temperature has a higher energy state than an identical lump at a lower temperature. Suppose we wish to reduce the energy of the material to its lowest possible value. Simply lowering the temperature to absolute zero will not necessarily ensure that the material is in its lowest possible energy configuration. Let's consider the example of a silicon boule being grown in a furnace to be used as a substrate for integrated-circuit devices. It is highly desirable that the crystal structure be a perfect, regular crystal lattice at ambient temperature. Once the silicon boule is formed, it must be properly cooled to ensure that the crystal lattice will form properly. Rapid cooling can result in many imperfections within the crystal structure, or in a substance that is glasslike, with no regular crystalline structure

at all. Both of these configurations have a higher energy than does the crystal
with the perfect lattice structure: They represent local energy minima.

An annealing process must be used to find the global energy minimum.
The temperature of the boule must be lowered gradually, giving atoms within
the structure time to rearrange themselves into the proper configuration. At
each temperature, sufficient time must be allowed so that the material reaches
an equilibrium. In equilibrium, the material follows the canonical probability
distribution:

$$P(E_r) \propto e^{-E_r/k_B T} \tag{5.18}$$

To understand how this annealing process helps the crystal to avoid a local
minimum, we shall employ an intuitive argument used by Hinton and Sejnowski
in their discussion of simulated annealing [3]. Consider the simple energy
landscape shown in Figure 5.1. The ball bearing described in the figure caption
has insufficient energy initially to roll up the other side of the hill and down
into the global minimum. If we *shake* the whole system, we might give the ball
enough of a push to get it up the hill. The harder we shake, the more likely it
is that the ball will be given enough energy to get over that hill. On the other
hand, vigorous shaking might also push the ball from the valley with the global
minimum *back* over to the local minimum side.

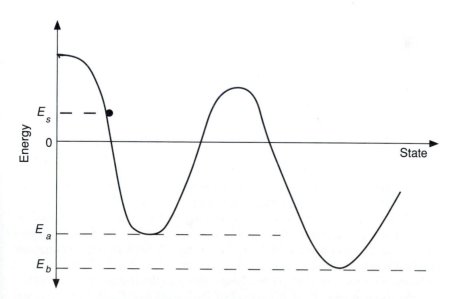

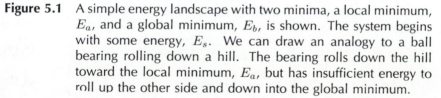

Figure 5.1   A simple energy landscape with two minima, a local minimum,
E_a, and a global minimum, E_b, is shown. The system begins
with some energy, E_s. We can draw an analogy to a ball
bearing rolling down a hill. The bearing rolls down the hill
toward the local minimum, E_a, but has insufficient energy to
roll up the other side and down into the global minimum.

If we give the system a gentle shaking, then, once the ball gets to the global minimum side, it is less likely to acquire sufficient energy to get back across to the local minimum side. However, because of the gentle shaking, it might take a very long time before the ball gets just the right push to get it over to the global minimum side in the first place.

Annealing represents a compromise between vigorous shaking and gentle shaking. At high temperatures, the large thermal energy corresponds to vigorous shaking; low temperatures correspond to gentle shaking. To anneal an object, we raise the temperature, then gradually lower it back to ambient temperature, allowing the object to reach equilibrium at each stop along the way. The technique of gradually lowering the temperature is the best way to ensure that a local minimum can be avoided without having to spend an infinite amount of time waiting for a transition out of a local minimum.

Exercise 5.4: Beginning with Eq. (5.18), find an equation that expresses the relative probability of the system being in the energy states, E_a or E_b, at some given temperature, T. Use this result to prove that, as $T \to 0$, the lower energy state is highly favored over the higher energy state.

We can postulate that it is possible to extend the analogy between information theory and statistical mechanics to allow us to place our neural network (information system) in contact with a *heat reservoir* at some, as yet undefined, *temperature*. If so, then we can perform a **simulated annealing** process whereby we gradually lower the system temperature while processing takes place in the network, in the hopes of avoiding a local minimum on the energy landscape.

To perform this process, we must simulate the effects of temperature on our system. In a physical system, molecules have an average kinetic energy proportional to the temperature of the system. Individual molecules may have more or less kinetic energy than the average, and random collisions may cause a molecule either to gain or to lose energy. We can simulate this behavior in a neural network by adding a stochastic element to the processing.

Let's look at an example from Chapter 4. Suppose we had a Hopfield network with binary outputs and we were seeking the network output with the lowest possible energy. According to the recipe in Chapter 4, each output node would be updated deterministically, depending on the sign of the net input to that unit and its current value. As we saw, this procedure usually leads to a solution at the nearest local minimum of energy. Instead of this deterministic procedure, let's *heat* the system to a temperature, T, and let the output value of each unit be determined stochastically according to the Boltzmann distribution.

For a single unit, x_i, if the energy of the *network* is E_a when $x_i = 1$, and E_b when $x_i = 0$, then, regardless of the previous state of x_i, let $x_i = 1$ with a probability of

$$p_i = \frac{e^{-E_a/k_B T}}{e^{-E_a/k_B T} + e^{-E_b/k_B T}} \tag{5.19}$$

$$p_i = \frac{1}{1 + e^{-\Delta E_i/k_B T}} \tag{5.20}$$

where $\Delta E_i = E_b - E_a$, and T is a parameter that is the analog of temperature. This operation ensures that, every so often, a unit will update so as to *increase* the energy of the system, thus helping the system get out of local-minimum valleys. Equation (5.19) results directly from the canonical distribution. Because only one unit is changing, there are only two potential states open to the system, which explains the two-term sum in the denominator.

As processing continues, the temperature is reduced gradually. In the end, there will be a high probability that the system is in a global energy minimum. The actual mechanics of this process will be discussed in the next section. Rather than continue using the Hopfield memory, we switch our attention to the particular network architecture known as the *Boltzmann machine*.

5.2   THE BOLTZMANN MACHINE

There are many similarities between the architecture and PEs of the **Boltzmann machine**, and those of other neural networks that we have discussed previously. However, there is a fundamental difference in the way we must think of the Boltzmann machine. The output of individual PEs in the Boltzmann machine is a stochastic function of the inputs, rather than a deterministic function: The output of a given node is calculated using probabilities, rather than a threshold or sigmoid output function. Moreover, we shall see that the training procedure does not depend solely on finding an energy minimum on an energy landscape. Rather, the learning algorithm will combine an energy minimization with an entropy maximization consistent with the use of the Boltzmann distribution to describe energy-state probabilities. These differences are a direct result of applying analogies from statistical mechanics to the neural network.

5.2.1   Basic Architecture and Processing

There are two different Boltzmann machine architectures of interest here. One we shall call the **Boltzmann completion** network, and the other we shall call the **Boltzmann input–output** network. For the moment, we shall concentrate on the Boltzmann completion architecture, which appears in Figure 5.2.

The function of the Boltzmann completion network is to learn a set of input patterns, and then to be able to supply missing parts of the patterns when a partial, or noisy, input pattern is processed. The input vectors are binary, with each component an element of $\{0, 1\}$.

As with the discrete Hopfield memory, the system energy can be calculated from

$$E = -\frac{1}{2} \sum_{i=1}^{n} \sum_{\substack{j=1 \\ j \neq i}}^{n} w_{ij} x_i x_j \qquad (5.21)$$

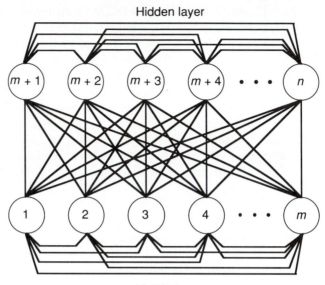

Figure 5.2   In the Boltzmann completion architecture, there are two layers of units: visible and hidden. The network is fully interconnected between layers and among units on each layer. The connections are bidirectional and the weights are symmetric, $w_{ij} = w_{ji}$.

where n is the total number of units in the network, and x_k is the output of the kth unit. The energy difference between the system with $x_k = 0$ and $x_k = 1$ is given by

$$\Delta E_k = (E_{x_k=0} - E_{x_k=1}) = \sum_{\substack{j=1 \\ j \neq k}}^{n} w_{kj} x_j \qquad (5.22)$$

Notice that the summation in Eq. (5.22) is identical to the usual definition of the net-input value to unit k, so that

$$\Delta E_k = \text{net}_k \qquad (5.23)$$

We shall assume for the moment that we already have an appropriate set of weights that encodes a set of binary vectors into the Boltzmann completion network. Suppose that the vector, $\mathbf{x} = (0, 1, 1, 0, 0, 1, 0)^t$, is one of the vectors learned by the network. We would like to be able to recall this vector given only partial knowledge, for example, the vector, $\mathbf{x}' = (0, u, 1, 0, u, 1, 0)^t$, where u represents an unknown component. The recall procedure will be performed using a simulated-annealing technique with $\mathbf{x}'$ as the starting vector on the visible units. The procedure is described by the following algorithm:

1. Force the outputs of all known visible units to the values specified by the initial input vector, $\mathbf{x}'$.

2. Assign all unknown visible units, and all hidden units, random output values from the set $\{1, 0\}$.

3. Select a unit, x_k, at random and calculate its net-input value, net$_k$.

4. Regardless of the current value of the unit, assign the output value, $x_k = 1$, with probability $p_k = 1 / \left(1 + e^{-\text{net}_k / T}\right)$. This stochastic choice can be implemented by comparison of the value of p_k to that of a number, z, selected randomly from a uniform distribution between zero and one. If $z \leq p_k$, then set $x_k = 1$. The parameter, T, acts as the temperature of the system. More will be said about the temperature in Section 5.2.3.

5. Repeat steps 3 and 4 until all units have had some probability of being selected for update. This number of unit-updates defines a **processing cycle**. For example, in a 10-unit network, 10 random unit selections would be a processing cycle. Completing a single processing cycle does not guarantee that every unit *has* been updated.

6. Repeat step 5 for several processing cycles, until **thermal equilibrium** has been reached at the given temperature, T. The number of processing cycles required to reach equilibrium is not easy to specify. Usually, we guess the number of processing cycles required to reach equilibrium.

7. Lower the temperature, T, and repeat steps 3 through 7.

Once the temperature has been reduced to a small value, the network will stabilize. The final result will be the outputs of the visible units.

The set of temperatures, along with the corresponding number of processing cycles at each temperature, constitute the **annealing schedule** for the network. For example, {2 processing cycles at a temperature of 10, 2 processing cycles at 8, 4 processing cycles at 6, 4 processing cycles at 4, 8 processing cycles at 2}, may be an appropriate annealing schedule for a certain problem.

By performing an annealing during pattern recall, we hope to avoid shallow, local minima. The final result should be a deeper, local minimum consistent with the known components of the initial input vector, $\mathbf{x}'$. We expect the final result to be the original vector, $\mathbf{x}$.

An alternative formulation of the Boltzmann machine is the Boltzmann input–output network shown in Figure 5.3. This network functions as a heteroassociative memory. During the recall process, the input-vector units are **clamped** permanently and are not updated during the annealing process. All hidden units and output units are updated according to the simulated-annealing procedure described previously for the Boltzmann completion network.

Hidden layer

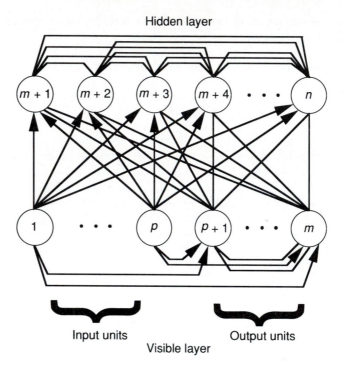

Input units   Output units
                    Visible layer

Figure 5.3   For the Boltzmann input–output network, the visible units
are separated into input and output units. There are no
connections among input units, and the connections from input
units to other units in the network are unidirectional. All other
connections are bidirectional, as in the Boltzmann completion
network.

5.2.2   Learning in Boltzmann Machines

Now that we have investigated the processing done to recall previously stored
patterns in Boltzmann-machine architectures, let's return to the problem of stor-
ing the patterns in the network. As was the case with pattern recall, learning
in Boltzmann machines is accomplished using a simulated-annealing technique.
This technique has fundamental differences from learning techniques investigated in previous chapters because of its stochastic nature. The learning algorithm for Boltzmann machines employs a gradient-descent technique, similar to
previous learning methods, although the function being minimized is no longer
identified with the energy of the network as described by Eq. (5.21).

Throughout this chapter, we have emphasized that the output values of
the processing elements have a probabilistic character. Thus, the output of
the network as a whole also has a probabilistic character. When training the
Boltzmann machine, we supply examples that are representative of the entire

population of possible input vectors. The learning algorithm that we employ must cause the network to form a model of the entire population of input patterns based on these examples. Unfortunately, there are often many different models that are consistent with the examples. The question is how to choose from among the various models.

One method of choosing among different models is to insist that the model of the population produced by the network will result in the most homogeneous distribution of input patterns consistent with the examples supplied. We can illustrate this concept with an example.

Suppose that we know that the first component of a three-component input vector will have a value of $+1$ in 40 percent of all vectors in the population. Out of eight possible three-component vectors, four have their first component as $+1$. There are an infinite number of ways that the probabilities of occurrence of those four vectors can combine to yield a total probability of 40 percent for the occurrence of $+1$ in the first position. One example is $P\{1,0,0\} = 10\%$, $P\{1,0,1\} = 4\%$, $P\{1,1,0\} = 8\%$, $P\{1,1,1\} = 18\%$. The most homogeneous distribution would be to assign equal probabilities to each of the four vectors, such that $P\{1,0,0\} = 10\%$, $P\{1,0,1\} = 10\%$, $P\{1,1,0\} = 10\%$, $P\{1,1,1\} = 10\%$. The rationale for this choice is that the information available gives us no reason to assign a higher probability of occurrence to any one of the vectors.

If a Boltzmann completion network learns the most homogeneous distribution, then repeated trials with an input vector of $P\{u,0,0\}$, where u is unknown, should result in a final output of $P\{1,0,0\}$ in approximately 10 trials out of every 100 (the more trials, the closer the results will be to 10 out of 100).

Recall from Section 5.1.1 that the asymmetric divergence,

$$G = \sum_{i=1}^{q} P_{1i} \log_2 \frac{P_{1i}}{P_{2i}}$$

measures the difference between an information source, S_1, with symbol probabilities, P_{1i}, and a source, S_2, with symbol probabilities, P_{2i}. Suppose the probabilities, P_{1i}, represent our knowledge of the probability distribution of a source. If the probabilities, P_{2i}, represent the most homogeneous distribution, then a learning algorithm that discovered a set of weights, w_{ij}, that minimized G would satisfy our desire to have the network learn the most homogeneous distribution consistent with what is known about the distribution. Such a learning algorithm would maximize the entropy of the system; so far, however, we have not said anything about the energy of the system. The following exercise is a prelude to that discussion.

Exercise 5.5: In the discussion of information theory in Section 5.1.1, we showed that the distribution with the maximum possible entropy was the one with equal symbol probabilities, $P_{2i} = 1/q$, where q is the number of symbols. Consider a physical system in equilibrium, at some finite temperature, T.

The distribution function for that physical system is the canonical distribution function given by Eq. (5.12). Show that, in the limit as $T \rightarrow \infty$, the physical system has equiprobable states, $P_r = 1/q$, where q is the number of possible states of the system.

As demonstrated in Exercise 5.5, an information system with equiprobable symbols is analogous to a physical system in equilibrium at an infinite temperature. If the temperature of the physical system is finite, the distribution with the maximum entropy (most homogeneous) is the canonical distribution. Furthermore, if the temperature is reduced gradually, lower-energy states will be favored (recall the discussion in Section 5.1.2). A reasonable approach to training the Boltzmann machine can now be constructed:

1. Artificially raise the temperature of the neural network to some finite value.

2. Anneal the system until equilibrium is reached at some low temperature value. (This minimum temperature should not be zero.)

3. Adjust the weights of the network so that the difference between the observed probability distribution and the canonical distribution is reduced (i.e., change the weights to reduce G).

4. Repeat steps 1 through 3 until the weights no longer change.

This procedure is a combination of gradient descent in the function, G, and simulated annealing as described in Section 5.2.1.

To perform a gradient descent in G, we must learn how changes in the weight values affect that function. Suppose we have a set of vectors, $\{\mathbf{V}_a\}$, that we would like a Boltzmann completion network to learn. These vectors would appear as the outputs of the visible units in the network. Define $\{\mathbf{H}_b\}$ as the set of vectors appearing on the hidden units.

We can impose our knowledge about the $\mathbf{V}_a$ vectors by *clamping* the outputs of the visible units to each $\mathbf{V}_a$ according to our knowledge of the probability of occurrence of $\mathbf{V}_a$. By *clamping*, we mean that the output values are fixed and do not change, even though other units may be changing according to the stochastic model presented earlier. Thus, the probability that the visible units will be clamped to the vector $\mathbf{V}_a$ is $P^+(\mathbf{V}_a)$, where the "+" superscript indicates that the visible units have been clamped. Units on the hidden layer may undergo change while a single vector is clamped to the visible units. The probability that vector $\mathbf{V}_a$ is clamped to the visible units, and that vector $\mathbf{H}_b$ appears on the hidden units, is $P^+(\mathbf{V}_a \wedge \mathbf{H}_b)$, and

$$P^+(\mathbf{V}_a) = \sum_b P^+(\mathbf{V}_a \wedge \mathbf{H}_b)$$

The reason that we must account for the hidden-layer vector is that the energy of the system depends on *all* of the units in the network, not just on the visible units. The total energy of the system with $\mathbf{V}_a$ on the visible units and

$\mathbf{H}_b$ on the hidden units is

$$E_{ab} = -\sum_{i<j} w_{ij} x_i^{ab} x_j^{ab} \qquad (5.24)$$

where x^{ab} can refer to either a visible unit or a hidden unit.

With none of the visible units clamped, the probability that $\mathbf{V}_a$ will appear on the visible units is given by

$$P^-(\mathbf{V}_a) = \sum_b P^-(\mathbf{V}_a \wedge \mathbf{H}_b)$$

where the "$-$" superscript indicates that the visible units are not clamped. Since this distribution represents a **free-running** (unclamped) system in equilibrium at some temperature, we can explicitly identify the probabilities as the canonical probabilities:

$$P^-(\mathbf{V}_a \wedge \mathbf{H}_b) = \frac{e^{-E_{ab}/T}}{\sum_{m,n} e^{-E_{mn}/T}} \qquad (5.25)$$

$$= \frac{e^{-E_{ab}/T}}{Z}$$

Then

$$P^-(\mathbf{V}_a) = \frac{\sum_b e^{-E_{ab}/T}}{\sum_{m,n} e^{-E_{mn}/T}} \qquad (5.26)$$

The explicit functional form of G now becomes

$$G = \sum_a P^+(\mathbf{V}_a) \ln \frac{P^+(\mathbf{V}_a)}{P^-(\mathbf{V}_a)}$$

where we have used the natural log rather than the base-2 log, for convenience. Differentiating G gives

$$\frac{\partial G}{\partial w_{ij}} = -\sum_a \frac{P^+(\mathbf{V}_a)}{P^-(\mathbf{V}_a)} \frac{\partial P^-(\mathbf{V}_a)}{\partial w_{ij}} \qquad (5.27)$$

Notice that the $P^+(\mathbf{V}_a)$ are independent of w_{ij} because the visible units are clamped to $\mathbf{V}_a$ and do not vary with changes in the w_{ij}.

From Eq. (5.26),

$$\frac{\partial P^-(\mathbf{V}_a)}{w_{ij}} = -\frac{1}{T} \sum_b \frac{e^{-E_{ab}/T}}{Z} \frac{\partial E_{ab}}{w_{ij}} - \sum_b \frac{e^{-E_{ab}/T}}{Z^2} \frac{\partial Z}{w_{ij}} \qquad (5.28)$$

The derivative of the energy function is

$$\frac{\partial E_{ab}}{w_{ij}} = -x_i^{ab} x_j^{ab} \qquad (5.29)$$

and the derivative of the partition function is

$$\frac{\partial Z}{w_{ij}} = \sum_{m,n}\left(-\frac{1}{T}\frac{\partial E_{mn}}{w_{ij}}e^{-E_{mn}/T}\right)$$

(5.30)

$$= \frac{1}{T}\sum_{m,n}x_i^{mn}x_j^{mn}e^{-E_{mn}/T}$$

Substituting Eqs. (5.29) and (5.30) into Eq. (5.28) yields

$$\frac{\partial P^-(\mathbf{V}_a)}{w_{ij}} = \frac{1}{T}\sum_b P^-(\mathbf{V}_a \wedge \mathbf{H}_b)x_i^{ab}x_j^{ab}$$

(5.31)

$$-\frac{P^-(\mathbf{V}_a)}{T}\frac{1}{T}\sum_{mn}P^-(\mathbf{V}_m \wedge \mathbf{H}_n)x_i^{mn}x_j^{mn}$$

where we have made use of the definition of $P^-(\mathbf{V}_a \wedge \mathbf{H}_b)$ and the definition of $P^-(\mathbf{V}_a)$.

Equation (5.31) can now be substituted into Eq. (5.27) to give

$$\frac{\partial G}{\partial w_{ij}} = -\frac{1}{T}\sum_{a,b}\frac{P^+(\mathbf{V}_a)}{P^-(\mathbf{V}_a)}P^-(\mathbf{V}_a \wedge \mathbf{H}_b)x_i^{ab}x_j^{ab}$$

(5.32)

$$+\frac{\sum_a P^+(\mathbf{V}_a)}{T}\sum_{mn}P^-(\mathbf{V}_m \wedge \mathbf{H}_n)x_i^{mn}x_j^{mn}$$

To simplify this equation, we first note that $\sum_a P^+(\mathbf{V}_a) = 1$. Next, we shall use a result from probability theory:

$$P^+(\mathbf{V}_a \wedge \mathbf{H}_b) = P^+(\mathbf{H}_b|\mathbf{V}_a)P^+(\mathbf{V}_a)$$

Stated in words, this equation means that the probability of having $\mathbf{V}_a$ on the visible layer *and* $\mathbf{H}_b$ on the hidden layer is equal to the probability of having $\mathbf{H}_b$ on the hidden layer *given* that $\mathbf{V}_a$ was on the visible layer, times the probability that $\mathbf{V}_a$ is on the visible layer. An analogous definition and statement can be made for $P^-(\mathbf{V}_a)$:

$$P^-(\mathbf{V}_a \wedge \mathbf{H}_b) = P^-(\mathbf{H}_b|\mathbf{V}_a)P^-(\mathbf{V}_a)$$

If $\mathbf{V}_a$ is on the visible layer, then the probability that $\mathbf{H}_b$ will occur on the hidden layer should not depend on whether $\mathbf{V}_a$ got there by being clamped to that state or by free-running to that state. Therefore, it must be true that

$$P^+(\mathbf{H}_b|\mathbf{V}_a) = P^-(\mathbf{H}_b|\mathbf{V}_a)$$

Then

$$\frac{P^-(\mathbf{V}_a \wedge \mathbf{H}_b)}{P^+(\mathbf{V}_a \wedge \mathbf{H}_b)} = \frac{P^-(\mathbf{V}_a)}{P^+(\mathbf{V}_a)}$$

and

$$P^-(\mathbf{V}_a \wedge \mathbf{H}_b)\frac{P^+(\mathbf{V}_a)}{P^-(\mathbf{V}_a)} = P^+(\mathbf{V}_a \wedge \mathbf{H}_b)$$

Using these results, we can write

$$\frac{\partial G}{\partial w_{ij}} = \frac{1}{T}(p_{ij}^- - p_{ij}^+)$$

where

$$p_{ij}^- = \sum_{a,b} P^-(\mathbf{V}_a \wedge \mathbf{H}_b)x_i^{ab}x_j^{ab} \qquad (5.33)$$

and

$$p_{ij}^+ = \sum_{a,b} P^+(\mathbf{V}_a \wedge \mathbf{H}_b)x_i^{ab}x_j^{ab} \qquad (5.34)$$

The interpretation of Eqs. (5.33) and (5.34) will be given shortly. For now, recall that weight changes occur in the direction of the negative gradient of G. Weight updates are calculated according to

$$\Delta w_{ij} = \epsilon(p_{ij}^+ - p_{ij}^-) \qquad (5.35)$$

where ϵ is a constant.

The quantities, p_{ij}^- and p_{ij}^+ are called **co-occurrence probabilities** because they compute the frequency that x_i^{ab} and x_j^{ab} are both active (an output value of 1) averaged over all possible combinations of the patterns, $\mathbf{V}_a$ and $\mathbf{H}_b$. Thus, p_{ij}^+ is the co-occurrence probability when the $\mathbf{V}_a$ patterns are being clamped on the visible units, and p_{ij}^- is the co-occurrence probability when the network is free-running. As seen in Eq. (5.35), the weights will continue to change as long as the two co-occurrence probabilities differ.

Several paragraphs ago, we described a simple algorithm for training a Boltzmann machine. We shall now expand that algorithm to include the method for determining the weight-update values as specified by Eq. (5.35):

1. Clamp one training vector to the visible units of the network.

2. Anneal the network according to the annealing schedule until equilibrium is reached at the desired minimum temperature.

3. Continue to run the network for several more processing cycles. After each processing cycle, determine which pairs of connected units are on simultaneously.

4. Average the co-occurrence results from step 3.

5. Repeat steps 1 through 4 for all training vectors, and average the co-occurrence results to get an estimate of p_{ij}^+ for each pair of connected units.

6. Unclamp the visible units, and anneal the network until equilibrium is reached at the desired minimum temperature.

7. Continue to run the network for several more processing cycles. After each processing cycle, determine which pairs of connected units are on simultaneously.

8. Average the co-occurrence results from step 7.

9. Repeat steps 6 through 8 for the same number of times as was done in step 5, and average the co-occurrence results to get an estimate of p_{ij}^- for each pair of connected units.

10. Calculate and apply the appropriate weight changes. (The entire sequence from step 1 to step 10 defines a **sweep**.)

11. Repeat steps 1 through 10 until $p_{ij}^+ - p_{ij}^-$ is sufficiently small.

An alternative way to decide when to halt training is to perform a test procedure after each sweep. Clamp partial or noisy input vectors to the visible units, anneal the network, and see how well the network reproduces the correct vector. When the performance is adequate, training can be stopped.

Although it is not possible to give an exact procedure for determining the annealing schedule, it is possible to provide guidelines and suggestions. The next section provides these guidelines, with other practical information about the simulation of the Boltzmann machine.

Exercise 5.6: Modify the Boltzmann learning algorithm to accommodate the Boltzmann input–output network described in Section 5.2.1.

5.2.3   Practical Considerations

If there is a single word that describes the learning process in a Boltzmann machine simulation, that word is *slow*. Even relatively small networks may require thousands of processing cycles to learn a set of input patterns adequately. This situation is exacerbated by the fact that the annealing schedule must incorporate a very slow reduction in temperature if the global minimum is to be found. Studies performed on simulated annealing by Geman and Geman showed that the temperature must be reduced in proportion to the inverse log of the temperature:

$$T(t_n) = \frac{T_0}{1 + \ln t_n}$$

where T_0 is the starting temperature, and the discrete-time variable, t_n, represents the nth processing cycle [2]. Annealing a single input pattern from a temperature of 40 to a temperature of 0.5 requires an impractical e^{80} processing cycles to ensure that the global minimum has been found (at $T = 0.5$).

Fortunately, we do not need to follow this prescription to obtain good results, but, other than the results of Geman and Geman, annealing schedules must be determined ad hoc.

Examples of annealing schedules used to solve a few small problems are given in a paper by Ackley, Hinton, and Sejnowski [1]. In a problem called the 8-3-8 encoder problem, they used a Boltzmann input–output network with 16 visible units and three hidden units. They clamped an eight-bit binary number to the input nodes. Only one of the bits in the input vector was allowed to be on at any given time. The problem was to train the network to reproduce the identical vector on the output nodes. Thus, the three hidden nodes learned a three-digit binary code for the eight possible input vectors. The annealing schedule was {2 processing cycles at a temperature of 20, 2 at 15, 2 at 12, 4 at 10}. Several thousand sweeps were required to train the network to perform the encoding task.

The annealing technique that we have described is not the only possible method. The bibliography at the end of this chapter contains references that describe other methods. One method in particular that we wish to note here is described by Szu [8]. Szu's method is based on the Cauchy distribution, rather than the Boltzmann distribution. The Cauchy distribution has the same general shape as the Boltzmann distribution, but does not fall off as sharply at large energies. The implication is that the **Cauchy machine** may occasionally take a rather large jump out of a local minimum. The advantage of this approach is that the global minimum can be reached with a much shorter annealing schedule. For the Cauchy machine, the annealing temperature should follow the inverse of the time:

$$T(t_n) = \frac{T_0}{1 + t_n}$$

This annealing schedule is much faster than is the one for the corresponding Boltzmann machine.

5.3 THE BOLTZMANN SIMULATOR

As you may have inferred from the previous discussion, simulating the Boltzmann network on a conventional computer will consume enormous amounts of both system memory and CPU time. For these reasons (as well as for brevity), we will limit our discussion of the simulator to only the most important data structures and algorithms needed to implement the Boltzmann network. The development of the less difficult or application-specific algorithms is left to you. We begin by defining the data structures that we must add to our generic simulator to implement the Boltzmann network. We then develop the algorithms that will be used to run the network simulator, and conclude the chapter with a presentation of an example problem that the Boltzmann network can be used to solve.

5.3.1   The Modified Boltzmann Network

The Boltzmann network, as we have discussed throughout this chapter, is similar in structure to the BAM and Hopfield networks described in Chapter 4. In particular, the Boltzmann network consists of a set of PEs, each completely interconnected with every other unit in the network.[2] This type of network arrangement is usually diagrammed as a set of units with bidirectional connections to every other unit, as illustrated earlier in Figure 5.2. For purposes of simulation, however, we will instead create the network structure with a single layer of PEs, each having a unidirectional input connection from every other unit. We adopt this convention because it offers us many insights into how to go about implementing the Boltzmann simulator program. However, you should note that this alternative model is functionally identical to the network containing bidirectional connections.

As an example, consider the two different views of the same Boltzmann network illustrated in Figure 5.4. Notice that, in the modified view shown in Figure 5.4(b), the network structure is much busier (and more confusing) than it is in the standard arrangement. If we look beneath the surface though, and consider only the processing going on at the level of each network unit, the modified view reveals that each PE behaves in a familiar manner; an aggregate input stimulation provided by many modulated input signals is converted to a single output that is, in turn, modulated to provide an input to every other network unit. This type of processing is exactly what our simulator is designed to model efficiently.

Based on this observation, our basic data structures for the network simulator will not require modification. We need only to introduce some new structures to account for how the network learns, and to incorporate them into the algorithms that we must develop to propagate signals through the network.

5.3.2   Boltzmann Data Structures

There are two significant differences between the structure of the Boltzmann network and that of other ANS networks we have discussed previously. The Boltzmann model is trained by using an annealing schedule to determine how many training passes to complete at every temperature interval, and the Boltzmann network is not a *layered* network. We will account for these differences separately as we modify our simulator data structures to implement the Boltzmann network. We begin by implementing a mechanism that will allow the simulator to follow an annealing schedule during signal propagation and training.

Since it is impractical for us, as program designers, to try to accommodate every possible application by implementing a universal annealing schedule, we

---

[2]The Boltzmann input–output model is an exception, due to its lack of interconnection between input units.

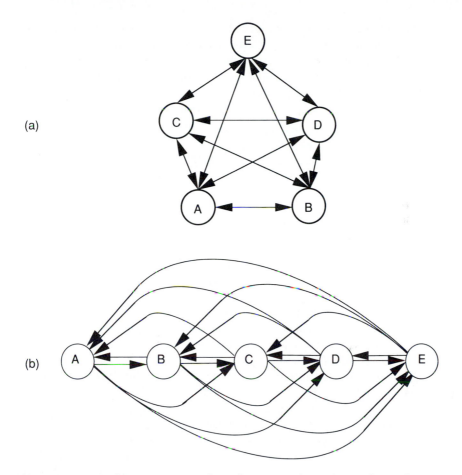

Figure 5.4 A Boltzmann network is shown, (a) from the traditional view, and (b) modified to conform to the unidirectional connection format.

will instead require the user to provide the annealing schedule for each application. The implementation of the schedule is relatively simple if we observe that the latter is nothing more than a variable length set of ordered pairs of *temperature* and *training passes*. Thus, we can construct an annealing schedule of indefinite size if we define a record structure to store each ordered pair, and dynamically allocate an array of these records to create the schedule. Our structure for the annealing pair is given by the declaration:

```
record ANNEAL =
  TEMPERATURE : float;      {temperature}
  PASSES : integer;         {training passes}
end record;
```

We complete the annealing schedule by defining an array of ANNEAL records, each specified by the user. As in the case of other dynamically allocated arrays discussed in this text, we do not presuppose the use of any particular computer language; therefore, the actual specification and mechanism for initialization of the SCHEDULE array is left to you. For purposes of discussion, however, the declaration of a typical annealing schedule array might take the form

```
record SCHEDULE (SIZE)=
   LENGTH : integer = SIZE;
   STEP : array[1..SIZE] of ANNEAL;
end record;
```

where SIZE is the user-provided length of the array.

Before we can define the remaining data structures needed to implement the Boltzmann network, we must take into account the second difference between the Boltzmann and other ANS network models we have discussed previously. Specifically, the Boltzmann machine is a nonlayered network, and has dedicated input and output units that are *subsets of units within the same layer*. Moreover, the inputs and outputs may overlap, as in the case of the Boltzmann completion network, in which the input units *are* the output units. An example of this type of network is the one that will simply fill in missing data elements from an incomplete input. On the other hand, the network may have two discrete sets of units, one acting as dedicated input units, the other as dedicated output units.

To account for these differences, we can make use of the fact that the outputs from all of the units in the network will be modeled as a linearly sequential array of data values in the computer memory, arranged from first to last, going from low memory toward high memory. This fact holds true because, as we have observed, the Boltzmann network can be thought of as containing a *single layer* of units. Furthermore, this sequential structure holds for all of the intermediate network structures that we must use (e.g., the unit weights array). If we therefore adopt the convention that all units in the network must be arranged sequentially, with the visible units occurring first, we can simply locate the first unit of the network input by using an integer index. Once the first unit is found, all other input units will follow in sequence. The same technique can be used to locate the network outputs as well. An additional benefit derived from the use of this method is the ability to provide either discrete or overlapping network inputs and outputs.

Unfortunately, our convention will introduce some other difficulties, because the number of units dedicated to input and output is no longer defined explicitly by the number of elements in an array, as it is in other network models. We must therefore compensate for the loss of layer identity by constructing one additional record that will be used to locate and size the network input and output units. This record will take the form

```
record DEDICATED =
   FIRST : integer;        {index to first dedicated unit}
   LENGTH : integer;       {number of units needed}
end record;
```

We will also need another structure to help us determine the required weight changes for the network during training. Since this network adapts its connections as a function of the probability that any two units are on simultaneously, we must have a means of collecting the statistics about how often that situation occurs *for every two units* in the network. The most straightforward approach to collecting these statistics is to construct an array that will be used to store and calculate the co-occurrence parameters, p_{ij}^+ and p_{ij}^-. For purposes of simulation, we must maintain a count value for every combination of two units in the network. Thus, we must be able to store information about the relationships between N units taken two at a time. The storage required for all this information will consume an array of dimension $N(N-1)/2$, with each element a floating-point number that will be used as both a count and an average. We will elaborate on this dual functionality as part of the discussion of the Boltzmann learning algorithms (see Section 5.3.3). For now, the declaration for this structure will again be dependent on the language of implementation; for that reason, it will not be presented here. For clarity, we will name the array CO_OCCURRENCE; the declaration of the SCHEDULE.STEP array provided earlier is an example of how this array might be constructed.

Having created an array to collect the CO_OCCURRENCE statistics about our Boltzmann machine, we now observe that it alone will not be sufficient for our simulation. A single array will allow us to accumulate the frequency with which any two network units are on together; however, these statistics must be gathered and averaged for every training pattern, as well as for the aggregate. Furthermore, we must collect network statistics during different runs (clamped to compute p_{ij}^+ and unclamped for p_{ij}^-). Fortunately, all these statistics can be combined, thus minimizing the amount of storage needed to preserve the data. However, the information from each run must be isolated so that the appropriate Δw can be computed, according to Eq. (5.35). We shall therefore allocate two such arrays, and shall create another record to locate each at run time. Such a record is given by

```
record CO_OCCURRENCE =
  CLAMPED : ^float[];
                     {locate array for p+ calculation}
  UNCLAMPED : ^float[];
                     {locate array for p- calculation}
end record;
```

Before pressing on, let us consider how to utilize effectively the arrays we have just created. To organize each array such that it is both meaningful and efficient, we must determine a means of associating array locations, and therefore computer memory, with network connections. This association is best accomplished implicitly, by allocating the first $N-1$ locations in the array to the connections between the first and all other network units. The next $N-2$ slots will be given to the second unit, and so on. As an example, consider a network with five units, labeled A through E; such a network is depicted in

Co-occurence

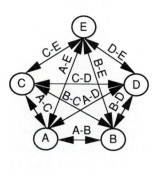

| A-B |
| A-C |
| A-D |
| A-E |
| B-C |
| B-D |
| B-E |
| C-D |
| C-E |
| D-E |

↑
Low memory

High memory
↓

(a)   (b)

Figure 5.5 The CO_OCCURRENCE array is shown (a) depicted as a sequential memory array, and (b) with its mapping to the connections in the Boltzmann network.

Figure 5.5(a). The first four entries in the CO_OCCURRENCE array for this network would be mapped to the connections between units A–B, A–C, A–D, and A–E, as shown in Figure 5.5(b). Likewise, the next three slots would be mapped to the connections between units B–C, B–D, and B–E; the next two to C–D, and C– E; and the last one to D–E. By using the arrays in this manner, we can collect co-occurrence statistics about the network by starting at the first input unit and sequentially scanning all other units in the network. After completing this initial pass, we can complete the network scan by merely incrementing our array pointer to access the second unit, then the third, fourth, ..., nth units.

We can now specify the remaining data structures needed to implement the Boltzmann network simulator. We begin by defining the top-level record structure used to define the Boltzmann network:

```
record BOLTZMANN =
    UNITS : integer;                {number of units in network}
    CLAMPED : boolean;         {true=clamped; false=unclamped}
    INPUTS : DEDICATED;        {locate and size network input}
    OUTPUTS : DEDICATED;  {locate and size network output}
    NODES : ^layer;                {pointer to layer structure}
    TEMPERATURE : float;       {current network temperature}
    CURRENT : integer;            {step in annealing schedule}
```

```
ANNEALING :  ^SCHEDULE[];
                        {pointer to user-defined schedule}
STATISTICS : CO_OCCURRENCE;
                        {pointers to statistics arrays}
end record;
```

Figure 5.6 provides an illustration of how the values in the BOLTZMANN structure interact to specify a Boltzmann network. Here, as in other network models, the layer structure is the gateway to the network specific data structures. All that is needed to gain access to the layer-specific data are pointers to the appropriate arrays. Thus, the structure for the layer record is given by

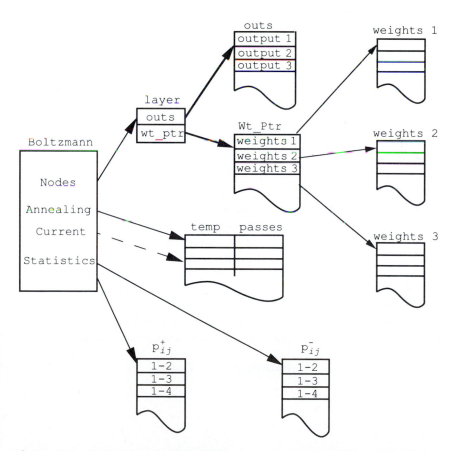

Figure 5.6 Organization of the Boltzmann network using the defined data structure is shown. In this example, the input and output units are the same, and the network is in the third step of its annealing schedule.

```
record LAYER =
  outs : ^float[];        {pointer to unit outputs array}
  weights : ^^float[];    {pointers in weight_ptr array}
end record;
```

where `outs` is a pointer used to locate the beginning of the unit outputs array in memory, and `weights` is a pointer to the intermediate `weight_ptr` array, which is used in turn to locate each of the input connection arrays in the system. Since the Boltzmann network requires only one layer of PEs, we will need only one `layer` pointer in the `BOLTZMANN` record. All these low-level data structures are exactly the same as those specified in the generic simulator discussed in Chapter 1.

5.3.3 Boltzmann Algorithms

Let us assume, for now, that our network data structures contain valid weights for all the connections, and that the user has initialized the annealing schedule to contain the information given in Table 5.1; in other words, the network data structures represent a trained network. We must now create the programs that the host computer will execute to simulate the network in production mode. We shall start by developing the information-recall routines.

Boltzmann Production Algorithms. Remember that information recall in the Boltzmann network consists of a sequence of steps where we first apply an input to the network, raise the temperature to some predefined level, and anneal the network while slowly lowering the temperature. In this example, we would initially raise the temperature to 5 and would perform four stochastic signal propagations; we would then lower the temperature to 4 and would perform six signal propagations, and so on. After completing the four required signal propagations when the temperature of the network is 1, we can consider the network annealed. At this point, we simply read the output values from the visible units.

If, however, we think about the process we just described, we can decompose the information-recall problem into three lower-level subroutines:

Temperature	Passes
5	4
4	6
3	7
2	6
1	4

Table 5.1   The annealing schedule for the simulator example.

apply_input A routine used to take a user-provided or training input and
apply it to the network, and to initialize the output from all unknown units
to a random state.

anneal A routine used to stimulate the Boltzmann network according to the
previously initialized annealing schedule.

get_output A function used to locate the start of the output array in the
computer memory, so that the network response can be accessed.

Since the anneal routine is the place where most of the processing is
accomplished, we shall concentrate on the development of just that routine,
leaving the design of the other two algorithms to you. The mathematics of
the Boltzmann network tells us that the annealing process, in production mode,
consists of two major functions that are repeated until the network has stabilized
at a low temperature. These functions, described next, can each be implemented
as subroutines that are called by the parent anneal process.

set_temp A procedure used to set the current network temperature and annealing schedule pass count to values specified in the overall annealing
schedule.

propagate A function used to perform one signal propagation through the
entire network, using the current temperature and probabilistic unit selection. This routine should be capable of performing the signal propagation
regardless of the network state (clamped or unclamped).

Signal Propagation in the Boltzmann Network. We shall now define the
most basic of the needed subroutines, the propagate procedure. The algorithm for this procedure, which follows, presumes that the user-provided
apply_input and not-yet-defined set_temp functions have been executed
to initialize the outputs of the network's units and temperature parameter
to the desired states.

```
procedure propagate (NET:BOLTZMANN)
{perform one signal propagation pass through network.}

var unit : integer;              {randomly selected unit}
    p : float;              {probability of unit being on}
    neti : float;                   {net input to unit}
    threshold : integer;   {point at which unit turns on}
    i, j : integer;                 {iteration counters}
    inputs : ^float[];     {pointer to unit outputs array}
    connects : ^float[]; {pointer to unit weights array}
    unclamped : integer; {index to first unclamped unit}
    firstc : integer;         {index to first connection}

begin
{locate the first nonvisible unit, assuming first
                                          index = 1}
  unclamped = NET.OUTPUTS.FIRST + NET.OUTPUTS.LENGTH - 1;
```

```
    if (NET.INPUTS.FIRST = NET.OUTPUTS.FIRST)
    then firstc = NET.INPUTS.FIRST    {Boltzmann completion}

    else firstc = NET.INPUTS.LENGTH + 1;
                                        {Boltzmann input-output}
    end if;

    for i = 1 to NET.UNITS  {for as many units in network}
      do
        if (NET.CLAMPED)            {if network is clamped}
        then                     {select an unclamped unit}

            unit = random(NET.UNITS - unclamped)
                    + unclamped;
        else                          {select any unit}
            unit = random(NET.UNITS);
        end if;

        neti = 0;                     {initialize input}
        inputs = NET.NODES^.OUTS;        {locate inputs}
        connects = NET.NODES^.WEIGHTS[unit]:
                                      {and connections}

        for j = firstc to NET.UNITS
                            {all connections to unit}
          do                {compute sum of products}
              neti = neti + inputs[j] * connects[j];
          end do;

    {this next statement is used to improve
                    performance, as described in the text}

        if (NET.INPUTS.FIRST = NET.OUTPUTS.FIRST)
        or (i >= firstc)
        then
          neti = neti - inputs[units] * connects[i];
                                      {no connection}
        end if;

        p = 1.0 / (1.0 + exp(-neti / NET.TEMPERATURE));
        threshold = round (p * 10000); {convert to integer}

        if (random(10000) <= threshold))
                                      {should unit be on?}
        then
          inputs[unit] = 1;                {if so, set to 1}
        else
          inputs[unit] = 0;           {otherwise, set to 0}
        end if;
      end do;
end procedure;
```

Before we move on to the next routine, there are three aspects of the `propagate` procedure that bear further discussion: the selection mechanism for unit update, the computation of the `neti` term, and the method we have chosen for determining when a unit is or is not active.

In the first case, the Boltzmann network must be able to run with its inputs either clamped or free-running. So that we do not need to have different `propagate` routines for each mode, we simply use a Boolean variable in the network record to indicate the current mode of operation, and enable the `propagate` routine to select a unit for update accordingly. If the network is *clamped*, we cannot select an input or output unit for update. We account for these differences by assuming that the visible units to the network are the first N units in the layer. We thus can be assured that the visible units will not change if we simply select a random unit from the set of units that do not include the first N units. We accomplish this selection by decreasing the range of the random-number generator to the number of network units minus N, and then adding N to the result. Since we have decided that all our arrays will use the first N indices to locate the visible units, generating a random index greater than N will always select a random unit beyond the range of the visible units. However, if the network is *unclamped*, any unit must be available for update. Inspection of the algorithm for `propagate` will reveal that these two cases are handled by the `if-then-else` clause at the beginning of the routine.

Second, there are two salient points regarding the computation of the `neti` term with respect to the `propagate` routine. The first point is that connections between input units are processed only when the network is configured as a Boltzmann completion network. In the Boltzmann input–output mode, connections between input units do not exist. This structure conforms to the mathematical model described earlier. The second point about the calculation of the `neti` term is that we have obviously wasted computer time by processing a connection from each unit to itself twice, once as part of the summation loop during the calculation of the `neti` value, and once to subtract it out after the total `neti` has been calculated. The reason we have chosen to implement the algorithm in this manner is, again, to improve performance. Even though we have consumed computer time by processing a nonexistent connection for every unit in the network, we have used far less time than would be required to disallow the computation of the missing connection selectively during *every iteration* of the summation loop. Furthermore, we can easily eliminate the error introduced in the input summation by processing the nonexistent connection by subtracting out just that term after completing the loop, prior to updating the output of the unit. You might also observe that we have wasted memory by allocating space for the connections between each unit and itself. We have chosen to implement the network in this fashion to simplify processing, and thus to improve performance as described.

As an example of why it is desirable to optimize the code at the expense of wasted memory, consider the alternative case where only valid connections are modeled. Since no unit has a connection to itself, but all units have outputs maintained in the same array, the code to process all input connections to a unit would have to be written as two different loops: one for those input PEs that precede the current unit, where the array indices for outputs and connections correspond one-to-one, and one loop for inputs from units that follow, where unit outputs are displaced by one array entry from the corresponding connection. This situation occurs because we have organized the unit outputs and connections as linearly sequential arrays in memory. Such a situation is illustrated in Figure 5.7.

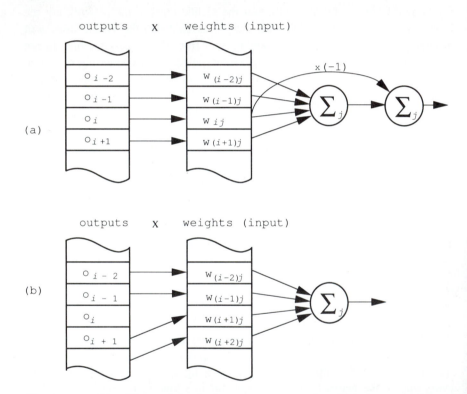

Figure 5.7 The illustration shows array processing (a) when memory is allocated for all possible connections, and (b) when memory is not allocated for intra-unit connections. In (a), the code necessary to perform this input summation simply computes the input value for all connections, then eliminates the error introduced by processing the nonexistent connection to itself. In (b), the code must be more selective about accessing connections, since the one-to-one mapping of connections to units is lost. Obviously, approach (a) is our preferred method, since it will execute much faster than approach (b).

Finally, with respect to deciding when to activate the output of a unit, recall that the Boltzmann network differs from the other networks that we have studied in that PEs are activated stochastically rather than deterministically. Recall that the equation

$$p_k = 1/(1 + e^{-\text{net}_k/T})$$

defines how we calculate the probability that a unit x_k is active with respect to its input stimulation (net_k). However, simply knowing the probability that a unit will generate an output does not guarantee that the unit *will* generate an output. We must therefore implement a mechanism that allows the computer to translate the calculated probability into a unit output that occurs with the same probability; in effect, we must let the computer *roll the dice* to determine when an output is active and when it is not.

One method for doing this is to make use of the pseudorandom-number generator available in most high-level computer languages. Here, we take advantage of the fact that the computed probability, p_k, will always be a fractional number ranging between zero and one, as illustrated by the graph depicted in Figure 5.8. We can map p_k to an integer *threshold* value between zero and some arbitrarily large number by simply multiplying the ceiling value by the computed probability and rounding the result into an integer. We then generate a random number between zero and the selected ceiling, and, if the probability does not exceed the threshold value just computed, the output of the unit is set to one. Assuming that the pseudorandom-number generator has a uniform probability distribution across the interval of interest, the random number produced will not exceed the threshold value with a probability equal to the specified value, p_k. Thus, we now have a means of stochastically activating unit outputs in the network.

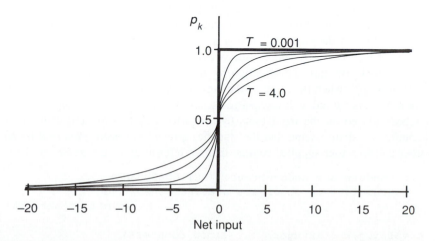

Figure 5.8 Shown here is a graph of the probability, p_k, that the kth unit is on at five different temperatures, T.

Boltzmann Learning Algorithms. There are five additional functions that must be defined to train the Boltzmann network:

set_temp A function used to update the parameters in the BOLTZMANN record to reflect the network temperature at the current step, as specified in the annealing schedule.

pplus A function used to compute and average the co-occurrence probabilities for a network with clamped inputs after it has reached equilibrium at the minimum temperature.

pminus A function similar to pplus, but used when the network is free-running.

update_connections The procedure that modifies the connection weights in the network to train the Boltzmann simulator.

The implementation of the set_temp function is straightforward, as defined here:

```
procedure set_temp (NET:BOLTZMANN; N:integer)
{set the temperature and schedule step}

begin
  NET.CURRENT = N;          {set current step}
  NET.TEMPERATURE = NET.ANNEALING^.STEP[N].TEMPERATURE;
end procedure;
```

On the other hand, the estimation of the p_{ij}^{+} and p_{ij}^{-} terms is complex, and each must be accomplished in two steps: in the first, statistics about the co-occurrence between network units must be gathered and averaged for *each* training pattern; in the second, the statistics across *all* training patterns are collected. This separation provides a natural breakpoint for algorithm development. We can therefore define two algorithms, sum_cooccurrence and pplus, that respectively address the two steps identified.

We shall now turn our attention to the computation of the co-occurrence probability, p_{ij}^{+}, when the input to the network is clamped to an arbitrary input vector, $\mathbf{V}_a$. As we did with propagate, we will assume that the input pattern has been placed on the input units by an earlier call to set_inputs. Furthermore, we shall assume that the statistics arrays have been initialized by an earlier call to a user-supplied routine that we refer to as zero_statistics.

```
procedure sum_cooccurrence (NET:BOLTZMANN)
{accumulate co-occurence statistics for the
                                 specified network}

var i,j,k : integer;       {loop counters}
    connect : integer;     {co-occurence index}
    stats : ^float[];      {pointer to statistics array}
```

```
begin
   if (NET.CLAMPED)          {if network is clamped}
   then stats = NET.STATISTICS.CLAMPED
   else stats = NET.STATISTICS.UNCLAMPED;
   end if;

   for i = 1 to 5            {arbitrary number of cycles}
      do
         propagate (NET);    {run the network once}

         connect = 1;        {start at first pair}
         for j = 1 to NET.UNITS
                             {for all units in network}

         do
            if (NET.NODES.OUTS^[j] = 1)    {if unit is on}
            then
              for k = j + 1 to NET.UNITS
                             {for rest of units}
                do
                   if (NET.NODES.OUTS^[k] = 1)
                   then
                      stats^[connect] = stats^[connect] + 1;
                   end if;

                   connect = next (connect);
                end do;

            else                      {skip to next unit connect}
               connect = connect + (NET.UNITS - j);
            end if;

         end do;
      end do;
   end procedure;
```

Notice that the sum_cooccurrence routine does not average the accumulated results after completing the examination. We delay this computation to the pplus routine so that we can continue to use the clamped array to collect statistics across all patterns. If we averaged the results after each cycle, we would be forced to maintain different arrays for each pattern, thus increasing the need for storage at a near-exponential rate. In addition, note that, by using a pointer to the appropriate statistics array, we have generalized the routine so that it may be used to collect statistics for the network in either the clamped or unclamped modes of operation.

Before we define the algorithm needed to estimate the p_{ij}^+ term for the Boltzmann network, we will make a few assumptions. Since the total number of training patterns that the network must learn will depend on the application, we must write the code so that the computer will calculate the co-occurrence statistics for a variable number of training patterns. We must therefore assume that the training data are available to the simulator from some external source (such as a global array or disk file) that we will refer to as PATTERNS, and that the total number of training patterns contained in this source is obtainable through a call to an application-defined function that we will call how_many. We also presume that you will provide the routines to initialize the co_occurrence arrays to zero, and set the outputs of the input network units to the state specified by the *i*th pattern in the PATTERNS data source. We will refer to these procedures as initialize_arrays and set_inputs, respectively. Based on these assumptions, we shall now define our algorithm for computing pplus:

```
procedure pplus (NET:BOLTZMANN)

var trials : integer;                  {average over trials}
    i : integer;                              {loop counter}

begin
  trials = how_many (PATTERNS) * 5;
                                    {five sums per pattern}
  for i = 1 to trials                      {for all trials}
    do
       NET.STATISTICS.CLAMPED^[i] =    {average results}
          NET.STATISTICS.CLAMPED^[i] / trials;
    end do;
end procedure;
```

The implementation of pminus is similar to the pplus algorithm, and is left to you as an exercise.

5.3.4   The Complete Boltzmann Simulator

Now that we have defined all the lower-level functions needed to implement the Boltzmann network, we shall describe the algorithms needed to tie everything together. As previously stated, the two user-provided routines (set_inputs and get_outputs) are assumed to initialize and recover input and output data to or from the simulator for an external process. However, we have yet to define the two intermediate routines that will be used to perform the network simulation given the externally provided inputs. We now begin to correct that deficiency by describing the algorithm for the anneal process.

```
procedure anneal (NET:BOLTZMANN)
{perform one pass through annealing schedule for
                                          current input}
var passes : integer;   {passes at current temperature}
    steps : integer;       {number of steps in schedule}
    i, j : integer;                        {loop counters}
```

```
begin
  steps = NET.ANNEALING^.LENGTH;    {steps in schedule}

  for i = 1 to steps         {for all steps in schedule}
    do
      passes = NET.ANNEALING^.STEP[i].PASSES;
      set_temp (NET, i);  {set current annealing step}

      for j = 1 to passes     {for all passes in step}
        do
          propagate (NET);
                     {perform required processing cycles}
        end do;
    end do;
end procedure;
```

All that remains to complete the learning-mode algorithms is a routine to update the connection weights in the network according to the statistics collected during the annealing process. This routine will compute and apply the Δw term for each connection in the network. To simplify the program, we assume that the ϵ constant contained in Eq. (5.35) will always be 0.3.

```
procedure update_connections (NET:BOLTZMANN)
{update all connections based on cooccurence statistics}

var connect : ^float[];  {pointer to connection array}
    pp, pm : float[];              {statistics arrays}
    dupconnect : ^float[];
                      {pointer to duplicate connection}
    i, j, stat : integer;         {iteration indices}

begin
  pp = NET.STATISTICS.CLAMPED^;
                           {locate pplus statistics}
  pm = NET.STATISTICS.UNCLAMPED^;
                           {locate pminus statistics}
  stat = 1;                {start at first statistic}

  for i = 1 to NET.UNITS    {for all units in network}
    do
      connect = NET.NODES.WEIGHTS^[i];
                               {locate connections}

      for j = (i + 1) to NET.UNITS
                               {for all connections}
        do
          connect^[j] = 0.3 * (pp[stat] - pm[stat]);
          stat = stat + 1;            {next statistic}
          dupconnect = NET.NODES.WEIGHTS^[j];
                                      {locate twin}
```

```
                    dupconnect^[i] = connect^[j];
                                                        {copy to twin}
                end do;
            end do;
        end procedure;
```

Notice that the update_connections routine modifies two connection values during every iteration, because we are modeling bidirectional connections as two unidirectional connections, and each must always contain the same value. Given the data structures we have defined for our simulator, we must preserve the bidirectional nature of the network connections by always modifying the values in two different arrays, such that these arrays always contain the same data. The algorithm for update_connections satisfies this requirement by locating the associated twin connection during every update cycle, and copying the new value from the current connection to the twin connection, as illustrated in Figure 5.9.

We shall now describe the algorithm used to train the Boltzmann simulator. Here, as before, we assume that the training patterns to be learned are contained in a globally accessible storage array named PATTERNS, and that the number of patterns in this array is obtainable through a call to an application-defined routine, how_many. Notice that in this function, we call the user-supplied routine, zero_statistics, to initialize the statistics arrays.

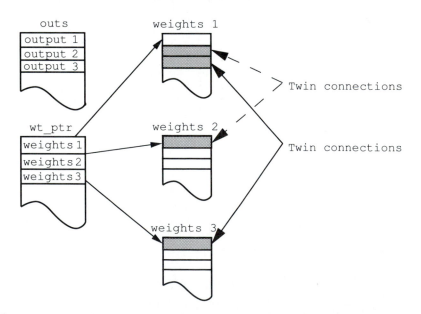

Figure 5.9   Updating of the connections in the Boltzmann simulator is shown. The weights in the arrays highlighted by the darkened boxes represent connections modified by one pass through the update_connections procedure.

```
function learn (NET:BOLTZMANN)
{cause network to learn input PATTERNS}

var i : integer;                    {iteration counters}

begin
  NET.CLAMPED = true;                 {clamp visible units}
  zero_statistics (NET);          {init statistics arrays}

  for i = 1 to how_many (PATTERNS)
    do
      set_inputs (NET, PATTERNS, i);
      anneal (NET);             {apply annealing schedule}
      sum_cooccurrence (NET);        {collect statistics}
    end do;

  pplus (NET);                              {estimate p+}
  NET.CLAMPED = false;            {unclamp visible units}
  for i = 1 to how_many (PATTERNS)
    do
      set_inputs (NET, PATTERNS, i);
      anneal (NET);             {apply annealing schedule}
      sum_cooccurrence (NET);        {collect statistics}
    end do;

  pminus (NET);                             {estimate p-}
  update_connections (NET);       {modify connections}
end procedure;
```

The algorithm necessary to have the network recall a pattern given an input pattern (production mode) is straightforward, and now depends on only the routines defined by the user to apply the new input pattern to the network and to read the resulting output. These routines, `apply_inputs` and `get_outputs`, respectively, are combined with `anneal` to generate the desired output, as shown next:

```
procedure recall (NET:BOLTZMANN; INVEC,OUTVEC:^float[])
{stimulate the network to generate an output from input}

begin
  apply_inputs (NET, INVEC);       {set the input}
  anneal (NET);                    {generate output}
  get_output (NET, OUTVEC);        {return output}
end procedure;
```

5.4 USING THE BOLTZMANN SIMULATOR

With the exception of the backpropagation network described in Chapter 3, the Boltzmann network is probably the most general-purpose network of those discussed in this text. It can be used either as an associative memory or as a mapping network, depending only on whether the output units overlap the input units. These two operating modes encompass most of the common problems to which ANS systems have been successfully applied. Unfortunately, the Boltzman network also has the distinction of being the slowest of all the simulators. Nevertheless, there are several applications that can be addressed using the Boltzmann network; in this section, we describe one.

This application uses the Boltzmann input–output model to associate patterns from "symptom" space with patterns in "diagnosis" space.

5.4.1   Boltzmann Symptom-Diagnosis Application

Let's consider a specific example of a symptom-diagnosis application. We will use an automobile diagnostic application as the basis for our example. Specifically, we will focus on an application that will diagnose why a car will not start. We first define the various symptoms to be considered:

- Does nothing: Nothing happens when the key is turned in the ignition switch.

- Clicks: A loud clicking noise is generated when the key is turned.

- Grinds: A loud grinding noise is generated when the key is turned.

- Cranks: The engine cranks as though trying to start, but the engine does not run on its own.

- No spark: Removing one of the spark-plug wires and holding the terminal near the block while cranking the engine produces no spark.

- Cable hot: After the engine has been cranked, the cable running from the battery to the starter solenoid is hot.

- No gas: Removing the fuel line from the carburetor (fuel injector) and cranking the engine produces no gas flow out of the fuel line.

Next, we consider the possible causes of the problem, based on the symptoms:

- Battery: The battery is dead.

- Solenoid: The starter solenoid is defective.

- Starter: The starter motor is defective.

- Wires: The ignition wires are defective.

- Distributor: The distributor rotor or cap is corroded.

- Fuel pump: The fuel pump is defective.

Although our list is not a complete representation of all possible problems, any one or a combination of these problems could be indicated by the symptoms. To complete our example, we shall construct a matrix indicating the

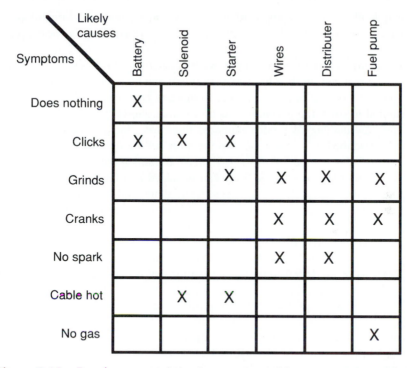

Figure 5.10 For the automobile diagnostic problem, we map symptoms to causes.

mapping of the symptoms to the probable causes. This matrix is illustrated in Figure 5.10.

An examination of this matrix indicates the variety of problems that can be indicated by any one symptom. The matrix also illustrates the problem we encounter when we attempt to program a system to perform the diagnostic function: There rarely is a one-to-one correspondence between symptoms and causes. To be successful, our automated diagnostic system must be able to correlate many different symptoms, and, in the event that some symptoms may be overlooked or absent, must be able to "fill in the blanks" of the problem based on just the indicated symptoms.

5.4.2 The Boltzmann Solution

We will now examine how a Boltzmann network can be applied to the symptom-diagnosis example we have created. The first step is to construct the network architecture that will solve the problem for us. Since we would like to be able to provide the network with observed symptoms, and to have it respond with probable cause, a good candidate architecture would be to map each symptom directly to an individual input PE, and each probable causes to an individual output PE. Since our application requires outputs that are different from the inputs, we select the Boltzmann input–output network as the best candidate.

Using the data from our example, we will need a network with seven input units and six output units. That leaves only the number of internal units undetermined. In this case, there is nothing to indicate how many hidden units will be required to solve the problem, and no external interface considerations that will limit the number of hidden units (as there were in the data-compression example described in Chapter 3). We therefore arbitrarily size the Boltzmann network such that it contains 14 internal units. If training indicates that we need more units in order to converge, they can be added at a later time. If we need fewer units, the extras can be eliminated later, although there is no overwhelming reason to remove them in such a small network other than improving the performance of the simulator.

Next, we must define the data sets to be used to train the network. Referring again to our example matrix, we can consider the data in the row vectors of the matrix as seven-dimensional input patterns; that is, for each probable-cause output that we would like the network to learn, there are seven possible symptoms that indicate the problem by their existence or absence. This approach will provide six training-vector pairs, each consisting of a seven-element symptom pattern and a six-element problem-indication pattern.

We let the existence of a symptom be indicated by a 1, and the absence of a symptom be represented by a 0. For any given input vector, the correct cause (or causes) is indicated by a logic 1 in the proper position of the output vector. The training-vector pairs produced by the mapping in the symptom-problem matrix for this example are illustrated in Figure 5.11. If you compare Figures 5.11 and 5.10, you will notice slight differences. You should convince yourself that the differences are justified.

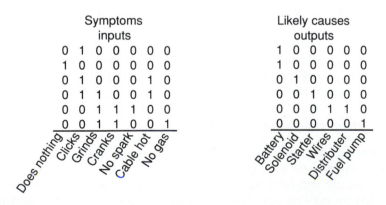

Figure 5.11   These training-vector pairs are used for the automobile diagnostic problem.

All that remains from this point is to train the network on these data pairs using the Boltzmann algorithms. Once trained, the network will produce an output identifying the probable cause indicated by the input symptom map. The network will do this when the input is equivalent to one of the training inputs, as expected, *and* it will produce an output indicating the *likely* cause of the problem when the input is similar to, but different from, any training input. This application illustrates the "best-guess" capability of the network and highlights the network's ability to deal with noisy or incomplete data inputs.

Programming Exercises

5.1. Develop the pseudocode design for the `set_inputs`, `apply_inputs`, and
`get_outputs` routines.

5.2. Develop the pseudocode design for the `pminus` routine.

5.3. The `pplus` and `pminus` as described are largely redundant and can be combined into a single routine. Develop the pseudocode design for such a routine.

5.4. Implement the Boltzmann simulator and test it with the automotive diagnostic data described in Section 5.4. Compare your results with ours, and discuss reasons for any differences.

5.5. Implement the Boltzmann simulator and test it on an application of your own choosing. Describe the application and your choice of training data, and discuss reasons why the test did or did not succeed.

5.6. Modify the simulator to contain two additional variable parameters, epsilon (ϵ) and `cycles`, as part of the network record structure. Epsilon will be used to calculate the connection-weight change, instead of the hard-coded 0.3 constant described in the text, and `cycles` should be used to specify the number of iterations performed during the `sum_cooccurrence` routine (instead of the five we specified). Retrain the network using the automotive diagnostic data with a different value for `epsilon`, then change `cycles`, and then change both parameters. Describe any performance variations that you observed.

Suggested Readings

The origin of modern information theory is described in a paper by Shannon, which is itself reprinted in a collection of papers on the mathematical theory of communications [7]. A good textbook on statistical mechanics is the one by Reif [6]. A detailed development of the learning algorithm for the Boltzmann machine is given in the paper by Hinton and Sejnowski in the PDP series [3]. Another worthwhile paper is the one by Ackley, Hinton, and Sejnowski [1]. An early account of using simulated annealing to solve optimization problems is given in a paper by Kirkpatrick, Gelatt, and Vecchi [5]. The concept of using the Cauchy distribution to speed the annealing process is discussed in a paper by Szu [8]. A *Byte* magazine article by Hinton contains an algorithm for the Boltzmann machine that is slightly different from the one presented in this chapter [4].

Bibliography

[1] David H. Ackley, Geoffrey E. Hinton, and Terrence J. Sejnowski. A learning algorithm for Boltzmann machines. In James A. Anderson and Edward Rosenfeld, editors, *Neurocomputing*. MIT Press, Cambridge, MA, pages 638–650, 1988. Reprinted from *Cognitive Science* 9:147–169, 1985.

[2] Stuart Geman and Donald Geman. Stochastic relaxation, Gibbs distributions, and the Bayesian restoration of images. In James A. Anderson and Edward Rosenfeld, editors, *Neurocomputing*. MIT Press, Cambridge, MA, pages 614–634, 1988. Reprinted from *IEEE Transactions of Pattern Analysis and Machine Intelligence* PAMI-6: 721–741, 1984.

[3] G. E. Hinton and T. J. Sejnowski. Learning and relearning in Boltzmann machines. In David E. Rumelhart and James L. McClelland, editors, *Parallel Distributed Processing: Explorations in the Microstructure of Cognition*. MIT Press, Cambridge, MA, pages 282–317, 1986.

[4] Geoffrey E. Hinton. Learning in parallel networks. *Byte*, 10(4):265–273, April 1985.

[5] S. Kirkpatrick, Jr., C. D. Gelatt, and M. P. Vecchi. Optimization by simulated annealing. In James A. Anderson and Edward Rosenfeld, editors, *Neurocomputing*. MIT Press, Cambridge, MA, pages 554–568, 1988. Reprinted from *Science* 220: 671–680, 1983.

[6] F. Reif. *Fundamentals of Statistical and Thermal Physics*. McGraw-Hill series in fundamental physics. McGraw-Hill, New York, 1965.

[7] C. E. Shannon. The mathematical theory of communication. In C. E. Shannon and W. Weaver, editors, *The Mathematical Theory of Communication*. University of Illinois Press, Urbana, IL, pages 29–125, 1963.

[8] Harold Szu. Fast simulated annealing. In John S. Denker, editor, *Neural Networks for Computing*. American Institute of Physics, New York, pages 420–425, 1986.

The Counterpropagation Network

The counterpropagation network (CPN) is the most recently developed of the models that we have discussed so far in this text. The CPN is not so much a new discovery as it is a novel combination of previously existing network types. Hecht-Nielsen synthesized the architecture from a combination of a structure known as a *competitive* network and Grossberg's *outstar* structure [5, 6]. Although the network architecture, as it appears in its originally published form in Figure 6.1, seems rather formidable, we shall see that the operation of the network is quite straightforward.

Given a set of vector pairs, $(\mathbf{x}_1, \mathbf{y}_1), (\mathbf{x}_2, \mathbf{y}_2), \ldots, (\mathbf{x}_L, \mathbf{y}_L)$, the CPN can learn to associate an $\mathbf{x}$ vector on the input layer with a $\mathbf{y}$ vector at the output layer. If the relationship between $\mathbf{x}$ and $\mathbf{y}$ can be described by a continuous function, Φ, such that $\mathbf{y} = \Phi(\mathbf{x})$, the CPN will learn to approximate this mapping for any value of $\mathbf{x}$ in the range specified by the set of training vectors. Furthermore, if the inverse of Φ exists, such that $\mathbf{x}$ is a function of $\mathbf{y}$, then the CPN will also learn the inverse mapping, $\mathbf{x} = \Phi^{-1}(\mathbf{y})$.[1] For a great many cases of practical interest, the inverse function does not exist. In these situations, we can simplify the discussion of the CPN by considering only the forward-mapping case, $\mathbf{y} = \Phi(\mathbf{x})$.

In Figure 6.2, we have reorganized the CPN diagram and have restricted our consideration to the forward-mapping case. The network now appears as

---

[1] We are using the term *function* in its strict mathematical sense. If y is a function of x, then every value of x corresponds to one and only one value of y. Conversely, if x is a function of y, then every value of y corresponds to one and only one value of x. An example of a function whose inverse is not a function is, $y = x^2, -\infty < x < \infty$. A somewhat more abstract, but perhaps more interesting, situation is a function that maps images of animals to the name of the animal. For example, "CAT" $= \Phi$("picture of cat"). Each picture represents only one animal, but each animal corresponds to many different pictures.

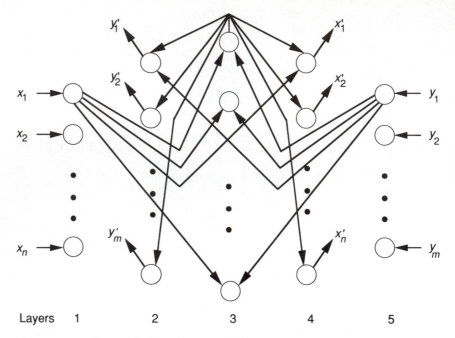

Layers   1   2   3   4   5

Figure 6.1   This spiderlike diagram of the CPN architecture has five layers:
two input layers (1 and 5), one hidden layer (3), and two
output layers (2 and 4). The CPN gets its name from the fact
that the input vectors on layers 1 and 2 appear to propagate
through the network in opposite directions. *Source: Reprinted
with permission from Robert Hecht-Nielsen, "Counterpropagation
networks."   In* Proceedings of the IEEE First International
Conference on Neural Networks. *San Diego, CA, June 1987.*
©*1987 IEEE.*

a three-layer architecture, similar to, but not exactly like, the backpropagation
network discussed in Chapter 3. An input vector is applied to the units on
layer 1. Each unit on layer 2 calculates its net-input value, and a competition
is held to determine which unit has the largest net-input value. That unit is
the only unit that sends a value to the units in the output layer. We shall
postpone a detailed discussion of the processing until we have examined the
various components of the network.

   CPNs are interesting for a number of reasons. By combining existing network types into a new architecture, the CPN hints at the possibility of forming
other, useful networks from bits and pieces of existing structures. Moreover,
instead of employing a single learning algorithm throughout the network, the
CPN uses a different learning procedure on each layer. The learning algorithms
allow the CPN to train quite rapidly with respect to other networks that we have
studied so far. The tradeoff is that the CPN may not always yield sufficient

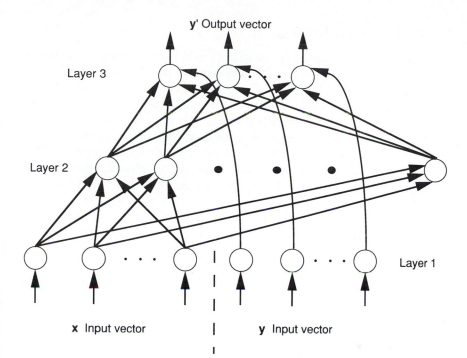

Figure 6.2 The forward-mapping CPN is shown. Vector pairs from the training set are applied to layer 1. After training is complete, applying the vectors $(\mathbf{x}, \emptyset)$ to layer 1 will result in an approximation, $\mathbf{y}'$, to the corresponding $\mathbf{y}$ vector, at the output layer, layer 3. See Section 6.2 for more details of the training procedure.

accuracy for some applications. Nevertheless, the CPN remains a good choice for some classes of problems, and it provides an excellent vehicle for rapid prototyping of other applications. In the next section, we shall examine the various building blocks from which the CPN is constructed.

6.1 CPN BUILDING BLOCKS

The PEs and network structures that we shall study in this section play an important role in many of the subsequent chapters in this text. For that reason, we present this introductory material in some detail. There are four major components: an input layer that performs some processing on the input data, a processing element called an **instar**, a layer of instars known as a **competitive network**, and a structure known as an **outstar**. In Section 6.2, we shall return to the discussion of the CPN.

6.1.1 The Input Layer

Discussions of neural networks often ignore the input-layer processing elements, or consider them simply as pass-through units, responsible only for distributing input data to other processing elements. Computer simulations of networks usually arrange for all input data to be scaled or normalized to accommodate calculations by the computer's CPU. For example, input-value magnitudes may have to be scaled to prevent overflow error during the sum-of-product calculations that dominate most network simulations. Biological systems do not have the benefits of such preprocessing; they must rely on internal mechanisms to prevent saturation of neural activities by large input signals. In this section, we shall examine a mechanism of interaction among processing elements that overcomes this **noise-saturation dilemma** [2]. Although the mechanism has some neurophysiological plausibility, we shall not examine any of the biological implications of the model.

Examine the layer of processing elements shown in Figure 6.3. There is one input value, I_i, for each of the n units on the layer. The total input pattern intensity is given by $I = \sum_i I_i$. Corresponding to each I_i, we shall define a quantity

$$\Theta_i = I_i \left(\sum_i I_i \right)^{-1} \tag{6.1}$$

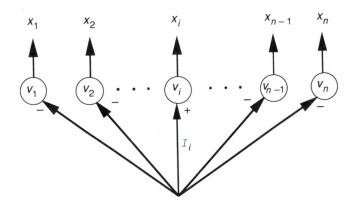

Figure 6.3 This layer of input units has n processing elements, $\{v_1, v_2, \ldots, v_n\}$. Each input value, I_i, is connected with an excitatory connection (arrow with a plus sign) to its corresponding processing element, v_i. Each I_i is connected also to every other processing element, v_k, $k \neq i$, with an inhibitory connection (arrow with a minus sign). This arrangement is known as *on-center, off-surround*. The output of the layer is proportional to the normalized reflectance pattern.

The vector, $(\Theta_1, \Theta_2, \ldots, \Theta_n)^t$, is called a **reflectance pattern**. Notice that this pattern is normalized in the sense that $\sum_i \Theta_i = 1$.

The reflectance pattern is independent of the total intensity of the corresponding input pattern. For example, the reflectance pattern corresponding to the image of a person's face would be independent of whether the person were being viewed in bright sunlight or in shade. We can usually recognize a familiar person in a wide variety of lighting conditions, even if we have not seen her previously in the identical situation. This experience suggests that our memory stores and recalls reflectance patterns.

The outputs of the processing elements in Figure 6.3 are governed by the set of differential equations,

$$\dot{x}_i = -Ax_i + (B - x_i)I_i - x_i \sum_{k \neq i} I_k \qquad (6.2)$$

where $0 < x_i(0) < B$, and $A, B > 0$. Each processing element receives a net excitation (on-center) of $(B - x_i)I_i$ from its corresponding input value, I_i. The addition of inhibitory connections (off-surround), $-x_i I_k$, from other units is responsible for preventing the activity of the processing element from rising in proportion to the absolute pattern intensity, I_i.

Once an input pattern is applied, the processing elements quickly reach an equilibrium state ($\dot{x}_i = 0$) with

$$x_i^{eq} = \Theta_i \frac{BI}{A + I} \qquad (6.3)$$

where we have used the definition of Θ_i in Eq. (6.1). The output pattern is normalized, since

$$\sum_i x_i = \frac{BI}{A + I} = B\left(\frac{A}{I} + 1\right)^{-1}$$

which is always less than B. Thus, the pattern of activity that develops across the input units is proportional to the reflectance pattern, rather than to the original input pattern.

After the input pattern is removed, the activities of the units do not remain at their equilibrium values, nor do they return immediately to zero. The activity pattern persists for some time while the term $-Ax_i$ reduces the activities gradually back to a value of zero.

An input layer of the type discussed in this section is used for both the **x**-vector and **y**-vector portions of the CPN input layer shown in Figure 6.1. When performing a digital simulation of the CPN, we can simplify the program by normalizing the input vectors in software. Whether the input-pattern normalization is accomplished using Eq. (6.2), or by some preprocessing in software, depends on the particular implementation of the network.

Exercise 6.1:

1. Solve Eq. (6.2) to find $x_i(t)$ explicitly, assuming $x_i(0) = 0$ and a constant input pattern, **I**.

2. Assume that the input pattern is removed at $t = t'$, and find $x_i(t)$ for $t > t'$.

3. Draw the graph of $x_i(t)$ from $t = 0$ to some $t \gg t'$. What determines how quickly $x_i(t)$ (a) reaches its equilibrium value, and (b) decays back to zero after the input pattern is removed?

Exercise 6.2: Investigate the equations

$$\dot{x}_i = -Ax_i + (B - x_i)I_i$$

as a possible alternative to Eq. (6.2) for the input-layer processing elements. For a constant reflectance pattern, what happens to the activation of each processing element as the total pattern intensity, I, increases?

Exercise 6.3: Consider the equations

$$\dot{x}_i = -Ax_i + (B - x_i)I_i - (x_i + C)\sum_{k \neq i} I_k$$

which differ from Eq. (6.2) by an additional inhibition term, $C\sum_{k \neq i} I_k$:

1. Suppose $I_i = 0$, but $\sum_{k \neq i} I_k > 0$. Show that x_i can assume a negative value. Does this result make sense? (Consider what it means for a real neuron to have zero activation in terms of the neuron's resting potential.)

2. Show that the system suppresses noise by requiring that the reflectance values, Θ_i, be greater than some minimum value before they will excite a positive activity in the processing element.

6.1.2   The Instar

The hidden layer of the CPN comprises a set of processing elements known as *instars*. In this section, we shall discuss the instar individually. In the following section, we shall examine the set of instars that operate together to form the CPN hidden layer.

The **instar** is a single processing element that shares its general structure and processing functions with many other processing elements described in this text. We distinguish it by the specific way in which it is trained to respond to input data.

Let's begin with a general processing element, such as the one in Figure 6.4(a). If the arrow representing the output is ignored, the processing element can be redrawn in the starlike configuration of Figure 6.4(b). The inward-pointing arrows identify the instar structure, but we restrict the use of the term *instar* to those units whose processing and learning are governed by the

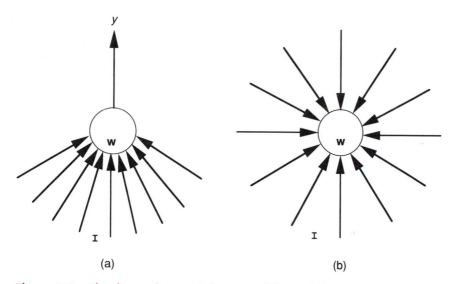

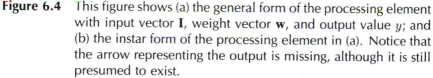

(a)   (b)

Figure 6.4   This figure shows (a) the general form of the processing element
with input vector **I**, weight vector **w**, and output value y; and
(b) the instar form of the processing element in (a). Notice that
the arrow representing the output is missing, although it is still
presumed to exist.

equations in this section. The net-input value is calculated, as usual, by the dot
product of the input and weight vectors, net $= \mathbf{I} \cdot \mathbf{w}$. We shall assume that the
input vector, **I**, and the weight vector, **w**, have been normalized to a length of 1.
    The output of the instar is governed by the equation

$$\dot{y} = -ay + b\,\text{net} \tag{6.4}$$

where $a, b > 0$. The dynamic behavior of y is illustrated in Figure 6.5.
    We can solve Eq. (6.4) to get the output as a function of time. Assuming
the initial output is zero, and that a nonzero input vector is present from time
$t = 0$ until time t,

$$y(t) = \frac{b}{a}\text{net}\left(1 - e^{-at}\right) \tag{6.5}$$

The equilibrium value of $y(t)$ is

$$y^{eq} = \frac{b}{a}\text{net} \tag{6.6}$$

If the input vector is removed at time t', after equilibrium has been reached,
then

$$y(t) = y^{eq}e^{-a(t-t')} \tag{6.7}$$

for $t > t'$.

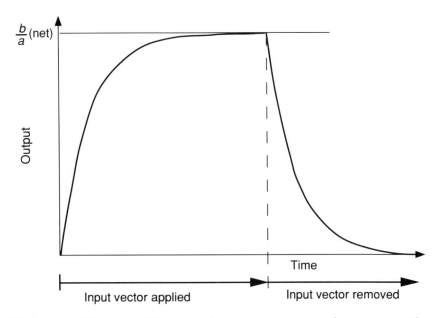

Figure 6.5 This graph illustrates the output response of an instar. When the input vector is nonzero, the output rises to an equilibrium value of (b/a)net. If the input vector is removed, the output falls exponentially with a time constant of $1/a$.

Notice that, for a given a and b, the output at equilibrium will be larger when the net-input value is larger. Figure 6.6 shows a diagram of the weight vector, **w**, of an instar, and an input vector, **I**. The net-input value determines how close to each other the two vectors are as measured by the angle between them, θ. The largest equilibrium output will occur when the input and weight vectors are perfectly aligned ($\theta = 0$).

If we want the instar to respond maximally to a particular input vector, we must arrange that the weight vector be made identical to the desired input vector. The instar can learn to respond maximally to a particular input vector if the initial weight vector is allowed to change according to the equation

$$\dot{\mathbf{w}} = -c\,\mathbf{w} + d\,\mathbf{I}\,y \tag{6.8}$$

where y is the output of the instar, and $c, d > 0$. Notice the relationship between Eq. (6.8) and the Hebbian learning rule discussed in Chapter 1. The second term on the right side of Eq. (6.8) contains the product of the input and the output of a processing element. Thus, when both are large, the weight on the input connection is reinforced, as predicted by Hebb's theory.

Equation 6.8 is difficult to integrate because y is a complex function of time through Eq. (6.5). We can try to simplify the problem by assuming that y

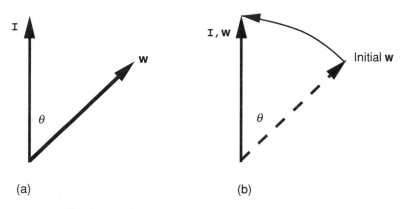

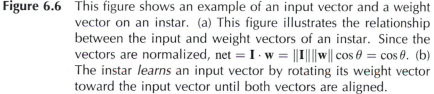

Figure 6.6   This figure shows an example of an input vector and a weight vector on an instar. (a) This figure illustrates the relationship between the input and weight vectors of an instar. Since the vectors are normalized, $\text{net} = \mathbf{I} \cdot \mathbf{w} = \|\mathbf{I}\|\|\mathbf{w}\| \cos\theta = \cos\theta$. (b) The instar *learns* an input vector by rotating its weight vector toward the input vector until both vectors are aligned.

reaches its equilibrium value much faster than changes in $\mathbf{w}$ can occur. Then, $y = y^{eq} = (b/a)\text{net}$. Because $\text{net} = \mathbf{w} \cdot \mathbf{I}$, Eq. (6.8) becomes

$$\dot{\mathbf{w}} = -c\mathbf{w} + d\,\mathbf{I}(\mathbf{w} \cdot \mathbf{I}) \qquad (6.9)$$

where we have absorbed the factor b/a into the constant d. Although Eq. (6.9) is still not directly solvable, the assumption that changes to weights occur more slowly than do changes to other parameters is important. We shall see more of the utility of such an assumption in Chapter 8. Figure 6.7 illustrates the solution to Eq. (6.9) for a simple two-dimensional case.

An alternative approach to Eq. (6.8) begins with the observation that, in the absence of an input vector, $\mathbf{I}$, the weight vector will continuously decay away toward zero ($\dot{\mathbf{w}} = -c\mathbf{w}$). This effect can be considered as a forgetfulness on the part of the processing element. To avoid this forgetfulness, we can modify Eq. (6.8) such that any change to the weight vector depends on whether there is an input vector there to be learned. If an input vector is present, then $\text{net} = \mathbf{w} \cdot \mathbf{I}$ will be nonzero. Instead of Eq. (6.8), we can use as the learning law,

$$\dot{\mathbf{w}} = (-c\mathbf{w} + d\mathbf{I})U(\text{net}) \qquad (6.10)$$

where

$$U(\text{net}) = \begin{cases} 1 & \text{net} > 0 \\ 0 & \text{net} = 0 \end{cases}$$

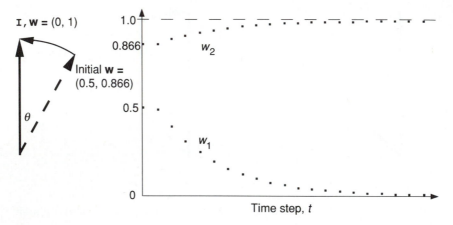

Figure 6.7 Given an input vector $\mathbf{I} = (0, 1)$ and an initial weight vector, $\mathbf{w}(0) = (0.5, 0.866)$, the components, w_1 and w_2, of the weight vector evolve in time according to Eq. (6.9), as shown in the graph. The weight vector eventually aligns itself to the input vector such that $\mathbf{w} = (0, 1) = \mathbf{I}$. For this example, $c = d = 1$.

Equation (6.10) can be integrated directly for $U(\text{net}) = 1$. Notice that $\mathbf{w}^{eq} = (d/c)\mathbf{I}$, making $c = d$ a condition that must be satisfied for $\mathbf{w}$ to evolve toward an exact match with $\mathbf{I}$. Using this fact, we can rewrite Eq. (6.10) in a form more suitable for later digital simulations:

$$\Delta\mathbf{w} = \alpha(\mathbf{I} - \mathbf{w}) \qquad (6.11)$$

In Eq. (6.11), we have used the approximation $d\mathbf{w}/dt \approx \Delta\mathbf{w}/\Delta t$, and have let $\alpha = c\Delta t$. An approximate solution to Eq. (6.10) would be

$$\mathbf{w}(t + 1) = \mathbf{w}(t) + \alpha(\mathbf{I} - \mathbf{w}(t)) \qquad (6.12)$$

for $\alpha < 1$; see Figure 6.8.

A single instar learning a single input vector does not provide an interesting case. Let's consider the situation where we have a number of input vectors, all relatively close together in what we shall call a *cluster*. A cluster might represent items of a single class. We would like the instar to learn some form of representative vector of the class: the average, for example. Figure 6.9 illustrates the idea.

Learning takes place in an iterative fashion:

1. Select an input vector, I_i, at random, according to the probability distribution of the cluster. (If the cluster is not uniformly distributed, you should select input vectors more frequently from regions where there is a higher density of vectors.)

2. Calculate $\alpha(\mathbf{I} - \mathbf{w})$, and update the weight vector according to Eq. (6.12).

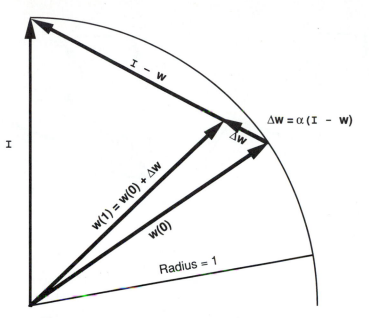

Figure 6.8   The quantity $(\mathbf{I} - \mathbf{w})$ is a vector that points from $\mathbf{w}$ toward $\mathbf{I}$. In Eq. (6.12), $\mathbf{w}$ moves in discrete timesteps toward $\mathbf{I}$. Notice that $\mathbf{w}$ does not remain normalized.

3. Repeat steps 1 and 2 for a number of times equal to the number of input vectors in the cluster.

4. Repeat step 3 several times.

The last item in this list is admittedly vague. There is a way to calculate an average error as learning proceeds, which can be used as a criterion for halting the learning process (see Exercise 6.4). In practice, error values are rarely used, since the instar is never used as a stand-alone unit, and other criteria will determine when to stop the training.

It is also a good idea to reduce the value of α as training proceeds. Once the weight vector has reached the *middle* of the cluster, outlying input vectors might pull $\mathbf{w}$ out of the area if α is very large.

When the weight vector has reached an average position within the cluster, it should stay generally within a small region around that average position. In other words, the average change in the weight vector, $\langle \Delta \mathbf{w} \rangle$, should become very small. Movements of $\mathbf{w}$ in one direction should generally be offset by movements in the opposite direction. If we assume $\langle \Delta \mathbf{w} \rangle = 0$, then Eq. (6.11) shows that

$$\langle \mathbf{w} \rangle = \langle \mathbf{I} \rangle$$

which is what we wanted.

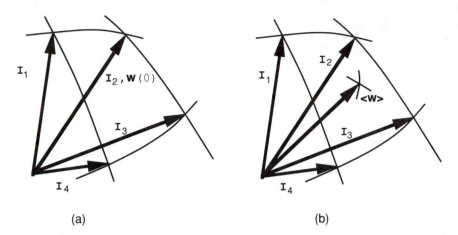

Figure 6.9   This figure illustrates how an instar learns to respond to a cluster of input vectors. (a) To learn a cluster of input vectors, we select the initial weight vector to be equal to some member of the cluster. This initialization ensures that the weight vector is in the right region of space. (b) As learning proceeds, the weight vector will eventually settle down to some small region that represents an average, $\langle \mathbf{w} \rangle$, of all the input vectors.

Now that we have seen how an instar can learn the average of a cluster of input vectors, we can talk about layers of instars. Instars can be grouped together into what is known as a **competitive network**. The competitive network forms the middle layer of the CPN and is the subject of the next section.

Exercise 6.4: For a given input vector, we can define the instar error as the magnitude of the difference between the input vector and the weight vector: $\varepsilon = \|\mathbf{I}_i - \mathbf{w}\|$. Show that the mean squared error can be written as

$$\langle \varepsilon^2 \rangle = 2(1 - \langle \cos \theta_i \rangle)$$

where θ_i is the angle between $\mathbf{I}_i$ and $\mathbf{w}$.

6.1.3   Competitive Networks

In the previous section, we saw how an individual instar could learn to respond to a certain group of input vectors clustered together in a region of space. Suppose we have several instars grouped in a layer, as shown in Figure 6.10, each of which responds maximally to a group of input vectors in a different region of space. We can say that this layer of instars *classifies* any input vector, because the instar with the strongest response for any given input identifies the region of space in which the input vector lies.

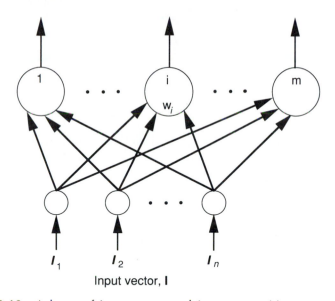

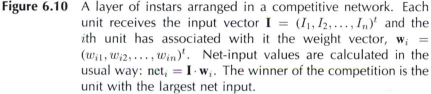

Input vector, I

Figure 6.10 A layer of instars arranged in a competitive network. Each unit receives the input vector $\mathbf{I} = (I_1, I_2, \ldots, I_n)^t$ and the ith unit has associated with it the weight vector, $\mathbf{w}_i = (w_{i1}, w_{i2}, \ldots, w_{in})^t$. Net-input values are calculated in the usual way: $\text{net}_i = \mathbf{I} \cdot \mathbf{w}_i$. The winner of the competition is the unit with the largest net input.

Rather than our examining the response of each instar to determine which is the largest, our task would be simpler if the instar with the largest response were the *only* unit to have a nonzero output. This effect can be accomplished if the instars compete with one another for the privilege of turning on. Since there is no external judge to decide which instar has the largest net input, the units must decide among themselves who is the winner. This decision process requires communication among all the units on the layer; it also complicates the analysis, since there are more inputs to each unit than just the input from the previous layer. In the following discussion, we shall be focusing on unit activities, rather than on unit output values.

Figure 6.11 illustrates the interconnections that implement competition among the instars. The unit activations are determined by differential equations. There is a variety of forms that these differential equations can take; one of the simplest is

$$\dot{x}_i = -Ax_i + (B - x_i)[f(x_i) + \text{net}_i] - x_i \left[\sum_{k \neq i} f(x_k) + \sum_{k \neq i} \text{net}_k \right] \quad (6.13)$$

where $A, B > 0$ and $f(x_i)$ is an output function that we shall specify shortly [2]. This equation should be compared to Eq. (6.2). We can convert Eq. (6.2) to

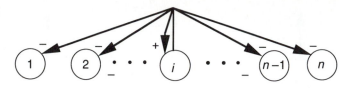

Figure 6.11   An   on-center   off-surround   system   for   implementing
competition among a group of instars. Each unit receives a
positive feedback signal to itself and sends an inhibitory signal
to all other units on the layer. The unit whose weight vector
most closely matches the input vector sends the strongest
inhibitory signals to the other units and receives the largest
positive feedback from itself.

Eq. (6.13) by replacing every occurrence of I_j in Eq. (6.2) with $f(x_j) + \text{net}_j$,
for all j. The relationship between the constants A and B, and the form of the
function, $f(x_j)$, determine how the solutions to Eq. (6.13) evolve in time. We
shall now look at specific cases.

Equation (6.13) is somewhat easier to analyze if we convert it to a pair
of equations: one that describes the reflectance variables, $X_i = x_i / \sum_k x_k$,
and one that describes the total pattern intensity, $x = \sum_k x_k$. First, rearrange
Eq. (6.13) as follows:

$$\dot{x}_i = -Ax_i + B[f(x_i) + \text{net}_i] - x_i \left[\sum_k f(x_k) + \sum_k \text{net}_k \right]$$

Next, sum over i to get

$$\dot{x} = -Ax + (B - x) \left[\sum_k f(xX_k) + \sum_k \text{net}_k \right] \tag{6.14}$$

Now substitute xX_i into Eq. (6.13) and use Eq. (6.14) to simplify the result. If
we make the definition $g(w) = w^{-1}f(w)$, then we get

$$x\dot{X}_i = BxX_i \sum_k X_k[g(xX_i) - g(xX_k)] + B(1 - X_i)\text{net}_i - BX_i \sum_{k \neq i} \text{net}_k \tag{6.15}$$

We can now evaluate the asymptotic behavior of Eqs. (6.14) and (6.15).
Let's begin with the simple, linear case of $f(w) = w$. Since $g(w) = w^{-1}f(w)$,
$g(w) = 1$ and the first term on the right of Eq. (6.15) is zero. The reflectance
variables stabilize at

$$X_i = \frac{\text{net}_i}{\sum_k \text{net}_k}$$

so the activities become

$$x_i = x^{eq} \frac{\text{net}_i}{\sum_k \text{net}_k}$$

where x^{eq} comes from setting Eq. (6.14) equal to zero. This equation shows that the units will accurately register any pattern presented as an input. Now let's look at what happens after the input pattern is removed.

Let $net_i = 0$ for all i. Then, $\dot{X}_i$ is identically zero for all time and the reflectance variables remain constant. The unit activations now depend only on x, since $x_i = xX_i$. Equation (6.14) reduces to

$$\dot{x} = (B - A - x)x$$

If $B \leq A$, then $\dot{x} < 0$ and $x \to 0$. However, if $B > A$, then $x \to B - A$ and the activity pattern becomes stored permanently on the units. This behavior is unlike the behavior of the input units described by Eq. (6.2), where removal of the input pattern always resulted in a decay of the activities. We shall call this storage effect **short-term memory** (STM). Even though the effect appears to be permanent, we can assume the existence of a reset mechanism that will remove the current pattern so that another can be stored. Figure 6.12 illustrates a simple example for the linear output function.

For our second example, we assume a faster-than-linear output function, $f(w) = w^2$. In this case $g(w) = w$. Notice that the first term on the right of Eq. (6.15) contains the factor $[g(xX_i) - g(xX_k)]$. For the quadratic output function, this expression reduces to $x[X_i - X_k]$. If $X_i > X_k$ for all values of $k \neq i$, then the first term in Eq. (6.14) is an excitatory term. If $X_i < X_k$ for $k \neq i$, then the first term in Eq. (6.14) becomes an inhibitory term. Thus, this network tends to enhance the activity of the unit with the largest value of X_i. This effect is illustrated in Figure 6.13. After the input pattern is removed, $\dot{X}_i$ will be greater than zero for only the unit with the largest value of X_i.

Exercise 6.5: Use Eq. (6.14) to show that, after the input pattern has been removed, the total activity of the network, x, is bounded by the value of B.

We now have an output function that can be used to implement a winner-take-all competitive network. The quadratic output function (or, for that matter, any function $f(w) = w^n$, where $n > 1$) can be used in off-surround, inhibitory connections to suppress all inputs except the largest. This effect is the ultimate in noise suppression: The network assumes that everything except the largest signal is noise.

It is possible to combine the qualities of noise suppression with the ability to store an accurate representation of an input vector: Simply arrange for the output function to be faster than linear for small activities, and linear for larger activities. If we add the additional constraint that the unit output must be bounded at all times, we must have the output function increase at a less-than-linear rate for large values of activity. This combination results in a sigmoid output function, as illustrated in Figure 6.14.

The mathematical analysis of Eqs. (6.14) and (6.15) with a sigmoid output function is considerably more complicated than it was for the other twocases. All the cases considered here, as well as many others, are treated in depth by

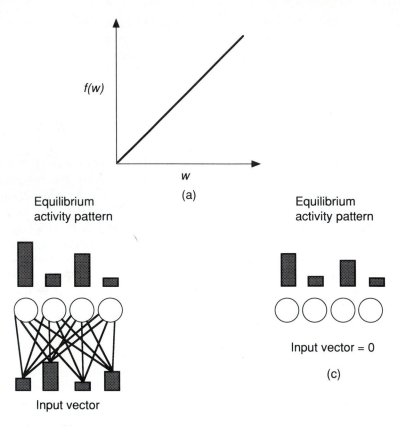

Figure 6.12   This series of figures shows the result of applying a certain input vector to units having a linear output function. (a) The graph of the output function, $f(w) = w$. (b) This figure shows the result of the sustained application of the input vector. The units reach equilibrium activities as shown. (c) After removal of the input vector, the units reach an equilibrium such that the pattern is stored in STM.

Grossberg [4].   Use of the sigmoid results in the existence of a **quenching threshold** (QT). Units whose net inputs are above the QT will have their activities enhanced.   The effect is one of **contrast enhancement**.   An extreme example is illustrated in Figure 6.14.

Reference back to Figure 6.1 or 6.2 will reveal that there are no obvious interconnections among the units on the competitive middle layer. In a digital simulation of a competitive network, the actual interconnections are unnecessary. The CPU can act as an external judge to determine which unit has the largest net-

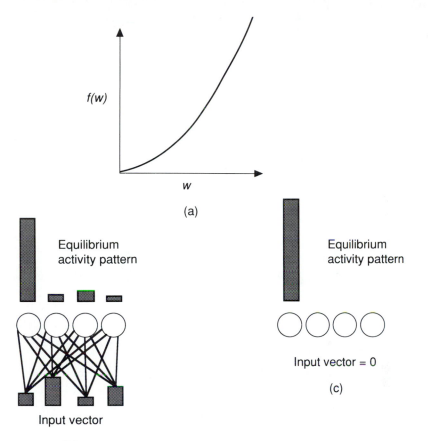

Figure 6.13 This series of figures is analogous to those in Figure 6.12, but with units having a quadratic output function. (a) The graph of the quadratic output function. (b) While the input vector is present, the network tends to enhance the activity of the unit with the largest activity. For the given input pattern, the unit activities reach the equilibrium values shown. (c) After the input pattern is removed, all activities but the largest decay to zero.

input value. The winning unit would then be assigned an output value of 1. The situation is similar for the input layer. In a software simulation, we do not need on-center off-surround interactions to normalize the input vector; that can also be done easily by the CPU. These considerations aside, attention to the underlying theory is essential to understanding. When digital simulations give way to neural-network integrated circuitry, such an understanding will be required.

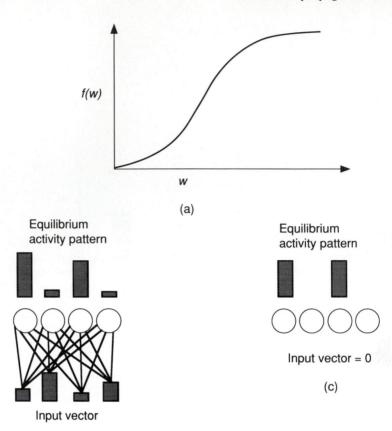

Figure 6.14   This figure is analogous to Figures 6.12 and 6.13, but with
units having a sigmoid output function. (a) The sigmoid
output function combines noise suppression at low activities,
linear pattern storage at intermediate values, and a bounded
output at large activity values. (b) When the input vector
is present, the unit activities reach an equilibrium value, as
shown. (c) After removal of the input vector, the activities
above a certain threshold are enhanced, whereas those below
the threshold are suppressed.

6.1.4   The Outstar

The final leg of our journey through CPN components brings us to Grossberg's
outstar structure. As Figure 6.15 shows, an outstar is composed of all of the
units in the CPN outer layer and a single hidden-layer unit. Thus, the outer-layer
units participate in several different outstars: one for each unit in the middle
layer.

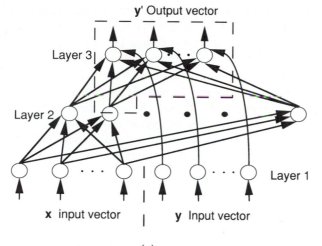

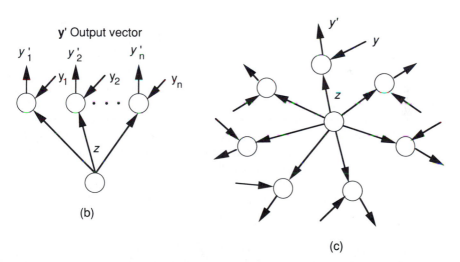

Figure 6.15 This figure illustrates the *outstar* and its relationship to the CPN architecture. (a) The dotted line encompasses one of the outstar structures in the CPN. The line is intentionally drawn through the middle-layer unit to indicate the dual functionality of that unit. Each middle-layer unit combines with the outer layer to form an individual outstar. (b) A single outstar unit is shown. The output units of the outstar have two inputs: z, from the connecting unit of the previous layer, and y_i, which is the training input. The training input is present during only the learning period. The output of the outstar is the vector $\mathbf{y}' = (y_1', y_2', \ldots, y_n')^t$. (c) The outstar is redrawn in a suggestive configuration. Note that the arrows point outward in a configuration that is complementary to the instar.

In Chapter 1, we gave a brief description of Pavlovian conditioning in terms of Hebbian learning. Grossberg argues that the outstar is the minimal neural architecture capable of classical conditioning [3]. Consider the outstar shown in Figure 6.16. Initially, the **conditioned stimulus** (CS) (e.g., a ringing bell) is assumed to be unable to elicit a response from any of the units to which it is connected. An **unconditioned stimulus** (UCS) (the sight of food) can cause an **unconditioned response** (UCR) (salivation). If the CS is present while the UCS is causing the UCR, then the strength of the connection from the CS unit to the UCR unit will also be increased, in keeping with Hebb's theory (see Chapter 1). Later, the CS will be able to cause a **conditioned response** (CR) (the same as the UCR), even if the UCS is absent.

The behavior of the outstars in the CPN resembles this classical conditioning. During the training period, the winner of the competition on the hidden layer turns on, providing a single CS to the output units. The UCS is supplied by the **y**-vector portion of the input layer. Because we want the network to learn the actual **y** vector, the UCR will be the same as the **y** vector, within a constant multiplicative factor. After training is complete, the appearance of the CS will cause the CR value (the **y**′ vector) to appear at the output units, even though the UCS values will be all zero.

In the CPN, the hidden layer participates in both the instar and outstar structures of the network. The function of the competitive instars is to recognize an input pattern through a winner-take-all competition. Once a winner has been declared, that unit becomes the CS for an outstar. The outstar associates some value or identity with the input pattern. The instar and outstar complement each other in this fashion: The instar recognizes an input pattern and classifies it; the outstar identifies or names the selected class. This behavior led one researcher to note that the instar is dumb, whereas the outstar is blind [9].

The equations that govern the processing and learning of the outstar are similar in form to those for the instar. During the training process, the output values of the outstar can be calculated from

$$\dot{y}'_i = -ay'_i + by_i + c\,\text{net}_i$$

which is similar to Eq. (6.4) for the instar except for the additional term due to the training input, y_i. The parameters a, b, and c, are all assumed to be positive. The value of net_i is calculated in the usual way as the sum of products of weights and input values from the connecting units. For the outstar and the CPN, only a single connecting unit has a nonzero output at any given time. Even though each output unit of the outstar has an entire weight vector associated with it, the net input reduces to a single term, $w_{ij}z$, where z is the output of the connecting unit. In the case of the CPN, $z = 1$. Therefore, we can write

$$\dot{y}'_i = -ay'_i + by_i + cw_{ij} \qquad \qquad (6.16)$$

where the jth unit on the hidden layer is the connecting unit. In its most general form, the parameters a, b, and c in Eq. (6.16) are functions of time. Here, we

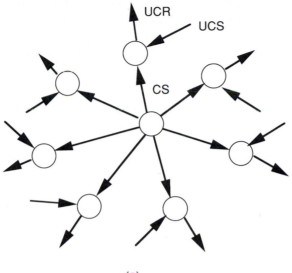

(a)

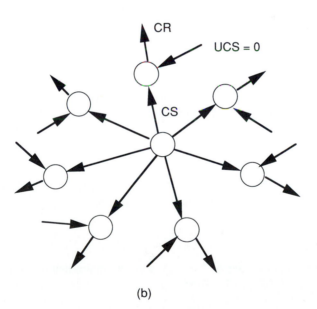

(b)

Figure 6.16   This figure shows an implied classical-conditioning scenario. (a) During the conditioning period, the CS and the UCS excite one of the output units simultaneously. (b) After conditioning, the presence of the CS alone can excite the CR without exciting any of the other output units.

shall consider them to be constants for simplicity. For the remainder of this discussion, we shall drop the j subscript from the weight.

After training is complete, no further changes in w_i take place and the training inputs, y_i, are absent. Then, the output of the outstar is

$$\dot{y}'_i = -ay'_i + cw_i^{eq} \tag{6.17}$$

where w_i^{eq} is the fixed weight value found during training.

The weights evolve according to an equation almost identical to Eq. (6.10) for the instar:

$$\dot{w}_i = (-dw_i + ey_i z)U(z) \tag{6.18}$$

Notice that the second term in Eq. (6.18) contains the training input, y_i, not the unit output, y'_i. The $U(z)$ function ensures that no unlearning takes place when there is no training input present, or when the connecting unit is off ($z = 0$). Since both z and $U(z)$ are 1 for the middle-layer unit that wins the competition, Eq. (6.18) becomes

$$\dot{w}_i = -dw_i + ey_i \tag{6.19}$$

for the connections from the winning, middle-layer unit. Connections from other middle-layer units do not participate in the learning.

Recall that a given instar can learn to recognize a cluster of input vectors. If the desired CPN outputs (the y_is) corresponding to each vector in the cluster are all identical, then the weights eventually reach the equilibrium values:

$$w_i^{eq} = \frac{e}{d} y_i$$

If, on the other hand, each input vector in the cluster has a slightly different output value associated with it, then the outstar will learn the average of all of the associated output values:

$$w_i^{eq} = \frac{e}{d} \langle y_i \rangle$$

Using the latter value for the equilibrium weight, Eq. (6.17) shows that the output after training reaches a steady state value of

$$y_i'^{eq} = \frac{c}{a} \frac{e}{d} \langle y_i \rangle.$$

Since we presumably want $y_i'^{eq} = \langle y_i \rangle$, we can require that $a = c$ in Eq. (6.17) and that $d = e$ in Eq. (6.18). Then,

$$y_i'^{eq} = \langle y_i \rangle = w_i^{eq} \tag{6.20}$$

For the purpose of digital simulation, we can approximate the solution to Eq. (6.19) by

$$w_i(t + 1) = w_i(t) + \beta(y_i - w_i(t)) \tag{6.21}$$

following the same procedure that led to Eq. (6.12) for the instar.

6.2   CPN DATA PROCESSING

We are now in a position to combine the component structures from the previous section into the complete CPN. We shall still consider only the forward-mapping CPN for the moment. Moreover, we shall assume that we are performing a digital simulation, so it will not be necessary to model explicitly the interconnects for the input layer or the competitive layer.

6.2.1   Forward Mapping

Assume that all training has occurred and that the network is now in a production mode. We have an input vector, $\mathbf{I}$, and we would like to find the corresponding $\mathbf{y}$ vector. The processing is depicted in Figure 6.17 and proceeds according to the following algorithm:

1. Normalize the input vector, $x_i = I_i/(\sqrt{\sum_n I_n^2})$.

2. Apply the input vector to the $\mathbf{x}$-vector portion of layer 1. Apply a zero vector to the $\mathbf{y}$-vector portion of layer 1.

3. Since the input vector is already normalized, the input layer only distributes it to the units on layer 2.

4. Layer 2 is a winner-take-all competitive layer. The unit whose weight vector most closely matches the input vector wins and has an output value of 1. All other units have outputs of 0. The output of each unit can be calculated according to

$$z_i = \begin{cases} 1 & \|\text{net}_i\| > \|\text{net}_j\| \text{ for all } j \neq i \\ 0 & \text{otherwise} \end{cases} \qquad (6.22)$$

5. The single winner on layer 2 excites an outstar.

Each unit in the outstar quickly reaches an equilibrium value equal to the value of the weight on the connection from the winning layer 2 unit [see Eq. (6.20)]. If the ith unit wins on the middle layer, then the output layer produces an output vector $\mathbf{y}' = (w_{1i}, w_{2i}, \ldots, w_{mi})^t$, where m represents the number of units on the output layer. A simple way to view this processing is to realize that the equilibrium output of the outstar is equal to the outstar's net input,

$$y_k'^{eq} = \sum_j w_{kj} z_j \qquad (6.23)$$

Since $z_j = 0$ unless $j = i$, then $y_k'^{eq} = w_{ki} z_i = w_{ki}$, which is consistent with the results obtained in Section 6.1.

This simple algorithm uses equilibrium, or asymptotic, values of node activities and outputs. We thus avoid the need to solve numerically all the corresponding differential equations.

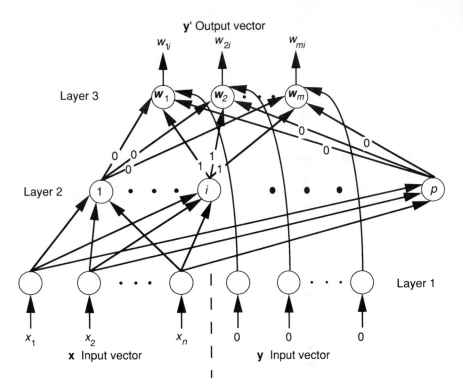

Figure 6.17 This figure shows a summary of the processing done on an input vector by the CPN. The input vector, $(x_1, x_2, \ldots, x_n)^t$ is distributed to all units on the competitive layer. The ith unit wins the competition and has an output of 1; all other competitive units have an output of 0. This competition effectively selects the proper output vector by exciting a single connection to each of the outstar units on the output layer.

6.2.2 Training the CPN

Here again, we assume that we are performing a digital simulation of the CPN. Although this assumption does not eliminate the need to find numerical solutions to the differential equations, we can still take advantage of prenormalized input vectors and an external judge to determine winners on the competitive layer. We shall also assume that a set of training vectors has been defined adequately. We shall have more to say on that subject in a later section.

Because there are two different learning algorithms in use in the CPN, we shall look at each one independently. In fact, it is a good idea to train the competitive layer completely before beginning to train the output layer.

The competitive-layer units train according to the instar learning algorithm described in Section 6.1. Since there will typically be many instars on the competitive layer, the iterative training process described earlier must be amended slightly. Here, as in Section 6.1, we assume that a cluster of input vectors forms a single class. Now, however, we have the situation where we may have several clusters of vectors, each cluster representing a different class. Our learning procedure must be such that each instar learns (wins the competition) for all the vectors in a single cluster. To accomplish the correct classification for each class of input vectors, we must proceed as follows:

1. Select an input vector from among all the input vectors to be used for training. The selection should be random according to the probability distribution of the vectors.

2. Normalize the input vector and apply it to the CPN competitive layer.

3. Determine which unit wins the competition by calculating the net-input value for each unit and selecting the unit with the largest (the unit whose weight vector is closest to the input vector in an inner-product sense).

4. Calculate $\alpha(\mathbf{x} - \mathbf{w})$ for the winning unit only, and update that unit's weight vector according to Eq. (6.12):

$$\mathbf{w}(t + 1) = \mathbf{w}(t) + \alpha(\mathbf{x} - \mathbf{w})$$

5. Repeat steps 1 through 4 until all input vectors have been processed once.

6. Repeat step 5 until all input vectors have been classified properly. When this situation exists, one instar unit will win the competition for all input vectors in a certain cluster. Note that there might be more that one cluster corresponding to a single class of input vectors.

7. Test the effectiveness of the training by applying input vectors from the various classes that were *not* used during the training process itself. If any misclassifications occur, additional training passes through step 6 may be required, even though all the training vectors are being classified correctly. If training ends too abruptly, the **win region** of a particular unit may be offset too much from the center of the cluster, and outlying vectors may be misclassified. We define an instar's *win region* as the region of vector space containing vectors for which that particular instar will win the competition. (See Figure 6.18.)

An issue that we have overlooked in our discussion is the question of initialization of the weight vectors. For all but the simplest problems, random initial weight vectors will not be adequate. We already hinted at an initialization method earlier: Set each weight vector equal to a representative of one of the clusters. We shall have more to say on this issue in the next section.

Once satisfactory results have been obtained on the competitive layer, training of the outstar layer can occur. There are several ways to proceed based on the nature of the problem.

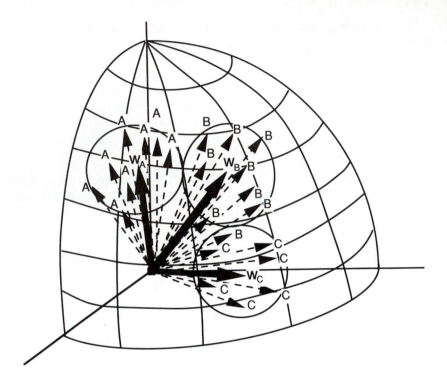

Figure 6.18   In this drawing, three clusters of vectors represent three distinct classes: A, B, and C. Normalized, these vectors end on the unit hypersphere. After training, the weight vectors on the competitive layer have settled near the centroid of each cluster. Each weight vector has a *win region* represented, although not accurately, by the circles drawn on the surface of the sphere around each cluster. Note that one of the B vectors encroaches into C's win region indicating that erroneous classification is possible in some cases.

Suppose that each cluster of input vectors represents a class, and all of the vectors in a cluster map to the identical output vector. In this case, no iterative training algorithm is necessary. We need only to determine which hidden unit wins for a particular class. Then, we simply assign the weight vector on the appropriate connections to the output layer to be equal to the desired output vector. That is, if the ith hidden unit wins for all input vectors of the class for which $\mathbf{A}$ is the desired output vector, then we set $w_{ki} = A_k$, where w_{ki} is the weight on the connection from the ith hidden unit to the kth output unit.

If each input vector in a cluster maps to a different output vector, then the outstar learning procedure will enable the outstar to reproduce the average of those output vectors when any member of the class is presented to the inputs of the CPN. If the average output vector for each class is known or can be calculated in advance, then a simple assignment can be made as in the previous paragraph: Let $w_{ki} = \langle A_k \rangle$.

If the average of the output vectors is not known, then an iterative procedure can be used based on Eq. (6.21).

1. Apply a normalized input vector, $\mathbf{x}_k$, and its corresponding output vector, $\mathbf{y}_k$, to the $\mathbf{x}$ and $\mathbf{y}$ inputs of the CPN, respectively.

2. Determine the winning competitive-layer unit.

3. Update the weights on the connections from the winning competitive unit to the output units according to Eq. (6.21):

$$w_i(t+1) = w_i(t) + \beta(y_{ki} - w_i(t))$$

4. Repeat steps 1 through 3 until all vectors of all classes map to satisfactory outputs.

6.2.3 Practical Considerations

In this section, we shall examine several aspects of CPN design and operation that will influence the results obtained using this network. The CPN is deceptively simple in its operation and there are several pitfalls. Most of these pitfalls can be avoided through a careful analysis of the problem being solved before an attempt is made to model the problem with the CPN. We cannot cover all eventualities in this section. Instead, we shall attempt to illustrate the possibilities in order to raise your awareness of the need for careful analysis.

The first consideration is actually a combination of two: the number of hidden units required, and the number of exemplars, or training vectors, needed for each class. It stands to reason that there must be at least as many hidden nodes as there are classes to be learned. We have been assuming that each class of input vectors can be identified with a cluster of vectors. It is possible, however, that two completely disjoint regions of space contain vectors of the same class. In such a situation, more than one competitive node would be required to identify the input vectors of a single class. Unfortunately, for problems with large dimensions, it may not always be possible to determine that such is the case in advance. This possibility is one reason why more than one representative for each class should be used during training, and also why the training should be verified with other representative input vectors.

Suppose that a misclassification of a test vector does occur after all of the training vectors are classified correctly. There are several possible reasons for this error. One possibility is that the set of exemplars did not adequately represent the class, so the hidden-layer weight vector did not find the true centroid. Equivalently, training may not have continued for a sufficient time to center the weight vector properly; this situation is illustrated in Figure 6.19.

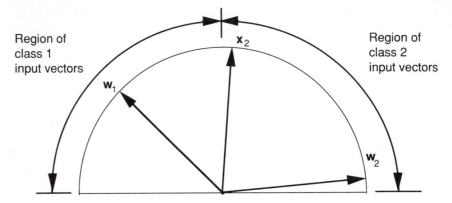

Figure 6.19   In this example, weight vector $\mathbf{w}_1$ learns class 1 and $\mathbf{w}_2$ learns
class 2.   The input vectors of each class extend over the
regions shown.   Since $\mathbf{w}_2$ has not learned the true centroid
of class 2, an outlying vector, $\mathbf{x}_2$, is actually closer to $\mathbf{w}_1$ and
is classified erroneously as a member of class 1.

One solution to these situations is to add more units on the competitive layer.
Caution must be used, however, since the problem may be exacerbated. A unit
added whose weight vector appears at the intersection between two classes may
cause misclassification of many input vectors of the original two classes. If a
threshold condition is added to the competitive units, a greater amount of control
exists over the partitioning of the space into classes. A threshold prevents a unit
from winning if the input vector is not within a certain minimum angle, which
may be different for each unit. Such a condition has the effect of limiting the
size of the win region of each unit.

There are also problems that can occur during the training period itself. For
example, if the distribution of the vectors of each class changes with time, then
competitive units that were coded originally for one class may get recoded to
represent another. Moreover, after training, moving distributions will result in
serious classification errors. Another situation is illustrated in Figure 6.20. The
problem there manifests itself in the form of a **stuck vector**; that is, one unit
that never seems to win the competition for any input vector.

The stuck-vector problem leads us to an issue that we touched on earlier: the
initialization of the competitive-unit weight vectors. We stated in the previous
section that a good strategy for initialization is to assign each weight vector to be
identical to one of the prototype vectors for each class. The primary motivation
for using this strategy is to avoid the stuck-vector problem.

The extreme case of the stuck-vector problem can occur if the weight vectors
are initialized to random values. Training with weight vectors initialized in this
manner could result in *all but one* of the weight vectors becoming stuck. A

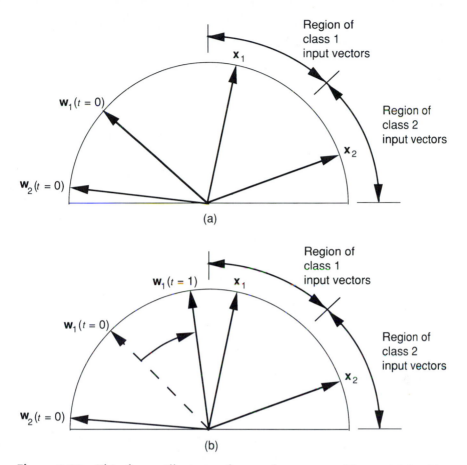

(a)

(b)

Figure 6.20   This figure illustrates the *stuck-vector* problem.   (a) In this
example, we would like w_1 to learn the class represented by
x_1, and w_2 to learn x_2. (b) Initial training with x_1 has brought
w_1 closer to x_2 than w_2 is. Thus, w_1 will win for either x_1 or
x_2, and w_2 will never win.

single weight vector would win for every input vector, and the network would
not learn to distinguish between any of the classes on input vectors.

This rather peculiar occurrence arises due to a combination of two factors:
(1) in a high-dimensional space, random vectors are all nearly orthogonal to one
another (their dot products are near 0), and (2) it is not unlikely that all input
vectors for a particular problem are clustered within a single region of space. If
these conditions prevail, then it is possible that only one of the random weight
vectors lies within the same region as the input vectors. Any input vector would
have a large dot product with that one weight vector only, since all other weight
vectors would be in orthogonal regions.

Another approach to dealing with a stuck vector is to endow the competitive units with a **conscience**. Suppose that the probability that a particular unit wins the competition was inversely proportional to the number of times that unit won in the past. If a unit wins too often, it simply shuts down, allowing others to win for a change. Incorporating this feature can *unstick* a stuck vector resulting from a situation such as the one shown in Figure 6.20.

In contrast to the competitive layer, the layer of outstars on the output layer has few potential problems. Weight vectors can be randomized initially, or set equal to 0 or to some other convenient value. In fact, the only real concern is the value of the parameter, β, in the learning law, Eq. (6.21). Since Eq. (6.21) is a numerical approximation to the solution of a differential equation, β should be kept suitably small, ($0 \leq \beta \ll 1$), to keep the solution well-behaved. As learning proceeds, β can be increased somewhat as the difference term, $(y_i - w_i(t))$, becomes smaller.

The parameter α in the competitive-layer learning law can start out somewhat larger than β. A larger initial α will bring weight vectors into alignment with exemplars more quickly. After a few passes, α should be *reduced* rather than increased. A smaller α will prevent outlying input vectors from pulling the weight vector very far from the centroid region.

A final caveat concerns the types of problems suitable for the CPN. We stated at the beginning of the chapter that the CPN is useful in many situations where other networks, especially backpropagation, are also useful. There is, however, one class of problems that can be solved readily by the BPN that cannot be solved at all by the CPN. This class is characterized by the need to perform a generalization on the input vectors in order to discover certain features of the input vectors that correlate to certain output values. The parity problem discussed in the next paragraph illustrates the point.

A backpropagation network with an input vector having, say, eight bits can learn easily to distinguish between vectors that have an even or odd number of 1s. A BPN with eight input units, eight hidden units, and one output unit suffices to solve the problem [10]. Using a representative sample of the 256 possible input vectors as a training set, the network learns essentially to count the number of 1s in the input vector. This problem is particularly difficult for the CPN because the network must separate vectors that differ by only a single bit. If your problem requires this kind of generalization, use a BPN.

6.2.4   The Complete CPN

Our discussion to this point has focused on the forward-mapping CPN. We wish to revisit the complete, forward- and reverse-mapping CPN described in the introduction to this chapter. In Figure 6.21, the full CPN (see Figure 6.1) is redrawn in a manner similar to Figure 6.2. Describing in detail the processing done by the full CPN would be largely repetitive. Therefore, we present a summary of the equations that govern the processing and learning.

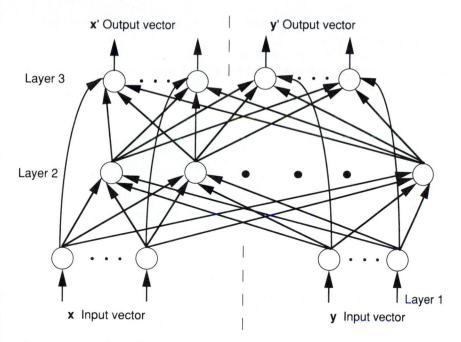

Figure 6.21 The full CPN architecture is redrawn from Figure 6.1. Both **x** and **y** input vectors are fully connected to the competitive layer. The **x** inputs are connected to the **x'** output units, and the **y** inputs are connected to the **y'** outputs.

Both **x** and **y** input vectors must be normalized for the full CPN. As in the forward-mapping CPN, both **x** and **y** are applied to the input units during the training process. After training, inputs of $(\mathbf{x}, \emptyset)$ will result in an output of $\mathbf{y}' = \Phi(\mathbf{x})$, and an input of $(\emptyset, \mathbf{y})$ will result in an output of $\mathbf{x}'$.

Because both **x** and **y** vectors are connected to the hidden layer, there are two weight vectors associated with each unit. One weight vector, **r**, is on the connections from the **x** inputs; another weight vector, **s**, is on the connections from the **y** inputs.

Each unit on the competitive layer calculates its net input according to

$$\text{net}_i = \mathbf{r} \cdot \mathbf{x} + \mathbf{s} \cdot \mathbf{y}$$

The output of the competitive layer units is

$$z_i = \begin{cases} 1 & \text{net}_i = \max\{\text{net}_k\} \\ 0 & \text{otherwise} \end{cases}$$

During the training process

$$\dot{\mathbf{r}}_i = \alpha_x(\mathbf{x} - \mathbf{r}_i)z_i$$
$$\dot{\mathbf{s}}_i = \alpha_y(\mathbf{y} - \mathbf{s}_i)z_i$$

As with the forward-mapping network, only the winning unit is allowed to learn for a given input vector.

Like the input layer, the output layer is split into two distinct parts. The $\mathbf{y}'$ units have weight vectors $\mathbf{w}_i$, and the $\mathbf{x}'$ units have weight vectors $\mathbf{v}_i$. The learning laws are

$$\dot{w}_{ij} = (-cw_{ij} + dy_i)z_j$$

and

$$\dot{v}_{ij} = (-ev_{ij} + fx_i)z_j$$

Once again, only weights for which $z_j \neq 0$ are allowed to learn.

Exercise 6.6: What will be the result, after training, of an input of $(\mathbf{x}_a, \mathbf{y}_b)$, where $\mathbf{x}_a = \Phi^{-1}(\mathbf{y}_a)$ and $\mathbf{y}_b = \Phi(\mathbf{x}_b)$?

6.3   AN IMAGE-CLASSIFICATION EXAMPLE

In this section, we shall look at an example of how the CPN can be used to classify images into categories. In addition, we shall see how a simple modification of the CPN will allow the network to perform some interpolation at the output layer.

The problem is to determine the angle of rotation of the principal axis of an object in two dimensions, directly from the raw video image of the object [1]. In this case, the object is a model of the Space Shuttle that can be rotated 360 degrees about a single axis of rotation. Numerical algorithms as well as pattern-matching techniques exist that will solve this problem. The neural-network solution possesses some interesting advantages, however, that may recommend it over these traditional approaches.

Figure 6.22 shows a diagram of the system architecture for the spacecraft orientation system. The video camera, television monitor, and robot all interface to a desktop computer that simulates the neural network and houses a video frame-grabber board. The architecture is an example of how a neural network can be embedded as a part of an overall system.

The system uses a CPN having 1026 input units (1024 for the image and 2 for the training inputs), 12 hidden units, and 2 output units. The units on the middle layer learn to divide the input vectors into different classes. There are 12 units in this layer, and 12 different input vectors are used to train the network. These 12 vectors represent images of the shuttle at 30-degree increments ($0°, 30°, \ldots, 330°$). Since there are 12 categories and 12 training vectors, training of the competitive layer consists of setting each unit's weight equal to one of the (normalized) input vectors. The output layer units learn to associate the correct sine and cosine values with each of the classes represented on the middle layer.

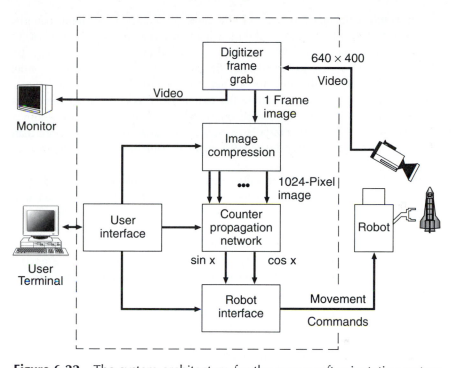

Figure 6.22 The system architecture for the spacecraft orientation system
is shown. The video camera and frame-grabber capture a
256-by-256-pixel image of the model. That image is reduced
to 32-by-32 pixels by a pixel-averaging technique, and is
then thresholded to produce a binary image. The resulting
1024-component vector is used as the input to the neural
network, which responds by giving the sine and cosine of
the rotation angle of the principal axis of the model. These
output values are converted to an angle that is sent as part
of a command string to a mechanical robot assembly. The
command sequence causes the robot to reach out and pick
up the model. The angle is used to roll the robot's wrist
to the proper orientation, so that the robot can grasp the
model perpendicular to the long axis. *Source: Reprinted
with permission from James A. Freeman, "Neural networks
for machine vision: the spacecraft orientation demonstration."*
e^{x}ponent: Ford Aerospace Technical Journal, *Fall 1988.*

It would seem that this network is limited to classifying all input patterns into only one of 12 categories. An input pattern representing a rotation of 32 degrees, for example, probably would be classified as a 30-degree pattern by this network. One way to remedy this deficiency would be to add more units on the middle layer, allowing for a finer categorization of the input images. An alternative approach is to allow the output units to perform an interpolation for patterns that do not match one of the training patterns to within a certain tolerance. For this interpolative scheme to be accomplished, more than one unit on the competitive layer must share in winning for each input vector.

Recall that the output-layer units calculate their output values according to Eq. (6.23): $y'_k = \sum_j w_{kj} z_j$. In the normal case, where the ith hidden unit wins, $y'_k = w_{ki}$, since $z_j = 1$ for $j = i$ and $z_j = 0$ otherwise. Suppose two competitive units shared in winning—the ones with the two closest matching patterns. Further, let the output of those units be proportional to how close the input pattern is; that is, $z_j \propto \cos\theta_j$ for the two winning units. If we restrict the total output from the middle layer to unity, then the output values from the output layer would be

$$y'_k = w_{ki} z_i + w_{kj} z_j$$

where the ith and jth units on the middle layer were the winners, and

$$z_i + z_j = 1$$

The network output is a linear interpolation of the outputs that would be obtained from the two patterns that exactly matched the two hidden units that shared the victory.

Using this technique, the network will classify successfully input patterns representing rotation angles it had never seen during the training period. In our experiments, the average error was approximately $\pm 3°$. However, since a simple linear interpolation scheme is used, the error varied from almost 0 to as much as 10 degrees. Other interpolation schemes could result in considerably higher accuracy over the entire range of input patterns.

One of the benefits of using the neural-network approach to pattern matching is robustness in the presence of noise or of contradictory data. An example is shown in Figure 6.23, where the network was able to respond correctly, even though a substantial portion of the image was obscured.

It is unlikely that someone would use a neural network for a simple orientation determination. The methodology can be extended to more realistic cases, however, where the object can be rotated in three dimensions. In such cases, the time required to construct and train a neural network may be significantly less than the time required for development of algorithms that perform the identical tasks.

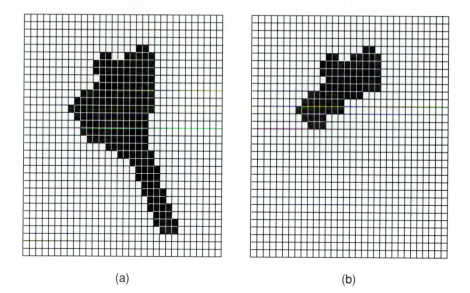

(a)   (b)

Figure 6.23   These figures show 32-by-32-pixel arrays of two different
input vectors for the spacecraft-orientation system. (a) This
is a bit-mapped image of the space-shuttle model at an
angle of 150° as measured clockwise from the vertical.
(b) The obscured image was used as an input vector to
the spacecraft-orientation system. The CPN responded with
an angle of 149°. *Source: Reprinted with permission from
James A. Freeman, "Neural networks for machine vision:
the spacecraft orientation demonstration."* e^xponent: Ford
Aerospace Technical Journal, *Fall 1988.*

6.4   THE CPN SIMULATOR

Even though it utilizes two different learning rules, the CPN is perhaps the least
complex of the layered networks we will simulate, primarily because of the
aspect of competition implemented on the single hidden layer. Furthermore, if
we assume that the host computer system ensures that all input pattern vectors are
normalized prior to presentation to the network, it is only the hidden layer that
contains any special processing considerations: the input layer is simply a fan-
out layer, and each unit on the output layer merely performs a linear summation
of its active inputs. The only complication in the simulation is the determination
of the *winning* unit(s), and the generation of the appropriate output for each of
the hidden-layer units. In the remainder of this section, we will describe the
algorithms necessary to construct the restricted CPN simulator. Then, we shall
describe the extensions that must be made to implement the complete CPN. We
conclude the chapter with thoughts on alternative methods of initializing and
training the network.

6.4.1   The CPN Data Structures

Due to the similarity of the CPN simulator to the BPN discussed in Chapter 3, we will use those data structures as the basis for the CPN simulator. The only modification we will require is to the top-level network record specification. The reason for this modification should be obvious by now; since we have consistently used the network record as the repository for all network specific parameters, we must include the CPN-specific data in the CPN's top level declaration. Thus, the CPN can be defined by the following record structure:

```
record CPN =
    INPUTS : ^layer;   {pointer to input layer record}
    HIDDENS : ^layer;  {pointer to hidden layer record}
    OUTPUTS : ^layer;  {pointer to output layer record}
    ALPHA : float;     {Kohonen learning parameter}
    BETA : float;      {Grossberg learning parameters}
    N : integer;       {number of winning units allowed}
end record;
```

where the layer record and all lower-level structures are identical to those defined in Chapter 3. A diagram illustrating the complete structure defined for this network is shown in Figure 6.24.

6.4.2   CPN Algorithms

Since forward signal propagation through the CPN is easiest to describe, we shall begin with that aspect of our simulator. Throughout this discussion, we will assume that

- The network simulator has been initialized so that the internal data structures have been allocated and contain valid information

- The user has set the outputs of the network input units to a normalized vector to be propagated through the network

- Once the network generates its output, the user application reads the output vector from the appropriate array and uses that output accordingly

Recall from our discussion in Section 6.2.1 that processing in the CPN essentially starts in the hidden layer. Since we have assumed that the input vector is both normalized and available in the network data structures, signal propagation begins by having the computer calculate the total input stimulation received by each unit on the hidden layer. The unit (or units, in the case where $N > 1$) with the largest aggregate input is declared the winner, and the output from that unit is set to 1. The outputs from all losing units are simultaneously set to 0.

Once processing on the hidden layer is complete, the network output is calculated by performance of another sum-of-products at each unit on the output layer. In this case, the dot product between the connection weight vector to the unit in question and the output vector formed by all the hidden-layer units is

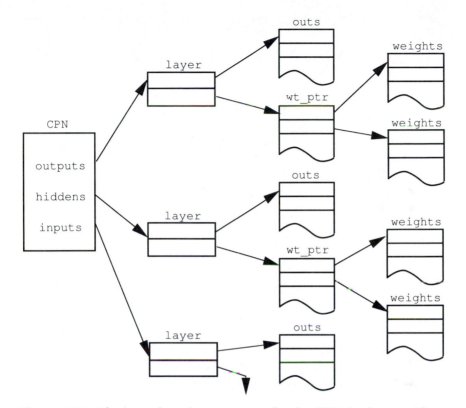

Figure 6.24 The complete data structure for the CPN is shown. These structures are representative of all the layered networks that we simulate in this text.

computed and used directly as the output for that unit. Since the hidden layer in the CPN is a competitive layer, the input computation at the output layer takes on a significance not usually found in an ANS; rather than combining feature indications from many units, which may be either excitatory or inhibitory (as in the BPN), the output units in the CPN are merely recalling features as *stored in the connections* between the winning hidden unit(s) and themselves. This aspect of memory recall is further illustrated in Figure 6.25.

Armed with this knowledge of network operation, there are a number of things we can do to make our simulation more efficient. For example, since we know that only a limited number of units (normally only one) in the hidden layer will be allowed to win the competition, there is really no point in forcing the computer to calculate the total input to every unit in the output layer. A much more efficient approach would be simply to allow the computer to *remember* which hidden layer unit(s) won the competition, and to restrict the

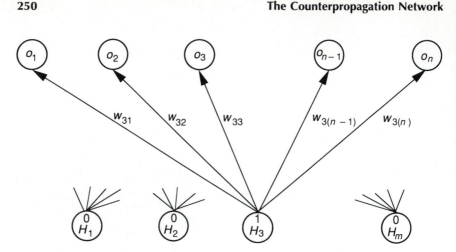

Figure 6.25   This figure shows the process of information recall in the output layer of the CPN. Each unit on the output layer receives an active input only from the winning unit(s) on the hidden layer. Since the connections between the winning hidden unit and each unit on the output layer contain the output value that was associated with the input pattern that won the competition during training, the process of computing the input at each unit on the output layer is nothing more than a selection of the appropriate output pattern from the set of available patterns stored in the input connections.

input calculation at each output unit to that unit's connections to the winning unit(s).

Also, we can consider the process of determining the winning hidden unit(s). In the case where only one unit is allowed to win ($N = 1$), determining the winner can be done easily as part of calculating the input to each hidden-layer unit; we simply need to compare the input just calculated to the value saved as the previously largest input. If the current input exceeds the older value, the current input replaces the older value, and processing continues with the next unit. After we have completed the input calculation for all hidden-layer units, the unit whose output matches the largest value saved can be declared the winner.[2]

On the other hand, if we allow more than one unit to win the competition ($N > 1$), the problem of determining the winning hidden units is more complicated. One problem we will encounter is the determination of *how many* units will be allowed to win simultaneously. Obviously, we will never have to allow all hidden units to win, but for how many possible winners must we account in

---

[2]This approach ignores the case where ties between hidden-layer units confuse the determination of the winner. In such an event, other criteria must be used to select the winner.

will be allowed to win simultaneously. Obviously, we will never have to allow all hidden units to win, but for how many possible winners must we account in our simulator design? Also, we must address the issue of ranking the hidden-layer units so that we may determine which unit(s) had a greater response to the input; specifically, should we simply process all the hidden-layer units first, and sort them afterward, or should we attempt to rank the units as we process them?

The answer to these questions is truly application dependent; for our purposes, however, we will assume that we must account for no more than three winning units ($0 < N < 4$) in our simulator design. This being the case, we can also assume that it is more efficient to keep track of up to three winning units as we go, rather than trying to sort through all hidden units afterward.

CPN Production Algorithms. Using the assumptions described, we are now ready to construct the algorithms for performing the forward signal propagation in the CPN. Since the processing on each of the two active layers is different (recall that the input layer is fan-out only), we will develop two different signal-propagation algorithms: prop_to_hidden and prop_to_output.

```
procedure prop_to_hidden
(NET:CPN; FIRST,SECOND,THIRD:INTEGER)
{propagate to hidden layer, returning indices to
                                         3 winners}

var units : ^float[];          {pointer to unit outputs}
    invec : ^float[];           {pointer to input units}
    connects : ^float[];   {pointer to connection array}
    i, j : integer;              {iteration counters}

begin
  units = NET.HIDDENS^.OUTS;       {locate output array}

  for i = 1 to length (units)
    do                               {for all hidden units}
      units[i] = 0;                {initialize accumulator}
      invec = NET.INPUTS^.OUTS;      {locate input array}
      connects = NET.HIDDENS^.WEIGHTS[i]^;
                                           {locate inputs}

      for j = 1 to length (connects) do
          units[i] = units[i] + connects[j] * invec[j];
      end do;

      rank (units[i], FIRST, SECOND, THIRD);
    end do;

  compete (NET.HIDDENS^.OUTS, FIRST, SECOND, THIRD);
end procedure;
```

This procedure makes calls to two as-yet-undefined routines, rank and compete. The purpose of these routines is to sort the current input with the current best three choices, and to generate the appropriate output for all units in the specified layer, respectively. Because the design of the rank procedure is fairly straightforward, it is left to you as an exercise. On the other hand, the compete process must do the right thing no matter how many winners are allowed, making it somewhat involved. We therefore present the design for compete in its entirety.

```
procedure compete
(UNITS:^float[]; FIRST,SECOND,THIRD:INTEGER)
{generate outputs for all UNITS using competitive
                                          function}

var outputs : ^float[];      {step through output array}
    sum : float;                   {local accumulator}
    win, place, show : float;        {store outputs}
    i : integer;                   {iteration counter}
begin
  outputs = UNITS;                 {locate output array}
  sum = outputs[FIRST];         {initialize accumulator}
  win = outputs[FIRST];            {save winning value}

  if (SECOND != 0)                   {if a second winner}
  then                          {add its contribution}
    sum = sum + outputs[SECOND];
    place = outputs[SECOND]; {save second place value}

    if (THIRD != 0)            {if a third place winner}
    then                          {add its contribution}
      sum = sum + outputs[THIRD];
      show = outputs[THIRD];  {save third place value}
    end if;
  end if;

  for i = 1 to length (units)    {for all hidden units}
    do
      outputs[i] = 0;               {set outputs to zero}
    end do;

  outputs[FIRST] = win / sum;      {set winners output}

  if (SECOND != 0)            {now update second winner}
  then
    outputs[SECOND] = place / sum;

    if (THIRD != 0)                     {and third place}
    then
      outputs[THIRD] = show / sum;
    end if;
  end if;
end procedure;
```

Before we move on to the `prop_to_output` routine, you should note that the `compete` procedure relies on the fact that the values of SECOND and THIRD are nonzero if and only if more than one unit wins the competition. Since it is assumed that these values are set as part of the `rank` procedure, you should take care to ensure that these variables are manipulated according to the number of winning units indicated by the value in the NET.N variable.

Let us now consider the process of propagating information to the output layer in the CPN. Once we have completed the signal propagation to the hidden layer, the outputs on the hidden layer will be nonzero only from the winning units. As we have discussed before, we could now proceed to perform a complete input summation at every unit on the output layer, but that would prove to be needlessly time-consuming. Since we have designed the `prop_to_hidden` procedure to return the index of the winning unit(s), we can assume that the top-level routine to propagate information through the network completely will have access to that information prior to calling the procedure to propagate information to the output layer. We can therefore code the `prop_to_output` procedure so that only those connections between the winning units and the output units are processed. Also, notice that the successful use of this procedure relies on the values of the SECOND and THIRD variables being nonzero only if more than one winner was allowed.

```
procedure prop_to_output
(NET:CPN; FIRST,SECOND,THIRD:INTEGER)
{generate outputs for units on the output layer}

var units : ^float[];              {locate output units}
    hidvec : ^float[];             {locate hidden units}
    connects : ^float[];            {locate connections}
    i : integer;                      {iteration counter}

begin
  units = NET.OUTPUTS^.OUTS;    {start of output array}
  hidvec = NET.HIDDENS^.OUTS;    {start of hidden array}

  for i = 1 to length (units)    {for all output units}
    do
      connects = NET.OUTPUTS^.WEIGHTS[i]^;
      units[i] = hidvec[FIRST] * connects[FIRST];

      if (SECOND != 0)
                  {if there is a second winning unit}
      then
        units[i] = units[i] + hidvec[SECOND]
                        * connects[SECOND];

        if (THIRD != 0)
                    {if there is a third winning unit}
```

```
            then
              units[i] = units[i] + hidvec[THIRD]
                                    * connects[THIRD];
            end if;
         end if;
      end do;
   end procedure;
```

You may now be asking yourself how we can be assured that the hidden-layer units will be using the appropriate output values for any number of winning units. To answer this question, we recall that we specified that at least one unit is guaranteed to win, and that at most, three will share in the victory. Inspection of the `compete` and `prop_to_output` routines shows that, with only one winning unit, the output of all non-winning units will be 0, whereas the winning unit will generate a 1. As we increase the number of units that we allow to win, the strength of the output from each of the winning units is proportionally decreased, so that the relative contribution from all winning units will linearly interpolate between output patterns the network was trained to produce.

Now we are prepared to define the top-level algorithm for forward signal propagation in the CPN. As before, we assume that the input vector has been set previously by an application-specific input routine.

```
      procedure propagate (NET:CPN)
      {perform a forward signal propagation in the CPN}

      var first,
          second
          third : integer;          {indices for winning units}

      begin
        prop_to_hidden (NET, first, second, third);
        prop_to_output (NET, first, second, third);
      end procedure;
```

CPN Learning Algorithms. There are two significant differences between forward signal propagation and learning in the CPN: during learning, only one unit on the hidden layer can win the competition, and, quite obviously, the network connection weights are updated. Yet, even though they are different, much of the activity that must be performed during learning is identical to the forward signal propagation. As you will see, we will be able to reuse the production-mode algorithms to a large extent as we develop our learning-mode procedures.

We shall begin by training the hidden-layer units to recognize our input patterns. Having completed that activity, we will proceed to train the output layer to reproduce the target outputs from the specified inputs. Let us first consider the process of training the hidden layer in the CPN. Assuming the input layer units have been initialized to contain a normalized vector to be learned, we can define the learning algorithm for the hidden-layer units in the following manner.

```
procedure learn_input (NET:CPN)
{update the connections to the winning hidden unit}

var winner : integer;     {used to locate winning unit}
    dummy1, dummy2 : integer;
                     {dummy variables for second and third}
    connects : ^float[];      {locate connection array}
    units : ^float[];             {locate input array}
    i : integer;                  {iteration counter}

begin
   dummy1 = 0;                       {no need for second or}
   dummy2 = 0;                       {third winning unit}
   prop_to_hidden (NET, winner, dummy1, dummy2);
   units = NET.INPUTS^.OUTS;         {locate input array}
   connects = NET.HIDDENS^.WEIGHTS[winner]^;
                                     {locate connections}

   for i = 1 to length (connects)
                     {for all connections to winner}
   do
      connects[i] = connects[i] +
               NET.ALPHA * (units[i] - connects[i]);
      end do;
end procedure;
```

Notice that this algorithm has no access to information that would indicate when the competitive layer has been trained sufficiently. Unlike in many of the other networks we have studied, there is no error measure to indicate convergence. For that reason, we have chosen to design this training algorithm so that it performs only one training pass in the competitive layer. A higher-level routine to train the entire network must therefore be coded such that it can reasonably determine when the competitive layer has completed its training.

Moving on to the output layer, we will construct our training algorithm for this part of the network such that only those connections from the winning hidden unit to the output layer are adapted. This approach will allow us to complete the training of the competitive layer before starting the training on the accretive layer. Hopefully, the use of this approach will enable the CPN to classify inputs correctly as it is training outputs, to avoid confusing the network.

```
procedure learn_output (NET:CPN; TARGET:^float[])
{train the output layer to reproduce the specified
                                            vector}

var winner : integer;     {used to locate winning unit}
    dummy1, dummy2 : integer;
                     {dummy variables for second & third}
```

```
      connects : ^float[];        {locate connection array}
      units : ^float[];           {locate output array}
      i : integer;                {iteration counter}

begin
   dummy1 = 0;                     {no need for second or}
   dummy2 = 0;                     {third winning unit}

   prop_to_hidden (NET, winner, dummy1, dummy2);
   units = NET.OUTPUTS^.OUTS;      {locate output array}

   for i = 1 to length (units)    {for all output units}
      do
         connects = NET.OUTPUTS^.WEIGHTS^[i];
                                     {locate connections}
         connects[winner] = connects[winner] +
                            NET.BETA * (TARGET[i] -
                                  connects[winner]);
      end do;
end procedure;
```

As with `learn_input`, `learn_output` performs only one training pass and makes no assessment of error. When the CPN is used, it is the application that makes the determination as to when training is complete. As an example, consider the spacecraft-orientation system described in Section 6.3. This network was constructed to learn the image of the space shuttle at 12 different orientations, producing the scaled sine and cosine of the angle between the reference position and the image position as output. Using our CPN algorithms, the training process for this application might have taken the following form:

```
procedure learn (NET:CPN; IMAGEFILE:disk file)
{teach the NET using data in the IMAGEFILE}

var iopairs : array [1..12,1..1026] of float;
    target : array [1..2] of float;
    status : array [1..12] of boolean;
    done : boolean;
    i, j : integer;

begin
   NET.N = 1;                          {force only one winner}
   READ_INPUT_FILE (IMAGEFILE, iopairs[1,1]);
                                        {init array}

   done = false;                       {train at least once}
   SET_FALSE (status);                 {initialize status array}

   while (not done)                    {until training complete}
      do
         for i = 1 to 12               {for each training pair}
```

```
            do
               j = random (12);
                              {select a pattern at random}
               SET_INPUT (CPN, iopairs[j, 1];
               learn_input (CPN); {train competitive layer}
            end do;

         TEST_IF_INPUT_LEARNED (status, done);
      end do;

   done = false;               {train output at least once}
   SET_FALSE (status);           {initialize status array}

   while (not done)            {until training complete}
      do
         for i = 1 to 12         {for each training pair}
            do                    {train accretive layer}
               SET_INPUT (CPN, iopairs[i, 1];
               GET_TARGET (target, iopairs[i, 1025]);
               learn_output (CPN, target);
            end do;

         TEST_IF_OUTPUT_LEARNED (status, done);
      end do;
end procedure;
```

where the application provided routines test_if_input_learned and
test_if_output_learned perform the function of deciding when the CPN
has been trained sufficiently. In the case of testing the competitive layer,
this determination was accomplished by verifying that all 12 input patterns
caused different hidden-layer units to win the competition. Similarly, the output
test indicated success when no output unit generated an actual output different by more than 0.001 from the desired output for each of the 12 patterns.
The other routines used in the application, READ_INPUT_FILE, SET_FALSE,
SET_INPUT, and GET_TARGET, merely perform housekeeping functions for
the system. The point is, however, that there is no general heuristic that we
can use to determine when to stop training the CPN simulator. If we had had
many more training pairs than hidden-layer units, the functions performed by
TEST_IF_INPUT_LEARNED and TEST_IF_OUTPUT_LEARNED might have
been altogether different.

6.4.3   Simulating the Complete CPN

Now that we have completed our discussion of the restricted CPN, let us turn
our attention for a moment to the full CPN. In terms of simulating the complete
network, there are only two differences between the restricted and complete
network implementations:

1. The size of the network, in terms of number of units and connections

2. The use of the network from the applications perspective

Quite obviously, the number of units in the network has grown from $N + H + M$, where N and M specify the number of units in the input and output layers, respectively, to $2(N+M)+H$. Similarly, the number of connections that must be maintained has doubled, expanding from $H(N + M)$ to $2H(N + M)$. Therefore, the extension from the restricted to the complete CPN has slightly less than doubled the amount of computer memory needed to simulate the network. In addition, the extra units and connections place an enormous overhead on the amount of computer time needed to perform the simulation, in that there are now $N + M$ extra connections to be processed at every hidden unit.

As illustrated in Figure 6.26, the complete CPN requires no modification to the algorithms we have just developed, other than to present both the input and output patterns as target vectors for the output layer. This assertion holds true assuming the user abides by the observation that, when going from input to output, the extra M units on the input layer are *zeroed* prior to performing the signal propagation. This being the case, the inputs from the extra units contribute nothing to the dot-product calculation at each hidden unit, effectively eliminating them from consideration in determining the winning unit. By the same token, the original N units must be zeroed prior to performance of the counterpropagation from the M new units to recover the original input.

6.4.4   Practical Considerations for the CPN Simulator

We earlier promised a discussion of the practical considerations of which we might take advantage when simulating the CPN. We shall now live up to that promise by offering insights into improving the performance of the CPN simulator.

Many times, a CPN application will require the network to function as an associative memory; that is, we expect the network to recall a specific output when presented with an input that is similar to a training input. Such an input could be the original input with noise added, or with part of the input missing. When constructing a CPN to act in this capacity, we usually create it with *as many hidden units as there are items to store*. In doing so, and in allowing only one unit to win the competition, we ensure that the network will always generate the exact output that was associated with the training input that most closely resembles the current input.

Having made this observation, we can now see how it is possible to reduce the amount of time needed to train the CPN by eliminating the need to train the competitive layer. We can do this reduction by *initializing* the connections to each hidden unit such that each input training pattern is mapped onto the connections of only one hidden unit. In essence, we will have trained the competitive layer by initializing the connections, in a manner similar to the process of initializing the BAM, described in Chapter 4. All that remains from

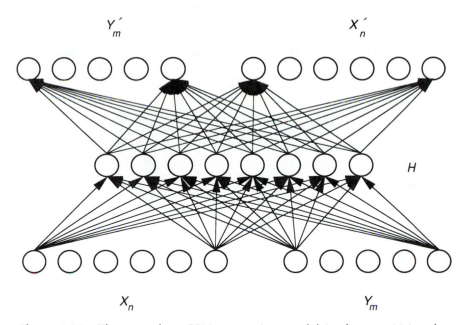

Figure 6.26 The complete CPN processing model is shown. Using the algorithms developed for the limited CPN, processing begins with the application of an input pattern on the X_n units *and* by zeroing of the extra Y_m units, which we use to represent the output. In this case, the output units (Y'_m) will produce the output pattern associated with the given input pattern during training. Now, to produce the counterpropagation effect, the opposite situation occurs. The given output pattern is applied to the input units previously zeroed (Y_m), while the X_n units are zeroed. The output of the network, on the X'_n units, represent the input pattern associated with the given output pattern during training.

this point is the training of the output layer, which ought to conclude in fairly short order. An example of this type of training is shown in Figure 6.27.

Another observation about the operation of the CPN can provide us with insight into improving the ability of the network to discriminate between similar vectors. As we have discussed, the competitive layer acts to select between one of the many input patterns the network was trained to recognize. It does this selection by computing the dot product between the input vector, **I**, and the connection weight vector, **w**. Since these two vectors are normalized, the resulting value represents the cosine of the angle between them in n-space. However, this approach can lead to problems if we allow the use of the null vector, **∅**, as a valid input. Since **∅** cannot be normalized, another method of

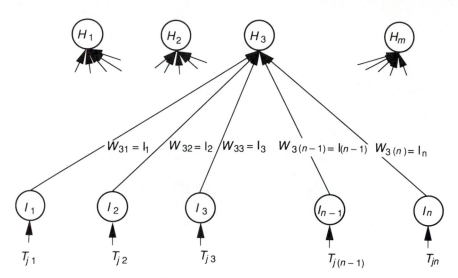

Figure 6.27 A restricted CPN initialized to eliminate the training of the competitive layer is shown. Note that the number of hidden units is exactly equal to the number of training patterns to be learned.

propagating signals to the hidden layer must be found. One alternative method that has shown promising results is to use the magnitude of the difference vector between the unnormalized **I** and **w** vectors as the input computation for each hidden unit. Specifically, let

$$\text{net}_i = (\sum_{j=0}^{n} (|W_{ij} - I_j|)^2)^{\frac{1}{2}}$$

be the input activation calculation performed at each hidden unit, rather than the traditional sum-of-products.

Use of this method prevents the CPN from creating duplicate internal mappings for similar, but different, input vectors. It also allows use of the null vector as a valid training input, something that we have found to be quite useful. Finally, at least one other researcher has indicated that this alternative method can improve the ability of the network to learn by reducing the number of training presentations needed to have the network classify input patterns properly [11].

Programming Exercises

6.1. Implement the CPN simulator described in the text and test it by training it to recognize the 36 uppercase ASCII characters from a pixel matrix representing the image of the character. For example, the 6×5 matrix illustrated next represents the pixel image of the character **A**. The equivalent ASCII code for that character is 41_{16}. Thus, the ordered pair $(08A8FE31_{16},41_{16})$ represent one training pair for the network. Complete this example by training the network to recognize the other 35 alphanumeric characters from their pixel image. How many hidden-layer units are needed to precisely recall all 36 characters?

```
..x..
.x.x.
x...x
xxxxx    =    00100 01010 10001 11111 10001 10001
x...x
x...x
```

6.2. Without resizing the network, retrain the CPN described in Programming Exercise 6.1 to recognize both the upper- and lowercase ASCII alphabetic characters. Describe how accurately the CPN identifies all characters after training. Include in your discussion any reasons you might have to explain why the CPN misclassifies some characters.

6.3. Repeat Programming Exercise 6.1, but allow two hidden units to win the competition during production. Explain the network's behavior under these circumstances.

6.4. Recreate the spacecraft-orientation example in Section 6.3 using your CPN simulator. You may simplify the problem by using a smaller matrix to represent the video image. For example, the 5×5 matrix shown next might be used to represent the shuttle image in the vertical position. Train the network to recognize your image at 45-degree rotational increments around the circle. Let two units win the competition, as in the example, and let the two output units produce the scaled sine and cosine of the image angle. Test your network by obscuring the image (enter a vector with 0s in place of 1s), and describe the results.

```
..x..
..x..
..x..
.xxx.    =    00100 00100 00100 01110 11111
xxxxx
```

6.5. Describe what would happen in Programming Exercise 6.4 if you only allowed one unit to win the competition. Describe what would happen if three units were allowed to win.

6.6. Implement the complete CPN simulator using the guidelines provided in the text. Train the network using the spacecraft-orientation data, and exercise the simulator in both the forward-propagation and counterpropagation modes. How well does the simulator produce the desired *input* pattern when given sine and cosine values that are not on a 45 degree angle?

Suggested Readings

The papers and book by Hecht-Nielsen are good companions to the material in this chapter on the CPN [5, 6, 8]. Hecht-Nielsen also has a paper that discusses some applications areas appropriate to the CPN [7].

The instar, outstar, and avalanche networks are discussed in detail in the papers by Grossberg in the collection *Studies of Mind and Brain* [4]. Individual papers from this collection are listed in the bibliography.

Bibliography

[1] James A. Freeman. Neural networks for machine vision applications: The spacecraft orientation demonstration. e^x*ponent: Ford Aerospace Technical Journal*, pp. 16–20, Fall 1988.

[2] Stephen Grossberg. How does a brain build a cognitive code. In Stephen Grossberg, editor, *Studies of Mind and Brain*. D. Reidel Publishing, Boston, pp. 1–52, 1982.

[3] Stephen Grossberg. Learning by neural networks. In Stephen Grossberg, editor, *Studies of Mind and Brain*. D. Reidel Publishing, Boston, pp. 65–156, 1982.

[4] Stephen Grossberg, editor. *Studies of Mind and Brain*, volume 70 of *Boston Studies in the Philosophy of Science*. D. Reidel Publishing Company, Boston, 1982.

[5] Robert Hecht-Nielsen. Counterpropagation networks. *Applied Optics*, 26(23):4979–4984, December 1987.

[6] Robert Hecht-Nielsen. Counterpropagation networks. In Maureen Caudill and Charles Butler, editors, *Proceedings of the IEEE First International Conference on Neural Networks*, Piscataway, NJ, pages II–19–II–32, June 1987. IEEE.

[7] Robert Hecht-Nielsen. Applications of counterpropagation networks. *Neural Networks*, 1(2):131–139, 1988.

[8] Robert Hecht-Nielsen. *Neurocomputing*. Addison-Wesley, Reading, MA, 1990.

[9] David Hestenes. How the brain works: The next great scientific revolution. Presented at the Third Workshop on Maximum Entropy and Bayesian Methods in Applied Statistics, University of Wyoming, August 1983.

[10] D. E. Rumelhart, G. E. Hinton, and R. J. Williams. Learning internal representations by error propagation. In David E. Rumelhart and James L. McClelland, editors, *Parallel Distributed Processing*, Chapter 8. MIT Press, Cambridge, MA, pp. 318–362, 1986.

[11] Donald Woods. Back and counter propagation aberrations. In *Proceedings of the IEEE First International Conference on Neural Networks*, pp. I–473–I–479, IEEE, San Diego, CA, June 1987.

C H A P T E R

Self-Organizing Maps

The cerebral cortex is arguably the most fascinating structure in all of human physiology. Although vastly complex on a microscopic level, the cortex reveals a consistently uniform structure on a macroscopic scale, from one brain to another. Centers for such diverse activities as thought, speech, vision, hearing, and motor functions lie in specific areas of the cortex, and these areas are located consistently relative to one another. Moreover, individual areas exhibit a logical ordering of their functionality. An example is the so-called tonotopic map of the auditory regions, where neighboring neurons respond to similar sound frequencies in an orderly sequence from high pitch to low pitch. Another example is the somatotopic map of motor nerves, represented artistically by the homunculus illustrated in Figure 7.1. Regions such as the tonotopic map and the somatotopic map can be referred to as **ordered feature maps**. The purpose of this chapter is to investigate a mechanism by which these ordered feature maps might develop naturally.

It appears likely that our genetic makeup predestines our neural development to a large extent. Whether the mechanisms that we shall describe here play a major or a minor role in the organization of neural tissue is not an issue for us. It was, however, an interest in discovering how such an organization might be learned that led Kohonen to develop many of the ideas that we present in this chapter [2].

The cortex is essentially a large (approximately 1-meter-square, in adult humans) thin (2-to-4-millimeter thick) sheet consisting of six layers of neurons of varying type and density. It is folded into its familiar shape to maximize packing density in the cranium. Since we are not so much concerned with the details of anatomy here, we shall consider an adequate model of the cortex to be a two-dimensional sheet of processing elements.

We saw in the previous chapter how on-center off-surround interactions among competitive processing elements could be used to construct a network that could classify clusters of input vectors. If you have not done so, please

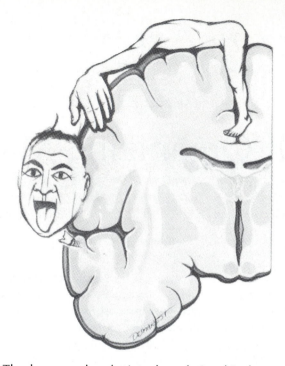

Figure 7.1   The homunculus depicts the relationship between regions of the somatotopic area of the cortex and the parts of the body that they control. Although somewhat distorted, the basic structure of the body is reflected in the organization of the cortex in this region. *Source: Reprinted with permission of McGraw-Hill, Inc. from Charles R. Noback and Robert J. Demarest*, The Human Nervous System: Basic Principles of Neurobiology, ©*1981 by McGraw-Hill, Inc.*

read Sections 6.1.1 through 6.1.3, as they are prerequisites to the material in this chapter.

In the simple competitive layer of the counterpropagation network, units learn by a process of self-organization. Learning was accomplished by the application of input data alone; no expected-output data was used as a teacher to signal the network that it had made an error. We call this type of learning **unsupervised learning**, and the input data are called **unlabeled data**. In the CPN, there was also no indication that the physical position of units in the competitive layer reflected any special relationship among the classes of data being learned. Thus, we say that there was a **random map** of input classes to competitive units.

In contrast to our discussion of random mapping, here we shall see how a simple extension of the competitive algorithms from Chapter 6 result in a

topology-preserving map of the input data to the competitive units.[1] Because of Kohonen's work in the development of the theory of competition, competitive processing elements are often referred to as **Kohonen units**.

As a simplified definition, we can say that, in a topology-preserving map, units located physically next to each other will respond to classes of input vectors that are likewise next to each other. Although it is easy to visualize units next to each other in a two-dimensional array, it is not so easy to determine which classes of vectors are next to each other in a high-dimensional space. Large-dimensional input vectors are, in a sense, projected down on the two-dimensional map in a way that maintains the natural order of the input vectors. This dimensional reduction could allow us to visualize easily important relationships among the data that otherwise might go unnoticed.

In the next section, we shall formalize some of the definitions presented in this section, and shall look at the mathematics of the topology-preserving map. Henceforth, we shall refer to the topology-preserving map as a **self-organizing map** (SOM).

7.1   SOM DATA PROCESSING

Lateral interactions among processing elements in the on-center off-surround scheme were modeled in Chapter 6 as a single positive-feedback connection to a central unit, and negative-feedback connections to all other units in the layer. In this chapter, we shall modify that model such that, during the learning process, the positive feedback will extend from the central (winning) unit to other units in some finite neighborhood around the central unit. In the competitive layer of the CPN, only the winning unit (the one whose weight vector most closely matched the input vector) was allowed to learn; in the SOM, all the units in the neighborhood that receive positive feedback from the winning unit participate in the learning process. Even if a neighboring unit's weight is orthogonal to the input vector, its weight vector will still change in response to the input vector. This simple addition to the competitive process is sufficient to account for the ordered mapping discussed in the previous section.

7.1.1   Unit Activations

The activations of the processing elements are defined by the set of equations

$$\dot{y}_i = -r_i(y_i) + \text{net}_i + \sum_j z_{ij} y_j \tag{7.1}$$

The function $r_i(y_i)$ is a general form of a loss term. In previous equations describing competitive interactions we have typically used $r_i(y_i) = Ay_i$ with A constant (cf. Eq. 6.13), but $r_i(y_i)$ could be a more complicated function of y_i.

---

[1] In fact, the development of the theory of competition among processing elements, and the theory of the topology-preserving map, predates the CPN by many years.

The term net$_i$ is the net input to unit i calculated in the usual manner as the dot product of the input vector and the weight vector of the unit. The final term in Eq. (7.1) models the lateral interactions between units. The sum extends over all units in the system. If z_{ij} takes the form of the **Mexican-hat function**, as shown in Figure 7.2(a), then the network will exhibit a *bubble* of activity around the unit with the largest value of net input. Although the unit with the largest net-input value is technically the winner in the competitive system, neighboring units *share* in that victory.

7.1.2   The SOM Learning Algorithm

During the training period, each unit with a positive activity within the neighborhood of the winning unit participates in the learning process in a manner identical to the instar discussed in Chapter 6. We can describe the learning process by the equations

$$\dot{\mathbf{w}}_i = \alpha(t)(\mathbf{x} - \mathbf{w}_i)U(y_i) \tag{7.2}$$

where $\mathbf{w}_i$ is the weight vector of the ith unit and $\mathbf{x}$ is the input vector. The function $U(y_i)$ is zero unless $y_i > 0$ in which case $U(y_i) = 1$, ensuring that only those units with positive activity participate in the learning process. The factor $\alpha(t)$ is written as a function of time to anticipate our desire to change it as learning progresses (see the discussion in Section 6.2.3).

In the remainder of the discussion, we shall not explicitly show the inhibitory connections between units, and we shall ignore the far-reaching excitatory interactions as a first approximation. The resultant interaction function is shown in Figure 7.2(b).

To demonstrate the formation of an ordered feature map, we shall use an example in which units are trained to recognize their relative positions in two-dimensional space. The scenario is illustrated in the sequence in Figure 7.3. Each processing element is identified by its coordinates, (u, v), in two-dimensional space. Weight vectors for this example are also two dimensional and are initially assigned to the processing elements randomly.

As with other competitive structures, a winning processing element is determined for each input vector based on the similarity between the input vector and the weight vector. For an input vector $\mathbf{x}$, the winning unit can be determined by

$$\|\mathbf{x} - \mathbf{w}_c\| = \min_i \{\|\mathbf{x} - \mathbf{w}_i\|\} \tag{7.3}$$

where the index c refers to the winning unit. To keep subscripts to a minimum, we identify each unit in the two-dimensional array by a single subscript, as in Eq. (7.3).

Instead of updating the weights of the winning unit only, we define a physical **neighborhood** around the unit, and all units within this neighborhood participate in the weight-update process. As learning proceeds, the size of the neighborhood is diminished until it encompasses only a single unit. If c is the

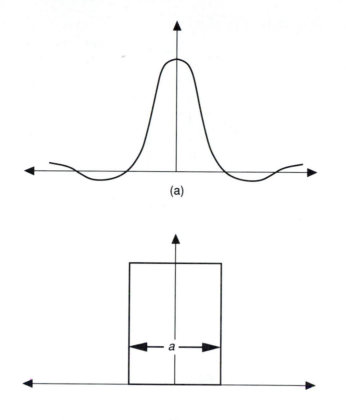

(a)

(b)

Figure 7.2 These graphics illustrate two different models of lateral interactions among network units. (a) This curve, characteristic of the lateral interactions between certain neurons in the cortex, is referred to as the *Mexican-hat function*. A centrally excited processing element excites a small neighborhood around it with positive feedback connections. As the lateral distance from the central node increases, the degree of excitation falls until it becomes an inhibition. This inhibition continues for a significantly longer distance. Finally, a weak positive feedback extends a considerable distance away from the central node. (b) We shall use this simple function as a first approximation to the Mexican-hat function. The distance, a, defines a neighborhood of units around the central unit that participate in learning along with the central unit.

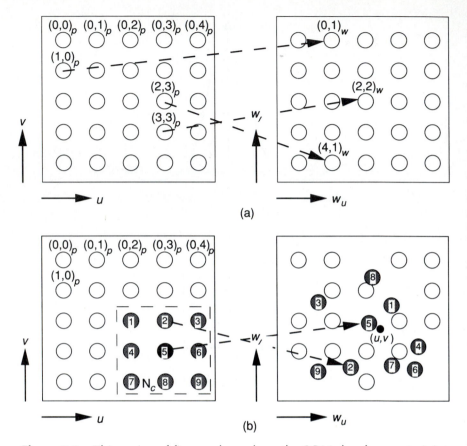

Figure 7.3 This series of figures shows how the SOM develops as training takes place. (a) Processing elements on the SOM are arranged in a two-dimensional array at discrete points, $(u, v)_p$ within the

winning unit, and N_c is the list of unit indices that make up the neighborhood, then the weight-update equations are

$$\mathbf{w}_i(t + 1) = \begin{cases} \mathbf{w}_i(t) + \alpha(t)(\mathbf{x} - \mathbf{w}_i(t)) & i \in N_c \\ 0 & \text{otherwise} \end{cases} \qquad (7.4)$$

Each weight vector participating in the update process rotates slightly toward the input vector, $\mathbf{x}$. Once training has progressed sufficiently, the weight vector on each unit will converge to a value that is representative of the coordinates of the points near the physical location of the unit.

Exercise 7.1: In Eq. (7.3), the winning unit is determined by the minimum of the quantity $\|\mathbf{x} - \mathbf{w}_i\|$. In Chapter 6, the winning unit was determined by the maximum of the quantity $net_i = \mathbf{x} \cdot \mathbf{w}_i$. Under what circumstances are these two conditions equivalent?

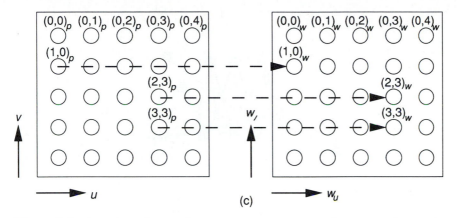

Figure 7.3   **(continued)** continuous space.   A two-dimensional weight
vector $(w_u, w_v)_w$ is assigned to each unit. The weight values
correspond to physical locations within the space occupied by
the processing elements, but they are assigned at random to the
units. Thus, neighboring units in physical space may occupy
unrelated locations in weight space.   (b) During training, a
point (u, v) is selected at random to be the input vector. A
winning unit is determined by a simple Euclidean distance
measure between the selected point and the unit's weight
vector, and a neighborhood, N_c, is defined around the winning
unit in physical space. The weight vectors in all units within
the neighborhood change slightly toward the value of the
input, (u, v). As training continues with different input points,
the size of the neighborhood is decreased gradually until it
encompasses only a single unit.   (c) At the completion of
training, the weight vector for each unit will be approximately
equal to the physical coordinates of the unit.

Exercise 7.2: Is it acceptable to initialize the weight vectors on an SOM unit
to random, unnormalized values? Explain your answer.

Kohonen has developed a clever way to illustrate the dynamics of the learning process for examples of the type described in Figure 7.3. Instead of plotting
the position of the processing elements according to their physical location, we
can plot them according to their location in weight space. We then draw connecting lines between units that are neighbors in physical space; Figure 7.4 illustrates
this idea. As training progresses, the map evolves, as shown in Figure 7.5.

We have assumed throughout this discussion that the input points are selected at random from a uniformly distributed set within the rectangular area
occupied by the processing elements. Suppose that the input points were selected from a different distribution, as illustrated in Figure 7.6. In this example,
input points are selected from a uniform, triangular distribution. The process-

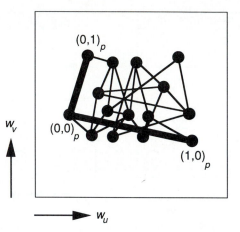

Figure 7.4 Each unit is identified by two sets of coordinates: fixed, physical-space coordinates in $(u, v)_p$ space and modifiable weight-space coordinates in $(w_u, w_v)_w$ space. A plot is made of points according to their position in weight space. Units are joined by lines according to their position in physical space. Neighboring units $(0, 0)_p, (0, 1)_p,$ and $(1, 0)_p$ would be connected as shown with the thick lines.

ing elements themselves are still in a two-dimensional physical array, but the weights form a map of the triangular region. Remember that the units do not change their physical location during training.

In the introduction to this chapter, we spoke of using the SOM to perform a dimensional reduction on the input data by mapping high-dimensional input vectors onto the two-dimensional map. We can illustrate this idea graphically by mapping a two-dimensional region of points onto a one-dimensional array of processing elements. Figure 7.7 illustrates the case for two different distributions of input points. Remember that the input and weight vectors are both two dimensional, whereas the physical location of each processing element is on a one-dimensional array.

All our examples to this point have used input points that are uniformly distributed within some region. There is nothing sacred about the uniform distribution. Input points can be distributed according to any distribution function. Once the SOM has been trained, the weight vectors will be organized into an approximation of the distribution function of the input vectors. Stated in more formal terms,

> The point density function of the weight vectors tends to approximate the probability density function $p(x)$ of the input vectors, x, and the weight vectors tend to be ordered according to their mutual similarity. [2]

We shall not attempt to prove that the prescription described here will result in a topology-preserving map. Even for the simple one-dimensional case, such a

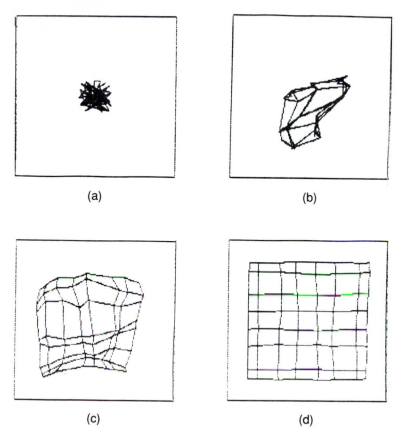

(a)   (b)

(c)   (d)

Figure 7.5 In this series of figures, a two-dimensional SOM develops from a space of input points selected randomly from a uniform-rectangular distribution. (a) In the initial map, weight vectors have random values near the center of the map coordinates. (b) As the map begins to evolve, weights spread out from the center. (c) Eventually, the final structure of the map begins to emerge. (d) In the end, the relationship between the weight vectors mimics the relationship between the physical coordinates of the processing elements.

proof is extremely long and complex. You should consult Kohonen's excellent book on SOMs for details [2].

7.1.3 The Feature Map Classifier

An advantage of the SOM is that large numbers of unlabeled data can be organized quickly into a configuration that may illuminate underlying structure within the data. Following the self-organization process, it may be desirable

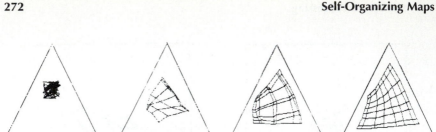

Figure 7.6 This sequence of diagrams illustrates the evolution of the map for a uniform, triangular distribution of input points. Notice that, in the final map, neighboring points in physical space end up with neighboring weights in weight space. This feature is the essence of the topology-preserving map.

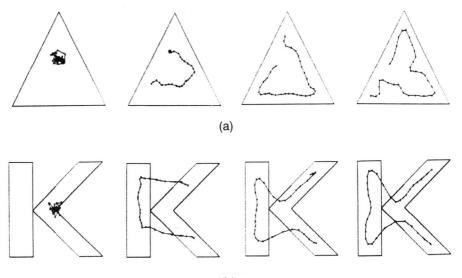

(a)

(b)

Figure 7.7 These figures illustrate one-dimensional maps for two different input probability distributions.   (a) This sequence shows the evolution of the one-dimensional SOM for a uniform distribution of points in a triangular region.   Notice how processing elements that are physical neighbors (indicated by connecting lines) form weight vectors that are distributed in an orderly fashion throughout the input space. (b) For this sequence, input points are uniformly distributed within the K-shaped region. Because of the concavities, weight vectors can have values that are outside of the actual space of input points.

to associate certain inputs with certain output values, such as is done with the backpropagation and counterpropagation networks.

The architecture of the SOM can be extended by the addition of an association layer, as shown in Figure 7.8. We refer to this structure as a **feature map classifier** (FMC). Units on the output layer can be trained by any of several methods including the delta rule, described in Chapter 2, or by the outstar procedure described in Chapter 6. An alternate training method, called **maximum-likelihood training** is described by Huang and Lippmann [1].

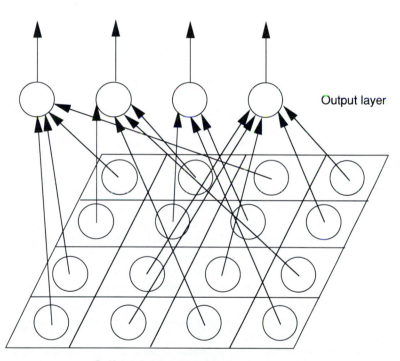

Output layer

Self-organizing map layer

Figure 7.8 In this representation of the feature map classifier, a layer of output units has been added to a two-dimensional SOM. The output units associate desired output values with certain input vectors. The SOM acts as a competitive network that classifies input vectors. The processing done by the FMC is virtually identical to that done by the forward-mapping CPN (see Chapter 6). Unlike in the CPN, it is not necessary to have the units on the competitive layer fully connected to the units on the output layer.

7.2   APPLICATIONS OF SELF-ORGANIZING MAPS

In this section, we discuss two applications that employ the SOM network. Each application illustrates a significantly different way in which the SOM can be used effectively.

7.2.1   The Neural Phonetic Typewriter

It has long been a goal of computer scientists to endow a machine with the ability to recognize and understand human speech. The possibilities for such a machine seem endless. Some progress has been made, yet the goal has been elusive. Despite many years of research, currently available commercial products are limited by their small vocabularies, by dependence on extensive training by a particular speaker, or by both.

The neural phonetic typewriter demonstrates the potential for neural networks to aid in the endeavor to build speaker-independent speech recognition into a computer. Moreover, it shows how neural-network technology can be merged with traditional signal processing and standard techniques in artificial intelligence to solve a particular problem. This device can transcribe speech into written text from an *unlimited* vocabulary, in real time, and with an accuracy of 92 to 97 percent [3]. It is therefore correctly called a *typewriter;* it does not purport to understand the meaning of the speech. Nevertheless, the neural phonetic typewriter should have a significant effect in the modern office. Training for an individual speaker requires the dictation of only about 100 words, and requires about 10 minutes of time on a personal computer.[2]

For this device, a two-dimensional array of nodes is trained using, as inputs, 15-component spectral analyses of spoken words sampled every 9.83 milliseconds. These input vectors are produced from a series of preprocessing steps performed on the audible sound. This preprocessing includes the use of a noise-canceling microphone, a 12-bit analog-to-digital conversion, a 256-point fast Fourier transform performed every 9.83 milliseconds, grouping of the spectral channels into 15 groups, and additional filtering and normalization of the resultant 15-component input vector.

Using Kohonen's clustering algorithm, nodes in a two-dimensional array were allowed to organize themselves in response to the input vectors. After training, the resulting map was calibrated by using the spectra of phonemes as input vectors. Even though phonemes were not used explicitly to train the network, most nodes responded to a single phoneme, as shown in Figure 7.9. This response to phonemes is all the more striking since the phonemes last from 40 milliseconds to 400 milliseconds, in contrast to the 9.83-millisecond sampling frequency used to train the network.

---

[2]Unfortunately for those of us whose native language is English, the only languages supported at present are Finnish and Japanese.

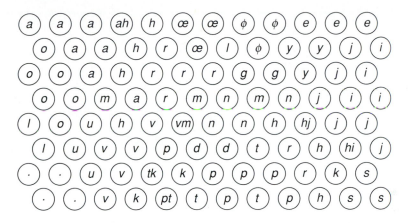

Figure 7.9 This figure is a phonotopic map with the neurons, shown as circles, and the phonemes to which they learned to respond. A double label means that the node responds to more than one phoneme. Some phonemes—such as the plosives represented by *k, p,* and *t*—are difficult for the network to distinguish and are most prone to misclassification by the network. *Source: Reprinted with permission from Teuvo Kohonen, "The neural phonetic typewriter."* IEEE Computer, *March 1988. ©1988 IEEE.*

As a word is spoken, it is sampled, analyzed, and submitted to the network as a sequence of input vectors. As the nodes in the network respond, a path is traced on the map that corresponds to the sequence of input patterns. See Figure 7.10 for an example; the arrows in the figure correspond to the sampling time of 9.83 milliseconds. This path results in a phonetic transcription of the word, which can then be compared with known words or used as input to a rule-based system. The analysis can be carried out quickly and efficiently using a variety of techniques, including neural-network associative memories.

As words are spoken into the microphone, their transcription appears on the computer screen. We eagerly await the English-language version.

7.2.2 Learning Ballistic Arm Movements

In our second example, we describe a method developed by Ritter and Schulten that uses an SOM that learns how to perform ballistic movements of a simple robot arm [4, 5, 6]. Ballistic movements are initiated by short-duration torques applied at the joints of the arm. Once the torques have been applied, motion of the arm proceeds freely (hence the term *ballistic* movement). Since the torques are of such short duration, there is no control of the motion by way of a feedback

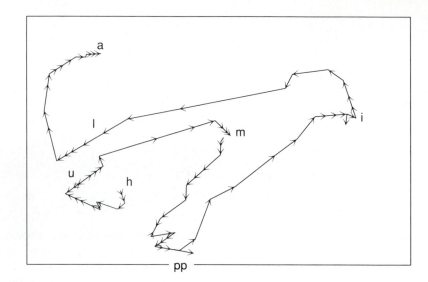

Figure 7.10   This illustration shows the sequence of responses from the phonotopic map resulting from the spoken Finnish word *humppila*. (Do not bother to look up the meaning of this word in your Finnish–English dictionary: *humppila* is the name of a place.) *Source: Reprinted with permission from Teuvo Kohonen, "The neural phonetic typewriter." IEEE Computer, March 1988. ©1988 IEEE.*

mechanism; thus, the torques that cause a particular motion must be known in advance. Figure 7.11 illustrates the simple, two-dimensional robot-arm model used in this example.

For a particular starting position, **x**, and a particular, desired end-effector velocity, $\mathbf{u}_{\mathrm{desired}}$, the required torques can be found from

$$\tau = \mathbf{A}(\mathbf{x})\mathbf{u}_{\mathrm{desired}} \tag{7.5}$$

where τ is the vector $(\tau_1, \tau_2)^t$.[3] The tensor quantity, **A** (here, simply a two-dimensional matrix) is determined by the details of the arm and its configuration. Ritter and Schulten use Kohonen's SOM algorithm to learn the $\mathbf{A}(\mathbf{x})$ quantities. A mechanism for learning the **A** tensors would be useful in a real environment where aging effects and wear might alter the dynamics of the arm over time.

The first part of the method is virtually identical to the two-dimensional mapping example discussed in Section 7.1. Recall that, in that example, units

---

[3]Torque itself is a vector quantity, defined as the time-rate of change of the angular momentum vector. Our vector τ is a composite of the magnitudes of two torque vectors, τ_1 and τ_2. The directions of τ_1 and τ_2 can be accounted for by their signs: $\tau > 0$ implies a counterclockwise rotation of the joint, and $\tau < 0$ implies a clockwise rotation.

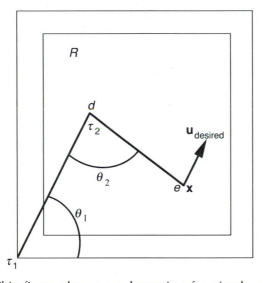

Figure 7.11   This figure shows a schematic of a simple robot arm and
its space of permitted movement. The arm consists of two
massless segments of length 1.0 and 0.9, with unit, point
masses at its distal joint, d, and its end effector, e. The end
effector begins at some randomly selected location, **x**, within
the region R. The joint angles are θ_1 and θ_2. The desired
movement of the arm is to have the end effector move at
some randomly selected velocity, $\mathbf{u}_{\text{desired}}$. For this movement
to be accomplished, torques τ_1 and τ_2 must be applied at the
joints.

learned to organize themselves such that their two-dimensional weight vectors
corresponded to the physical coordinates of the associated unit. An input vector
of (x_1, x_2) would then cause the largest response from the unit whose physical
coordinates were closest to (x_1, x_2).

Ritter and Schulten begin with a two-dimensional array of units identified by their integer coordinates, (i, j), within the region R of Figure 7.11.
Instead of using the coordinates of a selected point as inputs, they use the
corresponding values of the joint angles. Given suitable restrictions on the
values of θ_1 and θ_2, there will be a one-to-one correspondence between the
joint-angle vector, $\theta = (\theta_1, \theta_2)^t$, and the coordinate vector, $\mathbf{x} = (x_1, x_2)^t$.
Other than this change of variables, and the use of a different model for the
Mexican-hat function, the development of the map proceeds as described in
Section 7.1:

1. Select a point **x** within R according to a uniform random distribution.

2. Determine the corresponding $\theta^* = \theta(\mathbf{x})$.

3. Select the winning unit, $\mathbf{y}^*$, such that

$$\|\theta(\mathbf{y}^*) - \theta^*\| = \min_{\mathbf{y}} \|\theta(\mathbf{y}) - \theta^*\|$$

4. Update the **theta** vector for all units according to

$$\theta(\mathbf{y}, t+1) = \theta(\mathbf{y}, t) + h_1(\mathbf{y} - \mathbf{y}^*, t)\big(\theta^* - \theta(\mathbf{y}, t)\big)$$

The function $h_1(\mathbf{y} - \mathbf{y}^*, t)$ defines the model of the Mexican-hat function: It is a Gaussian function centered on the winning unit. Therefore, the *neighborhood* around the winning unit that gets to share in the victory encompasses all of the units. Unlike in the example in Section 7.1, however, the magnitude of the weight updates for the neighboring units decreases as a function of distance from the winning unit. Also, the width of the Gaussian is decreased as learning proceeds.

So far, we have not said anything about how the $\mathbf{A}(\mathbf{x})$ matrices are learned. That task is facilitated by association of one $\mathbf{A}$ tensor with each unit of the SOM network. Then, as winning units are selected according to the procedure given, $\mathbf{A}$ matrices are updated right along with the θ vectors.

We can determine how to adjust the $\mathbf{A}$ matrices by using the difference between the desired motion, $\mathbf{u}_{\text{desired}}$, and the actual motion, $\mathbf{v}$, to determine successive approximations to $\mathbf{A}$. In principle, we do not need a SOM to accomplish this adjustment. We could pick a starting location, then investigate all possible velocities starting from that point, and iterate $\mathbf{A}$ until it converges to give the expected movements. Then, we would select another starting point and repeat the exercise. We could continue this process until all starting locations have been visited and all $\mathbf{A}$s have been determined.

The advantage of using a SOM is that *all* $\mathbf{A}$ matrices are updated simultaneously, based on the corrections determined for only one starting location. Moreover, the magnitude of the corrections for neighboring units ensures that their $\mathbf{A}$ matrices are brought close to their correct values quickly, perhaps even before their associated units have been selected via the θ competition. So, to pick up the algorithm where we left off,

5. Select a desired velocity, $\mathbf{u}$, with random direction and unit magnitude, $\|\mathbf{u}\| = 1$. Execute an arm movement with torques computed from $\tau = \mathbf{A}(\mathbf{x})\mathbf{u}$, and observe the actual end-effector velocity, $\mathbf{v}$.

6. Calculate an improved estimate of the $\mathbf{A}$ tensor for the winning unit:

$$\mathbf{A}(\mathbf{y}^*, t+1) = \mathbf{A}(\mathbf{y}^*, t) + \epsilon \mathbf{A}(\mathbf{y}^*, t)(\mathbf{u} - \mathbf{v})\mathbf{v}^t$$

where ϵ is a positive constant less than 1.

7. Finally, update the $\mathbf{A}$ tensor for all units according to

$$\mathbf{A}(\mathbf{y}, t+1) = \mathbf{A}(\mathbf{y}, t) + h_2(\mathbf{y} - \mathbf{y}^*, t)\big(\mathbf{A}(\mathbf{y}^*, t+1) - \mathbf{A}(\mathbf{y}, t)\big)$$

where h_2 is a Gaussian function whose width decreases with time.

The result of using a SOM in this manner is a significant decrease in the convergence time for the **A** tensors. Moreover, the investigators reported that the system was more robust in the sense of being less sensitive to the initial values of the **A** tensors.

7.3 SIMULATING THE SOM

As we have seen, the SOM is a relatively uncomplicated network in that it has only two layers of units. Therefore, the simulation of this network will not tax the capacity of the general network data structures with which we have, by now, become familiar. The SOM, however, adds at least one interesting twist to the notion of the layer structure used by most other networks; this is the first time we have dealt with a layer of units that is organized as a two-dimensional matrix, rather than as a simple one-dimensional vector. To accommodate this new dimension, we will decompose the matrix conceptually into a single vector containing all the row vectors from the original matrix. As you will see in the following discussion, this matrix decomposition allows the SOM simulator to be implemented with minimal modifications to the general data structures described in Chapter 1.

7.3.1 The SOM Data Structures

From our theoretical discussion earlier in this chapter, we know that the SOM is structured as a two-layer network, with a single vector of input units providing stimulation to a rectangular array of output units. Furthermore, units in the output layer are interconnected to allow lateral inhibition and excitation, as illustrated in Figure 7.12(a). This network structure will be rather cumbersome to simulate if we attempt to model the network precisely as illustrated, because we will have to iterate on the row and column offsets of the output units. Since we have chosen to organize our network connection structures as discrete, single-dimension arrays accessed through an intermediate array, there is no straightforward means of defining a matrix of connection arrays without modifying most of the general network structures. We can, however, reduce the complexity of the simulation task by conceptually unpacking the matrix of units in the output layer, reforming them as a single layer of units organized as a long vector composed of the concatenation of the original row vectors.

In so doing, we will have essentially restructured the network such that it resembles the more familiar two-layer structure, as shown in Figure 7.12(b). As we shall see, the benefit of restructuring the network in this manner is that it will enable us to efficiently locate, and update, the *neighborhood* surrounding the winning unit in the competition.

If we also observe that the connections between the units in the output layer can be simulated on the host computer system as an algorithmic determination of the winning unit (and its associated neighborhood), we can reduce the processing

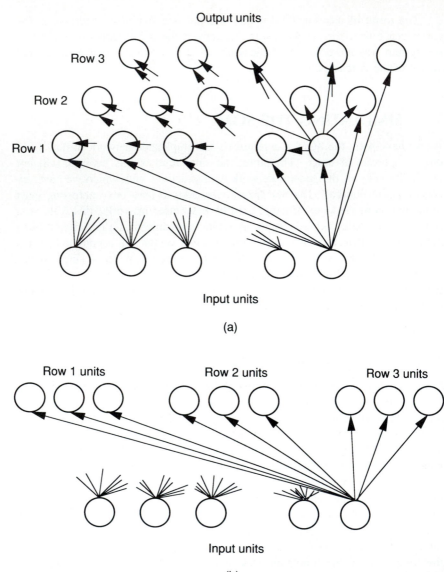

Figure 7.12 The conceptual model of the SOM is shown, (a) as described by the theoretical model, and (b) restructured to ease the simulation task.

model of the SOM network to a simple two-layer, feedforward structure. This reduction allows us to simulate the SOM by using exactly the data structures described in Chapter 1. The only network-specific structure needed to implement the simulator is then the top-level network-specification record. For the SOM, such a record takes the following form:

```
record SOM =
  ROWS : integer;          {number of rows in output layer}
  COLS : integer;                      {ditto for columns}
  INPUTS : ^layer;    {pointer to input layer structure}
  OUTPUTS : ^layer; {pointer to output layer structure}
  WINNER : integer;              {index to winning unit}
  deltaR : integer;          {neighborhood row offset}
  deltaC : integer;       {neighborhood column offset}
  TIME : integer;                  {discrete timestep}
end record;
```

7.3.2 SOM Algorithms

Let us now turn our attention to the process of implementing the SOM simulator. As in previous chapters, we shall begin by describing the algorithms needed to propagate information through the network, and shall conclude this section by describing the training algorithms. Throughout the remainder of this section, we presume that you are by now familiar with the data structures we use to simulate a layered network. Anyone not comfortable with these structures is referred to Section 1.4.

SOM Signal Propagation. In Section 6.4.4, we described a modification to the counterpropagation network that used the magnitude of the difference vector between the unnormalized input and weight vectors as the basis for determining the activation of a unit on the competitive layer. We shall now see that this approach is a viable means of implementing competition, since it is the basic method of stimulating output units in the SOM.

In the SOM, the input layer is provided only to store the input vector. For that reason, we can consider the process of forward signal propagation to be a matter of allowing the computer to visit all units in the output layer sequentially. At each output-layer unit, the computer calculates the magnitude of the difference vector between the output of the input layer and the weight vector formed by the connections between the input layer and the current unit. After completion of this calculation, the magnitude will be stored, and the computer will move on to the next unit on the layer. Once all the output-layer units have been processed, the forward signal propagation is finished, and the output of the network will be the matrix containing the magnitude of the difference vector for each unit in the output layer.

If we also consider the training process, we can allow the computer to store locally an index (or pointer) to locate the output unit that had the smallest difference-vector magnitude during the initial pass. That index can then be used to identify the winner of the competition. By adopting this approach, we can also use the routine used to forward propagate signals in the SOM during training with no modifications.

Based on this strategy, we shall define the forward signal-propagation algorithm to be the combination of two routines: one to compute the difference-vector magnitude for a specified unit on the output layer, and one to call the first routine for every unit on the output layer. We shall call these routines `prop` and `propagate`, respectively. We begin with the definition of `prop`.

```
function prop (NET:SOM; UNIT:integer) return float
{compute the magnitude of the difference vector for UNIT}

var invec, connects : ^float[];          {locate arrays}
    sum, mag : float;               {temporary variables}
    i : integer;                      {iteration counter}

begin
  invec = NET.INPUTS^.OUTS^;       {locate input vector}
  connects = NET.OUTPUTS^.WEIGHTS^[UNIT]; {connections}
  sum = 0;                              {initialize sum}

  for i = 1 to length(invec)            {for all inputs}
    do                              {square of difference}
      sum = sum + sqr(invec[i] - connect[i]);
    end do;

  mag = sqrt(sum);                   {compute magnitude}
  return (mag);                       {return magnitude}
end function;
```

Now that we can compute the output value for any unit on the output layer, let us consider the routine to generate the output for the entire network. Since we have defined our SOM network as a standard, two-layer network, the pseudocode definition for `propagate` is straightforward.

```
function propagate (NET:SOM) return integer
{propagate forward through the SOM, return the index to
                                            winner}

var outvec : ^float[];              {locate output array}
    winner : integer;                {winning unit index}
    smallest, mag : float            {temporary storage}
    i : integer;                      {iteration counter}

begin
  outvec = NET.OUTPUTS^.OUTS^;       {locate output array}
  winner = 0;                          {initialize winner}
  smallest = 10000;                     {arbitrarily high}

  for i = 1 to length(outvec)           {for all outputs}
```

```
     do
        mag = prop(NET, i);              {activate unit}
        outvec[i] = mag;                 {save output}

        if (mag < smallest)      {if new winner is found}
        then
           winner = i;                   {mark new winner}
           smallest = mag;         {save winning value}
        end if;
     end do;

   NET.WINNER = winner;          {store winning unit id}
   return (winner);                   {identify winner}
   end function;
```

SOM Learning Algorithms. Now that we have developed a means for performing the forward signal propagation in the SOM, we have also solved the largest part of the problem of training the network. As described by Eq. (7.4), learning in the SOM takes place by updating of the connections to the set of output units that fall within the *neighborhood* of the winning unit. We have already provided the means for determining the winner as part of the forward signal propagation; all that remains to be done to train the network is to develop the processes that define the neighborhood (N_c) and update the connection weights.

Unfortunately, the process of determining the neighborhood surrounding the winning unit is likely to be application dependent. For example, consider the two applications described earlier, the neural phonetic typewriter and the ballistic arm movement systems. Each implemented an SOM as the basic mechanism for solving their respective problems, but each also utilized a neighborhood-selection mechanism that was best suited to the application being addressed. It is likely that other problems would also require alternative methods better suited to determining the size of the neighborhood needed for each application. Therefore, we will not presuppose that we can define a universally acceptable function for N_c.

We will, however, develop the code necessary to describe a typical neighborhood-selection function, trusting that you will learn enough from the example to construct a function suitable for your applications. For simplicity, we will design the process as two functions: the first will return a true–false flag to indicate whether a certain unit is within the neighborhood of the winning unit at the current timestep, and the second will update the connection values at an output unit, if the unit falls within the neighborhood of the winning unit.

The first of these routines, which we call neighbor, will return a true flag if the row and column coordinates of the unit given as input fall within the range of units to be updated. This process proves to be relatively easy, in that the routine needs to perform only the following two tests:

$$(R_w - \Delta R) \le R \le (R_w + \Delta R)$$
$$(C_w - \Delta C) \le C \le (C_w + \Delta C)$$

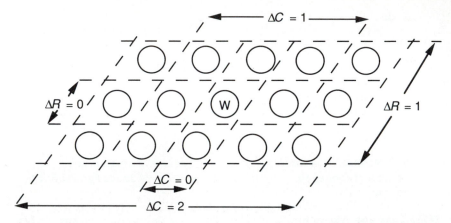

Figure 7.13   A simple scheme is shown for dynamically altering the size of the neighborhood surrounding the winning unit. In this diagram, **W** denotes the winning unit for a given input vector. The neighborhood surrounding the winning unit is then given by the values contained in the variables deltaR and deltaC contained in the SOM record. As the values in deltaR and deltaC approach zero, the neighborhood surrounding the winning unit shrinks, until the neighborhood is precisely the winning unit.

where (R_w, C_w) are the row and column coordinates of the winning unit, $(\Delta R, \Delta C)$ are the row and column offsets from the winning unit that define the neighborhood, and (R, C) the row and column coordinates of the unit being tested.

For example, consider the situation illustrated in Figure 7.13. Notice that the boundary surrounding the winner's neighborhood shrinks with successively smaller values for $(\Delta R, \Delta C)$, until the neighborhood is limited to the winner when $(\Delta R, \Delta C) = (0, 0)$. Thus, we need only to alter the values for $(\Delta R, \Delta C)$ in order to change the size of the winner's neighborhood.

So that we can implement this mechanism of neighborhood determination, we have incorporated two variables in the SOM record, which we have named deltaR and deltaC, which allow the network record to keep the current values for the ΔR and ΔC terms. Having made this observation, we can now define the algorithm needed to implement the neighbor function.

```
function neighbor (NET:SOM; R,C,W:integer) return boolean
{return true if (R,C) is in the neighborhood of W}

var row, col,                    {coordinates of winner}
    dR1, dC1,              {coordinates of lower boundary}
    dR2, dC2 : integer; {coordinates of upper boundary}

begin
```

```
row = (W-1) / NET.COLS;
                        {convert index of winner to row}

col = (W-1) % NET.COLS;
                        {modulus finds column of winner}
dR1 = max(1, (row - NET.deltaR));
dR2 = min(NET.ROWS, (row + NET.deltaR));
dC1 = max(1, (col - NET.deltaC));
dC2 = min(NET.COLS, (col + NET.deltaC));

return (((dR1 <= R) and (R <= dR2)) and
         ((dC1 <= C) and (C <= dC2)));
end function;
```

Note that the algorithm for `neighbor` relies on the fact that the array indices for the winning unit (`W`) and the number of rows and columns in the SOM output layer are presumed to start at 1 and to run through n. If the first index is presumed to be zero, the determination of the `row` and `col` values described must be adjusted, since zero divided by anything is zero. Similarly, the `min` and `max` functions utilized in the algorithm are needed to protect against the case where the winning unit is located on an "edge" of the network output.

Now that we can determine whether or not a unit is in the neighborhood of the winning unit in the SOM, all that remains to complete the implementation of the training algorithms is the function needed to update the weights to all the units that require updating. We shall design this algorithm to return the number of units updated in the SOM, so that the calling process can determine when the neighborhood around the winning unit has shrunk to just the winning unit (i.e., when the number of units updated is equal to 1). Also, to simplify things, we shall assume that the $\alpha(t)$ term given in the weight-update equation (Eq. 7.2) is simply a small constant value, rather than a function of time. In this example algorithm, we define the $\alpha(t)$ parameter as the value A.

```
function update (NET:SOM) return integer
{update the weights to all winning units,
                returning the number of winners updated}

constant A : float = 0.3; {simple activation constant}

var winner, unit, upd : integer;
                                {indices to output units}
    invec : ^float[];
                            {locate unit output arrays}

    connect : ^float[];      {locate connection array}
    i, j, k : integer;              {iteration counters}

begin
  winner = propagate (NET); {propagate and find winner}
  unit = 1;                  {start at first output unit}
  upd = 0;                        {no updates yet}
```

```
for i = 1 to NET.ROWS                        {for all rows}
  do
    for j = 1 to NET.COLS                  {and all columns}
      do
        if (neighbor (NET,i,j,winner))
        then
        {first locate the appropriate connection array}
          connect = NET.OUTPUTS^.WEIGHTS^[unit];
            {then locate the input layer output array}
          invec = NET.INPUTS^.OUTS^;
          upd = upd + 1;          {count another update}

          for k = 1 to length(connect)
                                    {for all connections}
            do
              connect[k] = connect[k]
                          + (A*(invec[k]-connect[k]));
            end do;
        end if;
        unit = unit + 1;                {access next unit}

      end do;
  end do;

  return (upd);                        {return update count}
end function;
```

7.3.3 Training the SOM

Like most other networks, the SOM will be constructed so that it initially contains random information. The network will then be allowed to self-adapt by being shown example inputs that are representative of the desired topology. Our computer simulation ought to mimic the desired network behavior if we simply follow these same guidelines when constructing and training the simulator.

There are two aspects of the training process that are relatively simple to implement, and we assume that you will provide them as part of the implementation of the simulator. These functions are the ones needed to initialize the SOM (initialize) and to apply an input vector (set_input) to the input layer of the network.

Most of the work to be done in the simulator will be accomplished by the previously defined routines, and we need to concern ourselves now with only the notion of deciding how and when to collapse the winning neighborhood as we train the network. Here again, this aspect of the design probably will be influenced by the specific application, so, for instructional purposes, we will restrict ourselves to a fairly easy application that allows each of the output layer units to be uniquely associated with a specific input vector.

For this example, let us assume that the SOM to be simulated has four rows of five columns of units in the output layer, and two units providing input. Such

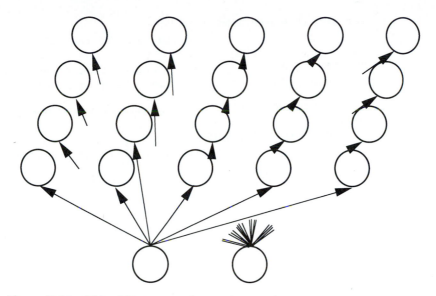

Figure 7.14 This SOM network can be used to capture organization of a two-dimensional image, such as a triangle, circle, or any regular polygon. In the programming exercises, we ask you to simulate this network structure to test the operation of your simulator program.

a network structure is depicted in Figure 7.14. We will code the SOM simulator so that the entire output layer is initially contained in the neighborhood, and we shall shrink the neighborhood by two rows and two columns after every 10 training patterns.

For the SOM, there are two distinct training sessions that must occur. In the first, we will train the network until the neighborhood has shrunk to the point that only one unit wins the competition. During the second phase, which occurs after all the training patterns have been allocated to a winning unit (although not necessarily *different* units), we will simply continue to run the training algorithm for an arbitrarily large number of additional cycles. We do this to try to ensure that the network has stabilized, although there is no absolute guarantee that it has. With this strategy in mind, we can now complete the simulator by constructing the routine to initialize and train the network.

```
procedure train (NET:SOM;  NP:integer)
{train the network for each of NP patterns}

begin
  initialize(NET);                {reader-provided routine}

  for i = 1 to NP                 {for all training patterns}
    do
```

```
NET.deltaR = NET.ROWS / 2;
                          {initialize the row offset}
NET.deltaC = NET.COLS / 2;      {ditto for columns}
NET.TIME = 0;                   {reset time counter}
set_inputs(NET,i);             {get training pattern}

while (update(NET) > 1)    {loop until one winner}
   do
      NET.TIME = NET.TIME + 1;
                          {advance training counter}

      if (NET.TIME % 10 = 0)        {if shrink time}
      then
      {shrink the neighborhood, with a floor
                                          of (0,0)}
         NET.deltaR = max (0, NET.deltaR - 1);
         NET.deltaC = max (0, NET.deltaC - 1);
      end if;
   end do;
end do;

{now that all patterns have one winner, train
                                          some more}

for i = 1 to 1000               {for arbitrary passes}
   do
      for j = 1 to NP                  {for all patterns}
         do
            set_inputs(NET, j);   {set training pattern}
            dummy = update(NET);       {train network}
         end do;
   end do;
end procedure;
```

Programming Exercises

7.1. Implement the SOM simulator. Test it by constructing a network similar to the one depicted in Figure 7.14. Train the network using the Cartesian coordinates of each unit in the output layer as training data. Experiment with different time periods to determine how many training passes are optimal before reducing the size of the neighborhood.

7.2. Repeat Programming Exercise 7.1, but this time extend the simulator to plot the network dynamics using Kohonen's method, as described in Section 7.1. If you do not have access to a graphics terminal, simply list out the connection-weight values to each unit in the output layer as a set of ordered pairs at various timesteps.

7.3. Repeat Programming Exercise 7.2, this time using three input units. Configure the output layer appropriately, and train the network to learn to map a three-dimensional cube in the first quadrant (all vertices should contain positive coordinates). Do not put the vertices of the cube at integer coordinates. Does the network do as well as the network in Programming Exercise 7.2?

Suggested Readings

The best supplement to the material in this chapter is Kohonen's text on self-organization [2]. Now in its second edition, that text also contains general background material regarding various learning methods for neural networks, as well as a review of the necessary mathematics.

Bibliography

[1] Willian Y. Huang and Richard P. Lippmann. Neural net and traditional classifiers. In *Proceedings of the Conference on Neural Information Processing Systems*, Denver, CO, November 1987.

[2] Teuvo Kohonen. *Self-Organization and Associative Memory*, volume 8 of *Springer Series in Information Sciences*. Springer-Verlag, New York, 1984.

[3] Teuvo Kohonen. The "neural" phonetic typewriter. *Computer*, 21(3):11–22, March 1988.

[4] H. Ritter and K. Schulten. Topology conserving mappings for learning motor tasks. In John S. Denker, editor, *Neural Networks for Computing*. American Institute of Physics, pp. 376–380, New York, 1986.

[5] H. Ritter and K. Schulten. Extending Kohonen's self-organizing mapping algorithm to learn ballistic movements. In Rolf Eckmiller and Christoph v.d. Malsburg, editors. *Neural Computers*. Springer-Verlag, Heidelberg, pp. 393–406, 1987.

[6] Helge J. Ritter, Thomas M. Martinetz, and Klaus J. Schulten. Topology-conserving maps for learning visuo-motor-coordination. *Neural Networks*, 2(3):159–168, 1989.

Adaptive Resonance Theory

One of the nice features of human memory is its ability to learn many new things without necessarily forgetting things learned in the past. A frequently cited example is the ability to recognize your parents even if you have not seen them for some time and have learned many new faces in the interim. It would be highly desirable if we could impart this same capability to an ANS. Most networks that we have discussed in previous chapters will tend to forget old information if we attempt to add new information incrementally.

When developing an ANS to perform a particular pattern-classification operation, we typically proceed by gathering a set of exemplars, or training patterns, then using these exemplars to train the system. During the training, information is encoded in the system by the adjustment of weight values. Once the training is deemed to be adequate, the system is ready to be put into production, and no additional weight modification is permitted.

This operational scenario is acceptable provided the problem domain has well-defined boundaries and is stable. Under such conditions, it is usually possible to define an adequate set of training inputs for whatever problem is being solved. Unfortunately, in many realistic situations, the environment is neither bounded nor stable.

Consider a simple example. Suppose you intend to train a BPN to recognize the silhouettes of a certain class of aircraft. The appropriate images can be collected and used to train the network, which is potentially a time-consuming task depending on the size of the network required. After the network has learned successfully to recognize all of the aircraft, the training period is ended and no further modification of the weights is allowed.

If, at some future time, another aircraft in the same class becomes operational, you may wish to add its silhouette to the store of knowledge in your network. To do this, you would have to retrain the network with the new pattern *plus* all of the previous patterns. Training on only the new silhouette could result in the network learning that pattern quite well, but forgetting previously learned patterns. Although retraining may not take as long as the initial training, it still could require a significant investment.

Moreover, if an ANS is presented with a previously unseen input pattern, there is generally no built-in mechanism for the network to be able to recognize the novelty of the input. The ANS doesn't know that it doesn't know the input pattern.

We have been describing what Stephen Grossberg calls the **stability–plasticity dilemma** [5]. This dilemma can be stated as a series of questions [6]: How can a learning system remain adaptive (plastic) in response to significant input, yet remain stable in response to irrelevant input? How does the system know to switch between its plastic and its stable modes? How can the system retain previously learned information while continuing to learn new things?

In response to such questions, Grossberg, Carpenter, and numerous colleagues developed **adaptive resonance theory** (ART), which seeks to provide answers. ART is an extension of the competitive-learning schemes that have been discussed in Chapters 6 and 7. The material in Section 6.1 especially, should be considered a prerequisite to the current chapter. We will draw heavily from those results, so you should review the material, if necessary, before proceeding.

In the competitive systems discussed in Chapter 6, nodes compete with one another, based on some specified criteria, and the winner is said to classify the input pattern. Certain instabilities can arise in these networks such that different nodes might respond to the same input pattern on different occasions. Moreover, later learning can wash away earlier learning if the environment is not statistically stationary or if novel inputs arise [9].

A key to solving the stability–plasticity dilemma is to add a feedback mechanism between the competitive layer and the input layer of a network. This feedback mechanism facilitates the learning of new information without destroying old information, automatic switching between stable and plastic modes, and stabilization of the encoding of the classes done by the nodes. The results from this approach are two neural-network architectures that are particularly suited for pattern-classification problems in realistic environments. These network architectures are referred to as ART1 and ART2. ART1 and ART2 differ in the nature of their input patterns. ART1 networks require that the input vectors be binary. ART2 networks are suitable for processing analog, or gray-scale, patterns.

ART gets its name from the particular way in which learning and recall interplay in the network. In physics, resonance occurs when a small-amplitude vibration of the proper frequency causes a large-amplitude vibration in an electrical or mechanical system. In an ART network, information in the form of processing-element outputs reverberates back and forth between layers. If the proper patterns develop, a stable oscillation ensues, which is the neural-network equivalent of resonance. During this resonant period, learning, or adaptation, can occur. Before the network has achieved a resonant state, no learning takes place, because the time required for changes in the processing-element weights is much longer than the time that it takes the network to achieve resonance.

A resonant state can be attained in one of two ways. If the network has learned previously to recognize an input vector, then a resonant state will be achieved quickly when that input vector is presented. During resonance, the adaptation process will reinforce the memory of the stored pattern. If the input vector is not immediately recognized, the network will rapidly search through its stored patterns looking for a match. If no match is found, the network will enter a resonant state whereupon the new pattern will be stored for the first time. Thus, the network responds quickly to previously learned data, yet remains able to learn when novel data are presented.

Much of Grossberg's work has been concerned with modeling actual macroscopic processes that occur within the brain in terms of the average properties of collections of the microscopic components of the brain (neurons). Thus, a Grossberg processing element may represent one or more actual neurons. In keeping with our practice, we shall not dwell on the neurological implications of the theory. There exists a vast body of literature available concerning this work. Work with these theories has led to predictions about neurophysiological processes, even down to the chemical-ion level, which have subsequently been proven true through research by neurophysiologists [6]. Numerous references are listed at the end of this chapter.

The equations that govern the operation of the ART networks are quite complicated. It is easy to lose sight of the forest while examining the trees closely. For that reason, we first present a qualitative description of the processing in ART networks. Once that foundation is laid, we shall return to a detailed discussion of the equations.

8.1 ART NETWORK DESCRIPTION

The basic features of the ART architecture are shown in Figure 8.1. Patterns of activity that develop over the nodes in the two layers of the attentional subsystem are called short-term memory (STM) traces because they exist only in association with a single application of an input vector. The weights associated with the bottom-up and top-down connections between F_1 and F_2 are called long-term memory (LTM) traces because they encode information that remains a part of the network for an extended period.

8.1.1 Pattern Matching in ART

To illustrate the processing that takes place, we shall describe a hypothetical sequence of events that might occur in an ART network. The scenario is a simple pattern-matching operation during which an ART network tries to determine

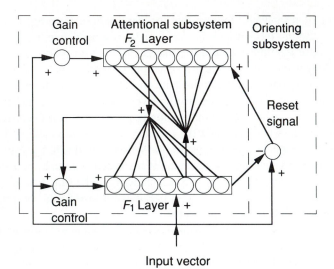

Input vector

Figure 8.1   The ART system is diagrammed. The two major subsystems are
the attentional subsystem and the orienting subsystem. F_1 and
F_2 represent two layers of nodes in the attentional subsystem.
Nodes on each layer are fully interconnected to the nodes on
the other layer. Not shown are interconnects among the nodes
on each layer. Other connections between components are
indicated by the arrows. A plus sign indicates an excitatory
connection; a minus sign indicates an inhibitory connection.
The function of the gain control and orienting subsystem is
discussed in the text.

whether an input pattern is among the patterns previously stored in the network.
Figure 8.2 illustrates the operation.

In Figure 8.2(a), an input pattern, **I**, is presented to the units on F_1 in the
same manner as in other networks: one vector component goes to each node.
A pattern of activation, **X**, is produced across F_1. The processing done by the
units on this layer is a somewhat more complicated form of that done by the
input layer of the CPN (see Section 6.1). The same input pattern excites both the
orienting subsystem, A, and the gain control, G (the connections to G are not
shown on the drawings). The output pattern, **S**, results in an inhibitory signal
that is also sent to A. The network is structured such that this inhibitory signal
exactly cancels the excitatory effect of the signal from **I**, so that A remains
inactive. Notice that G supplies an excitatory signal to F_1. The same signal
is applied to each node on the layer and is therefore known as a **nonspecific
signal**. The need for this signal will be made clear later.

The appearance of **X** on F_1 results in an output pattern, **S**, which is sent
through connections to F_2. Each F_2 unit receives the entire output vector, **S**,

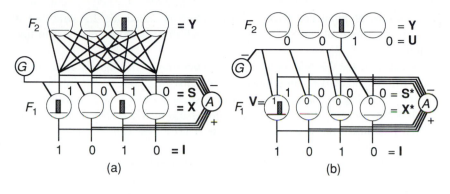

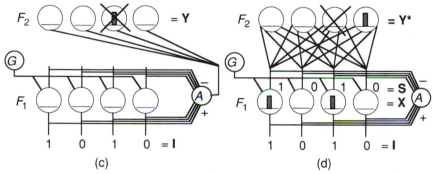

Figure 8.2   A pattern-matching cycle in an ART network is shown. The process evolves from the initial presentation of the input pattern in (a) to a pattern-matching attempt in (b), to reset in (c), to the final recognition in (d). Details of the cycle are discussed in the text.

from F_1. F_2 units calculate their net-input values in the usual manner by summing the products of the input values and the connection weights. In response to inputs from F_1, a pattern of activity, **Y**, develops across the nodes of F_2. F_2 is a competitive layer that performs a contrast enhancement on the input signal like the competitive layer described in Section 6.1. The gain control signals to F_2 are omitted here for simplicity.

In Figure 8.2(b), the pattern of activity, **Y**, results in an output pattern, **U**, from F_2. This output pattern is sent as an inhibitory signal to the gain control system. The gain control is configured such that if it receives any inhibitory signal from F_2, it ceases activity. **U** also becomes a second input pattern for the F_1 units. **U** is transformed by LTM traces on the top-down connections from F_2 to F_1. We shall call this transformed pattern **V**.

Notice that there are three possible sources of input to F_1, but that only two appear to be used at any one time. The units on F_1 (and F_2 as well) are constructed so that they can become active only if two out of the possible three sources of input are active. This feature is called the **2/3 rule** and it plays an important role in ART, which we shall discuss more fully later in this section.

Because of the 2/3 rule, only those F_1 nodes receiving signals from both **I** and **V** will remain active. The pattern that remains on F_1 is $\mathbf{I} \cap \mathbf{V}$, the intersection of **I** and **V**. In Figure 8.2(b), the patterns mismatch and a new activity pattern, $\mathbf{X}^*$, develops on F_1. Since the new output pattern, $\mathbf{S}^*$, is different from the original pattern, **S**, the inhibitory signal to A no longer cancels the excitation coming from **I**.

In Figure 8.2(c), A has become active in response to the mismatch of patterns on F_1. A sends a nonspecific reset signal to all of the nodes on F_2. These nodes respond according to their present state. If they are inactive, they do not respond. If they are active, they become inactive *and they stay that way for an extended period of time*. This sustained inhibition is necessary to prevent the same node from winning the competition during the next matching cycle. Since **Y** no longer appears, the top-down output and the inhibitory signal to the gain control also disappear.

In Figure 8.2(d), the original pattern, **X**, is reinstated on F_1, and a new cycle of pattern matching begins. This time a new pattern, $\mathbf{Y}^*$, appears on F_2. The nodes participating in the original pattern, **Y**, remain inactive due to the long term effects of the reset signal from A.

This cycle of pattern matching will continue until a match is found, or until F_2 runs out of previously stored patterns. If no match is found, the network will assign some uncommitted node or nodes on F_2 and will begin to learn the new pattern.[1] Learning takes place through the modification of the weights, or the LTM traces. It is important to understand that this learning process does not start or stop, but rather continues even while the pattern matching process takes place. Anytime signals are sent over connections, the weights associated with those connections are subject to modification. Why then do the mismatches not result in loss of knowledge or the learning of incorrect associations? The reason is that the time required for significant changes to occur in the weights is very long with respect to the time required for a complete matching cycle. The connections participating in mismatches are not active long enough to affect the associated weights seriously.

When a match does occur, there is no reset signal and the network settles down into a resonant state as described earlier. During this stable state, connections remain active for a sufficiently long time so that the weights are strengthened. This resonant state can arise only when a pattern match occurs, or during the enlistment of new units on F_2 in order to store a previously unknown pattern.

---

[1]In an actual ART network, the pattern-matching cycle may not visit all previously stored patterns before an uncommitted F_2 node is chosen.

8.1.2   Gain Control in ART

Before continuing with a look at the dynamics of ART networks, we want to examine more closely the need for the gain-control mechanism. In the simple example discussed in the previous section, the existence of a gain control and the 2/3 rule appear to be superfluous. They are, however, quite important features of the system, as the following example illustrates.

Suppose the ART network of the previous section was only one in a hierarchy of networks in a much larger system. The F_2 layer might be receiving inputs from a layer above it as well as from the F_1 layer below. This hierarchical structure is thought to be a common one in biological neural systems. If the F_2 layer were stimulated by an upper layer, it could produce a top-down output and send signals back to the F_1 layer. It is possible that this top-down signal would arrive at F_1 before an input signal, $\mathbf{I}$, arrived at F_1 from below. A premature signal from F_2 could be the result of an **expectation** arising from a higher level in the hierarchy. In other words, F_2 is indicating what it expects the next input pattern to be, before the pattern actually arrives at F_1. Biological examples of this expectation phenomenon abound. For example, how often have you anticipated the next word that a person was going to say during a conversation?

The appearance of an early top-down signal from F_2 presents us with a small dilemma. Suppose F_1 produced an output in response to any single input vector, no matter what the source. Then, the expectation signal arriving from F_2 would elicit an output from F_1 and the pattern-matching cycle would ensue without ever having an input vector to F_1 from below. Now let's add in the gain control and the 2/3 rule.

According to the discussion in the previous section, if G exists, any signal coming from F_2 results in an inhibition of G. Recall that G nonspecifically arouses every F_1 unit. With the 2/3 rule in effect, inhibition of G means that a top-down signal from F_2 cannot, by itself, elicit an output from F_1. Instead, the F_1 units become preconditioned, or sensitized, by the top-down pattern. In the biological language of Grossberg, the F_1 units have received a **subliminal** stimulation from F_2. If now the expected input pattern is received on F_1 from below, this preconditioning results in an immediate resonance in the network. Even if the input pattern is not the expected one, F_1 will still provide an output, since it is receiving inputs from two out of the three possible sources, $\mathbf{I}, G$, and F_2.

If there is no expectation signal from F_2, then F_1 remains completely quiescent until it receives an input vector from below. Then, since G is not inhibited, F_1 units are again receiving inputs from two sources and F_1 will send an output up to F_2 to begin the matching cycle.

G and the 2/3 rule combine to permit the F_1 layer to distinguish between an expectation signal from above, and an input signal from below. In the former case, F_1's response is subliminal; in the latter case, it is **supraliminal**—that is, it generates a nonzero output.

In the next section, we shall examine the equations that govern the operation of the ART1 network. We shall see explicitly how the gain control and 2/3 rule influence the processing-element activities. In Section 8.3, we shall extend the result to encompass the ART2 architecture.

Exercise 8.1: Based on the discussion in this section, describe how the gain control signal on the F_2 layer would function.

8.2 ART1

The ART1 architecture shares the same overall structure as that shown in Figure 8.1. Recall that all inputs to ART1 must be binary vectors; that is, they must have components that are elements of the set $\{0, 1\}$. This restriction may appear to limit the utility of the network, but there are many problems having data that can be cast into binary format. The principles of operation of ART1 are similar to those of ART2, where analog inputs are allowed. Moreover, the restrictions and assumptions that we make for ART1 will simplify the mathematics a bit. We shall examine the attentional subsystem first, including the STM layers F_1 and F_2, and the gain-control mechanism, G.

8.2.1 The Attentional Subsystem

The dynamic equations for the activities of the processing elements on layers F_1 and F_2 both have the form

$$\epsilon \dot{x}_k = -x_k + (1 - Ax_k)J_k^+ - (B + Cx_k)J_k^- \tag{8.1}$$

J_k^+ is an excitatory input to the kth unit and J_k^- is an inhibitory input. The precise definitions of these terms, as well as those of the parameters $A, B,$ and C, depend on which layer is being discussed, but all terms are assumed to be greater than zero. Henceforth we shall use x_{1i} to refer to activities on the F_1 layer, and x_{2j} for activities on the F_2 layer. Similarly, we shall add numbers to the parameter names to identify the layer to which they refer: for example, B_1, A_2. For convenience, we shall label the nodes on F_1 with the symbol v_i and those on F_2 with v_j. The subscripts i and j will be used exclusively to refer to the layers F_1 and F_2, respectively.

The factor ϵ requires some explanation. Recall from the previous section that pattern-matching activities between layers F_1 and F_2 must occur much faster than the time required for the connection weights to change significantly. The ϵ factor in Eq. (8.1) embodies that requirement. If we insist that $0 \leq \epsilon \ll 1$, then $\dot{x}_k$ will be a fairly large value; that is, x_k will reach its equilibrium value quickly. Since x_k spends most of its time near its equilibrium value, we shall not have to concern ourselves with the time evolution of the activity values: We shall automatically set the activities equal to the asymptotic values. Under these conditions, the ϵ factor becomes superfluous, and we shall drop it from the equations that follow.

Exercise 8.2: Show that the activities of the processing elements described by Eq. (8.1) have their values bounded within the interval $[-BC, A]$, no matter how large the excitatory or inhibitory inputs may become.

Processing on F_1. Figure 8.3 illustrates an F_1 processing element with its various inputs and weight vectors. The units calculate a net-input value coming from F_2 in the usual way:[2]

$$V_i = \sum_j u_j z_{ij} \tag{8.2}$$

We assume the unit output function quickly rises to 1 for nonzero activities. Thus, we can approximate the unit output, s_i, with a binary step function:

$$s_i = h(x_{1i}) = \begin{cases} 1 & x_{1i} > 0 \\ 0 & x_{1i} \leq 0 \end{cases} \tag{8.3}$$

The total excitatory input, J_i^+, is given by

$$J_i^+ = I_i + D_1 V_i + B_1 G \tag{8.4}$$

where D_1 and B_1 are constants.[3] The inhibitory term, J_i^-, we shall set identically equal to 1. With these definitions, the equations for the F_1 processing elements are

$$\dot{x}_{1i} = -x_{1i} + (1 - A_1 x_{1i})(I_i + D_1 V_i + B_1 G) - (B_1 + C_1 x_{1i}) \tag{8.5}$$

The output, G, of the gain-control system depends on the activities on other parts of the network. We can describe G succinctly with the equation

$$G = \begin{cases} 1 & \text{if } \mathbf{I} \neq \mathbf{0} \text{ and } \mathbf{U} = \mathbf{0} \\ 0 & \text{otherwise} \end{cases} \tag{8.6}$$

In other words, if there is an input vector, and F_2 is *not* actively producing an output vector, then $G = 1$. Any other combination of activity on $\mathbf{I}$ and F_2 effectively inhibits the gain control from producing its nonspecific excitation to the units on F_1.[4]

---

[2]The convention on weight indices that we have utilized consistently throughout this text is opposite to that used by Carpenter and Grossberg. In our notation, z_{ij} refers to the weight on the connection *from* the jth unit *to* the ith unit. In Carpenter and Grossberg's notation, z_{ij} would refer to the weight on the connection *from* the ith node *to* the jth.

[3]Carpenter and Grossberg include the parameter, D_1, in their calculation of V_i. In their notation: $V_i = D_1 \sum_j u_j z_{ij}$. You should bear this difference in mind when reading their papers.

[4]In the original paper by Carpenter and Grossberg, the authors described four different ways of implementing the gain control system. The method that we have shown here was chosen to be consistent with the general description of ART given in the previous sections. [5]

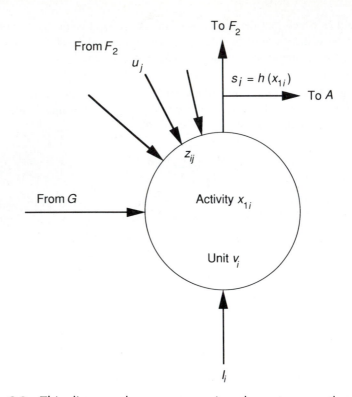

Figure 8.3   This diagram shows a processing element, v_i, on the F_1 layer
of an ART1 network. The activity of the unit is x_{1i}. It receives
a binary input value, I_i, from below, and an excitatory signal,
G, from the gain control. In addition, the top-down signals,
u_j, from F_2 are gated (multiplied by) weights, z_{ij}. Outputs,
s_i, from the processing element go up to F_2 and across to the
orienting subsystem, A.

Let's examine Eq. (8.5) for the four possible combinations of activity on
I and F_2. First, consider the case where there is no input vector and F_2 is
inactive. Equation (8.5) reduces to

$$\dot{x}_{1i} = -x_{1i} - (B_1 + C_1 x_{1i})$$

In equilibrium $\dot{x}_{1i} = 0$,

$$x_{1i} = \frac{-B_1}{1 + C_1} \tag{8.7}$$

Thus, units with no inputs are held in a negative activity state.

Now apply an input vector, **I**, but keep F_2 inactive for the moment. In this
case, both F_1 and the gain control receive input signals from below. Since F_2

is inactive, G is not inhibited. The equations for the F_1 units become

$$\dot{x}_{1i} = -x_{1i} + (1 - A_1 x_{1i})(I_i + B_1 G) - (B_1 + C_1 x_{1i})$$

When the units reach their equilibrium activities,

$$x_{1i} = \frac{I_i}{1 + A_1(I_i + B_1) + C_1} \tag{8.8}$$

where we have used $G = 1$. In this case, units that receive a nonzero input value from below also generate an activity value greater than zero and have a nonzero output value according to Eq. (8.3). Units that do not receive a nonzero input nevertheless have their activities raised to the zero level through the nonspecific excitation signal from G.

For the third scenario, we examine the case where an input pattern, **I**, and a top-down pattern, **V**, from F_2 are coincident on the F_1 layer. The equations for the unit activities are

$$\dot{x}_{1i} = -x_{1i} + (1 - A_1 x_{1i})(I_i + D_1 V_i) - (B_1 + C_1 x_{1i})$$

Here, the equilibrium value

$$x_{1i} = \frac{I_i + D_1 V_i - B_1}{1 + A_1(I_i + D_1 V_i) + C_1} \tag{8.9}$$

requires a little effort to interpret. Whether x_{1i} is greater than, equal to, or less than zero depends on the relative values of the quantities in the numerator in Eq. (8.9). We can distinguish three cases of interest, which are determined by application of the 2/3 rule.

If a unit has a positive input value, I_i, and a large positive net input from above, V_i, then the 2/3 rule says that the unit activity should be greater than zero. For this to be the case, it must be true that $I_i + D_1 V_i - B_1 > 0$ in Eq. (8.9). To analyze this relation further, we shall anticipate some results from the discussion of processing on the F_2 layer. Specifically, we shall assume that only a single node on F_2 has a nonzero output at any given time, the maximum output of an F_2 node is 1, and the maximum weight on any top-down connection is also 1. Since $V_i = \sum_j u_j z_{ij}$ and only one u_j is nonzero, then $V_i \leq 1$. Then, in the most extreme case with $V_i = 1$, and $I_i = 1$, we must have $1 + D_1 - B_1 > 0$, or

$$B_1 < D_1 + 1 \tag{8.10}$$

Any unit that does not receive a top-down signal from F_2 must have a negative activity, even if it receives an input from below. In this case, we must have, $I_i - B_1 < 0$, or

$$B_1 > 1 \tag{8.11}$$

Suppose F_2 is producing a top-down output (perhaps as a result of inputs from higher levels), but there is not yet an input vector **I**. G is still inhibited in this case. The equilibrium state is

$$x_{1i} = \frac{D_1 V_i - B_1}{1 + A_1 D_1 V_i + C_1} \tag{8.12}$$

If a unit receives no net input from F_2 ($V_i = 0$), then it remains at its most negative activity level, as in Eq. (8.7). If $V_i > 0$, then the unit's activity rises to some value above that of Eq. (8.7), but it must remain negative because we do not want the unit to have a nonzero output based on top-down inputs alone. Then, from the numerator of Eq. (8.12), we must have $D_1 - B_1 < 0$, or

$$B_1 > D_1 \tag{8.13}$$

Equations (8.10), (8.11), and (8.13) combine to give the overall condition,

$$\max\{D_1, 1\} < B_1 < D_1 + 1 \tag{8.14}$$

The ART1 parameters must satisfy the constraint of Eq. (8.14) to implement the 2/3 rule successfully and to distinguish between top-down and bottom-up input patterns.

Satisfying the constraints of Eq. (8.14) does not guarantee that a unit that receives both an input from below, I_i, and one from above, V_i, will have a positive value of activation. We must consider the case where V_i is less than its maximum value of 1 (even though $u_j = 1$, z_{ij} may be less than 1, resulting in $V_i < 1$). In such a case, the condition that Eq. (8.9) gives a positive value is

$$I_i + D_1 V_i - B_1 > 0$$

Since $I_i = 1$, this relation defines a condition on V_i:

$$V_i > \frac{B_1 - 1}{D_1} \tag{8.15}$$

Equation (8.15) tells us that the input to unit v_i due to a top-down signal from F_2 must meet a certain threshold condition to ensure a positive activation of v_i, even if v_i receives a strong input, I_i, from below. We shall return to this result when we discuss the weights, or LTM traces, from F_2 to F_1.

Processing on F_2. Figure 8.4 shows a typical processing element on the F_2 layer. The gain-control input and the connection from the orienting subsystem are shown but we shall not include them explicitly in the following analysis.

The unit activations are described by an equation of the form of Eq. (8.1). We can specify the various terms as follows.

The net input received from the F_1 layer is calculated as usual:

$$T_j = \text{net}_j = \sum_i s_i z_{ji} \tag{8.16}$$

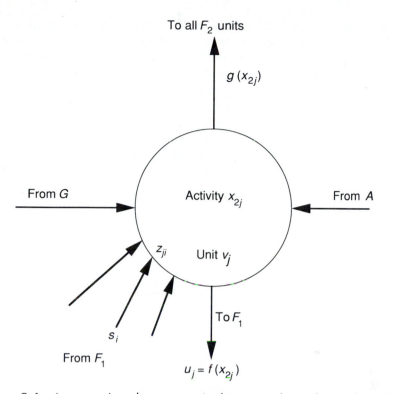

Figure 8.4 A processing element, v_j, is shown on the F_2 layer of an ART1 network. The activity of the unit is x_{2j}. The unit v_j receives inputs from the F_1 layer, the gain-control system, G, and the orienting subsystem, A. Bottom-up signals, s_i, from F_1 are gated by the weights, z_{ji}. Outputs, u_j, are sent back down to F_1. In addition, each unit receives a positive-feedback term from itself, $g(x_{2j})$ and sends an identical signal through an inhibitory connection to all other units on the layer.

The total excitatory input to v_j is

$$J_j^+ = D_2 T_j + g(x_{2j}) \tag{8.17}$$

The inhibitory input to each unit is

$$J_j^- = \sum_{k \neq j} g(x_{2k}) \tag{8.18}$$

Substituting these values into Eq. (8.1) yields

$$\dot{x}_{2j} = -x_{2j} + (1 - A_2 x_{2j})(D_2 T_j + g(x_{2j})) - (B_2 + C_2 x_{2j}) \sum_{k \neq j} g(x_{2k}) \tag{8.19}$$

Note the similarity between Eq. (8.19) and Eq. (6.13) from Section 6.1.3. Both equations describe a competitive layer with on-center off-surround interactions. In Section 6.1.3, we showed how the choice of the functional form of $g(x)$ influenced the evolution of the activities of the units on the layer.[5] Without repeating the analysis, we assume that the values of the various parameters in Eq. (8.19), and the functional form of $g(x)$ have been chosen to enhance the activity of the single F_2 node with the largest net-input value from F_1 according to Eq. (8.16). The activities of all other nodes are suppressed to zero. The output of this winning node is given a value of one. We can therefore express the output values of F_2 nodes as

$$u_j = f(x_{2j}) = \begin{cases} 1 & T_j = \max_k\{T_k\} \forall k \\ 0 & \text{otherwise} \end{cases} \tag{8.20}$$

We need to clarify one final point concerning Figure 8.4. The processing element in that figure appears to violate our standard of a single output per node: The node sends an output of $g(x_{2j})$ to the F_2 units, and an output of $f(x_{2j})$ to the F_1 units. We can reconcile this discrepancy by allowing Figure 8.4 to represent a composite structure. We can arrange for unit v_j to have the single output value x_{2j}. This output can then be sent to two other processing elements; one that gives an output of $g(x_{2j})$, and one that gives an output of $f(x_{2j})$. By assuming the existence of these intermediate nodes, or **interneurons**, we can avoid violating the single-output standard. The node in Figure 8.4 then represents a composite of the v_j nodes and the two intermediate nodes.

Top-Down LTM Traces. The equations that describe the top-down LTM traces (weights on connections from F_2 units to F_1 units) should be somewhat familiar from the study of Chapter 6:

$$\dot{z}_{ij} = (-z_{ij} + h(x_{1i}))f(x_{2j}) \tag{8.21}$$

Since $f(x_{2j})$ is nonzero for only one value of j (one F_2 node, v_j), Eq. (8.21) is nonzero only for connections leading down from that winning unit. If the jth F_2 node is active and the ith F_1 node is also active, then $\dot{z}_{ij} = -z_{ij} + 1$ and z_{ij} asymptotically approaches one. If the jth F_2 node is active and the ith F_1 node is not active, then $\dot{z}_{ij} = -z_{ij}$ and z_{ij} decays toward zero. We can summarize the behavior of z_{ij} as follows:

$$\dot{z}_{ij} = \begin{cases} -z_{ij} + 1 & v_j \text{ active and } v_i \text{ active} \\ -z_{ij} & v_j \text{ active and } v_i \text{ inactive} \\ 0 & v_j \text{ and } v_i \text{ both inactive} \end{cases} \tag{8.22}$$

Recall from Eq. (8.15) that, if F_2 is active, then v_i can be active only if it is receiving an input, I_i, from below and a *sufficiently large* net input, V_i,

---

[5]Caution! The function $g(x)$ in this section is the analog of $f(x)$ in Section 6.1.3. In Section 6.1.3, $g(x)$ was used to mean $x^{-1}f(x)$. In this section, $g(x)$ does not mean the same as $x^{-1}f(x)$.

from the F_2 layer. Since only one F_2 unit is active at a time, $V_i = u_j z_{ij} = z_{ij}$. Equation (8.15) now becomes a condition on the weight on the connection from v_j to v_i:

$$z_{ij} > \frac{B_1 - 1}{D_1} \tag{8.23}$$

Unless z_{ij} has a minimum value given by Eq. (8.23), it will decay toward zero even if v_j is active and v_i is receiving an input, I_i, from below.

From a practical standpoint, all top-down connection weights must be initialized to a value greater than the minimum given by Eq. (8.23) in order for *any* learning to take place on the network. Otherwise, any time a v_j is active on F_2, all connections from it to any unit on F_1 will decay toward zero; eventually, all the connection weights will be zero and the system will be useless.

If a resonant condition is allowed to continue for an extended period, top-down weights will approach their asymptotic values of 1 or 0, according to Eq. (8.22). For the purpose of our digital simulations, we shall assume that input patterns are maintained on F_1 for a sufficient time to permit top-down weights to equilibrate. Thus, as soon as a resonant state is detected, we can immediately set the appropriate top-down weights to their asymptotic values. If v_J is the winning F_2 node, then

$$z_{iJ} = \begin{cases} 1 & v_i \text{ active} \\ 0 & \text{otherwise} \end{cases} \tag{8.24}$$

Weights on connections from other nodes, v_j, $j \neq J$, are not changed. We refer to this model as **fast learning**. Weights on bottom-up connections also have a fast-learning model, which we shall discuss next.

Bottom-Up LTM Traces.   The equations that describe the bottom-up LTM traces are slightly more complicated than were those for the top-down LTM traces. The weight on the connection from v_i on F_1 to v_j on F_2 is determined by

$$\dot{z}_{ji} = K f(x_{2j})[(1 - z_{ji})Lh(x_{1i}) - z_{ji} \sum_{k \neq i} h(x_{1k})] \tag{8.25}$$

where K and L are constants, $f(x_{2j})$ is the output of v_j, and $h(x_{1i})$ is the output of v_i. As was the case with the top-down LTM traces, the factor $f(x_{2j})$ ensures that only weights on the winning node are allowed to change. Other than that, Eq. (8.25) is an equation for a competitive system with on-center off-surround interactions. In this case, however, it is the individual weights that are competing among one another, rather than individual units.

Let's assume v_j is the winning unit on F_2. There are two cases to consider. If v_i is active on F_1, then $h(x_{1i}) = 1$; otherwise, $h(x_{1i}) = 0$. Weights on connections to other F_2 units do not change since, for them, $f(x_{2k}) = 0$, $k \neq j$.

Before going further with Eq. (8.25), we wish to introduce a new notation. If the input pattern is **I**, then we shall define the magnitude of **I** as $|\mathbf{I}| = \sum_i I_i$.

Since I_i is either 0 or 1, the magnitude of $\mathbf{I}$ is equal to the number of nonzero inputs. The output of F_1 is the pattern $\mathbf{S}$: Its magnitude is $|\mathbf{S}| = \sum_i h(x_{1i})$, which is also just the number of nonzero outputs on F_1. The actual output pattern, $\mathbf{S}$, depends on conditions in the network:

$$\mathbf{S} = \begin{cases} \mathbf{I} & F_2 \text{ is inactive} \\ \mathbf{I} \cap \mathbf{V}^J & F_2 \text{ is active} \end{cases} \tag{8.26}$$

where the superscript on $\mathbf{V}^J$ means that v_J was the winning node on F_2. We can interpret $\mathbf{V}^J$ as meaning the binary pattern with a 1 at those positions where the input, V_i, from above is large enough to support the activation of v_i whenever v_i receives an input I_i from below.

Since $|\mathbf{S}| = \sum_i h(x_{1i})$, then $\sum_{k \neq i} h(x_{1k}) = \sum_k h(x_{1k}) - h(x_{1i})$ which will be equal to either $|\mathbf{S}| - 1$ or $|\mathbf{S}|$, depending on whether v_i is active. We can now summarize the three cases of Eq. (8.25) as follows:

$$\dot{z}_{ji} = \begin{cases} K[(1 - z_{ji})L - z_{ji}(|\mathbf{S}| - 1)] & \text{if } v_i \text{ and } v_j \text{ are active} \\ -K[z_{ji}|\mathbf{S}|] & \text{if } v_i \text{ is inactive and } v_j \text{ is active} \\ 0 & \text{if } v_j \text{ is inactive} \end{cases} \tag{8.27}$$

Remember, v_i can remain active only if it receives an input I_i from below *and* a sufficiently large input V_i from above. In the fast-learning case, weights on the winning F_2 node, v_J, take on the asymptotic values given by

$$z_{Ji} = \begin{cases} \frac{L}{L-1+|\mathbf{S}|} & \text{if } v_i \text{ is active} \\ 0 & \text{if } v_i \text{ is inactive} \end{cases} \tag{8.28}$$

where we have $L > 1$ in order to keep $L - 1 > 0$.

By defining the bottom-up weights as we have in this section, we impart to the ART1 network an important characteristic that we can elucidate with the following scenario. Suppose one F_2 node, v_{J1}, wins and learns during the presentation of an input pattern, $\mathbf{I}_1$, and another node, v_{J2}, wins and learns input pattern $\mathbf{I}_2$. Further, let input pattern $\mathbf{I}_1$ be a subset of pattern $\mathbf{I}_2$; that is, $\mathbf{I}_1 \subset \mathbf{I}_2$. When next we present either $\mathbf{I}_1$ or $\mathbf{I}_2$, we would like the appropriate node on F_2 to win. Equation (8.28) ensures that the proper node will win by keeping the weights on the node that learned the subset pattern sufficiently larger than the weights on the node that learned the superset pattern.

For the subset pattern, $\mathbf{I}_1$, weights on connections from active F_1 nodes all take on the value

$$z_{J1,i} = \frac{L}{L-1+|\mathbf{I}_1|}$$

where we have used the result $|\mathbf{S}| = |\mathbf{I}_1 \cap \mathbf{V}^J| = |\mathbf{I}_1|$. We have not yet shown that this result holds, but we will see shortly that it is true because of the way that we initialize the top-down weights on the F_1 layer.

For the superset pattern,

$$z_{J2,i} = \frac{L}{L-1+|\mathbf{I}_2|}$$

on connections from those active F_1 nodes. Now let's calculate the net input to the two nodes for each of the input patterns to verify that node v_{J1} wins for pattern $\mathbf{I}_1$ and node v_{J2} wins for pattern $\mathbf{I}_2$.

The net inputs to v_{J1} and v_{J2} for input pattern $|\mathbf{I}_1|$ are

$$T_{J1,1} = \sum_i z_{J1,i} h(x_{1i})_1$$

$$= \frac{L|\mathbf{I}_1|}{L - 1 + |\mathbf{I}_1|}$$

and

$$T_{J2,1} = \sum_i z_{J2,i} h(x_{1i})_1$$

$$= \frac{L|\mathbf{I}_1|}{L - 1 + |\mathbf{I}_2|}$$

respectively, where the extra subscript on T and $h(x_{1i})$ refers to the number of the pattern being presented. Since $\mathbf{I}_1 \subset \mathbf{I}_2$, $|\mathbf{I}_1| < |\mathbf{I}_2|$, and $T_{J2,1} < T_{J1,1}$, so v_{J1} wins as desired. When $\mathbf{I}_2$ is presented, the net inputs are

$$T_{J1,2} = \sum_i z_{J1,i} h(x_{1i})_2$$

$$= \frac{L|\mathbf{I}_1|}{L - 1 + |\mathbf{I}_1|}$$

and

$$T_{J2,2} = \sum_i z_{J2,i} h(x_{1i})_2$$

$$= \frac{L|\mathbf{I}_2|}{L - 1 + |\mathbf{I}_2|}$$

Notice that $|\mathbf{I}_1|$ appears in the numerator in the expression for $T_{J1,2}$ instead of $|\mathbf{I}_2|$. Recall that v_{J1} has learned only the subset pattern. Therefore, bottom-up weights on that node are nonzero only for F_1 units that represent the subset. This time, since $|\mathbf{I}_1| < |\mathbf{I}_2|$, we have $T_{J2,2} > T_{J1,2}$ so v_{J2} wins.

Exercise 8.3: The expression for the net-input values to the winning F_2 units has the form:

$$T(|\mathbf{I}|) = \frac{a|\mathbf{I}|}{b + |\mathbf{I}|}$$

where a and b are both positive. Show that this function, called a Weber function, is an increasing function of $|\mathbf{I}|$ for $|\mathbf{I}| > 1$.

On a network with uncommitted nodes in F_2 (i.e., nodes that have not yet participated in any learning), we must also ensure that their weights due to the initialization scheme are not so great that they *accidentally* win over a node that *has* learned the pattern. Therefore, we must keep all initial weights below a certain value. Since all patterns are a subset of the pattern containing all 1s, we should keep all initial weight values within the range

$$0 \le z_{ji}(0) \le \frac{L}{L - 1 + M} \tag{8.29}$$

where M is the number of nodes on F_1, and hence is the number of bottom-up connections to each F_2 node. This condition ensures that some uncommitted node does not accidentally win over a node that has learned a particular input pattern.

Exercise 8.4: Let F_2 node v_J learn an input pattern $\mathbf{I}$ according to Eq. (8.28). Assume that all other nodes have their weights initialized according to Eq. (8.29). Prove that presentation of $\mathbf{I}$ will activate v_J, rather than any other uncommitted node, $v_j, \ j \ne J$.

8.2.2 The Orienting Subsystem

The orienting subsystem in an ART network is responsible for sensing mismatches between bottom-up and top-down patterns on the F_1 layer. Its operation can be modeled by the addition of terms to the dynamic equations that describe the activities of the F_2 processing element. Since our discussion has evolved from the dynamic equations to their asymptotic solutions and the fast-learning case, we shall not return to the dynamic equations at this point.

There are many ways to model the dynamics of the orienting subsystem. One example is the development by Ryan and Winter, and by Ryan, Winter, and Turner, listed in the Suggested Readings section at the end of this chapter. Our approach here will be to describe the details of the matching and reset process and the effects on the F_2 units.

We can model the orienting subsystem as a single processing element, A, with an output to each unit on the F_2 layer. The inputs to A are the outputs of the F_1 units, $\mathbf{S}$, and the input vector, $\mathbf{I}$. The weights on the connections from the input vector are all equal to a value P; those on the connections from F_1 are all equal to a value $-Q$. The net input to A is then $P|\mathbf{I}| - Q|\mathbf{S}|$. The output of A switches on if the net input becomes nonzero:

$$P|\mathbf{I}| - Q|\mathbf{S}| > 0$$

or

$$P|\mathbf{I}| > Q|\mathbf{S}|$$
$$\frac{P}{Q} > \frac{|\mathbf{S}|}{|\mathbf{I}|}$$

The quantity P/Q is given the name **vigilance parameter** and is usually identified by the symbol, ρ. Thus, activation of the orienting subsystem is prevented if

$$\frac{|\mathbf{S}|}{|\mathbf{I}|} \ge \rho \tag{8.30}$$

Recall that $|\mathbf{S}| = |\mathbf{I}|$ when F_2 is inactive. The orienting subsystem must not send a reset signal to F_2 at that time. From Eq. (8.30), we get a condition on the vigilance parameter:

$$\rho \le 1$$

We also obtain a subsequent condition on P and Q:

$$P \le Q$$

The value of the vigilance parameter measures the degree to which the system discriminates between different classes of input patterns. Because of the way ρ is defined, it implements a *self-scaling* pattern match. By *self-scaling*, we mean that the presence or absence of a certain feature in two patterns may or may not cause a reset depending on the overall importance of that feature in defining the pattern class. Figure 8.5 illustrates an example of this self-scaling.

Stated another way, the value of ρ determines the granularity with which input patterns are classified by the network. For a given set of patterns to be classified, a large value of ρ will result in finer discrimination between classes than will a smaller value of ρ.

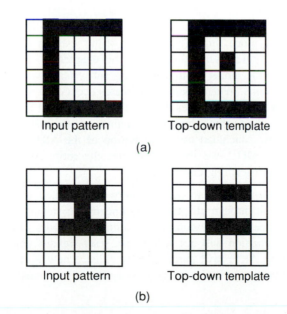

Input pattern   Top-down template

(a)

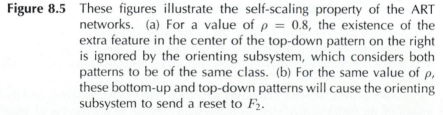

Input pattern   Top-down template

(b)

Figure 8.5 These figures illustrate the self-scaling property of the ART networks. (a) For a value of $\rho = 0.8$, the existence of the extra feature in the center of the top-down pattern on the right is ignored by the orienting subsystem, which considers both patterns to be of the same class. (b) For the same value of ρ, these bottom-up and top-down patterns will cause the orienting subsystem to send a reset to F_2.

Having a value of ρ that is less than one also permits the possibility that the top-down pattern that is coded by F_2 to represent a particular class may change as new input vectors are presented to the network. We can see this by reference back to Figure 8.5(a). We implicitly assumed that the top-down pattern on the right (with the extra dot) had been previously encoded (learned) by one of the F_2 nodes. The appearance of the bottom-up pattern on the left (without the extra dot) does not cause a reset, so a resonance is established between the F_1 layer and the winning node on F_2 that produced the top-down pattern. During this resonance, weights can be changed. The F_1 node corresponding to the feature of the center dot is *not* active, since that feature is missing from the input vector. According to Eq. (8.22), the top-down weight on that connection will decay away; in the fast-learning mode, we simply set it equal to zero. Similarly, the bottom-up weight on the F_2 node will decay according to Eq. (8.27).

The recoding of top-down template patterns described in the previous paragraph could lead to instabilities in the learning process. These instabilities could manifest themselves as a continual change in the class of input vectors recognized, or encoded, by each F_2 unit. Fortunately, ART was developed to combat this instability. We shall not prove it here, but it can be shown that category learning will stabilize in an ART1 network, after at most a few recodings. We shall demonstrate this result in the next section, where we look at a numerical example of ART1 processing. The stability of the learning is a direct result of the use of the 2/3 rule described earlier in this chapter.

To complete the model of the orienting subsystem, we must consider its effects on the F_2 units. When a pattern mismatch occurs, the orienting subsystem should inhibit the F_2 unit that resulted in the nonmatching pattern, and should maintain that inhibition throughout the remainder of the matching cycle.

We have now concluded our presentation of the ART1 network. Before proceeding on to ART2, we shall summarize the entire ART1 model for the asymptotic and fast-learning case.

Exercise 8.5: Assume that an input pattern has resulted in an unsuccessful search for a match through all previously encoded F_2 templates. On the next matching cycle, one of the previously uncommitted F_2 nodes will win by default. Show that this situation will not result in a reset signal from A. This proof demonstrates that ART1 will automatically enlist a new F_2 node if the input pattern cannot be categorized with previously learned patterns.

8.2.3   ART1 Processing Summary

For this summary we shall employ the asymptotic solutions to the dynamic equations and the fast-learning case for the weights. We shall also present a step-by-step calculation showing how the ART1 network learns and recalls patterns.

To begin with, we must determine the size of the F_1 and F_2 layers, and the values of the various parameters in the system. Let M be the number of units on F_1 and N be the number of units on F_2. Other parameters must be chosen according to the following constraints:

$$A_1 \geq 0$$
$$C_1 \geq 0$$
$$D_1 \geq 0$$
$$\max\{D_1, 1\} < B_1 < D_1 + 1$$
$$L > 1$$
$$0 < \rho \leq 1$$

Top-down weights ($v_j \to v_i$) are initialized according to

$$z_{ij}(0) > \frac{B_1 - 1}{D_1}$$

and bottom-up weights ($v_i \to v_j$) are initialized according to

$$0 < z_{ji}(0) < \frac{L}{L - 1 + M}$$

The activities on F_2 are initialized to zero, but, according to our chosen model, F_1 activities are initialized to

$$x_{1i}(0) = \frac{-B_1}{1 + C_1}$$

All input patterns must be binary: $I_i \in \{0, 1\}$. The magnitude of a vector is equal to the sum of the components: for example, $|\mathbf{I}| = \sum_i^M I_i$. Since we will be interested in the magnitude of only binary vectors, this sum will be equal to the number of nonzero components of the vector.

We are now ready to process data on the network. We proceed according to the following algorithm:

1. Apply an input vector $\mathbf{I}$ to F_1. F_1 activities are calculated according to

$$x_{1i} = \frac{I_i}{1 + A_1(I_i + B_1) + C_1}$$

2. Calculate the output vector for F_1,

$$s_i = h(x_{1i}) = \begin{cases} 1 & x_{1i} > 0 \\ 0 & x_{1i} \leq 0 \end{cases}$$

3. Propagate $\mathbf{S}$ forward to F_2 and calculate the activities according to

$$T_j = \sum_{i=1}^{M} s_i z_{ji}$$

4. Only the winning F_2 node has a nonzero output:

$$u_j = \begin{cases} 1 & T_j = \max_k\{T_k\} \forall k \\ 0 & \text{otherwise} \end{cases}$$

We shall assume that the winning node is v_J.

5. Propagate the output from F_2 back to F_1. Calculate the net inputs from F_2 to the F_1 units:

$$V_i = \sum_{j=1}^{N} u_j z_{ij}$$

6. Calculate the new activities according to

$$x_{1i} = \frac{I_i + D_1 V_i - B_1}{1 + A_1(I_i + D_1 V_i) + C_1}$$

7. Determine the new output values, s_i, as in step 2.

8. Determine the degree of match between the input pattern and the top-down template:

$$\frac{|\mathbf{S}|}{|\mathbf{I}|} = \frac{\sum_{i=1}^{M} s_i}{\sum_{i=1}^{M} I_i}$$

9. If $|\mathbf{S}|/|\mathbf{I}| < \rho$ mark v_J as inactive, zero the outputs of F_2, and return to step 1 using the original input pattern. If $|\mathbf{S}|/|\mathbf{I}| \geq \rho$, continue.

10. Update bottom-up weights on v_J only

$$z_{Ji} = \begin{cases} \frac{L}{L-1+|S|} & \text{if } v_i \text{ is active} \\ 0 & \text{if } v_i \text{ is inactive} \end{cases}$$

11. Update the top-down weights coming from v_J only to all F_1 units:

$$z_{iJ} = \begin{cases} 1 & \text{if } v_i \text{ is active} \\ 0 & \text{if } v_i \text{ is inactive} \end{cases}$$

12. Remove the input pattern. Restore all inactive F_2 units. Return to step 1 with a new input pattern.

To see this algorithm in operation, let's perform a step-by-step calculation for a small example problem. We will use this example to see how subset and superset patterns are handled by the network.

We shall choose the dimensions of F_1 and F_2 as $M = 5$ and $N = 6$, respectively. Other parameters in the system are $A_1 = 1, B_1 = 1.5, C_1 = 5, D_1 = 0.9, L = 3, \rho = 0.9$.

We initialize weights on F_1 units by adding a small, positive value (0.2, in this case) to $(B_1 - 1)/D_1$. Each unit on F_1 then has the weight vector

$$\mathbf{z}_i = (0.756, 0.756, 0.756, 0.756, 0.756, 0.756)^t$$

Since $L = 3$ and $M = 5$, weights on F_2 units are all initialized to slightly less than $L/(L-1+M)$. Each weight is given the value $0.429 - 0.1 = 0.329$. Each weight vector is then

$$\mathbf{z}_j = (0.329, 0.329, 0.329, 0.329, 0.329)^t$$

All F_2 units are initialized to zero activity. F_1 activities are initialized to $-B_1/(1 + C_1) = -0.25$:

$$\mathbf{X}(0) = (-0.25, -0.25, -0.25, -0.25, -0.25)^t$$

We can now begin actual processing. We shall start with the simple input vector,

$$\mathbf{I}_1 = (0, 0, 0, 1, 0)^t$$

Now, we follow the sequence of the algorithm:

1. After the input vector is applied, the F_1 activities become

$$\mathbf{X}_1 = (0, 0, 0, 0.118, 0)^t$$

2. The output vector is $\mathbf{S} = (0, 0, 0, 1, 0)^t$.

3. Propagating this output vector to F_2, the net inputs to all F_2 units will be identical:

$$T_j = \mathbf{z}_j \cdot \mathbf{S}$$

Then, $\mathbf{T} = (0.329, 0.329, 0.329, 0.329, 0.329, 0.329)^t$.

4. Since all unit activities are equal, simply take the first unit as our winner. Then, the output from F_2 is $\mathbf{U} = (1, 0, 0, 0, 0, 0)^t$.

5. Propagate back to F_1:

$$V_i = \mathbf{z}_i \cdot \mathbf{U}$$

Then, $\mathbf{V} = (0.756, 0.756, 0.756, 0.756, 0.756)^t$.

6. Calculate the new activity values on F_1 according to Eq. (8.9):

$$\mathbf{X} = (-0.123, -0.123, -0.123, 0.023, -0.123)^t$$

7. Only unit 4 has a positive activity, so the new outputs are $\mathbf{S} = (0, 0, 0, 1, 0)^t$.

8. $|\mathbf{S}|/|\mathbf{I}| = 1 > \rho$.

9. There is no reset: Resonance has been reached.

10. Update bottom-up weights on F_2 unit v_1 according to the fast-learning rule. Since $\frac{L}{L-1+|\mathbf{S}|} = 1$, $\mathbf{z}_1$ on F_2 becomes $(0, 0, 0, 1, 0)^t$. Thus, unit v_1 encodes the input vector exactly. It is actually in the *pattern* of nonzero weights that

we are interested here. The fact that the single nonzero weight matches the input value is purely coincidental, as we shall see shortly.

11. Update weights on top-down connections. Only the first weight on each F_1 unit changes. If each row describes the weights on one unit, then the weight matrix for F_1 units is

$$0 \ 0.756 \ 0.756 \ 0.756 \ 0.756 \ 0.756$$
$$0 \ 0.756 \ 0.756 \ 0.756 \ 0.756 \ 0.756$$
$$0 \ 0.756 \ 0.756 \ 0.756 \ 0.756 \ 0.756$$
$$1 \ 0.756 \ 0.756 \ 0.756 \ 0.756 \ 0.756$$
$$0 \ 0.756 \ 0.756 \ 0.756 \ 0.756 \ 0.756$$

That completes the cycle for the first input pattern. Now let's apply a second pattern that is orthogonal to the first—namely, $I_2 = (0,0,1,0,1)^t$. We shall abbreviate the calculation somewhat.

When the input pattern is propagated to F_2, the resultant activities are $T = (0.000, 0.657, 0.657, 0.657, 0.657, 0.657)^t$. Unit 1 definitely loses. We select unit 2 as the winner. The output of F_2 is $U = (0,1,0,0,0,0)^t$. Propagating back to F_1 we get $V = (0.756, 0.756, 0.756, 0.756, 0.756)^t$ and $X = (-0.123, -0.123, 0.0234, -0.123, 0.0234)^t$. The resulting output matches the input vector, $(0,0,1,0,1)^t$ so there is no reset.

Weights on the winning F_2 unit are set to $(0,0,0.75,0,0.75)^t$. The second weight on each F_1 unit is adjusted such that the new weight matrix on F_1 is

$$0 \ 0 \ 0.756 \ 0.756 \ 0.756 \ 0.756$$
$$0 \ 0 \ 0.756 \ 0.756 \ 0.756 \ 0.756$$
$$0 \ 1 \ 0.756 \ 0.756 \ 0.756 \ 0.756$$
$$1 \ 0 \ 0.756 \ 0.756 \ 0.756 \ 0.756$$
$$0 \ 1 \ 0.756 \ 0.756 \ 0.756 \ 0.756$$

For reference, the weight matrix on F_2 looks like

$$
\begin{array}{ccccc}
0 & 0 & 0 & 1 & 0 \\
0 & 0 & 0.75 & 0 & 0.75 \\
0.329 & 0.329 & 0.329 & 0.329 & 0.329 \\
0.329 & 0.329 & 0.329 & 0.329 & 0.329 \\
0.329 & 0.329 & 0.329 & 0.329 & 0.329 \\
0.329 & 0.329 & 0.329 & 0.329 & 0.329
\end{array}
$$

Now let's see what happens when we apply a vector that is a subset of I_2—namely, $I_3 = (0,0,0,0,1)^t$. When this pattern is propagated forward, the activities on F_2 become $(0, 0.75, 0.329, 0.329, 0.329, 0.329)^t$. Notice that the second unit wins the competition in this case so F_2 output is $(0,1,0,0,0,0)^t$. Going back to F_1, the net inputs from the top-down pattern are $V = (0,0,1,0,1)^t$.

In this case, the equilibrium activities are $\mathbf{X} = (-0.25, -0.25, -0.087, -0.25, 0.051)^t$ with only one positive activity. The new output pattern is $(0, 0, 0, 0, 1)^t$, which exactly matches the input pattern, so no reset occurs.

Even though unit 2 on F_2 had previously encoded an input pattern, it gets recoded now to match the new input pattern that is a subset of the original pattern. The new weight matrices appear as follows. For F_1,

$$
\begin{array}{cccccc}
0 & 0 & 0.756 & 0.756 & 0.756 & 0.756 \\
0 & 0 & 0.756 & 0.756 & 0.756 & 0.756 \\
0 & 0 & 0.756 & 0.756 & 0.756 & 0.756 \\
1 & 0 & 0.756 & 0.756 & 0.756 & 0.756 \\
0 & 1 & 0.756 & 0.756 & 0.756 & 0.756
\end{array}
$$

For F_2,

$$
\begin{array}{ccccc}
0 & 0 & 0 & 1 & 0 \\
0 & 0 & 0 & 0 & 1 \\
0.329 & 0.329 & 0.329 & 0.329 & 0.329 \\
0.329 & 0.329 & 0.329 & 0.329 & 0.329 \\
0.329 & 0.329 & 0.329 & 0.329 & 0.329 \\
0.329 & 0.329 & 0.329 & 0.329 & 0.329
\end{array}
$$

If we return to the superset vector, $(0, 0, 1, 0, 1)^t$, the initial forward propagation to F_2 yields activities of $(0.000, 1.000, 0.657, 0.657, 0.657, 0.657)^t$, so unit 2 wins again. Going back to F_1, $\mathbf{V} = (0, 0, 0, 0, 1)^t$, and the equilibrium activities are $(-0.25, -0.25, -0.071, -0.25, 0.051)^t$. The new outputs are $(0, 0, 0, 0, 1)^t$. This time, we get a reset signal, since $|\mathbf{S}|/|\mathbf{I}_2| = 0.5 < \rho$. Thus, unit 2 on F_2 is removed from competition, and the matching cycle is repeated with the original input vector restored on F_1.

Propagating forward a second time results in activities on F_2 of $(0.000, 0.000, 0.657, 0.657, 0.657, 0.657)^t$, where we have forced unit 2's activity to zero as a result of sustained inhibition from the orienting subsystem. We choose unit 3 as the winner this time, and it codes the input vector. On subsequent presentations of subset and superset vectors, each will access the appropriate F_2 unit directly without the need of a search. This result can be verified by direct calculation with the example presented in this section.

Exercise 8.6: Verify the statement made in the previous paragraph that the presentation of $(0, 0, 1, 0, 1)^t$ and $(0, 0, 0, 0, 1)^t$ result in immediate access to the corresponding nodes on F_2 without reset by performing the appropriate calculations.

Exercise 8.7: What does the weight matrix on F_2 look like after unit 3 encodes the superset vector given in the example in this section?

Exercise 8.8: What do you expect will happen if we apply $(0, 1, 1, 0, 1)^t$ to the example network? Note that the pattern is a superset to one already encoded. Verify your hypothesis by direct calculation.

8.3   ART2

On the surface, ART2 differs from ART1 only in the nature of the input patterns: ART2 accepts analog (or gray-scale) vector components as well as binary components. This capability represents a significant enhancement to the system.

Beyond the surface difference between ART1 and ART2 lie architectural differences that give ART2 its ability to deal with analog patterns. These differences are sometimes more complex, and sometimes less complex, than the corresponding ART1 structures.

Aside from the obvious fact that binary and analog patterns differ in the nature of their respective components, ART2 must deal with additional complications. For example, ART2 must be able to recognize the underlying similarity of identical patterns superimposed on constant backgrounds having different levels. Compared in an absolute sense, two such patterns may appear entirely different when, in fact, they should be classified as the same pattern.

The price for this additional capability is primarily an increase in complexity on the F_1 processing level. The ART2 F_1 level consists of several sublevels and several gain-control systems. Processing on F_2 is the same for ART2 as it was for ART1. As partial compensation for the added complexity on the F_1 layer, the LTM equations are a bit simpler for ART2 than they were for ART1.

The developers of the architecture, Carpenter and Grossberg, have experimented with several variations of the architecture for ART2. At the time of this writing, that work is continuing. The architecture we shall describe here is one of several variations reported by Carpenter and Grossberg [2].

8.3.1   ART2 Architecture

As we mentioned in the introduction to this section, ART2 bears a superficial resemblance to ART1. Both have an attentional subsystem and an orienting subsystem. The attentional subsystem of each architecture consists of two layers of processing elements, F_1 and F_2, and a gain-control system. The orienting subsystem of each network performs the identical function. Moreover, the basic differential equations that govern the activities of the individual processing elements are the same in both cases. To deal successfully with analog patterns in ART2, Carpenter and Grossberg have had to split the F_1 layer into a number of sublayers containing both feedforward and feedback connections. Figure 8.6 shows the resulting structure.

8.3.2   Processing on F_1

The activity of each unit on each sublayer of F_1 is governed by an equation of the form

$$\epsilon \dot{x}_k = -Ax_k + (1 - Bx_k)J_k^+ - (C + Dx_k)J_k^- \tag{8.31}$$

where A, B, C, and D are constants. Equation (8.31) is almost identical to Eq. (8.1) from the ART1 discussion in Section 8.2.1. The only difference is

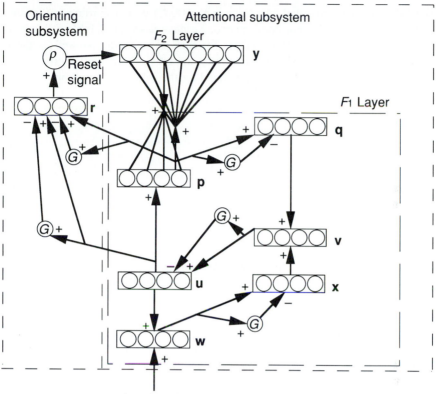

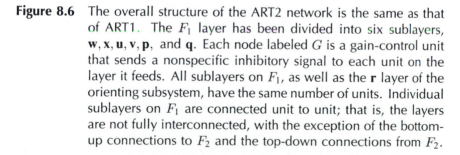

Input vector

Figure 8.6 The overall structure of the ART2 network is the same as that of ART1. The F_1 layer has been divided into six sublayers, $\mathbf{w}, \mathbf{x}, \mathbf{u}, \mathbf{v}, \mathbf{p}$, and $\mathbf{q}$. Each node labeled G is a gain-control unit that sends a nonspecific inhibitory signal to each unit on the layer it feeds. All sublayers on F_1, as well as the $\mathbf{r}$ layer of the orienting subsystem, have the same number of units. Individual sublayers on F_1 are connected unit to unit; that is, the layers are not fully interconnected, with the exception of the bottom-up connections to F_2 and the top-down connections from F_2.

the appearance of the multiplicative factor in the first term on the right-hand side in Eq. (8.31). For the ART2 model presented here, we shall set B and C identically equal to zero. As with ART1, J_k^+ and J_k^- represent net excitatory and inhibitory factors, respectively. Likewise, we shall be interested in only the asymptotic solution, so

$$x_k = \frac{J_k^+}{A + D J_k^-} \qquad (8.32)$$

The values of the individual quantities in Eq. (8.32) vary according to the sub-layer being considered. For convenience, we have assembled Table 8.1, which shows all of the appropriate quantities for each F_1 sublayer, as well as the **r** layer of the orienting subsystem. Based on the table, the activities on each of the six sublayers on F_1 can be summarized by the following equations:

$$w_i = I_i + au_i \tag{8.33}$$

$$x_i = \frac{w_i}{e + \|\mathbf{w}\|} \tag{8.34}$$

$$v_i = f(x_i) + bf(q_i) \tag{8.35}$$

$$u_i = \frac{v_i}{e + \|\mathbf{v}\|} \tag{8.36}$$

$$p_i = u_i + \sum_j g(y_j)z_{ij} \tag{8.37}$$

$$q_i = \frac{p_i}{e + \|\mathbf{p}\|} \tag{8.38}$$

We shall discuss the orienting subsystem **r** layer shortly. The parameter e is typically set to a positive number considerably less than 1. It has the effect

			Quantity	
Layer	**A**	**D**	J_i^+	J_i^-
w	1	1	$I_i + au_i$	0
x	e	1	w_i	$\|\mathbf{w}\|$
u	e	1	v_i	$\|\mathbf{v}\|$
v	1	1	$f(x_i) + bf(q_i)$	0
p	1	1	$u_i + \sum_j g(y_j)z_{ij}$	0
q	e	1	p_i	$\|\mathbf{p}\|$
r	e	1	$u_i + cp_i$	$\|\mathbf{u}\| + c\mathbf{p}\|$

Table 8.1   Factors in Eq. (8.32) for each F_1 sublayer and the **r** layer. I_i is the ith component of the input vector. The parameters $a, b, c,$ and e are constants whose values will be discussed in the text. y_j is the activity of the jth unit on the F_2 layer and $g(y)$ is the output function on F_2. The function $f(x)$ is described in the text.

of keeping the activations finite when no input is present in the system. We do not require the presence of e for this discussion so we shall set $e = 0$ for the remainder of the chapter.

The three gain control units in F_1 nonspecifically inhibit the $\mathbf{x}$, $\mathbf{u}$, and $\mathbf{q}$ sublayers. The inhibitory signal is equal to the magnitude of the input vector to those layers. The effect is that the activities of these three layers are normalized to unity by the gain control signals. This method is an alternative to the on-center off-surround interaction scheme presented in Chapter 6 for normalizing activities.

The form of the function, $f(x)$, determines the nature of the contrast enhancement that takes place on F_1 (see Chapter 6). A sigmoid might be the logical choice for this function, but we shall stay with Carpenter's choice of

$$f(x) = \begin{cases} 0 & 0 \le x \le \theta \\ x & x > \theta \end{cases} \tag{8.39}$$

where θ is a positive constant less than one. We shall use $\theta = 0.2$ in our subsequent examples.

It will be easier to see what happens on F_1 during the processing of an input vector if we actually carry through a couple of examples, as we did with ART1. We shall set up a five-unit F_1 layer. The constants are chosen as follows: $a = 10; b = 10; c = 0.1$. The first input vector is

$$\mathbf{I}_1 = (0.2, 0.7, 0.1, 0.5, 0.4)^t$$

We propagate this vector through the sublayers in the order of the equations given.

As there is currently no feedback from $\mathbf{u}$, $\mathbf{w}$ becomes a copy of the input vector:

$$\mathbf{w} = (0.2, 0.7, 0.1, 0.5, 0.4)^t$$

$\mathbf{x}$ is a normalized version of the same vector:

$$\mathbf{x} = (0.205, 0.718, 0.103, 0.513, 0.410)^t$$

In the absence of feedback from $\mathbf{q}$, $\mathbf{v}$ is equal to $f(\mathbf{x})$:

$$\mathbf{v} = (0.205, 0.718, 0, 0.513, 0.410)^t$$

Note that the third component is now zero, since its value fell below the threshold, θ. Because F_2 is currently inactive, there is no top-down signal to F_1. In that case, all the remaining three sublayers on F_1 become copies of $\mathbf{v}$:

$$\mathbf{u} = (0.205, 0.718, 0, 0.513, 0.410)^t$$
$$\mathbf{p} = (0.205, 0.718, 0, 0.513, 0.410)^t$$
$$\mathbf{q} = (0.205, 0.718, 0, 0.513, 0.410)^t$$

We cannot stop here, however, as both **u**, and **q** are now nonzero. Beginning again at **w**, we find:

$$\mathbf{w} = (2.263, 7.920, 0.100, 5.657, 4.526)^t$$
$$\mathbf{x} = (0.206, 0.722, 0.009, 0.516, 0.413)^t$$
$$\mathbf{v} = (2.269, 7.942, 0.000, 5.673, 4.538)^t$$

where **v** now has contributions from the current **x** vector and the **u** vector from the previous time step. As before, the remaining three layers will be identical:

$$\mathbf{u} = (0.206, 0.723, 0.000, 0.516, 0.413)^t$$
$$\mathbf{p} = (0.206, 0.723, 0.000, 0.516, 0.413)^t$$
$$\mathbf{q} = (0.206, 0.723, 0.000, 0.516, 0.413)^t$$

Now we can stop because further iterations through the sublayers will not change the results. Two iterations are generally adequate to stabilize the outputs of the units on the sublayers.

During the first iteration through F_1, we assumed that there was no top-down signal from F_2 that would contribute to the activation on the **p** sublayer of F_1. This assumption may not hold for the second iteration. We shall see later from our study of the orienting subsystem that, by initializing the top-down weights to zero, $z_{ij}(0) = 0$, we prevent reset during the initial encoding by a new F_2 unit. We shall assume that we are considering such a case in this example, so that the net input from any top-down connections sum to zero.

As a second example, we shall look at an input pattern that is a simple multiple of the first input pattern—namely,

$$\mathbf{I}_2 = (0.8, 2.8, 0.4, 2.0, 1.6)^t$$

which is each element of $\mathbf{I}_1$ times four. Calculating through the F_1 sublayers results in

$$\mathbf{w} = (0.800, 2.800, 0.400, 2.000, 1.600)^t$$
$$\mathbf{x} = (0.205, 0.718, 0.103, 0.513, 0.410)^t$$
$$\mathbf{v} = (0.205, 0.718, 0.000, 0.513, 0.410)^t$$
$$\mathbf{u} = (0.206, 0.722, 0.000, 0.516, 0.413)^t$$
$$\mathbf{p} = (0.206, 0.722, 0.000, 0.516, 0.413)^t$$
$$\mathbf{q} = (0.206, 0.722, 0.000, 0.516, 0.413)^t$$

The second time through gives

$$\mathbf{w} = (2.863, 10.020, 0.400, 7.160, 5.726)^t$$
$$\mathbf{x} = (0.206, 0.722, 0.0288, 0.515, 0.412)^t$$
$$\mathbf{v} = (2.269, 7.942, 0.000, 5.672, 4.538)^t$$
$$\mathbf{u} = (0.206, 0.723, 0.000, 0.516, 0.413)^t$$
$$\mathbf{p} = (0.206, 0.723, 0.000, 0.516, 0.413)^t$$
$$\mathbf{q} = (0.206, 0.723, 0.000, 0.516, 0.413)^t$$

Notice that, after the **v** layer, the results are identical to the first example. Thus, it appears that ART2 treats patterns that are simple multiples of each other as belonging to the same class. For analog patterns, this would appear to be a useful feature. Patterns that differ only in amplitude probably should be classified together.

We can conclude from our analysis that F_1 performs a straightforward normalization and contrast-enhancement function before pattern matching is attempted. To see what happens during the matching process itself, we must consider the details of the remainder of the system.

8.3.3 Processing on F_2

Processing on F_2 of ART2 is identical to that performed on ART1. Bottom-up inputs are calculated as in ART1:

$$T_j = \sum_i p_i z_{ji} \tag{8.40}$$

Competition on F_2 results in contrast enhancement where a single winning node is chosen, again in keeping with ART1.

The output function of F_2 is given by

$$g(y_j) = \begin{cases} d & T_j = \max_k\{T_k\} \forall k \\ 0 & \text{otherwise} \end{cases} \tag{8.41}$$

This equation presumes that the set $\{T_k\}$ includes only those nodes that have not been reset recently by the orienting subsystem.

We can now rewrite the equation for processing on the **p** sublayer of F_1 as (see Eq. 8.37)

$$p_i = \begin{cases} u_i & \text{if } F_2 \text{ is inactive} \\ u_i + dz_{iJ} & \text{if the } J\text{th node on } F_2 \text{ is active} \end{cases} \tag{8.42}$$

8.3.4 LTM Equations

The LTM equations on ART2 are significantly less complex than are those on ART1. Both bottom-up and top-down equations have the same form:

$$\dot{z}_{ji} = g(y_j)\left(p_i - z_{ji}\right) \tag{8.43}$$

for the bottom-up weights from v_i on F_1 to v_j on F_2, and

$$\dot{z}_{ij} = g(y_j)\left(p_i - z_{ij}\right) \tag{8.44}$$

for top-down weights from v_j on F_2 to v_i on F_1. If v_J is the winning F_2 node, then we can use Eq. (8.42) in Eqs. (8.43) and (8.44) to show that

$$\dot{z}_{Ji} = d\left(u_i + dz_{iJ} - z_{Ji}\right)$$

and similarly

$$\dot{z}_{iJ} = d(u_i + dz_{iJ} - z_{iJ})$$

with all other $\dot{z}_{ij} = \dot{z}_{ji} = 0$ for $j \neq J$. We shall be interested in the fast-learning case, so we can solve for the equilibrium values of the weights:

$$z_{Ji} = z_{iJ} = \frac{u_i}{1 - d} \qquad (8.45)$$

where we assume that $0 < d < 1$.

We shall postpone the discussion of initial values for the weights until after the discussion of the orienting subsystem.

8.3.5   ART2 Orienting Subsystem

From Table 8.1 and Eq. (8.32), we can construct the equation for the activities of the nodes on the **r** layer of the orienting subsystem:

$$r_i = \frac{u_i + cp_i}{\|\mathbf{u}\| + \|c\mathbf{p}\|} \qquad (8.46)$$

where we once again have assumed that $e = 0$. The condition for reset is

$$\frac{\rho}{\|\mathbf{r}\|} > 1 \qquad (8.47)$$

where ρ is the vigilance parameter as in ART1.

Notice that two F_1 sublayers, **p**, and **u**, participate in the matching process. As top-down weights change on the **p** layer during learning, the activity of the units on the **p** layer also changes. The **u** layer remains stable during this process, so including it in the matching process prevents reset from occurring while learning of a new pattern is taking place.

We can rewrite Eq. (8.46) in vector form as

$$\mathbf{r} = \frac{\mathbf{u} + c\mathbf{p}}{\|\mathbf{u}\| + c\|\mathbf{p}\|}$$

Then, from $\|\mathbf{r}\| = (\mathbf{r} \cdot \mathbf{r})^{1/2}$, we can write

$$\|\mathbf{r}\| = \frac{\left[1 + 2\|c\mathbf{p}\| \cos(\mathbf{u}, \mathbf{p}) + \|c\mathbf{p}\|^2\right]^{1/2}}{1 + \|c\mathbf{p}\|} \qquad (8.48)$$

where $\cos(\mathbf{u}, \mathbf{p})$ is the cosine of the angle between **u** and **p**. First, note that, if **u** and **p** are parallel, then Eq. (8.48) reduces to $\|\mathbf{r}\| = 1$, and there will be no reset. As long as there is no output from F_2, Eq. (8.37) shows that $\mathbf{u} = \mathbf{p}$, and there will be no reset in this case.

Suppose now that F_2 does have an output from some winning unit, and that the input pattern needs to be learned, or encoded, by the F_2 unit. We also do not want a reset in this case. From Eq. (8.37), we see that $\mathbf{p} = \mathbf{u} + d\mathbf{z}_J$, where the Jth unit on F_2 is the winner and $\mathbf{z}_J = (z_{1J}, z_{2J}, \ldots, z_{MJ})^t$. If we initialize all the top-down weights, z_{ij}, to zero, then the initial output from F_2 will have no effect on the value of $\mathbf{p}$; that is, $\mathbf{p}$ will remain equal to $\mathbf{u}$.

During the learning process itself, $\mathbf{z}_J$ becomes parallel to $\mathbf{u}$ according to Eq. (8.45). Thus, $\mathbf{p}$ also becomes parallel to $\mathbf{u}$, and again $\|\mathbf{r}\| = 1$ and there is no reset.

As with ART1, a sufficient mismatch between the bottom-up input vector and the top-down template results in a reset. In ART2, the bottom-up pattern is taken at the $\mathbf{u}$ sublevel of F_1 and the top-down template is taken at $\mathbf{p}$.

Before returning to our numerical example, we must finish the discussion of weight initialization. We have already seen that top-down weights must be initialized to zero. Bottom-up weight initialization is the subject of the next section.

8.3.6 Bottom-Up LTM Initialization

We have been discussing the modification of LTM traces, or weights, in the case of fast-learning. Let's examine the dynamic behavior of the bottom-up weights during a learning trial. Assume that a particular F_2 node has previously encoded an input vector such that $z_{ji} = u_i/(1-d)$, and, therefore, $\|\mathbf{z}_J\| = \|\mathbf{u}\|/(1-d) = 1/(1-d)$, where $\mathbf{z}_J$ is the vector of bottom-up weights on the Jth, F_2 node. Suppose the same node wins for a slightly different input pattern, one for which the degree of mismatch is not sufficient to cause a reset. Then, the bottom-up weights will be recoded to match the new input vector. During this dynamic recoding process, $\|\mathbf{z}_J\|$ can decrease before returning to the value $1/(1-d)$. During this decreasing period, $\|\mathbf{r}\|$ will also be decreasing. If other nodes have had their weight values initialized such that $\|\mathbf{z}_j(0)\| > 1/(1-d)$, then the network might switch winners in the middle of the learning trial.

We must, therefore, initialize the bottom-up weight vectors such that

$$\|\mathbf{z}\| < \frac{1}{1-d}$$

We can accomplish such an initialization by setting the weights to small random numbers. Alternatively, we could use the initialization

$$z_{ji}(0) \leq \frac{1}{(1-d)\sqrt{M}} \tag{8.49}$$

This latter scheme has the appeal of a uniform initialization. Moreover, if we use the equality, then the initial values are as large as possible. Making the initial values as large as possible biases the network toward uncommitted nodes. Even if the vigilance parameter is too low to cause a reset otherwise, the network will choose an uncommitted node over a badly mismatched node. This mechanism helps stabilize the network against constant recoding.

Similar arguments lead to a constraint on the parameters c and d; namely,

$$\frac{cd}{1-d} \le 1 \tag{8.50}$$

As the ratio approaches 1, the network becomes more sensitive to mismatches because the value of $\|\mathbf{r}\|$ decreases to a smaller value, all other things being equal.

8.3.7 ART2 Processing Summary

In this section, we assemble a summary of the processing equations and constraints for the ART2 network. Following this brief list, we shall return to the numerical example that we began two sections ago.

As we did with ART1, we shall consider only the asymptotic solutions to the dynamic equations, and the fast-learning mode. Also, as with ART1, we let M be the number of units in each F_1 sublayer, and N be the number of units on F_2. Parameters are chosen according to the following constraints:

$$
\begin{aligned}
a, b &> 0 \\
0 \le d &\le 1 \\
\frac{cd}{1-d} &\le 1 \\
0 \le \theta &\le 1 \\
0 \le \rho &\le 1 \\
e &\ll 1
\end{aligned}
$$

Top-down weights are all initialized to zero:

$$z_{ij}(0) = 0$$

Bottom-up weights are initialized according to

$$z_{ji}(0) \le \frac{1}{(1-d)\sqrt{M}}$$

Now we are ready to process data.

1. Initialize all layer and sublayer outputs to zero vectors, and establish a cycle counter initialized to a value of one.

2. Apply an input pattern, $\mathbf{I}$ to the $\mathbf{w}$ layer of F_1. The output of this layer is

$$w_i = I_i + au_i$$

3. Propagate forward to the $\mathbf{x}$ sublayer.

$$x_i = \frac{w_i}{e + \|\mathbf{w}\|}$$

4. Propagate forward to the **v** sublayer.

$$v_i = f(x_i) + bf(q_i)$$

Note that the second term is zero on the first pass through, as **q** is zero at that time.

5. Propagate to the **u** sublayer.

$$u_i = \frac{v_i}{e + \|\mathbf{v}\|}$$

6. Propagate forward to the **p** sublayer.

$$p_i = u_i + dz_{iJ}$$

where the Jth node on F_2 is the winner of the competition on that layer. If F_2 is inactive, $p_i = u_i$. Similarly, if the network is still in its initial configuration, $p_i = u_i$ because $z_{ij}(0) = 0$.

7. Propagate to the **q** sublayer.

$$q_i = \frac{p_i}{e + \|\mathbf{p}\|}$$

8. Repeat steps 2 through 7 as necessary to stabilize the values on F_1.

9. Calculate the output of the **r** layer.

$$r_i = \frac{u_i + cp_i}{e + \|\mathbf{u}\| + \|c\mathbf{p}\|}$$

10. Determine whether a reset condition is indicated. If $\rho/(e + \|\mathbf{r}\|) > 1$, then send a reset signal to F_2. Mark any active F_2 node as ineligible for competition, reset the cycle counter to one, and return to step 2. If there is no reset, and the cycle counter is one, increment the cycle counter and continue with step 11. If there is no reset, and the cycle counter is greater than one, then skip to step 14, as resonance has been established.

11. Propagate the output of the **p** sublayer to the F_2 layer. Calculate the net inputs to F_2.

$$T_j = \sum_{i=1}^{M} p_i z_{ji}$$

12. Only the winning F_2 node has nonzero output.

$$g(T_j) = \begin{cases} d & T_j = \max_k \{T_k\} \\ 0 & \text{otherwise} \end{cases}$$

Any nodes marked as ineligible by previous reset signals do not participate in the competition.

13. Repeat steps 6 through 10.

14. Modify bottom-up weights on the winning F_2 unit.

$$z_{Ji} = \frac{u_i}{1 - d}$$

15. Modify top-down weights coming from the winning F_2 unit.

$$z_{iJ} = \frac{u_i}{1 - d}$$

16. Remove the input vector. Restore all inactive F_2 units. Return to step 1 with a new input pattern.

8.3.8   ART2 Processing Example

We shall be using the same parameters and input vector for this example that we used in Section 8.3.2. For that reason, we shall begin with the propagation of the **p** vector up to F_2. Before showing the results of that calculation, we shall summarize the network parameters and show the initialized weights.

We established the following parameters earlier: $a = 10; b = 10; c = 0.1, \theta = 0.2$. To that list we add the additional parameter, $d = 0.9$. We shall use $N = 6$ units on the F_2 layer.

The top-down weights are all initialized to zero, so $z_{ij}(0) = 0$ as discussed in Section 8.3.5. The bottom-up weights are initialized according to Eq. (8.49): $z_{ji} = 0.5/(1 - d)\sqrt{M} = 2.236$, since $M = 5$.

Using $\mathbf{I} = (0.2, 0.7, 0.1, 0.5, 0.4)^t$ as the input vector, before propagation to F_2 we have $\mathbf{p} = (0.206, 0.722, 0, 0.516, 0.413)^t$. Propagating this vector forward to F_2 yields a vector of activities across the F_2 units of

$$\mathbf{T} = (4.151, 4.151, 4.151, 4.151, 4.151, 4.151)^t$$

Because all of the activities are the same, the first unit becomes the winner and the activity vector becomes

$$\mathbf{T} = (4.151, 0, 0, 0, 0, 0)^t$$

and the output of the F_2 layer is the vector, $(0.9, 0, 0, 0, 0, 0)^t$.

We now propagate this output vector back to F_1 and cycle through the layers again. Since the top-down weights are all initialized to zero, there is no change on the sublayers of F_1. We showed earlier that this condition will not result in a reset from the orienting subsystem; in other words, we have reached a resonant state. The weight vectors will now update according to the appropriate equations given previously. We find that the bottom-up weight matrix is

$$\begin{pmatrix} 2.063 & 7.220 & 0.000 & 5.157 & 4.126 \\ 2.236 & 2.236 & 2.236 & 2.236 & 2.236 \\ 2.236 & 2.236 & 2.236 & 2.236 & 2.236 \\ 2.236 & 2.236 & 2.236 & 2.236 & 2.236 \\ 2.236 & 2.236 & 2.236 & 2.236 & 2.236 \\ 2.236 & 2.236 & 2.236 & 2.236 & 2.236 \end{pmatrix}$$

and the top-down matrix is

$$\begin{pmatrix} 2.06284 \ 0 \ 0 \ 0 \ 0 \ 0 \\ 7.21995 \ 0 \ 0 \ 0 \ 0 \ 0 \\ 0.00000 \ 0 \ 0 \ 0 \ 0 \ 0 \\ 5.15711 \ 0 \ 0 \ 0 \ 0 \ 0 \\ 4.12568 \ 0 \ 0 \ 0 \ 0 \ 0 \end{pmatrix}$$

Notice the expected similarity between the first row of the bottom-up matrix and the first column of the top-down matrix.

We shall not continue this example further. You are encouraged to build an ART2 simulator and experiment on your own.

8.4 THE ART1 SIMULATOR

In this section, we shall present the design for the ART network simulator. For clarity, we will focus on only the ART1 network in our discussion. The development of the ART2 simulator is left to you as an exercise. However, due to the similarities between the two networks, much of the material presented in this section will be applicable to the ART2 simulator. As in previous chapters, we begin this section with the development of the data structures needed to implement the simulator, and proceed to describe the pertinent algorithms. We conclude this section with a discussion of how the simulator might be adapted to implement the ART2 network.

8.4.1 ART1 Data Structures

The ART1 network is very much like the BAM network described in Chapter 4 of this text. Both networks process only binary input vectors. Both networks use connections that are initialized by performance of a calculation based on parameters unique to the network, rather than a random distribution of values. Also, both networks have two layers of processing elements that are completely interconnected between layers (the ART network augments the layers with the gain control and reset units).

However, unlike in the BAM, the connections between layers in the ART network are not bidirectional. Rather, the network units here are interconnected by means of two sets of *uni*directional connections. As shown in Figure 8.7, one set ties all the outputs of the elements on layer F_1 to all the inputs on F_2, and the other set connects all F_2 unit outputs to inputs on layer F_1. Thus, for reasons completely different from those used to justify the BAM data structures, it turns out that the interconnection scheme used to model the BAM is identical to the scheme needed to model the ART1 network.

As we saw in the case of the BAM, the data structures needed to implement this view of network processing fit nicely with the processing model provided by the generic simulator described in Chapter 1. To understand why this is so, recall the discussion in Section 4.5.2 where, in the case of the BAM, we claimed it was desirable to split the bidirectional connections between layers into two sets of

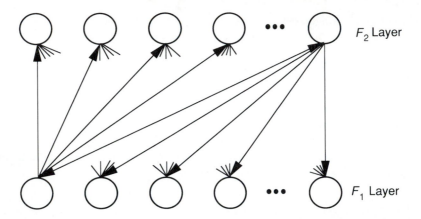

Figure 8.7   The diagram shows the interconnection strategy needed to simulate the ART1 network. Notice that only the connections between units on the F_1 and F_2 layers are needed. The host computer can perform the function of the gain control and reset units directly, thus eliminating the need to model these structures in the simulator.

unidirectional connections, and to process each individually. By organizing the network data structures in this manner, we were able to simplify the calculations performed at each network unit, in that the computer had only input values to process. In the case of the BAM, splitting the connections was done to improve performance at the expense of additional memory consumption. We can now see that there was another benefit to organizing the BAM simulator as we did: The data structures used to model the modified BAM network can be ported directly to the ART1 simulator.

By using the interconnection data structures developed for the BAM as the basis of the ART1 network, we eliminate the need to develop a new set of data structures, and now need only to define the top-level network structure used to tie all the ART1 specific parameters together. To do this, we simply construct a record containing the pointers to the appropriate layer structures and the learning parameters unique to the ART1 network. A good candidate structure is given by the following declaration:

```
record ART1 =                  {the network declaration}
   begin
      F1 : ^layer;             {locate F1 layer structure}
      F2 : ^layer;             {locate F2 layer structure}
      A1 : float;              {A parameters for layer F1}
      B1 : float;              {B parameters for layer F1}
      C1 : float;              {C parameters for layer F1}
      D1 : float;              {D parameters for layer F1}
      L  : float;              {L parameter for network}
```

```
     rho : float;              {vigilance parameter}
     F2W : integer;            {index of winner on F2 layer}
     INH : ^float[];           {F2 inhibited vector}
     magX : float;             {magnitude of vector on F1}
  end record;
```

where A, B, C, D, and L are network parameters as described in Section 8.2. You should also note that we have incorporated three items in the network structure that will be used to simplify the simulation process. These values—F2W, INH, and magX—are used to provide immediate access to the winning unit on F_2, to implement the inhibition mechanism from the attentional subsystem (A), and to store the computed magnitude of the template on layer F_1, respectively. Furthermore, we have not specified the dimension of the INH array directly, so you should be aware that we assume that this array contains as many values as there are units on layer F_2. We will use the INH array to selectively eliminate the input stimulation to each F_2 layer unit, thus performing the reset function. We will elaborate on the use of this array in the following section.

As illustrated in Figure 8.8, this structure for the ART1 network provides us with access to all the network-specific data that we will require to complete our simulator, we shall now proceed to the development of the algorithms necessary to simulate the ART1 network.

8.4.2 ART1 Algorithms

As discussed in Section 8.2, it is desirable to simplify (as much as possible) the calculation of the unit activity within the network during digital simulation. For that reason, we will restrict our discussion of the ART1 algorithms to the asymptotic solution for the dynamic equations, and will implement the fast-learning case for the network weights.

Further, to clarify the implementation of the simulator, we will focus on the processing described in Section 8.2.3, and will use the data provided in that example as the basis for the algorithm design provided here. If you have not done so already, please review Section 8.2.3.

We begin by presuming that the network simulator has been constructed in memory and initialized according to the example data. We can define the algorithm necessary to perform the processing of the input vector on layer F_1 as follows:

```
procedure prop_to_F1 (net:ART1; invec:^float[]);
{compute outputs for layer F1 for a given input vector}

var i : integer;                      {iteration counter}
    unit : ^float[];           {pointer to unit outputs}

begin
  unit = net.F1^.OUTS;               {locate unit outputs}
  for i = 1 to length(unit)             {for all F1 units}
```

```
        do
          unit[i] = invec[i] /
                  (1 + net.A1 * (invec[i] + net.B1) + net.C1);

          if (unit[i] > 0)   {convert activation to output}
          then unit[i] = 1
          else unit[i] = 0;
          end if;
        end do;
      end procedure;
```

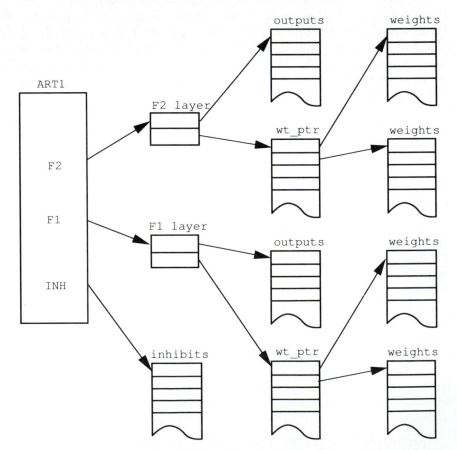

Figure 8.8   The complete data structure for the ART1 simulator is shown.
Notice that we have added an additional array to contain
the INHibit data that will be used to suppress invalid pattern
matches on the F_2 layer.   Compare this diagram with the
declaration in the text for the ART1 record, and be sure you
understand how this model implements the interconnection
scheme for the ART1 network.

Notice that the computation for the output of each unit on F_1 requires no modulating connection `weights`. This calculation is consistent with the processing model for the ART1 network, but it also is of benefit since we must use the input connection arrays to each unit on F_1 to hold the values associated with the connections from layer F_2. This makes the simulation process efficient, in that we can model two different kinds of connections (the inputs from the external world, and the top-down connections from F_2) in the memory space required for one set of connections (the standard input connections for a unit on a layer).

The next step in the simulation process is to propagate the signals from the F_1 layer to the F_2 layer. This signal propagation is the familiar sum-of-products operation, and each unit in the F_2 layer will generate a nonzero output only if it had the highest activation level on the layer. For the ART1 simulation, however, we must also consider the effect of the inhibit signal to each unit on F_2 from the attentional subsystem. We assume this inhibition status is represented by the values in the `INH` array, as initialized by a reader-provided routine to be discussed later, and further modified by network operation. We will use the values $\{0, 1\}$ to represent the inhibition status for the network, with a zero indicating the F_2 unit is inhibited, and a one indicating the unit is actively participating in the competition. Furthermore, as in the discussion of the counterpropagation network simulator, we will find it desirable to know, after the signal propagation to the competitive layer has completed, which unit won the competition so that it may be quickly accessed again during later processing.

To accomplish all of these operations, we can define the algorithm for the signal propagation to all units on layer F_2 as follows:

```
procedure prop_to_F2 (net:ART1);
{propagate signals from layer F1 to F2}

var i,j : integer;                    {iteration counters}
    unit : ^float[];          {pointer to F2 unit outputs}
    inputs : ^float[];        {pointer to F1 unit outputs}
    connects : ^float[];    {pointer to unit connections}
    largest : float;                  {largest activation}
    winner : integer;                   {index to winner}
    sum : float;                            {accumulator}

begin
    unit = net.F2^.OUTS;           {locate F2 output array}
    inputs = net.F1^.OUTS;         {locate F1 output array}
    largest = -100;            {initial largest activation}

    for i = 1 to length(unit)              {for all F2 units}
      do
        unit[i] = 0;                {deactivate unit output}
      end do;

    for i = 1 to length(unit)              {for all F2 units}
      do
```

```
        sum = 0;                          {reset accumulator}
        connects = net.F2^.WEIGHTS[i];
                                  {locate connection array}

        for j = 1 to length(inputs)
                                  {for all inputs to unit}

          do                        {compute activation}
            sum = sum + inputs[j] * connects[j];
          end do;

        sum = sum * net.INH[i];     {inhibit if necessary}

        if (sum > largest)            {if current winner}
        then
          winner = i;                 {remember this unit}
          largest = sum;          {mark largest activation}
        end if;
      end do;

    unit[winner] = 1;                          {mark winner}
    net.F2W = winner;                       {remember winner}
  end procedure;
```

Now we have to propagate from the winning unit on F_2 back to all the units on F_1. In theory, we perform this step by computing the inner product between the connection weight vector and the vector formed by the outputs from all the units on F_2. For our digital simulation, however, we can reduce the amount of time needed to perform this propagation by limiting the calculation to only those connections between the units on F_1 and the single winning unit on F_2. Further, since the output of the winning unit on F_2 was set to one, we can again improve performance by eliminating the multiplication and using the connection weight directly. This new input from F_2 is then used to calculate a new output value for the F_1 units. The sequence of operations just described is captured in the following algorithm.

```
procedure prop_back_to_F1 (net:ART1; invec:^float[]);
{propagate signals from F2 winner back to F1 layer}

var i : integer;                     {iteration counter}
    winner : integer;         {index of winning F2 unit}
    unit : ^float[];                  {locate F1 units}
    connects : ^float[];           {locate connections}
    X : float;                    {new input activation}
    Vi : float;                     {connection weight}

begin
  unit = net.F1^.OUTS;
                          {locate beginning of F1 outputs}
    winner = net.F2W;            {get index of winning unit}
```

```
for i = 1 to length(unit)              {for all F1 units}
   do
      connects = net.F1^.WEIGHTS;
                              {locate connection arrays}
      Vi = connects[i]^[winner];
                              {get connection weight}

      X = (invec[i] + net.D1 * Vi - net.B1) /
          (1 + net.A1 * (invec[i] + net.D1 * Vi) + net.C1);

      if (X > 0)               {is activation sufficient}
      then unit[i] = 1         {to turn on unit output?}
      else unit[i] = 0 ;             {if not, turn off}
   end do;
end procedure;
```

Now all that remains is to compare the output vector on F_1 to the original input vector, and to update the network accordingly. Rather than trying to accomplish both of these operations in one function, we shall construct two functions (named `match` and `update`) that will determine whether a match has occurred between bottom-up and top-down patterns, and will update the network accordingly. These routines will both be constructed so that they can be called from a higher-level routine, which we call `propagate`. We first compute the degree to which the two vectors resemble each other. We shall accomplish this comparison as follows:

```
function match (net:ART1; invec:^float[]) return float;
{compare input vector to activation values on F1}

var i : integer;                        {iteration counter}
    unit : ^float[];        {locate outputs of F1 units}
    magX : float;            {the magnitude of template}
    magI : float;            {the magnitude of the input}

begin
   unit = net.F1^.OUTS;              {access unit outputs}
   magX = 0;                    {initialize magnitude}
   magI = 0;                                    {ditto}

   for i = 1 to length(unit)
                           {for all component of input}
      do
         magX = magX + unit[i];
                           {compute magnitude of template}
         magI = magI + invec[i];   {same for input vector}
      end do;

   net.magX = magX;        {save magnitude for later use}
   return (magX / magI);       {return the match value}
end function;
```

Once resonance has been established (as indicated by the degree of the match found between the template vector and the input vector), we must update the connection weights in order to reinforce the memory of this pattern. This update is accomplished in the following manner.

```
procedure update (net:ART1);
{update the connection weights to remember a pattern}

var i : integer;                          {iteration counter}
    winner : integer;          {index of winning F2 unit}
    unit : ^float[];             {access to unit outputs}

    connects : ^float[]; {access to connection values}
    inputs : ^float[];         {pointer to outputs of F1}

begin
  unit = net.F2^.OUTS;   {update winning F2 unit first}
  winner = net.F2W;                 {index to winning unit}
  connects = net.F2^.WEIGHTS[winner];
                              {locate winners connections}
  inputs = net.F1^.OUTS;   {locate outputs of F1 units}

  for i = 1 to length(connects)
                      {for all connections to F2 winner}
    do
     {update the connections to the unit according to
        Eq. (8.28)}
      connects[i] = (net.L / (net.L - 1 + net.magX))
                      * inputs[i];
    end do;

  for i = 1 to length(unit) {now do connections to F1}
    do
      connects = net.F1^.WEIGHTS[i];
                                    {access connections}
      connects[winner] = inputs[i]; {update connections}
    end do;
end procedure;
```

You should note from inspection of the **update** algorithm that we have taken advantage of some characteristics of the ART1 network to enhance simulator performance in two ways:

- We update the connection weights to the winner on F_2 by multiplying the computed value for each connection by the output of the F_1 unit associated with the connection being updated. This operation makes use of the fact that the output from every F_1 unit is *always* binary. Thus, connections are updated correctly regardless of whether they are connected to an active or inactive F_1 unit.

• We update the top-down connections from the winning F_2 unit to the units on F_1 to contain the *output value of the F_1 unit to which they are connected.* Again, this takes advantage of the binary nature of the unit outputs on F_1 and allows us to eliminate a conditional test-and-branch operation in the algorithm.

With the addition of a top-level routine to tie them all together, the collection of algorithms just defined are sufficient to implement the ART1 network. We shall now complete the simulator design by presenting the implementation of the `propagate` routine. So that it remains consistent with our example, the top-level routine is designed to place an input vector on the network, and perform the signal propagation according to the algorithm described in Section 8.2.3. Note that this routine uses a reader-provided routine (`remove_inhibit`) to set all the values in the `ART1.INH` array to one. This routine is necessary in order to guarantee that all F_2 units participate in the signal-propagation activity for every new pattern presented to the network.

```
procedure propagate (net:ART1; invec:^float[]);
{perform a signal propagation with learning in the
                                             network}

var done : boolean;            {true when template found}

begin
  done = false;                            {start loop}
  remove_inhibit (net);          {enable all F2 units}

  while (not done)
    do
       prop_to_F1 (net, invec);       {update F1 layer}
       prop_to_F2 (net);           {determine F2 winner}
       prop_back_to_F1 (net, invec);
                                 {send template back to F1}

       if (match(net, invec) < net.rho)
                              {if pattern does not match}
       then net.INH[net.F2W] = 0      {inhibit winner}
       else done = true;              {else exit loop}
    end do;

  update (net);                     {reinforce template}
end procedure;
```

Note that the `propagate` algorithm does not take into account the case where all F_2 units have been encoded and *none* of them match the current input pattern. In that event, one of two things should occur: Either the algorithm should attempt to combine two already encoded patterns that exhibit some degree of similarity in order to free an F_2 unit (difficult to implement), or the simulator should allow for growth in the number of network units. This second option can be accomplished as follows:

1. When the condition exists that requires an additional F_2 unit, first allocate a new array of floats that contains enough room for all existing F_2 units, plus some number of extra units.

2. Copy the current contents of the output array to the newly created array so that the existing n values occupy the first n values in the new array.

3. Change the pointer in the ART1 record structure to locate the new array as the output array for the F_2 units.

4. Deallocate the old F_2 output array (optional).

The design and implementation of such an algorithm is left to you as an exercise.

8.5 ART2 SIMULATION

As we discussed earlier in this chapter, the ART2 model varies from the ART1 network primarily in the implementation of the F_1 layer. Rather than a single-layer structure of units, the F_1 layer contains a number of sublayers that serve to remove noise, to enhance contrast, and to normalize an analog input pattern. We shall not find this structure difficult to model, as the F_1 layer can be reduced to a superlayer containing many intermediate layer structures. In this case, we need only to be aware of the differences in the network structure as we implement the ART2 processing algorithms.

In addition, signals propagating through the ART2 network are primarily analog in nature, and hence must be modeled as floating-point numbers in our digital simulation. This condition creates a situation of which you must be aware when attempting to adapt the algorithms developed for the ART1 simulator to the ART2 model. Recall that, in several ART1 algorithms, we relied on the fact that network units were generating *binary* outputs in order to simplify processing. For example, consider the case where the input connection weights to layer F_2 are being modified during learning (algorithm `update`). In that algorithm, we multiplied the corrected connection weight *by the output of the unit from the F_1 layer*. We did this multiplication to ensure that the ART1 connections were updated to contain either the corrected connection value (if the F_1 unit was on) or to zero (if the F_1 unit was off). This approach will not work in the ART2 model, because F_1 layer units can now produce analog outputs.

Other than these two minor variations, the implementation of the ART2 simulator should be straightforward. Using the ART1 simulator and ART2 discussion as a guide, we leave it as an exercise for you to develop the algorithms and data structures needed to create an ART2 simulator.

Programming Exercises

8.1. Implement the ART1 simulator. Test it using the example data presented in Section 8.2.3. Does the simulator generate the same data values described in the example? Explain your answer.

8.2. Design and implement a function that can be incorporated in the `propagate` routine to account for the situation where all F_2 units have been used and a new input pattern does not match any of the encoded patterns. Use the guidelines presented in the text for this algorithm. Show the new algorithm, and indicate where it should be called from inside the `propagate` routine.

8.3. Implement the ART2 simulator. Test it using the example data presented in Section 8.3.2. Does the simulator behave as expected? Describe the activity levels at each sublayer on F_1 at different periods during the signal-propagation process.

8.4. Using the ART2 simulator constructed in Programming Exercise 8.3, describe what happens when all the inputs in a training pattern are scaled by a random noise function and are presented to the network after training. Does your ART2 network correctly classify the new input into the same category as it classifies the original pattern? How can you tell whether it does?

Suggested Readings

The most prolific writers of the neural-network community appear to be Stephen Grossberg, Gail Carpenter, and their colleagues. Starting with Grossberg's work in the 1970s, and continuing today, a steady stream of papers has evolved from Grossberg's early ideas. Many such papers have been collected into books. The two that we have found to be the most useful are *Studies of Mind and Brain* [10] and *Neural Networks and Natural Intelligence* [13]. Another collection is *The Adaptive Brain, Volumes I and II* [11, 12]. This two-volume compendium contains papers on the application of Grossberg's theories to models of vision, speech and language recognition and recall, cognitive self-organization, conditioning, reinforcement, motivation, attention, circadian rhythms, motor control, and even certain mental disorders such as amnesia. Many of the papers that deal directly with the adaptive resonance networks were coauthored by Gail Carpenter [1, 5, 2, 3, 4, 6].

A highly mathematical paper by Cohen and Grossberg proved a convergence theorem regarding networks and the latter's ability to learn patterns [8]. Although important from a theoretical standpoint, this paper is recommended for only the hardy mathematician.

Applications using ART networks often combine the basic ART structures with other, related structures also developed by Grossberg and colleagues. This fact is one reason why specific application examples are missing from this chapter. Examples of these applications can be found in the papers by Carpenter et al. [7], Kolodzy [15], and Kolodzy and van Allen [14]. An alternate method for modeling the orienting subsystem can be found in the papers by Ryan and Winter [16] and by Ryan, Winter, and Turner [17].

Bibliography

[1] Gail A. Carpenter and Stephen Grossberg. Associative learning, adaptive pattern recognition and cooperative-competetive decision making by neural networks. In H. Szu, editor. *Hybrid and Optical Computing*. SPIE, 1986.

[2] Gail A. Carpenter and Stephen Grossberg. ART 2: Self-organization of stable category recognition codes for analog input patterns. *Applied Optics*, 26(23):4919–4930, December 1987.

[3] Gail A. Carpenter and Stephen Grossberg. ART2: Self-organization of stable category recognition codes for analog input patterns. In Maureen Caudill and Charles Butler, editors, *Proceedings of the IEEE First International Conference on Neural Networks*, San Diego, CA, pp. II–727–II–735, June 1987. IEEE.

[4] Gail A. Carpenter and Stephen Grossberg. Invariant pattern recognition and recall by an attentive self-organizing ART architecture in a nonstationary world. In Maureen Caudill and Charles Butler, editors, *Proceedings of the IEEE First International Conference on Neural Networks*, San Diego, CA, pp. II–737–II–745, June 1987. IEEE.

[5] Gail A. Carpenter and Stephen Grossberg. A massively parallel architecture for a self-organizing neural pattern recognition machine. *Computer Vision, Graphics, and Image Processing*, 37:54–115, 1987.

[6] Gail A. Carpenter and Stephen Grossberg. The ART of adaptive pattern recognition by a self-organizing neural network. *Computer*, 21(3):77–88, March 1988.

[7] Gail A. Carpenter, Stephen Grossberg, and Courosh Mehanian. Invariant recognition of cluttered scenes by a self-organizing ART architecture: CORT-X boundary segmentation. *Neural Networks*, 2(3):169–181, 1989.

[8] Michael A. Cohen and Stephen Grossberg. Absolute stability of global pattern formation and parallel memory storage by competitive neural networks. *IEEE Transactions on Systems, Man, and Cybernetics*, SMC-13(5):815–826, September–October 1983.

[9] Stephen Grossberg. Adaptive pattern classsification and universal recoding, I: Parallel development and coding of neural feature detectors. In Stephen Grossberg, editor. *Studies of Mind and Brain*. D. Reidel Publishing, Boston, pp. 448–497, 1982.

[10] Stephen Grossberg. *Studies of Mind and Brain*, volume 70 of *Boston Studies in the Philosophy of Science*. D. Reidel Publishing Company, Boston, 1982.

[11] Stephen Grossberg, editor. *The Adaptive Brain, Vol. I: Cognition, Learning, Reinforcement, and Rhythm*. North Holland, Amsterdam, 1987.

[12] Stephen Grossberg, editor. *The Adaptive Brain, Vol. II: Vision, Speech, Language and Motor Control*. North Holland, Amsterdam, 1987.

[13] Stephen Grossberg, editor. *Neural Networks and Natural Intelligence*. MIT Press, Cambridge, MA, 1988.

[14] P. Kolodzy and E. J. van Allen. Application of a boundary contour neural network to illusions and infrared imagery. In *Proceedings of the IEEE First International Conference on Neural Networks*, San Diego, CA, pp. IV-193–IV-202, June 1987. IEEE.

[15] Paul J. Kolodzy. Multidimensional machine vision using neural networks. In *Proceedings of the IEEE First International Conference on Neural Networks*, San Diego, CA, pp. II-747–II-758, June 1987. IEEE.

[16] T. W. Ryan and C. L. Winter. Variations on adaptive resonance. In Maureen Caudill and Charles Butler, editors, *Proceedings of the IEEE First International Conference on Neural Networks*, San Diego, CA, pp. II-767–II-775, June 1987. IEEE.

[17] T. W. Ryan, C. L. Winter, and C. J. Turner. Dynamic control of an artificial neural system: the property inheritance network. *Applied Optics*, 21(23): 4961–4971, December 1987.

Spatiotemporal
Pattern Classification

Many ANS architectures, such as backpropagation, adaptive resonance, and others discussed in previous chapters of this text, are applicable to the recognition of spatial information patterns: a two-dimensional, bit-mapped image of a handwritten character, for example. Input vectors presented to such a network were not necessarily time correlated in any way; if they were, that time correlation was incidental to the pattern-classification process. Individual patterns were classified on the basis of information contained within the pattern itself. The previous or subsequent pattern had no effect on the classification of the current input vector.

We presented an example in Chapter 7 where a sequence of spatial patterns could be encoded as a path across a two-dimensional layer of processing elements (see Section 7.2.1, on the neural phonetic typewriter). Nevertheless, the self-organizing map used in that example was not conditioned to respond to any particular sequence of input patterns; it just reported what the sequence was.

In this chapter, we shall describe ANS architectures that can deal directly with both the spatial and the temporal aspects of input signals. These networks encode information relating to the time correlation of spatial patterns, as well as the spatial pattern information itself. We define a **spatiotemporal pattern** (STP) as a time-correlated sequence of spatial patterns.

There are several application domains where STP recognition is important. One that comes to mind immediately is speech recognition, for which the STP could be the time-varying power spectrum produced by a multichannel audio spectrum analyzer. A coarse example of such an analyzer is represented by the bar-graph display of a typical graphic equalizer used in many home stereo systems. Each channel of the graphic equalizer responds to the sound inten-

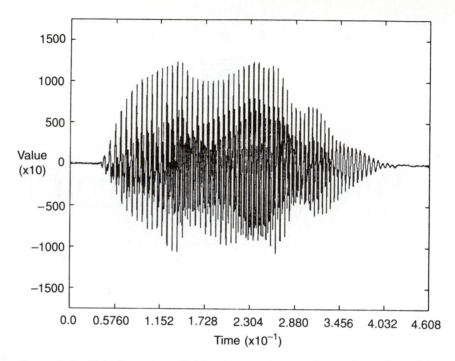

Figure 9.1   This figure is a digitized acoustic waveform of a male speaker
making the utterance "zero" in ambient conditions. The
sampling rate is 10 kHz. *Source: Courtesy of Kamil Grajski,
Loral Western Development Laboratories.*

sity within a certain frequency interval. Other applications, with characteristics
similar to the speech example, include radar and sonar echoes.

Figures 9.1 and 9.2 illustrate an example of an STP from a spoken word.
The waveform shown in Figure 9.1 has been converted into a sequence of
power spectra in Figure 9.2. Each individual spectrum is a spatial pattern. The
sequence of spatial patterns, one at each time slice, makes up the STP.

Much of the following discussion requires an understanding of the material
contained in Chapter 6. If you have not already studied that material, you should
do so before attempting to read this chapter.

9.1   THE FORMAL AVALANCHE

The foundation for the development of the network architectures in this chapter
is the formal avalanche structure developed by Grossberg [2]. The network is
shown in Figure 9.3. The structure of the network resembles the top two layers

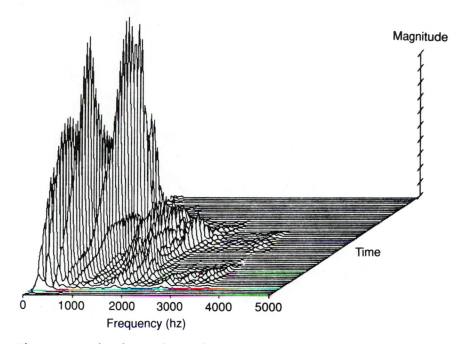

Figure 9.2 This figure shows the spectrogram made from the waveform in Figure 9.1. The horizontal axis represents frequency, and the vertical axis represents the power level of the signal at each frequency. Time extends *backward* into the figure. *Source: Courtesy of Kamil Grajski, Loral Western Development Laboratories.*

of the CPN described in Chapter 6. This resemblance is not coincidental: Both networks use multiple outstars.[1]

The CPN and the avalanche use their outstars in a slightly different manner. In the CPN, individual spatial patterns were presented to the input layer, a winning hidden-layer unit was found, and the corresponding outstar was excited. The outputs of the outstar were the previously learned mapping for the class of input pattern presented.

Instead of performing a recognition function, the avalanche demonstrates how a complex spatiotemporal pattern might be learned and recalled. An example would be the sequence of muscle contractions and extensions that result in the ability to play a particular piece on the piano. The pattern can be learned as follows (refer to Figure 9.3).

---

[1]We hasten to add that the development of the avalanche preceded that of the CPN by many years, even though we discussed the CPN first in this text.

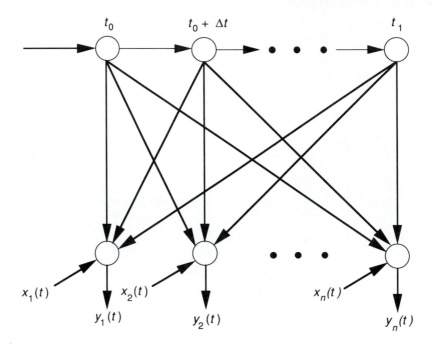

Figure 9.3   This figure shows Grossberg's formal avalanche structure. The network consists of multiple outstars, all sharing their output units. The network learns $\mathbf{y}(t) \approx \mathbf{x}(t)$. Once it is trained, the avalanche can replay $\mathbf{y}(t)$ in the proper sequence by exciting the outstars sequentially.

Assume $\mathbf{x}(t) = (x_1(t), x_2(t), \dots, x_n(t))^t$ is the set of muscle commands required at time t, $t_0 \leq t \leq t_1$. Activate the node labeled t_0 and apply $\mathbf{x}(t_0)$ to be learned by the outstar's output units. The second set of commands, $\mathbf{x}(t_0 + \Delta t)$ is applied while activating the second outstar, labeled $t_0 + \Delta t$. Continue this process by activating successive outstars until all of the muscle commands have been learned in sequence. Once learned, the entire series of commands can be recalled by activation of the outstars in the proper sequence, $t_0, t_0 + \Delta t, t_0 + 2\Delta t, \dots, t_1$, while a zero vector is applied to the x inputs.[2] Replay of the learned sequence can be initiated by stimulating the t_0 node. The t_0 node then stimulates the $t_0 + \Delta t$ node, and so forth.

For our purposes it does not matter whether the formal avalanche architecture bears much resemblance to actual biological systems; the mere fact that it represents a minimal architecture capable of learning and reproducing STPs makes this network structure interesting in its own right. In the next section, we

---

[2]See Section 6.1 for the details on the outstar training procedure.

shall return to a consideration of the pattern-recognition problem. We shall show how avalanche structures can be constructed that can identify complex STPs.

Exercise 9.1: The Moonlight Sonata requires approximately 13.5 minutes to perform. Assume that a formal avalanche structure is responsible for actuating the muscles that enable someone to perform this piece on the piano. Assume that the outstars are stimulated at a rate of one every 25 milliseconds. Estimate how many outstars would be required in the avalanche. Speculate on the likelihood that the formal avalanche is actually used in the brain for this purpose.

9.2 ARCHITECTURES OF SPATIOTEMPORAL NETWORKS (STNS)

We shall anchor the following discussion in familiar waters by using the example of speech recognition as the source for our STPs.

Figure 9.4 shows a simple experimental arrangement that generates STPs from spoken words. At each instant of time, the output of the spectrum analyzer consists of a vector whose components are the powers in the various channels. For example, at $t = t_1$,

$$\mathbf{P}_i(t_1) = (P_{i1}(t_1), P_{i2}(t_1), \ldots, P_{in}(t_1))^t$$

is the power spectrum for the ith word at time t_1. The STP for each word consists of a sequence of vectors of the form $\mathbf{P}_i(t_j)$. If P_i is the STP for the ith word, then

$$P_i = \{\mathbf{P}_i(t_1), \mathbf{P}_i(t_2), \ldots, \mathbf{P}_i(t_j)\}$$

Differences in volume can be accounted for by normalization of the individual power spectra: $\|\mathbf{P}_i(t_j)\| = 1$.

To complete the picture, we must specify the number of vectors in the set, P_i. To represent a time-varying signal accurately, we must sample the power spectrum at a frequency at least two times the bandwidth of the original signal. Although we have restricted ourselves to speech, we can accommodate other time-varying signals in a similar manner.

9.2.1 STN for Speech Recognition

We shall first construct a network that is tuned to recognize a single word. Then, we shall show how to expand the network to accommodate other words. Figure 9.5 shows the basic structure.

To tune the network for a specific word, we must first perform a spectral analysis while someone actually speaks the word. To tune it more generally, we might take the average of the spectra produced by several different speakers. If the time required to say the word is t and we must sample at a rate of ν per second, then we need $m = \nu t$ spectra to represent the word, and m PEs in our

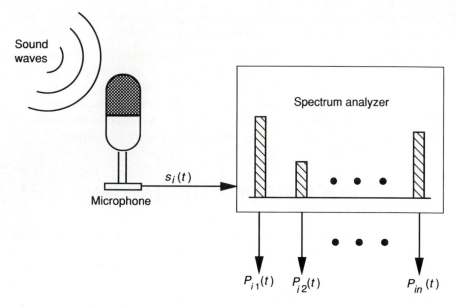

Figure 9.4   This diagram shows the generation of power spectra from speech. The microphone acts as a transducer producing the electrical signal, $s_i(t)$, from the sound-pressure waves. The subscript i identifies a single word. The spectrum analyzer measures the power contained in each of n frequency bins. $P_{i1}(t)$ is the power in frequency bin 1 for the ith spoken word.

network. Let

$$P_1 = \{\mathbf{P}_1(t_1), \mathbf{P}_1(t_2), \ldots, \mathbf{P}_1(t_m)\}$$

be the STP for the word. Assign weight vectors to the network units according to $\mathbf{z}_1 = \mathbf{P}_1(t_1), \mathbf{z}_2 = \mathbf{P}_1(t_2), \ldots, \mathbf{z}_m = \mathbf{P}_1(t_m)$, where $\|\mathbf{P}_1(t_j)\| = 1$. The dimension of the weight vectors and, therefore, the number of inputs to each processing element, is defined by the number of channels in the spectrum analyzer.

Now let's have someone repeat the word into the microphone as we apply the resultant STP to the network to verify its response. We have not as yet specified the processing performed by each unit, so we shall do that as we proceed. Let $Q_1 = \{\mathbf{Q}_1(t_1), \mathbf{Q}_1(t_2), \ldots, \mathbf{Q}_1(t_m)\}$ be the STP from the output of the spectrum analyzer. Assume that each $\mathbf{Q}_1(t_j)$ is normalized to one. To simplify the notation, we make the definition $\mathbf{Q}_{1i} = \mathbf{Q}_1(t_i)$.

Each $\mathbf{Q}_{1i}$ is applied to the inputs of *every* PE and is allowed to remain there for a time t equal to the sampling interval for the spectra. After that time, the next input vector, $\mathbf{Q}_{1,i+1}$ is applied, and so on. During the time that a particular input vector is present on the unit inputs, each PE dynamically adjusts its activation and output value according to the prescription that we shall now describe.

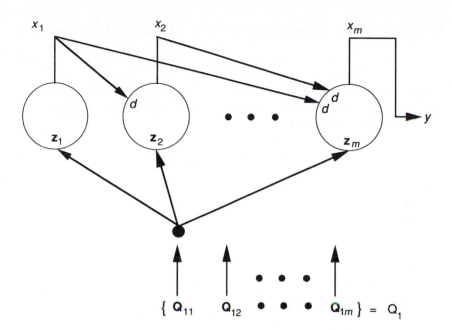

Figure 9.5 The avalanche network for single-word recognition is shown. The output of each unit is connected to each successive unit, from left to right, with a connection strength of d, where $0 < d < 1$. The dimension of the input vector is equal to the number of channels in the spectrum analyzer, and the number of units is equal to the number of times the power spectrum is sampled. Weight vectors associated with each unit are denoted by the z vectors. The network output is the single value, y. See the text for details of the operation of this network.

Like typical PEs in other networks, the units receive a net-input value from the dot product of the input vector and the unit's weight vector: in this case, $Q_{1i} \cdot z_i$, for the ith unit. In addition, each unit receives an input signal from the outputs of all units preceding it. By *preceding*, we mean those units to the left of a given unit, as depicted in Figure 9.5. Since the weights associated with the latter connections are all set to a constant, $d < 1$, the total input to the ith unit is given by

$$I_i = Q_{1i} \cdot z_i + d \sum_{k=1}^{i-1} x_k \qquad (9.1)$$

where x_k is the output of the kth unit. The output of the ith unit is modeled by a differential equation of the form

$$\dot{x}_i = A(-ax_i + b[I_i - \Gamma]^+) \qquad (9.2)$$

In Eq. (10.2), a and b are both positive constants. The function $[u]^+$ is defined by

$$[u]^+ = \begin{cases} u & \text{if } u > 0 \\ 0 & \text{if } u \le 0 \end{cases} \tag{9.3}$$

Γ takes on the role of a threshold value. For now, we will consider Γ to be some predefined constant value. The function $A(u)$ is called an **attack function**. It is defined by the equation

$$A(u) = \begin{cases} u & \text{if } u > 0 \\ cu & \text{if } u \le 0 \end{cases} \tag{9.4}$$

where $0 < c < 1$. The attack function has the effect of causing rise and fall times for the PE output values to differ from each other. The response of a PE to a finite input value exceeding the threshold is illustrated in Figure 9.6.

The output of the last unit, x_m, is defined as the network output value; that is, $y = x_m$. The equations for the network are defined such that the value of $y(t)$ at any time t provides a measure of how closely the STP being presented to the network matches the one previously stored in the network.

Unlike what we assumed for typical PEs in other networks, we shall not assume here that unit outputs can be approximated by the asymptotic values. In fact, we shall rely heavily on the dynamic nature of the output values for the successful operation of the network. Let's consider the case where $Q_1 = P_1$, by which we mean that $\mathbf{Q}_{1i} = \mathbf{P}_1(t_i)$ for all i. We shall analyze the network's response as we apply the input vectors of Q_1 in succession. Assume that Γ is sufficiently large (say, 0.9) such that a fairly close match between $\mathbf{Q}_{1i}$ and $\mathbf{z}_i$ is required before a PE produces a nonzero output.

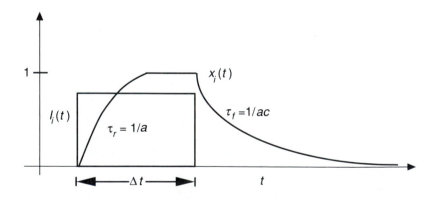

Figure 9.6 This graph shows the output of an STN PE in response to a net-input value above threshold. The total input, I_i, exceeds the threshold value for the duration Δt. The time constant for the rise is $\tau_r = 1/a$, but the time constant for the fall is $\tau_f = 1/ac$, which is longer than the rise time since $c < 1$. PEs are arbitrarily made to saturate at an output value of one.

The first input vector, $\mathbf{Q}_{11}$, matches $\mathbf{z}_1$ exactly, so x_1 begins to rise quickly. We shall assume that all other units remain quiescent. If $\mathbf{Q}_{11}$ remains long enough, x_1 will saturate. In any case, as soon as $\mathbf{Q}_{11}$ is removed and $\mathbf{Q}_{12}$ is applied, x_1 will begin to decay. At the same time, x_2 will begin to rise because $\mathbf{Q}_{12}$ matches the weight vector, $\mathbf{z}_2$. Moreover, since x_1 will not have decayed away completely, it will contribute to the positive input value to unit 2. When $\mathbf{Q}_{13}$ is applied, both x_1 and x_2 will contribute to the input to unit 3.

This cascade continues while all input vectors are applied to the network. Since the input vectors have been applied in the proper sequence, unit input values tend to be reinforced by the outputs of preceding units. By the time the final input vector is applied, the network output, represented by $y = x_m$, may already have reached saturation, even though contributions from units very early in the network may have decayed away.

To illustrate the effects of a pattern mismatch, let's examine the situation where the patterns of Q_1 are applied in reverse order. Since $\mathbf{Q}_{1m}$ matches $\mathbf{z}_m$, x_m will begin a quick rise toward saturation, although its output is not being reinforced by any other units in the network. When $\mathbf{Q}_{1.m-1}$ is applied, x_{m-1} turns on and sends its output value to contribute to x_m. The total input to the mth unit is dx_{m-1}, which, because $d < 1$, is unlikely to overcome the threshold Γ. Therefore, x_m will continue to decay away. By the time the last input vector is applied, x_m may have decayed away entirely, indicating that the network has not recognized the STP. Note that we have assumed here that $\mathbf{Q}_{1.m-1}$ is orthogonal to the weight vector z_m, and thus there is no contribution to the input to the mth unit from the dot product of these two vectors. This assumption is acceptable for this discussion to illustrate the concepts behind the network operation. In practice, these vectors will not necessarily be orthogonal.

Figure 9.7 shows a graphic example of unit outputs for a pattern recognition by a simple, four-unit STN. Results from applying the identical input vectors, but in a random order, are shown in Figure 9.8. Notice how the activity pattern appears to flow smoothly from left to right in the first figure.

Because of the relatively rapid rise time of the unit activity, followed by a longer decay time, the STN has the property of being somewhat insensitive to the speed at which the STP is presented. We know that different speakers pronounce the same word at slightly different rates; thus, tolerance of time variation is a desirable characteristic of STNs. Figure 9.9 shows the results of presenting an STP at two different rates to the same network.

Recall that the network we have been describing is capable of recognizing only a single STP. To distinguish words in some specified vocabulary, we would have to replicate the network for each word that we want the system to recognize. Figure 9.10 illustrates a system that can distinguish N words.

There are many aspects of the speech-recognition problem that we have overlooked in our discussion. For example, how do we account for both small words and large words? Moreover, some words are subsets of other words; will the system distinguish between a subset word spoken slowly and a superset

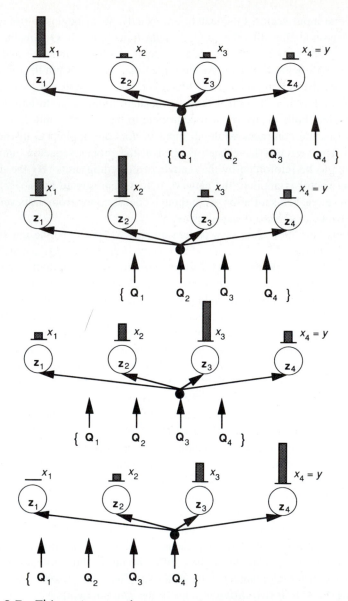

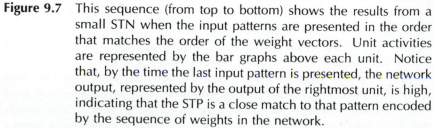

Figure 9.7 This sequence (from top to bottom) shows the results from a small STN when the input patterns are presented in the order that matches the order of the weight vectors. Unit activities are represented by the bar graphs above each unit. Notice that, by the time the last input pattern is presented, the network output, represented by the output of the rightmost unit, is high, indicating that the STP is a close match to that pattern encoded by the sequence of weights in the network.

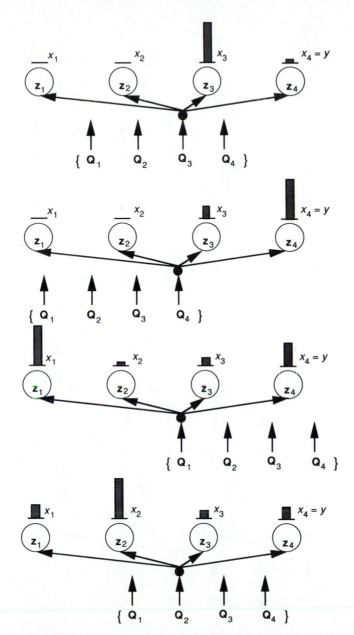

Figure 9.8 In this sequence, the network is the same as that shown in Figure 9.7, as are the input patterns. In this case, however, the input patterns are presented to the network out of sequence. By the time the last input pattern is presented, the network output is low, indicating that the network has not recognized the sequence.

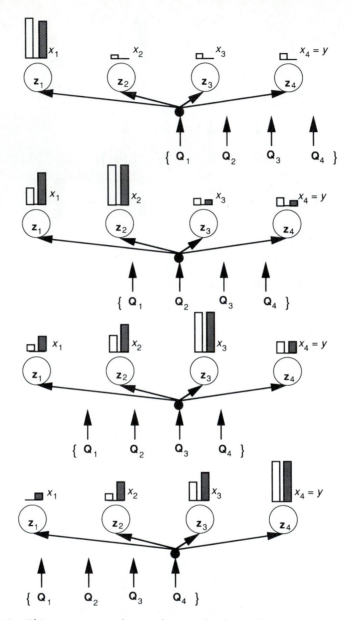

Figure 9.9 This sequence shows the results from the presentation of an STP at two different rates. The activities represented by the unshaded bar graphs are for the case where each spatial pattern is presented and held for a certain time, t, before the next pattern is presented. The activities represented by the shaded bar graphs are for the case where each spatial pattern is presented for a time, $t/2$. Note that, in both cases, the network output is high.

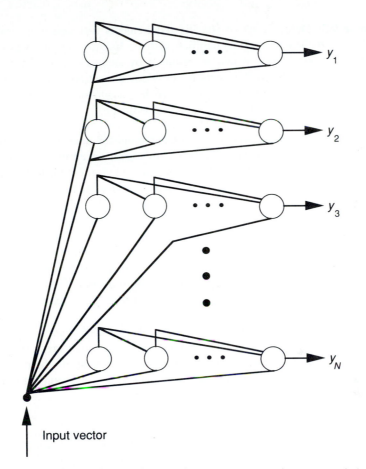

Figure 9.10 A layered STN for word recognition is shown. Each layer is tuned to recognize a single word. Each unit in each layer receives the identical series of input vectors as a word is spoken and analyzed by the spectrum analyzer. After each word is presented, the largest y value indicates the layer that most closely matched the STP.

word spoken quickly? Different words with the same ending could result in ambiguous results. The layered architecture that we have described represents only a conceptual foundation for a realistic speech-recognition system.

Exercise 9.2: With the system described in this section, two different STPs having the same final pattern vector could result in a large output from the same layer (since the rightmost unit is stimulated last in each case). Suggest modifications to the network that could alleviate this error.

Exercise 9.3: Define a set of specific requirements that you think should be met by any realistic speech-recognition system. Estimate the amount of computational resources that would be required by such a system, based on the architecture described in this section. Provide your answer in terms of *operations per second*, where an operation can be an add or a multiply. List all assumptions that you made to arrive at your estimate.

If we reflect on the architecture of our proposed speech-recognition system, it may appear somewhat inefficient to assign an entire layer of PEs to a single word. In the previous paragraph, we called attention to the fact that some words are subsets of others, so there is bound to be some redundancy in our system. Even at the level of individual PEs, there is likely to be a fair amount of repetition. By taking advantage of this fact, we might be able to reduce the computational load on our system. Figure 9.11 illustrates a simple example. Eliminating redundant units, as shown in the figure, will increase the efficiency of our network but may complicate the interpretation of the outputs from individual layers. For example, in the case of a subset word, the output of one entire layer may feed into the first unit of a layer representing the superset word.

Rather than continue this piecemeal analysis, we shall simply conclude that, ultimately, the most efficient network may be one in which many (or most, or all) units are connected to many (or most, or all) other units. In the next section, we shall describe such an architecture, and shall show a learning algorithm that allows a time sequence to be learned by the network.

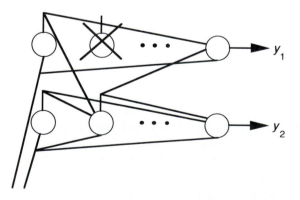

Figure 9.11   This figure shows how to eliminate a redundant unit in a layered STN. Unit 2 on layers 1 and 2 have the same weight vector. By reconnecting the units as shown, we can eliminate one unit from the network.

9.3 THE SEQUENTIAL COMPETITIVE AVALANCHE FIELD

The network in Figure 9.12 represents the logical extrapolation from eliminating redundant elements in the layered STN described in the previous section. The structure is called a sequential, competitive avalanche field (SCAF) [3]. It is illustrated here as a one-dimensional array of PEs, although it could be constructed as a two-dimensional array. In a two-dimensional configuration, the SCAF resembles Kohonen's SOM described in Chapter 7. Both the SCAF and the SOM are made up of competing units, but the mechanism for mediating that competition differs in each case.

You should note from the architecture diagram that there are no outputs corresponding to the y values in the layered architecture described in the previous section. This fact complicates the interpretation of the network response to any particular STP. We shall first examine how the network responds to an STP, then shall discuss how the weight vectors are determined.

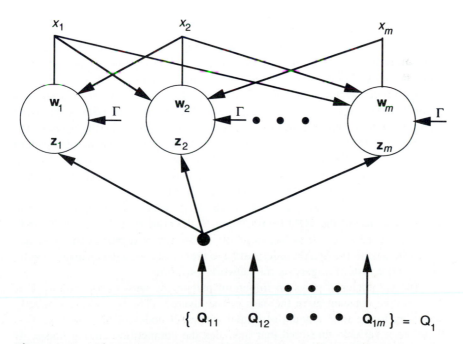

Figure 9.12 The sequential, competitive avalanche-field architecture. The output of each unit is connected to all other units through the weight vectors $\mathbf{w}_i$. The $\mathbf{z}_i$ are the weight vectors on the input connections. The global parameter Γ mediates the competition in the network as described in the text.

The equations that govern the response of individual processing elements on the SCAF are almost identical to those for the units on the layered STN. The input to the ith node has three components, $I_i^{(1)}$, $I_i^{(2)}$, and Γ where

$$I_i^{(1)} = \mathbf{z}_i \cdot \mathbf{Q} \tag{9.5}$$

$$I_i^{(2)} = \mathbf{w}_i \cdot \mathbf{x} \tag{9.6}$$

where $w_{ii} = 0$. Γ is called the system activity threshold; its value and function shall be described shortly. The total input to a node is calculated as

$$I_{i,\text{net}} = I_i - \Gamma \tag{9.7}$$

where

$$I_i = I_i^{(1)} + dI_i^{(2)} \tag{9.8}$$

and d represents a gain term on the contribution from other units. Typically, we shall want $0 < d \leq 1$.

The equation for the output of the node is given by the same attack function that we used on the single-layer STN in the previous section:

$$\dot{x}_i = A(-ax + b[I_i - \Gamma]^+)$$

where a and b are positive constants.

Note that the output of each unit is dependent on the current input vector, and on the recent history of the input vectors. The parameters of the attack function are adjusted such that the output quickly saturates in response to a matching input vector. Furthermore, the extended decay time of node outputs means that the network retains some knowledge of the input vectors that were presented within some recent time interval. This feature gives the network the ability to encode the time correlation of the input vectors. Instead of a pattern of activity that marches across a layer, as in the case of the layered STN, a **constellation** of activity develops over selected nodes in the SCAF. Figure 9.13 illustrates the response of a two-dimensional SCAF.

Once again, we shall point out the similarity between the SCAF response and the response of the SOM from Chapter 7, the primary difference being that, in the SOM, each unit fires and turns off before the next unit in the sequence fires, whereas, in the SCAF, units that have previously fired decay away slowly, so the entire pattern lingers on the network for a time.

The parameter Γ plays an important part in the network operation. Γ is not a simple constant as in the case of the layered STN, but it varies directly according to the total amount of output across all nodes of the network. Γ is therefore a variable threshold that mediates the competition among nodes. If recent input vectors find near matches, Γ rises quickly to keep the threshold high. If recent input vectors do not find matches, Γ decreases. In this way, Γ acts as an indicator of how closely incoming patterns match something the network has learned to recognize. A low value of Γ indicates that recent input pattern sequences are unknown to the network.

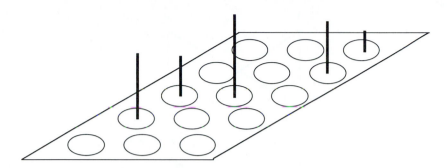

Figure 9.13   The response of a SCAF to a series of input vectors is shown. The vertical bars represent the output value of the associated node. Nodes with no bars have zero output. The constellation of activity that results can be associated with the identity of the most recent STP input.

Γ is calculated from the differential equation

$$\dot{\Gamma} = \alpha(S - T) + \beta\dot{S} \tag{9.9}$$

where T is a positive constant, called the **power-level target**, and

$$S = \sum_i x_i$$

is the total activity in the network. In practice, the choices of the parameters T, α, and β have a significant effect on the performance of the SCAF. You must adjust these parameters experimentally to tune the network.

9.3.1   Two-Node SCAF Example

To see how the behavior of the SCAF permits the network to distinguish between different time-sequences of patterns, we consider the simple case of a two-node system illustrated in Figure 9.14. We desire the system to distinguish between the two STPs, $Q_1 = \{\mathbf{Q}_{11}, \mathbf{Q}_{12}\}$ and $Q_2 = \{\mathbf{Q}_{12}, \mathbf{Q}_{11}\}$, where the position of the input vector in the list indicates the order of presentation.

Let us assume that the weights on unit 1, $\mathbf{z}_1$, are an exact match to the input pattern $\mathbf{Q}_{11}$, and that those on unit 2, $\mathbf{z}_2$, match $\mathbf{Q}_{12}$. This match can be arranged through training exactly like that done for the CPN, which this part of the SCAF resembles. Furthermore, we assume that $\mathbf{z}_1, \mathbf{z}_2, \mathbf{Q}_{11}$, and $\mathbf{Q}_{12}$ are normalized to unity, and that $\mathbf{z}_1$ and $\mathbf{Q}_{11}$ are orthogonal to $\mathbf{z}_2$ and $\mathbf{Q}_{12}$. We will also assume that the weight connecting the output of unit 1 to unit 2 is one, as indicated in the figure, and the weight connecting the output of unit 2 to unit 1

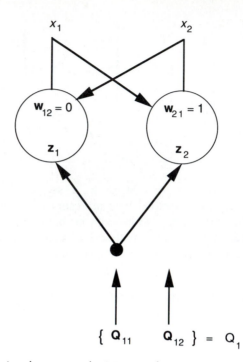

Figure 9.14   A simple two-node SCAF is shown.

is zero. The mechanism for training these weights will be described later. The final assumption is that the initial value for Γ is zero.

Consider what happens when $\mathbf{Q}_{11}$ is applied first. The net input to unit 1 is

$$
\begin{aligned}
I_{1,\text{net}} &= \mathbf{z}_1 \cdot \mathbf{Q}_{11} + w_{12}x_2 - \Gamma(t) \\
&= 1 + 0 - \Gamma(t)
\end{aligned}
$$

where we have explicitly shown gamma as a function of time. According to Eqs. (9.2) through (9.4), $\dot{x}_1 = -ax_1 + b(1 - \Gamma)$, so x_1 begins to increase, since Γ and x_1 are initially zero.

The net input to unit 2 is

$$
\begin{aligned}
I_{2,\text{net}} &= \mathbf{z}_2 \cdot \mathbf{Q}_{11} + w_{21}x_1 - \Gamma(t) \\
&= 0 + x_1 - \Gamma(t)
\end{aligned}
$$

Thus, $\dot{x}_2$ also begins to rise due to the positive contribution from x_1. Since both x_1 and x_2 are increasing from the start, the total activity in the network, $x_1 + x_2$, increases quickly. Under these conditions, $\Gamma(t)$ will begin to increase, according to Eq. (9.9).

After a short time, we remove $\mathbf{Q}_{11}$ and present $\mathbf{Q}_{12}$. x_1 will begin to decay, but slowly with respect to its rise time. Now, we calculate $I_{1,\text{net}}$ and $I_{2,\text{net}}$ again:

$$
\begin{aligned}
I_{1,\text{net}} &= \mathbf{z}_1 \cdot \mathbf{Q}_{12} + w_{12}x_2 - \Gamma(t) \\
&= 0 + 0 - \Gamma(t) \\
I_{2,\text{net}} &= \mathbf{z}_2 \cdot \mathbf{Q}_{12} + w_{21}x_1 - \Gamma(t) \\
&= 1 + x_1 - \Gamma(t)
\end{aligned}
$$

Using Eqs. (9.2) through (9.4) again, $\dot{x}_1 = -cax_1$ and $\dot{x}_2 = b(1 + x_1 - \Gamma)$, so x_1 continues to decay, but x_2 will continue to rise until $1 + x_1 < \Gamma(t)$. Figure 9.15(a) shows how x_1 and x_2 evolve as a function of time.

A similar analysis can be used to evaluate the network output for the opposite sequence of input vectors. When $\mathbf{Q}_{12}$ is presented first, x_2 will increase. x_1 remains at zero since $I_{1,\text{net}} = -\Gamma(t)$ and, thus, $\dot{x}_1 = -cax_1$. The total activity in the system is not sufficient to cause $\Gamma(t)$ to rise.

When $\mathbf{Q}_{11}$ is presented, the input to unit 1 is $I_1 = 1$. Even though x_2 is nonzero, the connection weight *is* zero, so x_2 does not contribute to the input to unit 1. x_1 begins to rise and $\Gamma(t)$ begins to rise in response to the increasing total activity. In this case, Γ does not increase as much as it did in the first example. Figure 9.15(b) shows the behavior of x_1 and x_2 for this example. The values of $\Gamma(t)$ for both cases are shown in Figure 9.15(c). Since $\Gamma(t)$ is the measure of recognition, we can conclude that $\mathbf{Q}_{11} \rightarrow \mathbf{Q}_{12}$ was recognized, but $\mathbf{Q}_{12} \rightarrow \mathbf{Q}_{11}$ was not.

9.3.2   Training the SCAF

As mentioned earlier, we accomplish training the weights on the connections from the inputs by methods already described for other networks. These weights encode the spatial part of the STP. We have drawn the analogy between the SOM and the spatial portion of the STN. In fact, a good method for training the spatial weights on the SCAF is with Kohonen's clustering algorithm (see Chapter 7). We shall not repeat the discussion of that training method here. We shall instead concentrate on the training of the temporal part of the SCAF.

Encoding the proper temporal order of the spatial patterns requires training the weights on the connections between the various nodes. This training uses the differential Hebbian learning law (also referred to as the Kosko–Klopf learning law):

$$
\dot{w}_{ij} = (-cw_{ij} + dx_ix_j)U(\dot{x}_i)U(-\dot{x}_j) \tag{9.10}
$$

where c and d are positive constants, and

$$
U(s) = \begin{cases} 1 & s > 0 \\ 0 & s \leq 0 \end{cases} \tag{9.11}
$$

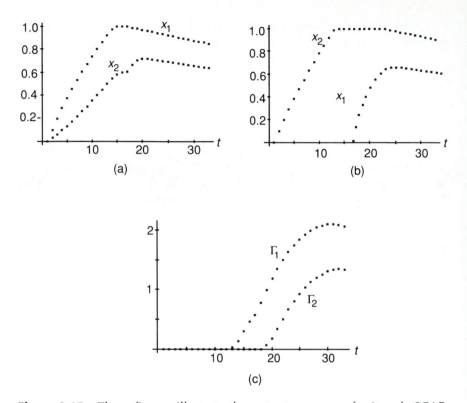

Figure 9.15   These figures illustrate the output response of a 2-node SCAF.
(a) This graph shows the results of a numerical simulation of
the two output values during the presentation of the sequence
$\mathbf{Q}_{11} \rightarrow \mathbf{Q}_{12}$. The input pattern changes at $t = 17$. (b) This
graph shows the results for the presentation of the sequence
$\mathbf{Q}_{12} \rightarrow \mathbf{Q}_{11}$. (c) This figure shows how the value of Γ evolves
in each case. Γ_1 is for the case shown in (a), and Γ_2 is for
the case shown in (b).

Without the U factors, Eq. (9.10) resembles the Grossberg outstar law. The
U factors ensure that learning can occur ($\dot{w}_{ij}$ is nonzero) only under certain
conditions. These conditions are that x_i is increasing ($\dot{x}_i > 0$) at the same time
that x_j is decreasing ($-\dot{x}_j > 0$). When these conditions are met, both U factors
will be equal to one. Any other combination of $\dot{x}_i$ and $\dot{x}_j$ will cause one, or
both, of the Us to be zero.

The effect of the differential Hebbian learning law is illustrated in Figure 9.16, which refers back to the two-node SCAF in Figure 9.14. We want
to train the network to recognize that pattern $\mathbf{Q}_{11}$ precedes pattern $\mathbf{Q}_{12}$. In the
example that we did, we saw that the proper response from the network was

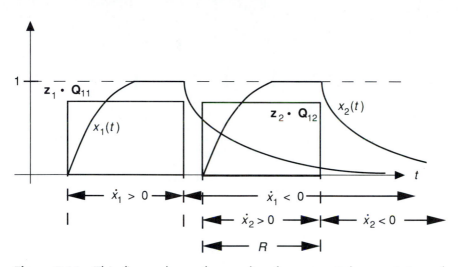

Figure 9.16 This figure shows the results of a sequential presentation of Q_{11} followed by Q_{12}. The net-input values of the two units are shown, along with the activity of each unit. Notice that we still consider that $\dot{x}_1 > 0$ and $\dot{x}_2 > 0$ throughout the periods indicated, even though the activity value is hard-limited to a maximum value of one. The region R indicates the time for which $\dot{x}_1 < 0$ and $\dot{x}_2 > 0$ simultaneously. During this time period, the differential Hebbian learning law causes w_{21} to increase.

achieved if $w_{12} = 0$ while $w_{21} = 1$. Thus, our learning law must be able to increase w_{21} without increasing w_{12}. Referring to Figure 9.16, you will see that the proper conditions will occur if we present the input vectors in their proper sequence during training. If we train the network by presenting Q_{11} followed by Q_{12}, then x_2 will be increasing while x_1 is decreasing, as indicated by the region, R, in Figure 9.16. The weight, w_{12}, remains at zero since the conditions are never right for it to learn. The weight, w_{21}, *does* learn, resulting in the configuration shown in Figure 9.14.

9.3.3 Time-Dilation Effects

The output values of nodes in the SCAF network decay slowly in time with respect to the rate at which new patterns are presented to the network. Viewed as a whole, the pattern of output activity across all of the nodes varies on a time scale somewhat longer than the one for the input patterns. This is a time-dilation effect, which can be put to good use.

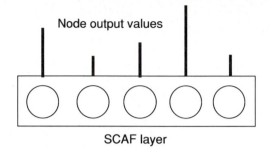

Figure 9.17   This representation of a SCAF layer shows the output values as vertical lines.

Figure 9.17 shows a representation of a SCAF with circles as the nodes. The vertical lines represent hypothetical output values for the nodes. As the input vectors change, the output of the SCAF will change: New units may saturate while others decay, although this decay will occur at a rate slightly slower than the rate at which new input vectors are presented. For STPs that are sampled frequently—say, every few milliseconds—the variation of the output values may still be too quick to be followed by a human observer. Suppose, however, that the output values from the SCAF were themselves used as input vectors to another SCAF. Since these outputs vary at a slower rate than the original input vectors, they can be sampled at a lower frequency. The output values of this second SCAF would decay even more slowly than those of the previous layer. Conceptually, this process can be continued until a layer is reached where the output patterns vary on a time scale that is equal to the total time necessary to present a complete sequence of patterns to the original network. The last output values would be essentially stationary. A single set of output values from the last slab would represent an entire series of patterns making up one complete STP. Figure 9.18 shows such a system based on a hierarchy of SCAF layers.

The stationary output vector can be used as the input vector to one of the spatial pattern-classification networks. The spatial network can learn to classify the stationary input vectors by the methods discussed previously. A complete spatiotemporal pattern-recognition and pattern-classification system can be constructed in this manner.

Exercise 9.4: No matter how fast input vectors are presented to a SCAF, the outputs can be made to linger if the parameters of the attack function are adjusted such that, once saturated, a node output decays very slowly. Such an arrangement would appear to eliminate the need for the layered SCAF architecture proposed in the previous paragraphs. Analyze the response of a SCAF to an arbitrary STP in the limiting case where saturated nodes never decay.

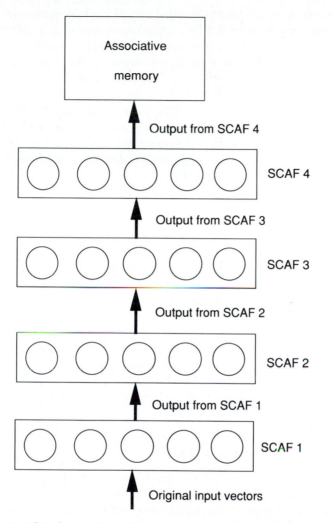

Figure 9.18 This hierarchy of SCAF layers is used for spatiotemporal pattern classification. The outputs from each layer are sampled at a rate slower than the rate at which inputs to that layer change. The output from the top layer, essentially a spatial pattern, can be used as an input to an associative network that classifies the original STP.

9.4 APPLICATIONS OF STNS

We suggested earlier in this chapter that STNs would be useful in areas such as speech recognition, radar analysis, and sonar-echo classification. To date, the dearth of literature indicates that little work has been done with this promising architecture.

A prototype sonar-echo classification system was built by General Dynamics Corporation using the layered STN architecture described in Section 9.2 [8]. In that study, time slices of the incoming sonar signals were converted to power spectra, which were then presented to the network in the proper time sequence. After being trained on seven civilian boats, the network was able to identify correctly each of these vessels from the latter's passive sonar signature.

The developers of the SCAF architecture experimented with a 30 by 30 SCAF, where outputs from individual units are connected randomly to other units. Apparently, the network performance was encouraging, as the developers are reportedly working on new applications. Details of those applications are not available at the time of this writing.

9.5   STN SIMULATION

In this section, we shall describe the design of the simulator for the spatiotemporal network. We shall focus on the implementation of a one-layer STN, and shall show how that STN can be extended to encompass multilayer (and multinetwork) STN architectures. The implementation of the SCAF architecture is left to you as an exercise.

We begin this section, as we have all previous simulation discussions, with a presentation of the data structures used to construct the STN simulator. From there, we proceed with the development of the algorithms used to perform signal processing within the simulator. We close this section with a discussion of how a multiple STN structure might be created to record a temporal sequence of related patterns.

9.5.1   STN Data Structures

The design of the STN simulator is reminiscent of the design we used for the CPN in Chapter 6. We therefore recommend that you review Section 6.4 prior to continuing here. The reason for the similarity between these two networks is that both networks fit precisely the processing structure we defined for performing competitive processing within a layer of units.[3] The units in both the STN and the competitive layer of the CPN operate by processing normalized input vectors, and even though competition in the CPN suppresses the output from all but the winning unit(s), all network units generate an output signal that is distributed to other PEs.

The major difference between the competitive layer in the CPN and the STN structure is related to the fact that the output from each unit in the STN becomes an input to all subsequent network units *on the layer*, whereas the lateral connections in the CPN simulation were handled by the host computer

---

[3]Although the STN is *not* competitive in the same sense that the hidden layer in the CPN is, we shall see that STN units respond actively to inputs in much the same way that CPN hidden-layer units respond.

system, and never were actually modeled. Similarly, the interconnections be-tween units on the layer in the STN can be accounted for by the processing algorithms performed in the host computer, so we do not need to account for those connections in the simulator design.

Let us now consider the top-level data structure needed to model an STN. As before, we will construct the network as a record containing pointers to the appropriate lower-level structures, and containing any network specific data parameters that are used globally within the network. Therefore, we can create an STN structure through the following record declaration:

```
record STN =
  begin
    UNITS : ^layer;        {pointer to network units}
    a, b, c, d : float;    {network parameters}
    gamma : float;         {constant value for gamma}
    upper : ^STN;          {pointer to next STN}
    lower : ^STN;          {pointer to previous STN}
    y : float;             {output of last STN element}
  end record;
```

Notice that, as illustrated in Figure 9.19, this record definition differs from all previous network record declarations in that we have included a means for

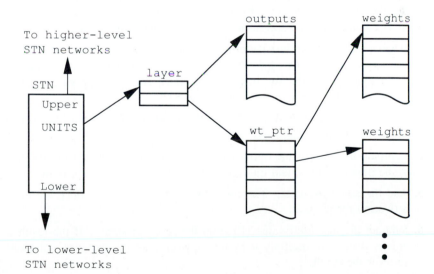

Figure 9.19   The data structure of the STN simulator is shown. Notice that, in this network structure, there are pointers to other network records above and below to accommodate multiple STNs. In this manner, the same input data can be propagated efficiently through multiple STN structures.

stacking multiple networks through the use of a doubly linked list of network record pointers. We include this capability for two reasons:

1. As described previously, a network that recognizes only *one* pattern is not of much use. We must therefore consider how to integrate *multiple networks* as part of our simulator design.

2. When multiple STNs are used to *time dilate* temporal patterns (as in the SCAF), the activity patterns of the network units can be used as input patterns to another network for further classification.

Finally, inspection of the STN record structure reveals that there is nothing about the STN that will require further modifications or extensions to the generic simulator structure we proposed in Chapter 1. We are therefore free to begin developing STN algorithms.

9.5.2   STN Algorithms

Let us begin by considering the sequence of operations that must be performed by the computer to simulate the STN. Using the speech-recognition example as described in Section 9.2.1 as the basis for the processing model, we can construct a list of the operations that must be performed by the STN simulator.

1. Construct the network, and initialize the input connections to the units such that the first unit in the layer has the first normalized input pattern contained in its connections, the second unit has the second pattern, and so on.

2. Begin processing the test pattern by zeroing the outputs from all units in the network (as well as the STN.y value, since it is a duplicate copy of the output value from the last network unit), and then applying the first normalized test vector to the input of the STN.

3. Calculate the inner product between the input test vector and the weight vector for the first unprocessed unit.

4. Compute the sum of the outputs from all units on the layer from the first to the previous units, and multiply the result by the network d term.

5. Add the result from step 3 to the result from step 4 to produce the input activation for the unit.

6. Subtract the threshold value (Γ) from the result of step 5. If the result is greater than zero, multiply it by the network b term; otherwise, substitute zero for the result.

7. Multiply the negative of the network a term by the previous output from the unit, and add the result to the value produced in step 6.

8. If the result of step 7 was less than or equal to zero, multiply it by the network c term to produce $\dot{x}$. Otherwise, use the result of step 7 without modification as the value for $\dot{x}$.

9. Compute the attack value for the unit by multiplying the $\dot{x}$ value calculated in step 8 by a small value indicating the network update rate (δt) to produce the update value for the unit output. Update the unit output by adding the computed attack value to the current unit output value.

10. Repeat steps 3 through 9 for each unit in the network.

11. Repeat steps 3 through 10 for the duration of the time step, Δt. The number of repetitions that occur during this step will be a function of the sampling frequency for the specific application.

12. Apply the next time-sequential test vector to the network input, and repeat steps 3 through 11.

13. After all the time-sequential test vectors have been applied, use the output of the last unit on the layer as the output value for the network for the given STP.

Notice that we have assumed that the network units update at a rate much more rapid than the sampling rate of the input (i.e., the value for δt is much smaller than the value of Δt). Since the actual sampling frequency (given by $\frac{1}{\Delta t}$) will always be application dependent, we shall assume that the network must update itself 100 times for each input pattern. Thus, the ratio of δt to Δt is 0.01, and we can use this ratio as the value for δt in our simulations.

We shall also assume that you will provide the routines necessary to perform the first two operations in the list. We therefore begin developing the simulator algorithms with the routine needed to propagate a given input pattern vector to a specified unit on the STN. This routine will encompass the operations described in steps 3 through 5.

```
function activation (net: STN; unumber:integer;
                     invec:^float[])
                return float;
{propagate the given input vector to the STN unit number}

var i : integer;                      {iteration counter}
    sum : float;                        {accumulator}
    others : float;               {unit output accumulator}
    connects : ^float[];          {locate connection array}
    unit : ^float[];                 {locate unit outputs}

begin
  sum = 0;                          {initialize accumulator}
  others = 0;                                      {ditto}
  unit = net.UNITS^.OUTS;          {locate unit arrays}
  connects = net.UNITS^.WEIGHTS[unumber];

  for i = 1 to length(invec)    {for all input elements}
    do                          {compute sum of products}
       sum = sum + connects[i] * invec[i];
    end do;
```

```
for i = 1 to (unumber - 1)  {sum other units outputs}
  do
    others = others + unit[i];
  end do;

return (sum + net.d * others);   {return activation}
end function;
```

The `activation` routine will allow us to compute the input-activation value for any unit in the STN. What we now need is a routine that will convert a given input value to the appropriate output value for any network unit. This service will be performed by the `Xdot` function, which we shall now define. Note that this routine performs the functions specified in steps 6 through 8 in the processing list above for any STN unit.

```
function Xdot (net:STN; unumber:integer; inval:float)
                return float;
{convert the input value for the specified unit to
                                  output value}

var outval : float;
   unit : ^float[];

begin
 unit = net.UNITS^.OUTS;    {access unit output array}
 outval = inval - net.gamma;    {threshold unit input}

 if (outval > 0)                        {if unit is on}
 then outval = outval * net.b {scale the unit output}
 else outval = 0;                       {else unit is off}

 outval = outval + unit[unumber] * -net.a;

 if (outval <= 0)                 {factor in decay term}
 then outval = outval * net.c;

 return (outval);                 {return delta x value}
end function;
```

All that remains at this point is to define a top-level procedure to tie together the signal-propagation routines, and to iterate for every unit in the network. These functions are embodied in the following procedure.

```
procedure propagate (net:STN; invec:^float[]);
{propagate an input vector through the STN}

const dt = 0.01;                  {network update rate}

var i : integer;                       {iteration counter}
   how_many : integer;        {number of units in STN}
   dx : float;                         {computed Xdot value}
   inval : float;                     {input activation}
   unit : ^float[];              {locate unit output array}
```

```
begin
unit = net.UNITS^.OUTS;      {locate the output array}
how_many = length(unit);        {save number of units}

for i = 1 to how_many       {for all units in the STN}
   do                         {generate output from input}
      inval = activation (net, i, invec);
      dx = Xdot (net, i, inval);
      unit[i] = unit[i] + (dx * dt);
   end do;

net.y = unit[how_many];         {save last unit output}
end procedure;
```

The propagate procedure will perform a complete signal propagation of *one* input vector through the entire STN. For a true spatiotemporal pattern-classification operation, propagate would have to be performed many times[4] for every Q_i patterns that compose the spatiotemporal pattern to be processed. If the network recognized the temporal pattern sequence, the value contained in the STN.y slot would be relatively high after all patterns had been propagated.

9.5.3 STN Training

In the previous discussion, we considered an STN that was *trained by initialization*. Training the network in this manner is fine if we know all the training vectors prior to building the network simulator. But what about those cases where it is preferable to defer training until after the network is operational? Such occurrences are common when the training environment is rather large, or when training-data acquisition is cumbersome. In such cases, is it possible to train an STN to record (and eventually to replay) data patterns collected at run time?

The answer to this question is a qualified "yes." The reason it is qualified is that the STN is not undergoing training in the same sense that most of the other networks described in this text are trained. Rather, we shall take the approach that an STN can be *constructed dynamically*, thus simulating the effect of training. As we have seen, the standard STN is constructed and *initialized* to contain the normalized form of the pattern to be encoded at each timestep in the connections of the individual network units. To *train* an STN, we will simply cause our program to *create a new STN* whenever a new pattern to be learned is available. In this manner, we construct specialized STNs that can then be exercised using all of the algorithms developed previously.

The only special consideration is that, with multiple networks in the computer simultaneously, we must take care to ensure that the networks remain accessible and consistent. To accomplish this feat, we shall simply link together

---

[4]It would have to be performed essentially $\frac{\Delta t}{\delta t}$ times, where Δt is the inverse of the sampling frequency for the application, and δt is the time that it takes the host computer to perform the propagate routine one time.

the network structures in a doubly linked list that a top-level routine can then access sequentially. A side benefit to this approach is that we have now created a means of collecting a number of *related* STPs, and have grouped them together sequentially. Thus, we can utilize this structure to encode (and recognize) a *sequence* of related patterns, such as the sonar signatures of different submarines, using the output from the most active STN as an indication of the type of submarine.

The disadvantage to the STN, as mentioned earlier, is that it will require many concurrent STN simulations to begin to tackle problems that can be considered nontrivial.[5] There are two approaches to solving this dilemma, both of which we leave to you as exercises. The first alternative method is to eliminate redundant network elements whenever possible, as was illustrated in Figure 9.11 and described in the previous section. The second method is to implement the SCAF network, and to combine many SCAF's with an associative-memory network (such as a BPN or CPN, as described in Chapters 3 and 6 respectively) to decode the output of the final SCAF.

Programming Exercises

9.1. Code the STN simulator and verify its operation by constructing multiple STNs, each of which is coded to recognize a letter sequence as a word. For example, consider the sequence "N E U R A L" versus the sequence "N E U R O N." Assume that two STNs are constructed and initialized such that each can recognize one of these two sequences. At what point do the STNs begin to fail to respond when presented with the wrong letter sequence?

9.2. Create several STNs that recognize letter sequences corresponding to different words. Stack them to form simple sentences, and determine which (if any) STNs fail to respond when presented with word sequences that are similar to the encoded sequences.

9.3. Construct an STN simulator that removes the redundant nodes for the word-recognition application described in Programming Exercise 9.1. Show listings for any new (or modified) data structures, as well as for code. Draw a diagram indicating the structure of the network. Show how your new data structures lend themselves to performing this simulation.

9.4. Construct a simulator for the SCAF network. Show the data structures required, and a complete listing of code required to implement the network. Be sure to allow multiple SCAFs to feed one another, in order to stack networks. Also describe how the output from your SCAF simulator would tie into a BPN simulator to perform the associative-memory function at the output.

---

[5]That is not to say that the STN should be considered a trivial network. There are many applications where the STN might provide an excellent solution, such as voiceprint classification for controlling access to protected environments.

9.5. Describe a method for training a BPN simulator to recognize the output of a SCAF. Remember that training in a BPN is typically completed before that network is first applied to a problem.

Suggested Readings

There is not a great deal of information available about Hecht-Nielsen's STN implementation. Aside from the papers cited in the text, you can refer to his book for additional information [4].

On the subject of STP recognition in general, and speech recognition in particular, there are a number of references to other approaches. For a general review of neural networks for speech recognition, see the papers by Lippmann [5, 6, 7]. For other methods see, for example, Grajski et al. [1] and Williams and Zipser [9].

Bibliography

[1] Kamil A. Grajski, Dan P. Witmer, and Carson Chen. A combined DSP and artificial neural network (ANN) approach to the classification of time series data. $e^x ponent$: *Ford Aerospace Technical Journal*, pages 20–25, Winter, 1989/1990.

[2] Stephen Grossberg. Learning by neural networks. In Stephen Grossberg, editor, *Studies of Mind and Brain*. D. Reidel Publishing, Boston, MA, pp. 65–156, 1982.

[3] Robert Hecht-Nielsen. Nearest matched filter classification of spatiotemporal patterns. Technical report, Hecht-Nielsen Neurocomputer Corporation, San Diego CA, June 1986.

[4] Robert Hecht-Nielsen. *Neurocomputing*. Addison-Wesley, Reading, MA, 1990.

[5] Richard P. Lippmann and Ben Gold. Neural-net classifiers useful for speech recognition. In *Proceedings of the IEEE First International Conference on Neural Networks*, San Diego, CA, pp. IV-417-IV-426, June 1987. IEEE.

[6] Richard P. Lippmann. Neural network classifiers for speech recognition. *The Lincoln Laboratory Journal*, 1(1):107–124, 1988.

[7] Richard P. Lippmann. Review of neural networks for speech recognition. *Neural Computation*, 1(1):1–38, Spring 1989.

[8] Robert L. North. Neurocomputing: Its impact on the future of defense systems. *Defense Computing*, 1(1), January–February 1988.

[9] Ronald J. Williams and David Zipser. A learning algorithm for continually running fully recurrent neural networks. *Neural Computation*, 1(2):270–280, 1989.

CHAPTER

The Neocognitron

ANS architectures such as backpropagation (see Chapter 3) tend to have general applicability. We can use a single network type in many different applications by changing the network's size, parameters, and training sets. In contrast, the developers of the neocognitron set out to tailor an architecture for a specific application: recognition of handwritten characters. Such a system has a great deal of practical application, although, judging from the introductions to some of their papers, Fukushima and his coworkers appear to be more interested in developing a model of the brain [4, 3].[1] To that end, their design was based on the seminal work performed by Hubel and Weisel elucidating some of the functional architecture of the visual cortex.

We could not begin to provide a complete accounting of what is known about the anatomy and physiology of the mammalian visual system. Nevertheless, we shall present a brief and highly simplified description of some of that system's features as an aid to understanding the basis of the neocognitron design.

Figure 10.1 shows the main pathways for neurons leading from the retina back to the area of the brain known as the visual, or striate, cortex. This area is also known as area 17. The optic nerve is made up of axons from nerve cells called retinal ganglia. The ganglia receive stimulation indirectly from the light-receptive rods and cones through several intervening neurons.

Hubel and Weisel used an amazing technique to discern the function of the various nerve cells in the visual system. They used microelectrodes to record the response of individual neurons in the cortex while stimulating the retina with light. By applying a variety of patterns and shapes, they were able to determine the particular stimulus to which a neuron was most sensitive.

The retinal ganglia and the cells of the lateral geniculate nucleus (LGN) appear to have circular receptive fields. They respond most strongly to circular

---

[1]This statement is intended not as a negative criticism, but rather as justification for the ensuing, short discussion of biology.

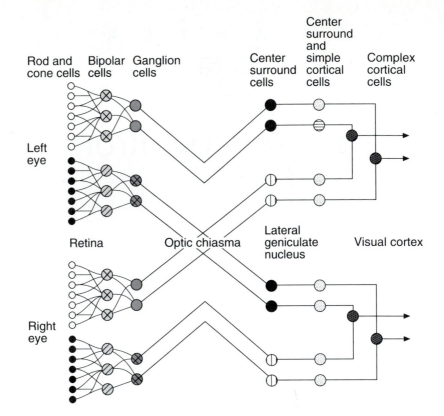

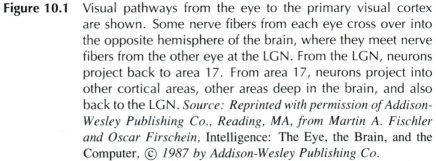

Figure 10.1 Visual pathways from the eye to the primary visual cortex are shown. Some nerve fibers from each eye cross over into the opposite hemisphere of the brain, where they meet nerve fibers from the other eye at the LGN. From the LGN, neurons project back to area 17. From area 17, neurons project into other cortical areas, other areas deep in the brain, and also back to the LGN. *Source: Reprinted with permission of Addison-Wesley Publishing Co., Reading, MA, from Martin A. Fischler and Oscar Firschein,* Intelligence: The Eye, the Brain, and the Computer, © *1987 by Addison-Wesley Publishing Co.*

spots of light of a particular size on a particular part of the retina. The part of the retina responsible for stimulating a particular ganglion cell is called the receptive field of the ganglion. Some of these receptive fields give an excitatory response to a centrally located spot of light, and an inhibitory response to a larger, more diffuse spot of light. These fields have an on-center off-surround response characteristic (see Chapter 6, Section 6.1). Other receptive fields have the opposite characteristic, with an inhibitory response to the centrally located spot—an off-center on-surround response characteristic.

The visual cortex itself is composed of six layers of neurons. Most of the neurons from the LGN terminate on cells in layer IV. These cells have circularly symmetric receptive fields like the retinal ganglia and the cells of the LGN. Further along the pathway, the response characteristic of the cells begins to increase in complexity. Cells in layer IV project to a group of cells directly above called **simple cells**. Simple cells respond to line segments having a particular orientation. Simple cells project to cells called **complex cells**. Complex cells respond to lines having the same orientation as their corresponding simple cells, although complex cells appear to integrate their response over a wider receptive field. In other words, complex cells are less sensitive to the position of the line on the retina than are the simple cells. Some complex cells are sensitive to line segments of a particular orientation that are moving in a particular direction.

Cells in different layers of area 17 project to different locations of the brain. For example, cells in layers II and III project to cells in areas 18 and 19. These areas contain cells called **hypercomplex cells**. Hypercomplex cells respond to lines that form angles or corners and that move in various directions across the receptive field.

The picture that emerges from these studies is that of a hierarchy of cells with increasingly complex response characteristics. It is not difficult to extrapolate this idea of a hierarchy into one where further data abstraction takes place at higher and higher levels. The neocognitron design adopts this hierarchical structure in a layered architecture, as illustrated schematically in Figure 10.2.

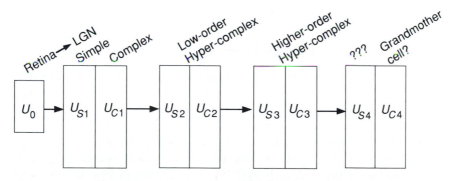

Figure 10.2 The neocognitron hierarchical structure is shown. Each box represents a level in the neocognitron comprising a simple-cell layer, U_{Si}, and a complex-cell layer, U_{Ci}, where i is the layer number. U_0 represents signals originating on the retina. There is also a suggested mapping to the hierarchical structure of the brain. The network concludes with single cells that respond to complex visual stimuli. These final cells are often called *grandmother cells* after the notion that there may be some cell in your brain that responds to complex visual stimuli, such as a picture of your grandmother.

We remind you that the description of the visual system that we have presented here is highly simplified. There is a great deal of detail that we have omitted. The visual system does not adhere to a strict hierarchical structure as presented here. Moreover, we do not subscribe to the notion that grandmother cells per se exist in the brain. We know from experience that strict adherence to biology often leads to a failed attempt to design a system to perform the same function as the biological prototype: Flight is probably the most significant example. Nevertheless, we do promote the use of neurobiological results if they prove to be appropriate. The neocognitron is an excellent example of how neurobiological results can be used to develop a new network architecture.

10.1 NEOCOGNITRON ARCHITECTURE

The neocognitron design evolved from an earlier model called the *cognitron*, and there are several versions of the neocognitron itself. The one that we shall describe has nine layers of PEs, including the retina layer. The system was designed to recognize the numerals 0 through 9, regardless of where they are placed in the field of view of the retina. Moreover, the network has a high degree of tolerance to distortion of the character and is fairly insensitive to the size of the character. This first architecture contains only feedforward connections. In Section 10.3.2, we shall describe a network that has feedback as well as feedforward connections.

10.1.1 Functional Description

The PEs of the neocognitron are organized into modules that we shall refer to as **levels**. A single level is shown in Figure 10.3. Each level consists of two **layers**: a layer of **simple cells**, or S-cells, followed by a layer of **complex cells**, or C-cells. Each layer, in turn, is divided into a number of **planes**, each of which consists of a rectangular array of PEs. On a given level, the S-layer and the C-layer may or may not have the same number of planes. All planes on a given layer will have the same number of PEs; however, the number of PEs on the S-planes can be different from the number of PEs on the C-planes at the same level. Moreover, the number of PEs per plane can vary from level to level. There are also PEs called V_S-cells and V_C-cells that are not shown in the figure. These elements play an important role in the processing, but we can describe the functionality of the system without reference to them.

We construct a complete network by combining an input layer, which we shall call the *retina*, with a number of levels in a hierarchical fashion, as shown in Figure 10.4. That figure shows the number of planes on each layer for the particular implementation that we shall describe here. We call attention to the

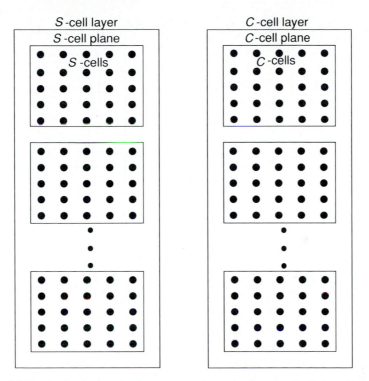

Figure 10.3   A single level of a neocognitron is shown. Each level consists of two layers, and each layer consists of a number of planes. The planes contain the PEs in a rectangular array. Data pass from the S-layer to the C-layer through connections that are not shown here. In neocognitrons having feedback, there also will be connections from the C-layer to the S-layer.

fact that there is nothing, in principle, that dictates a limit to the size of the network in terms of the number of levels.

The interconnection strategy is unlike that of networks that are fully interconnected between layers, such as the backpropagation network described in Chapter 3. Figure 10.5 shows a schematic illustration of the way units are connected in the neocognitron. Each layer of simple cells acts as a feature-extraction system that uses the layer preceding it as its input layer. On the first S-layer, the cells on each plane are sensitive to simple features on the retina—in this case, line segments at different orientation angles. Each S-cell on a single plane is sensitive to the same feature, but at different locations on the input layer. S-cells on different planes respond to different features.

As we look deeper into the network, the S-cells respond to features at higher levels of abstraction; for example, corners with intersecting lines at various

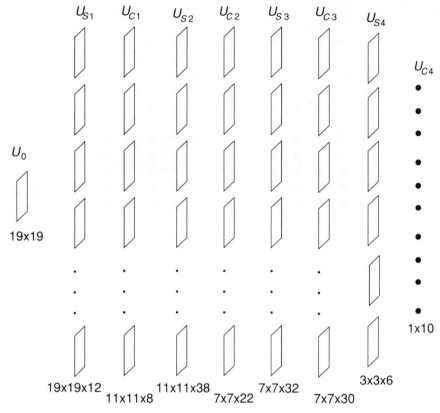

Figure 10.4   The figure shows the basic organization of the neocognitron
for the numeral-recognition problem. There are nine layers,
each with a varying number of planes. The size of each layer,
in terms of the number of processing elements, is given below
each layer. For example, layer U_{C2} has 22 planes of 7×7
processing elements arranged in a square matrix. The layer
of C-cells on the final level is made up of 10 planes, each
of which has a single element. Each element corresponds to
one of the numerals from 0 to 9. The identification of the
pattern appearing on the retina is made according to which
C-cell on the final level has the strongest response.

angles and orientations. The C-cells integrate the responses of groups of S-
cells. Because each S-cell is looking for the same feature in a different location,
the C-cells' response is less sensitive to the exact location of the feature on the
input layer. This behavior is what gives the neocognitron its ability to identify
characters regardless of their exact position in the field of the retina. By the
time we have reached the final layer of C-cells, the effective receptive field

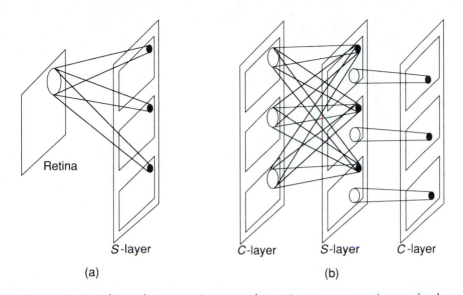

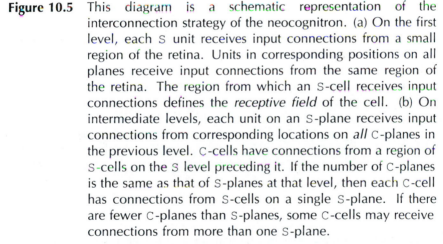

Figure 10.5   This diagram is a schematic representation of the interconnection strategy of the neocognitron. (a) On the first level, each S unit receives input connections from a small region of the retina. Units in corresponding positions on all planes receive input connections from the same region of the retina. The region from which an S-cell receives input connections defines the *receptive field* of the cell. (b) On intermediate levels, each unit on an S-plane receives input connections from corresponding locations on *all* C-planes in the previous level. C-cells have connections from a region of S-cells on the S level preceding it. If the number of C-planes is the same as that of S-planes at that level, then each C-cell has connections from S-cells on a single S-plane. If there are fewer C-planes than S-planes, some C-cells may receive connections from more than one S-plane.

of each cell is the entire retina. Figure 10.6 shows the character identification process schematically.

Note the slight difference between the first S-layer and subsequent S-layers in Figure 10.5. Each cell in a plane on the first S-layer receives inputs from a single input layer—namely, the retina. On subsequent layers, each S-cell plane receives inputs from each of the C-cell planes immediately preceding it. The situation is slightly different for the C-cell planes. Typically, each cell on a C-cell plane examines a small region of S-cells on a single S-cell plane. For example, the first C-cell plane on layer 2 would have connections to only a region of S-cells on the first S-cell plane of the previous layer. Ref-

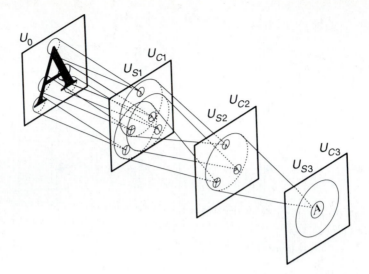

Figure 10.6   This figure illustrates how the neocognitron performs
                  its character-recognition function.   The neocognitron
                  decomposes the input pattern into elemental parts consisting
                  of line segments at various angles of rotation. The system
                  then integrates these elements into higher-order structures at
                  each successive level in the network. Cells in each level
                  integrate the responses of cells in the previous level over a
                  finite area. This behavior gives the neocognitron its ability to
                  identify characters regardless of their exact position or size
                  in the field of view of the retina. *Source: Reprinted with
                  permission from Kunihiko Fukushima, "A neural network for
                  visual pattern recognition."* IEEE Computer, *March 1988.* ©
                  1988 IEEE.

erence back to Figure 10.4 reveals that there is not necessarily a one-to-one
correspondence between C-cell planes and S-cell planes at each layer in the
system. This discrepancy occurs because the system designers found it advan-
tageous to combine the inputs from some S-planes to a single C-plane if the
features that the S-planes were detecting were similar. This tuning process
is evident in several areas of the network architecture and processing equations.

   The weights on connections to S-cells are determined by a training process
that we shall describe in Section 10.2.2. Unlike in many other network architectures (such as backpropagation), where each unit has a different weight vector,
all S-cells on a single plane share the same weight vector. Sharing weights
in this manner means that all S-cells on a given plane respond to the identical
feature in their receptive fields, as we indicated. Moreover, we need to train

only one S-cell on each plane, then to distribute the resulting weights to the other cells.

The weights on connections to C-cells are not modifiable in the sense that they are not determined by a training process. All C-cell weights are usually determined by being tailored to the specific network architecture. As with S-planes, all cells on a single C-plane share the same weights. Moreover, in some implementations, all C-planes on a given layer share the same weights.

10.2 NEOCOGNITRON DATA PROCESSING

In this section we shall discuss the various processing algorithms of the neocognitron cells. First we shall look at the S-cell data processing including the method used to train the network. Then, we shall describe processing on the C-layer.

10.2.1 *S*-Cell Processing

We shall first concentrate on the cells in a single plane of U_{S1}, as indicated in Figure 10.7. We shall assume that the retina, layer U_0, is an array of 19 by 19 pixels. Therefore, each U_{S1} plane will have an array of 19 by 19 cells. Each plane scans the entire retina for a particular feature. As indicated in the figure, each cell on a plane is looking for the identical feature but in a different location on the retina. Each S-cell receives input connections from an array of 3 by 3 pixels on the retina. The receptive field of each S-cell corresponds to the 3 by 3 array centered on the pixel that corresponds to the cell's location on the plane.

When building or simulating this network, we must make allowances for edge effects. If we surround the active retina with inactive pixels (outputs always set to zero), then we can automatically account for cells whose fields of view are centered on edge pixels. Neighboring S-cells scan the retina array displaced by one pixel from each other. In this manner, the entire image is scanned from left to right and top to bottom by the cells in each S-plane.

A single plane of V_C-cells is associated with the S-layer, as indicated in Figure 10.7. The V_C-plane contains the same number of cells as does each S-plane. V_C-cells have the same receptive fields as the S-cells in corresponding locations in the plane. The output of a V_C-cell goes to a single S-cell in every plane in the layer. The S-cells that receive inputs from a particular V_C-cell are those that occupy a position in the plane corresponding to the position of the V_C-cell. The output of the V_C-cell has an inhibitory effect on the S-cells. Figure 10.8 shows the details of a single S-cell along with its corresponding inhibitory cell.

Up to now, we have been discussing the first S-layer, in which cells receive input connections from a single plane (in this case the retina) in the previous layer. For what follows, we shall generalize our discussion to include the case

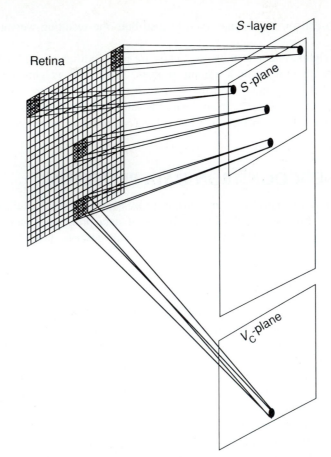

Figure 10.7   The retina, layer U_0, is a 19-by-19-pixel array, surrounded by inactive pixels to account for edge effects as described in the text. One of the S-planes is shown, along with an indication of the regions of the retina scanned by the individual cells. Associated with each S-layer in the system is a plane of V_C-cells. These cells receive input connections from the same receptive field as do the S-cells in corresponding locations in the plane. The processing done by these V_C-cells is described in the text.

of layers deeper in the network where an S-cell will receive input connections from all the planes on the previous C-layer.

Let the index k_l refer to the kth plane on level l. We can label each cell on a plane with a two-dimensional vector, with **n** indicating its position on the plane; then, we let the vector **v** refer to the *relative* position of a cell in the previous layer lying in the receptive field of unit **n**. With these definitions, we

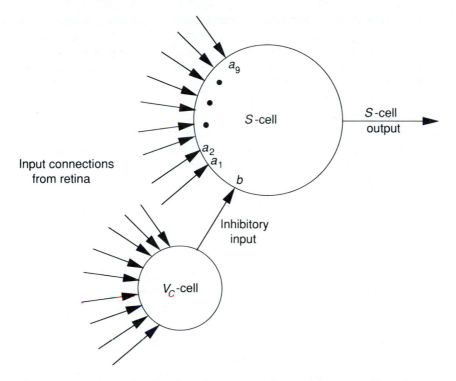

Figure 10.8   A single S-cell and corresponding inhibitory cell on the U_{S1} layer are shown. Each unit receives the identical nine inputs from the retina layer. The weights, a_i, on the S-cell determine the feature for which the cell is sensitive. Both the a_i weights on connections from the retina, and the weight, b, from the V_C-cells are modifiable and are determined during a training process, as described in the text.

can write the following equation for the output of any S-cell:

$$U_{S_l}(k_l, \mathbf{n}) =$$

$$r_l \cdot \phi \left[\frac{1 + \sum_{k_{l-1}=1}^{K_{l-1}} \sum_{\mathbf{v} \in A_l} a_l(k_{l-1}, \mathbf{v}, k_l) \cdot U_{C_{l-1}}(k_{l-1}, \mathbf{n} + \mathbf{v})}{1 + \frac{r_l}{1+r_l} b_l(k_l) \cdot V_{C_l}(\mathbf{n})} - 1 \right] \quad \textbf{(10.1)}$$

where the function ϕ is a linear threshold function given by

$$\phi(x) = \begin{cases} x & x \geq 0 \\ 0 & x < 0 \end{cases} \quad \textbf{(10.2)}$$

We have used the dot notation to indicate ordinary multiplication in Eq. (10.1), to enhance the readability of that expression.

Let's dissect these equations in some detail. The inner summation of Eq. (10.1) is the usual sum-of-products calculation of inputs, $U_{C_{l-1}}(k_{l-1}, \mathbf{n}+\mathbf{v})$, and weights, $a_l(k_{l-1}, \mathbf{v}, k_l)$. The sum extends over all units in the previous C-layer that lie within the receptive field of unit $\mathbf{n}$. Those units are designated by the vector $\mathbf{n}+\mathbf{v}$. Because we shall assume that all weights and cell output values are nonnegative, the sum-of-products calculation yields a measure of how closely the input pattern matches the weight vector on a unit.[2] We have labeled the receptive field A_l, indicating that the geometry of the receptive field is the same for all units on a particular layer. The outer summation of Eq. (10.1) extends over all of the K_{l-1} planes of the previous C-layer. In the case of U_{S1}, there would be no need for this outer summation.

The product, $b_l(k_l) \cdot V_{C_l}(\mathbf{n})$, in the denominator of Eq. (10.1), represents the inhibitory contribution of the V_C-cell. The parameter r_l, where $0 \leq r_l < \infty$, determines the cell's selectivity for a specific pattern. The factor $r_l/(1 + r_l)$ goes from zero to one as r_l goes from zero to infinity. Thus, for small values of r_l, the denominator of Eq. (10.1) could be relatively small compared to the numerator *even if the input pattern did not exactly match the weight vector*. This situation could result in a positive argument to the ϕ function. If r_l were large, then the match between the input pattern and the weights in the numerator of Eq. (10.1) would have to be more exact to overcome the inhibitory effects of the V_C-cell input. Notice also that this same r_l parameter appears as a multiplicative factor of the ϕ function. If r_l is small, and cell selectivity is small, this factor ensures that the output from the cell itself cannot become very large.

We can view the function of r_l in another way. We rewrite the argument of the function in Eq. (10.1) as

$$\frac{e - [r_l/(1 + r_l)]h}{1 + [r_l/(1 + r_l)]h}$$

where e is the net excitatory term and h is the net inhibitory term. According to Eq. (10.2), the S-cell output will be nonzero only if

$$e - \frac{r_l}{1 + r_l} h > 0$$

or,

$$\frac{e}{h} > \frac{r_l}{1 + r_l}$$

Thus, the quantity r_l determines the minimum relative strength of excitation versus inhibition that will result in a nonzero output of the unit. As r_l increases, $r_l/(1 + r_l) \rightarrow 1$. Therefore, a larger r_l requires a larger excitation relative to inhibition for a nonzero output.

---

[2]Although we have not said anything about normalizing the input vector or the weights, we could add this condition to our system design. Then, we could talk about *closeness* in terms of the angle between the input and weight vectors, as we did in Chapter 6.

Notice that neither of the weight expressions, $a_l(k_{l-1}, \mathbf{v}, k_l)$, or $b_l(k_l)$ depend explicitly on the position, $\mathbf{n}$, of the cell. Remember that all cells on a plane share the same weights, even the $b_l(k_l)$ weights, which we did not discuss previously.

We must now specify the output from the inhibitory nodes. The V_C-cell at position $\mathbf{n}$ has an output value of

$$V_{C_l}(\mathbf{n}) = \sqrt{\sum_{k_{l-1}=1}^{K_{l-1}} \sum_{\mathbf{v} \in A_l} c_l(\mathbf{v}) \cdot U^2_{C_{l-1}}(k_{l-1}, \mathbf{n} + \mathbf{v})} \qquad (10.3)$$

where $c_l(\mathbf{v})$ is the weight on the connection from a cell at position $\mathbf{v}$ of the V_C-cell's receptive field. These weights are not subject to training. They can take the form of any normalized function that decreases monotonically as the magnitude of $\mathbf{v}$ increases. One such function is [7]

$$c_l(\mathbf{v}) = \frac{1}{C(l)} \alpha_l^{r'(v)} \qquad (10.4)$$

where $r'(v)$ is the normalized distance between the cell located at position $\mathbf{v}$ and the center of the receptive field, and α_l is a constant less than 1 that determines the rate of falloff with increasing distance. The factor $C(l)$ is a normalization constant:

$$C(l) = \sum_{k_{l-1}}^{K_{l-1}} \sum_{\mathbf{v} \in A_l} \alpha_l^{r'(v)} \qquad (10.5)$$

The condition that the weights are normalized can be expressed as

$$\sum_{k_{l-1}}^{K_{l-1}} \sum_{\mathbf{v} \in A_l} c_l(\mathbf{v}) = 1 \qquad (10.6)$$

which is satisfied by Eqs. (10.4) and (10.5).[3] The form of the $c_l(\mathbf{v})$ function also affects the S-cells pattern selectivity by favoring patterns that are centrally located in the receptive field. We shall see in the next section that this same function modulates the weights, $a_l(k_{l-1}, \mathbf{v}, k_l)$, during learning. Thus, both excitatory inputs and inhibitory inputs will be stronger if the input pattern is centrally located in the cell's receptive field.

The particular form of Eq. (10.3) is that of a weighted, root-mean-square of the inputs to the V_C-cell. Looking back at Eq. (10.1), we can see that, in the S-cells, the net excitatory input to the cell is being compared to a measure of the average input signal. If the ratio of the net excitatory input to the net inhibitory input is greater than 1, the cell will have a positive output.

---

[3]If we impose the condition that the input vectors be normalized, as suggested in footnote 2, then we can relax the normalization condition on these weights.

Exercise 10.1: We can rewrite Eq. (10.1) for a single S-cell in the succinct form

$$U_S = r_l \phi \left[\frac{1+e}{1+h} - 1 \right] \tag{10.7}$$

where e and h represent total excitatory and inhibitory inputs to the cell, respectively, and we have absorbed the factor $r_l/(1 + r_l)$ into h. Show that, when the inhibitory input is very small, Eq. (10.7) can be written as

$$U_S \approx r_l \phi [e - h]$$

Exercise 10.2: Show that, when both e and h are very large in Eq. (10.7),

$$U_S \approx r_l \phi \left[\frac{e}{h} - 1 \right]$$

10.2.2   Training Weights on the S-Layers

There are several different methods for training the weights on the neocognitron. The method that we shall detail here is an unsupervised-learning algorithm designed by the original neocognitron designers. At the end of this section, we will mention a few alternatives to this approach.

Unsupervised Learning.   In principle, training proceeds as it does for many networks. First, an input pattern is presented at the input layer and the data are propagated through the network. Then, weights are allowed to make incremental adjustments according to the specified algorithm. After weight updates have occurred, a new pattern is presented at the input layer, and the process is repeated with all patterns in the training set until the network is classifying the input patterns properly.

In the neocognitron, sharing of weights on a given plane means that only a single cell on each plane needs to participate in the learning process. Once its weights have been updated, a copy of the new weight vector can be distributed to the other cells on the same plane. To understand how this works, we can think of the S-planes on a given layer as being stacked vertically on top of one another, aligned so that cells at corresponding locations are directly on top of one another. We can now imagine many overlapping columns running perpendicular to this stack. These columns define groups of S-cells, where all of the members in a group have receptive fields in approximately the same location of the input layer.

With this model in mind, we now apply an input pattern and examine the response of the S-cells in each column. To ensure that each S-cell provides a distinct response, we can initialize the a_l weights to small, positive random values. The b_l weights on the inhibitory connections can be initialized to zero. We first note the plane and position of the S-cell whose response is the strongest in each column. Then we examine the individual planes so that, if one plane contains two or more of these S-cells, we disregard all but the cell responding the strongest. In this manner, we will locate the S-cell on each plane whose response is the strongest, subject to the condition that each of those cells is in a different column. Those S-cells become the prototypes, or representatives, of all the cells on their respective planes. Likewise, the strongest responding V_C-cell is chosen as the representative for the other cells on the V_C-plane.

Once the representatives are chosen, weight updates are made according to the following equations:

$$\Delta a_l(k_{l-1}, \mathbf{v}, \hat{k}_l) = q_l c_{l-1}(\mathbf{v}) U_{C_{l-1}}(k_{l-1}, \hat{\mathbf{n}} + \mathbf{v}) \tag{10.8}$$

$$\Delta b_l(\hat{k}_l) = q_l V_{C_{l-1}}(\hat{\mathbf{n}}) \tag{10.9}$$

where q_l is the learning rate parameter, $c_{l-1}(\mathbf{v})$, is the monotonically decreasing function as described in the previous section, and the location of the representative for plane $\hat{k}_l$ is $\hat{\mathbf{n}}$.

Notice that the largest increases in the weights occur on those connections that have the largest input signal, $U_{C_{l-1}}(k_{l-1}, \hat{\mathbf{n}} + \mathbf{v})$. Because the S-cell whose weights are being modified was the one with the largest output, this learning algorithm implements a form of Hebbian learning. Notice also that weights can only increase, and that there is no upper bound on the weight value. The form of Eq. (10.1), for S-cell output, guarantees that the output value will remain finite, even for large weight values (see Exercise 10.2).

Once the cells on a given plane begin to respond to a certain feature, they tend to respond less to other features. After a short time, each plane will have developed a strong response to a particular feature. Moreover, as we look deeper into the network, planes will be responding to more complex features.

Other Learning Methods. The designers of the original neocognitron knew to what features they wanted each level, and each plane on a level, to respond. Under these circumstances, a set of training vectors can be developed for each layer, and the layers can be trained independently. Figure 10.9 shows the training patterns that were used to train the 38 planes on the second layer of the neocognitron illustrated previously in Figure 10.4.

It is also possible to select the representative cell for each plane in advance. Care must be taken, however, to ensure that the input pattern is presented in the proper location with respect to the representative's receptive field. Here again, some foreknowledge of the desired features is required.

Provided that the weight vectors and input vectors are normalized, weight updates to representative cells can be made according to the method described in Chapter 6 for competitive layers. To implement this method, you would essentially rotate the existing weight vector a little in the direction of the input

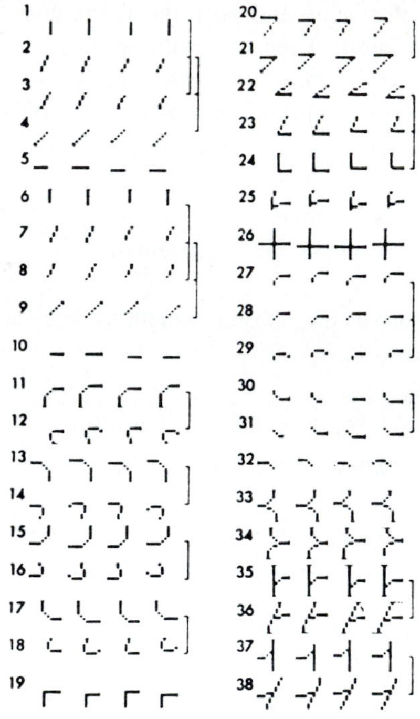

Figure 10.9 This figure shows the four patterns used to train each of the 38 planes on layer U_{S2} of the neocognitron designed to recognize the numerals 0 through 9. The square brackets indicate groupings of S-planes whose output connections converge on a single C-plane in the following layer. *Source: Reprinted with permission from Kunihiko Fukushima, Sei Miyake, and Takayuki Ito, "Neocognitron: a neural network model for a mechanism of visual pattern recognition." IEEE Transactions on Systems, Man, and Cybernetics, SMC-13(5), September/October 1983. © 1983 IEEE.*

vector. You would need to multiply the input vector by the monotonically decreasing function and renormalize first [6].

10.2.3 Processing on the *C*-Layer

The functions describing the C-cell processing are similar in form to those for the S-cells. Also like the S-layer, each C-layer has associated with it a single plane of inhibitory units that function in a manner similar to the V_C-cells on the S-layer. We label the output of these units $V_{S_l}(\mathbf{n})$.

Generally, units on a given C-plane receive input connections from one, or at most a small number of, S-planes on the preceding layer. V_S-cells receive input connections from all S-planes on the preceding layer.

The output of a C-cell is given by

$$U_{C_l}(k_l, \mathbf{n}) =$$
$$\psi\left[\frac{1 + \sum_{\kappa_l=1}^{K_l} j_l(\kappa_l, k_l) \sum_{\mathbf{v} \in D_l} d_l(\mathbf{v}) \cdot U_{S_l}(k_l, \mathbf{n} + \mathbf{v})}{1 + V_{S_l}(\mathbf{n})} - 1\right] \qquad \textbf{(10.10)}$$

where K_l is the number of S-planes at level l, $j_l(\kappa_l, k_l)$ is one or zero depending on whether S-plane κ_l is or is not connected to C-plane k_l, $d_l(\mathbf{v})$ is the weight on the connection from the S-cell at position $\mathbf{v}$ in the receptive field of the C-cell, and D_l defines the receptive-field geometry of the C-cell.

The function ψ is defined by

$$\psi(x) = \begin{cases} \dfrac{x}{\beta + x} & x \geq 0 \\ 0 & x < 0 \end{cases} \qquad \textbf{(10.11)}$$

where β is a constant. The output of the V_S-cells is given by

$$V_{S_l}(\mathbf{n}) = \frac{1}{K_l} \sum_{\kappa_l=1}^{K_l} \sum_{\mathbf{v} \in D_l} U_{S_l}(k_l, \mathbf{n} + \mathbf{v}) \cdot d_l(\mathbf{v}) \qquad \textbf{(10.12)}$$

The weights, $d_l(\mathbf{v})$, are fixed values with the same general form as the $c_l(\mathbf{v})$ described in the previous section, although Menon and Heinemann report satisfactory results if $d_l(\mathbf{v})$ is a uniform value across the receptive field [7].

Notice the absence of weights on the connection from the V_S-cell, as indicated in the denominator of Eq. (10.10). Also substitute Eq. (10.12) in Eq. (10.10) and notice the similarity between the numerator and denominator of the first term in the brackets. Equation (10.12) indicates that the V_S-cell is calculating the average input value for all the S-planes. In that case, Eq. (10.10) can have a nonzero value only if the excitatory response of the C-cell is greater than the average. This behavior is similar to that of the S-cells, although the measure of the average is different in each case.

In summary, only a certain percentage of S-cells and C-cells at each level respond with a positive output value. These are the cells whose excitation level exceeds that of the average cells.

10.3 PERFORMANCE OF THE NEOCOGNITRON

Figure 10.10 shows a typical response of cells in the nine-layer neocognitron trained to recognize handwritten numerals 0 through 9. This particular example shows the network being presented with the numeral 2. By the time the data have propagated back to the final layer, only two cells are giving any response at all. The cell corresponding to the numeral 2 shows the strongest response.

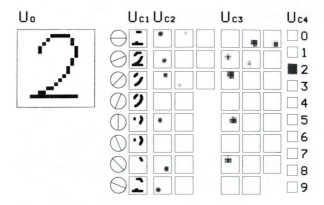

Figure 10.10   In this figure, the numeral 2 appears on the retina of the neocognitron. All the planes at each level are indicated by individual boxes. Cells within those planes that are responding to the input are indicated in black within the boxes. The planes on layer U_{C4} have only one cell per plane, each cell corresponding to one of the numbers from 0 to 9. The strength of the response from each unit on that layer is indicated by the degree of darkening in the associated box. *Source: Reprinted with permission of Addison-Wesley Publishing Co., Reading, MA, from Robert Hecht-Nielsen,* Neurocomputing, © *1990 by Addison-Wesley Publishing Co.*

Some examples of numerals that were recognized successfully appear in Figure 10.11. Finally, we show in Figure 10.12 an example of a pattern that results in a completely ambiguous response from the neocognitron. In the next section, we describe a method for resolving patterns such as the one in Figure 10.12.

10.4   ADDITION OF LATERAL INHIBITION AND FEEDBACK TO THE NEOCOGNITRON

There are two issues raised by the example of the superimposed patterns that we described at the end of the previous paragraph. The first deals with resolving the ambiguity so that the network makes a clear choice. The second deals with getting the network to recognize and identify *both* patterns present on the retina.

Arranging for the network to make a choice between the two patterns can be accomplished by the addition of lateral inhibition between neighboring cells on a layer. If each cell is inhibiting other cells, then minor differences in response will be magnified over time, and one cell in the final layer usually will emerge as the clear winner.

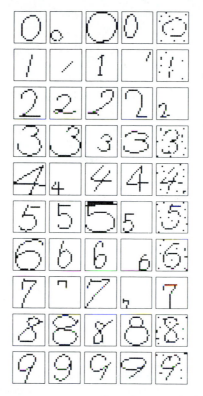

Figure 10.11   These are some examples of numerals that were successfully recognized by the neocognitron.   The patterns vary according to size, location on the retina, amount of distortion, and addition of noise. *Source: Reprinted with permission of Addison-Wesley Publishing Co., Reading, MA, from Robert Hecht-Nielsen,* Neurocomputing, © *1990 by Addison-Wesley Publishing Co.*

The second issue can be addressed by the addition of feedback paths in the network, along with other devices, such as gain controls on cells and variable threshold conditions. If a pattern such as the one in Figure 10.12 is presented, feedforward connections and lateral inhibition are allowed to function to choose a single responsive cell in the final layer of the network. This cell may represent either a 2 or a 4, and slightly different input patterns may alter the initial response.

Following this initial processing, signals are sent *back* toward the retina via other planes of cells, called w_S-cells and w_C-cells. During the feedforward process, only certain C-cells and S-cells remain active. These cells gate the

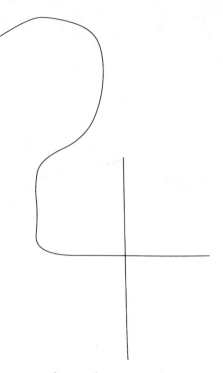

Figure 10.12   This pattern shows the numeral 4 superimposed on the numeral 2. This pattern cannot be identified unambiguously by the neocognitron that we have been describing.

feedback pathways so that feedback signals retrace the same pathways through the network back to the retina. In turn, the w_S-cells and w_C-cells facilitate the strengthening of responses by the active C-cells and S-cells by affecting changes in the thresholds and gains of these cells. Thus, a self-sustaining resonance effect ensues, which is remindful of the similar effect in the ART networks of Chapter 8.

   To cause the network to recognize the second pattern present on the retina, all that is necessary is to interrupt the feedback signals momentarily. This action causes the gain of all active C-cells to be lowered, as though by fatigue. As a result, other previously inactive cells can respond, and a second resonance will be established where the second pattern is identified on the last layer of the network. Once again, we are reminded of the orienting subsystem of ART and the sustained inhibitory signals used there to facilitate search.

   Although we have given only a cursory treatment to lateral inhibition and feedback here, we do not mean to give the impression that implementing these devices is easy. The architectural details and processing equations necessary are similar to those for the neocognitron, but are considerably more complex.

References at the end of this chapter will direct you to sources for the details, should you be interested in reading further.

Exercise 10.3: There are actually three numerals present in the pattern in Figure 10.12. What is the third numeral?

Suggested Readings

The original cognitron is described in an article by Fukushima [1]. Other articles by him and his colleagues are listed in the bibliography [4, 2, 3]. One of the clearest descriptions of the operation and training of the neocognitron appears in an article by Menon and Heinemann [7]. This paper also illustrates the use of the neocognitron architecture in a pattern-recognition application different from the numeral recognition application.

As we mentioned in the Preface, we chose not to include the pseudocode for the neocognitron simulator. If you wish to see an example of how complicated such a simulator can become, see the *HNC ANZA User's Manual* (Hecht-Nielsen Neurocomputing Corporation, San Diego, CA) [5].

Bibliography

[1] Kunihiko Fukushima. Cognitron: A self-organizing multilayered neural network. *Biological Cybernetics*, 20:121–136, 1975.

[2] Kunihiko Fukushima. Neural network model for selective attention in visual pattern recognition and associative recall. *Applied Optics*, 26(23):4985–4992, December 1987.

[3] Kunihiko Fukushima. A neural network for visual pattern recognition. *Computer*, 21(3):65–75, March 1988.

[4] Kunihiko Fukushima, Sei Miyake, and Takayuki Ito. Neocognitron: A neural network model for a mechanism of visual pattern recognition. *IEEE Transactions on Systems, Man, and Cybernetics*, SMC-13(5):826–834, September–October 1983.

[5] Robert Hecht-Nielsen. *ANZA User's Guide*. Hecht-Nielsen Neurocomputer Corporation, San Diego, CA, Release 1.0, July 1987.

[6] Robert Hecht-Nielsen. Counterpropagation networks. *Applied Optics*, 26(23):4979–4984, December 1987.

[7] Murali M. Menon and Karl G. Heinemann. Classification of patterns using a self-organizing neural network. *Neural Networks*, 1(3):201–215, 1988.

I N D E X